A HISTORY OF
White Metal
Transport Modelling
A Who's Who in the Industry

by Ray Strutt and David Wright

CONTENTS

Acknowledgements   IV

Foreword   V

Introduction   VI

Chapter One   Where did it all start?   1

Chapter Two   Making Models from White Metal   23

Chapter Three   Pattern Makers - The Heart of the Business   29

Chapter Four   The Early Pioneers   57

Chapter Five   The ModeleX Era   104

Chapter Six   International Connection   109

Chapter Seven   Commercial Break   144

Chapter Eight   On the Buses   157

Chapter Nine   Trains, Planes & Boats   163

Chapter Ten   Breaking the Records   173

Chapter Eleven   The Chequered Flag   182

Chapter Twelve   The Shop Front   190

Chapter Thirteen   The Volume Producers   212

Chapter Fourteen   The Parts Bin   226

Chapter Fifteen   The Adapters & Flatterers   231

Chapter Sixteen   The Influence of China & the 21st Century Scene   247

Appendix 1   Pattern Maker Network   253

Appendix 2   A White Metal Model timeline   257

Appendix 3   Sponsors   262

Index   Chapters and Profiles   264

ACKNOWLEDGEMENTS

Thanks to all contributors for their time and supplying their own photos,
in particular – Charles Barnett; Derek Barratt; Peter Cox;
Bryan Garfield Jones; Guy Harrison; Paul Lang; Kevin McGimpsey;
Colin Penn; Mike Richardson; Brian Salter; Mike Stanton; Roger Tennyson;
Max Tomlinson; Rod Ward; Bob Wills.
Also, for their assistance in the research – Anbrico; Mark Beesley;
Robert Forsythe; Clive Lawrence; Pat Jewell; Anthony Mosley; Randall Olson;
South London Press; The Model Rail Magazine; Vectis Auctions; Veloce
Publishing; Wayne Moyer; Joan Webber; Tony Wright.

FOREWORD
HRH The Duke of Gloucester KG GCVO

For the last 100 years the motor car has been the most potent symbol of personal transportation. Its development over the decades has brought many changes, making older models obsolete and the need for motorists to update their transport. Nostalgia can cause regret at the passing of a favourite and I suspect that many model cars are bought as a reminder of just such favourites.

There is no doubt that the first model cars were seen as toys and suitable presents for children. This would account for the unsuitable colours found on many early Dinky Toys – but as it became possible to make the models more true to life, with interiors, windows, accurate wheels and so on, it became obvious that many were bought by adults as a reminder of past times. Indeed, the advent of white metal models enabled collectors to purchase models of cars not otherwise available.

Real motorcars take up a lot of space and are expensive to maintain in good condition: model cars take up little space and have a zero maintenance cost. Collectors can go beyond just their own experience of motoring and can afford to collect models of real cars that were unaffected by the mundane needs of normal motoring. Whether they are racing cars or fantasy cars, the collector can select any without concern for practicality. They can collect those models which influenced the design of others, or can include motorcars they have never met before – prototypes, or those strange models that stayed behind the Iron Curtain, across the Atlantic, or in the Far East.

The use of white metal enabled manufacturers to make small production runs a viable possibility, but it required skill to estimate public demand for either completed models, or kits, that allowed the enthusiast to get the colours and variations just right.

Model cars cannot be obtained unless somebody chooses to make them. This book recounts the efforts of those who believed that there was a public demand for unusual scale models and shows their successes and failures. Some were very crude and cheap, others were beautifully produced and very expensive. In every case, the manufacturer had to estimate the strength of public demand; some proved too optimistic, some got it just right. I suspect the desire to do justice in making the miniature reflect the true shape and character of the original, increased the optimism of the pioneers of this cottage industry that has grown over the years to be a large international business.

This book by Ray Strutt and David Wright covers that interesting period when the pioneers demonstrated what was possible and what might then have proved to be too optimistic. They go on to record the histories of the multitude of producers that came in the later years, and bring the reader up to date with modern techniques and market forces.

INTRODUCTION

One day at a Windsor toy fair in 2008, Ray Strutt and David Wright, with many years of experience collecting model cars already behind them, found themselves considering the same topic. How could we document the development of the white metal model industry without creating an endless catalogue of the thousands of different model cars produced by so many enthusiasts, often working alone, over a period of 40 years or more?

We knew that no one else had thought this to be a worthwhile venture particularly as this field is quite a specialised one. However, our concern to commit to paper our combined knowledge, lest it be gone forever in the course of time, drove us forward.

Ray's background as the founder of the successful series of ModeleX shows in the 1990s, coupled with a unique window on the white metal world through regular reviews of the products for Collectors Gazette, meant his world wide knowledge was potentially encyclopaedic. David, on the other hand, has enjoyed the building of white metal kits since the early 1970s, culminating in a significant collection, from which he has written extensively for the trade magazines. Through searching for more obscure models he has encountered many small producers not all familiar with the ModeleX exposure.

Together, we considered the challenge! What should be included? Cars certainly were the prime motivator, but railways, trucks, buses, aeroplanes, figures, spare parts? All these have played a part in the evolution of the white metal field, and deserve a place in history. So who was first to make a white metal model car? It became clear that there was no easy answer to this and other questions, but the fun in exploring all the avenues was endless, and threatened to render the research infinite!

Over what period of time did the industry blossom, then become more specialist, and subsequently wane to serve a smaller but dedicated band of collectors? What were the influences that sparked its genesis, and what have been the challenges and new developments?

Seeking answers to these many questions prompted us to take a step back, consider the wider world, and remind ourselves of what is most important in our lives – the people. And so this book took on a mission, to explore the contributions that so many dedicated craftsmen have made to this specialist industry. Some have been flamboyant characters with remarkable life experiences, whilst others have preferred the obscurity that backroom roles, however skilled, afforded them.

Nevertheless, whilst this project has been principally about the people in this industry, it was too tempting to resist trying to list all the makers and their ranges known to them. However, in the end cataloguing accurately the 370+ ranges and makers was beyond the scope of this volume. So, we began seeking out craftsmen past and present, the pattern makers, mould makers, casters, assemblers, distributors and retailers who all had stories to tell.

We concentrated our efforts mostly in the United Kingdom, as from a practical standpoint, this was where most of the originators lived. However, we have successfully included key figures from many parts of the world, wherever the connection could be made. Indeed, some of the international figures we encountered can truly be said to be founding fathers of the industry.

As for subject matter, we make no apologies for majoring on 1:43 model cars, as this is our principal interest. However, a unique book of this kind would not be complete without the inclusion of other collectable scales, and the development of model buses, model railways and, indeed, both aircraft and boats, in the medium of white metal.

In the end, we both feel we have enriched our knowledge of both the people who created the models and the models themselves. Whilst professional connections between craftsmen were originally quite secretive, the camaraderie that we uncovered in our research and conversations was surprising, yet very satisfying. In many cases, the curiosity and continued interest in the fortunes of colleagues no longer involved was also very strong.

In looking back, we have so many people to thank for supporting the production of this book, and this must include all those key characters whose lives have been laid bear in these pages, and who gave such full accounts of their changing fortunes and difficulties, but to a man were keen to see this tome finished and published.

Indeed, all who took part agreed that the prime motivation was to ensure that the collective history and memories of pattern makers, casters, etc., should be deposited safely in one place, lest the combined knowledge be lost as we all inevitably move to the great toy fair in the sky! We have aimed at documenting not only the lives of those involved, but their manufacturing methods, what helped them get into the business, and in some cases took them out. Happily, many have stayed the course and are still in demand as model makers in one form or another.

At this point it is important to stress that the stories do not comprise a definitive listing of all who have played a part in this industry. Indeed, there are some who, due to personal circumstances, lack of available current contact details, or simply no longer being with us, we were unable to track down. A very small minority chose not to take part.

So, from Skinner to Tin Wizard, from Graphic Designers to Brooklin Models, we hope the reader will feel affection for those who have given collectors such joy in the miniature replicas of the various forms of transport through the ages.

Ray Stewitt   David Wright

CHAPTER ONE

WHERE DID IT ALL START?

Of all the specialist materials used to produce model cars and trucks, it is white metal that gets mentioned the most often, and certainly in Great Britain has been the most influential in the opening up of our hobby.

The Sussex firm of Wills Finecast began producing kits of railway locomotives as early as 1958, and this led to 1:24 scale kits of racing cars, of which the 1962 BRM was the first in the line. With its move from Thornton Heath to larger premises in Forest Row in 1964, Bob Wills added more car kits to its portfolio, and was certainly one of the first producers of 1:24 scale metal car kits, and therefore a true pioneer.

Bob's story is recounted elsewhere, but he does recall a company known as Replicars, which had experimented with 1:24 scale cars, including the Rolls Royce Silver Ghost. An article in the Modellers' World magazine of April 1985 explores these models, but Bob believes that their involvement was transient, and that it was he who started this industry in 1:24 scale. However, further investigation, with the help of an article by Max Tomlinson in Model Auto Review, confirms that Graphic Designers Ltd, the business

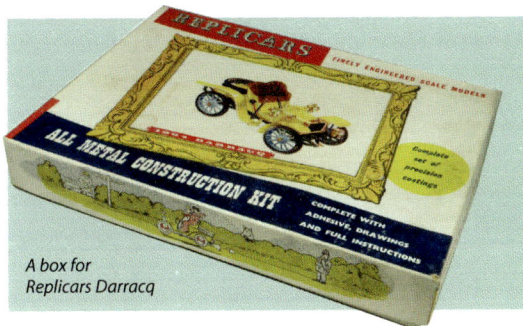

Bob Wills

started by Bill and Ted Friend, was producing 1:24 scale kits as early as 1955. Examples of these rest in the collections of Mike Richardson and Charles Barnett. The accolade for the first white metal model car should therefore be awarded to Designers' Replicars range described on page 10.

A box for
Replicars Darracq

We know from contributors that Auto-Kits Ltd, of 72, Finsbury Pavement EC2, (Telephone number Monarch 5506) was first started by Ian Smith, who used to work for Lotus. The directors were Ron Clover, R.S.H Platt and Ian Smith.

Prior to launching its own 1:24 scale white metal kits made by Bob Wills, Ron Platt produced 1:24 scale handbuilt models made from aluminium sheet pressed over a form. Brass provided the medium for the smaller parts, and the cars modelled were Lotus 7, Lotus 18, Lotus 20 and Lotus 23.

Around 1967, Reg Bishop, its pattern maker was working on the 1966 Brabham F1 car, but sadly died before he was able to finish it. Ron passed the pattern to Dick Ward. A few years later Auto-Kits had cash flow problems, and finally closed down, when Bob Wills purchased them.

However, if for the purposes of this research, we regard white metal as one of the alloys of tin, then thanks to Max Tomlinson we know that the French Paris-based company of S.R. (Simon et Rivolet) manufactured tin cast toy cars around 1910. Indeed, from 1890, it produced small pewter/tin cast items and trinkets for the Paris tourist trade, such as miniatures of the Eiffel Tower and Notre Dame. Model cars and tanks were produced between 1910 and 1914, and by 1918 and the end of World War 1, the company had become known as 'Successor et Rivolet' and moved to smaller premises. This name change implies the death of Monsieur Simon, and the continuance of the company by his wife. Some observers have noticed the similarity of craftsmanship and detail between these models and the early Tootsietoys, giving rise to speculation that the pattern maker may have left France for the United States.

Simon et Rivolet's pewter alloy /white metal car circa 1910

The first public signs of an emerging white metal kit market appeared in the pages of Modellers' World, a publication edited and published by Mike and Sue Richardson. Launched in October 1971, it wasn't until the following April that it carried an article about the kits made by the Rev. Paddy Stanley. As a padre to the forces overseas, many found it amazing that he found time to cast and produce kits and handbuilt models. He had been doing just this since 1967, and for providing further information, he used a forwarding address of Williams & Glynns Bank, Whitehall!

But two other names come to the fore in this competition for first in the race. Brian Jewell refers to his 1:43 scale white metal range known as Marc Europa, and the best known example is probably his 1962 Ferrari 250 GTO, in his book entitled Model Car Collecting, published in 1963. We can, therefore, safely assume that his small and unfinished range appeared prior to 1963. Also we have found out that it was Denzil Skinner who cast Brian's models for him, indeed it was Denzil Skinner who also crafted the

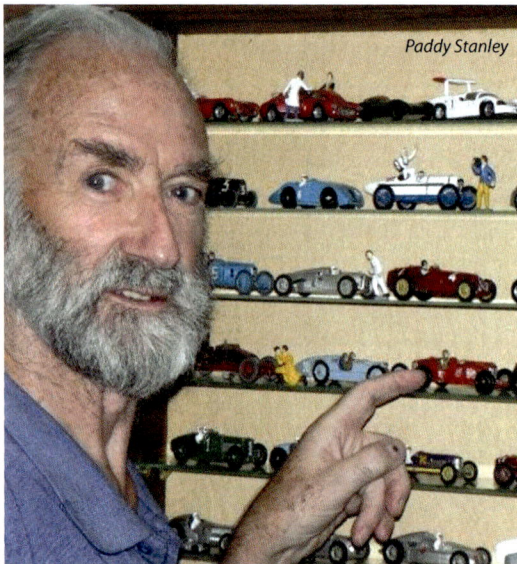

Paddy Stanley

master pattern for this model, but alas, was allegedly never paid for that or the very limited castings!

Denzil Skinner had been making small military models to a constant 1:100 scale since 1951. So, it seems that for the very first person who used white metal as a medium for casting any model in England, Denzil Skinner can claim the accolade. It looks like Brian Jewell can take the award for the first car in 1:43 scale.

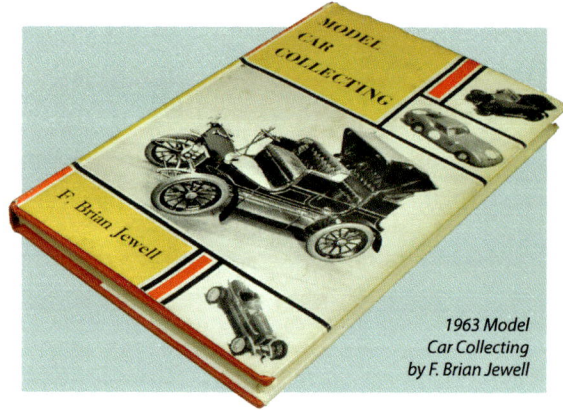

1963 Model Car Collecting by F. Brian Jewell

But were cars first?

Possibly the first manufacturer of white metal models may have been the 4mm railway wagons and parts and coach bogies by Nucro (Acro). It started in about 1949/50 but with fully finished wagons only slightly cheaper than a Tri-ang loco it was just not competitive.

It was followed by Keyser's, Wills, Gem and Bec, and those 4 carried on until l970 as almost the only source of w/m castings although CCW (O Gauge) must have had a machine as well. Most casters worked in much the same way. If you wanted a quantity of castings from your own patterns you "gave" it to one of the above who supplied a quantity free and kept the pattern for their own use!

This was obviously no great incentive to enthusiastic pattern makers and was, of course, the reason that enterprising pattern makers and casters such as Adrian Swain bought a casting machine for themselves as they soon realised there would never be any money in it otherwise.

Indeed, Adrian may have been the first to actually supply a casting service to other people on any sort of commercial basis, in addition to often getting them started by making the patterns as well!

The name K's kits, has been synonymous with model railway locomotives and rolling stock for many years. The company was N&K. C. Keyser Ltd, and it was as early as 1954 that Ken Keyser saw a jeweller's centrifugal casting machine, and realised the possibilities this would unlock for small scale production of white metal model railway components. Complete wagon kits in white metal appeared in 1956, about the same time as Bob Wills had arrived at the same production process a few months previously. However, according to 'A History of Locomotive Kits, Volume 1', K's launched their first complete 4mm locomotive kit a year later, this time beating Wills by a few months. We also know that they experimented with white metal model car kits, in 1967 and 1968, producing a Bugatti T59 and Ferrari Dino, both in 1:24 scale, examples of which are in the collection of Max Tomlinson. It is believed that the patterns for these were purchased by SMTS.

Whilst Keysers continued as K's for many years in the model railway field, and indeed employed some notable leading lights in the model car field too, Bob Wills was able to encompass both railway and motor cars very successfully, achieving a range of around 40 locomotive kits.

The Tanks of all Nations range

We have been extremely fortunate to have been able to speak personally with a number of these early "trailblazers" and to record their memories and challenges in what was an industry in its infancy.

Pete Atkinson
Acorn Models

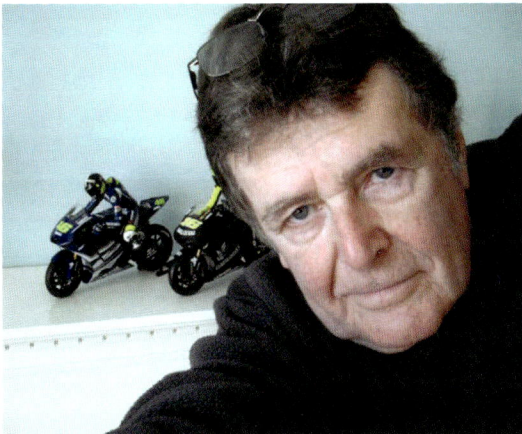

Some white metal stories are intertwined with many other achievements, and include a variety of materials used for models. Pete Atkinson's is one of those stories!

Pete was born into a family of gunsmiths, and his father had a group of 6 hunting, shooting and fishing sports shops around south Wales. His interest in cars began in the 1950s when Stock Car Racing came to Swansea, and his father decided to sponsor a local Stock car track. He was more into bikes, and had a Subbuteo speedway track, but he got interested in the cars, took his brothers' Dinky Toys and crushed them in the vice and painted them to resemble stock cars!

When Scalextric was first launched, Pete's father sold them in the family's shops, and he set one up on a table tennis table, charging customers 1 penny a go. He claims to have created the first pay and drive slot-cars!

Pete recalls that around 1957 he saw a picture in an American magazine for sidewalk surfboards. He promptly converted Mettoy Warwick Flyer roller skates into skateboards and claimed to have invented the name! This can be backed up historically with a picture in the South Wales Evening Post. Directly as a result, Mettoy sold thousands of them as the Warwick Skateboard. At just 14 years of age he was in business with royalties for years. This established a strong link with Mettoy and Corgi that endured for some years.

Some time later, he set up the first Welsh surfboard factory called Acorn Surfboards at the same time as his golf and model car shop.

Between 1960 and 1961, Pete got into racing bikes, especially scrambling, with a magnificent achievement in 1961 when he won a gold medal at the World International 6-Day Trials. He hated the gunsmith business, and decided to go his own way, so with £25 he bought a hairdressers shop, and enjoyed the swinging 60s to the full with all the 'chicks' who worked there!

Pete believes that he created a first by producing a limited edition collector's issue of the Corgi Austin Minivan with decals for his family shop, the Atkinsons Golf and Model Centre. Only 50 were made, and he knows where one still exists but he is unable to persuade the owner to part with it!

Continuing with the scrambling, he had a serious accident in 1963, and was in a coma for 6 months. His therapy became making model trials bikes from Britains motor cycles; his first foray into 'chopping'.

Once out of hospital, he opened a range of shops including boutiques and One-Arm bandit shops. This led to the purchase of 9 – 11 Picton Arcade, Swansea, in 1965, an old toy shop, which he re-opened as a golf and model car centre. Peter stocked Dinky and Corgi Toys, Tri-ang Spot-On, and slot racing systems by Wrenn, Scalextric, VIP and Airfix. Slot racing was all the rage, and Pete was so impressed with the Model Road Racing Car's racing centre's portable racing track that he bought it and installed it in the room above the shop. With suitable coin-operated mechanism, this established a very successful local club.

The shop flourished, and the stock was supplemented considerably by Pete beginning to correspond with an Italian collector and trader, who was keen to swap his Mercury, Politoys, Solido and other makes not available in the UK for Dinky Toys.

One day Ian Norris and Derek Slack walked into the shop. Both worked for Mettoy/Corgi in Swansea, Ian in management and Derek in design and development. They offered to give Pete access and use of Corgi's vac-form machine for making slot racing car bodies. The old system of barter then came into full swing when Pete met Barry Lester, as a result of advertising in Slot Car Magazine. Barry was seeking RIO models, and in order that he might produce vac-form slot racing bodies, Pete needed a model maker to create patterns. Barry thus made wooden "bucks" for the models, in 1:24, 1:32 and HO scales. The body sat on an aluminium chassis made at a local metal works known as Tom Smith & Clarke.

In addition to the slot racing shells, the Acorn name appeared on a 1:42 range, after none of the UK manufacturers were prepared to accept Pete's ideas for more unusual cars for collectors rather than children. How their view has since changed! However, both Corgi and Dinky were prepared to sell him the wheels and tyres, which guided his choice of subject. The name came from Acorn Lodge, where Pete was living at the time.

Acorn Models' Porsche 917 prototype

First to be launched was a Morgan Plus 4, based on Pete's mother's car, with an option for the Le Mans winning car no. 41. These were featured in Model Cars and Miniature Auto World.

With encouragement from Noel Stanbury, founder of the Mini Seven Racing Club, who was also seeking models of his cars, the next model was the Lotus Formula Ford. All the models were packed in the cellar under the house by a local woman working for Pete. By 1968, a total of 15 models had been made in this range of Acorn models, and thousands had been sold all over the world.

The business grew, and began to include model railways too. Occasional visitors to the shop included a local piano tuner named Mr Hustle, who would bring in old toys and lead soldiers from his travels. Pete also appeared on local BBC Welsh radio promoting toy collecting.

During those heydays of Corgi production at Swansea, everyone knew an employee of Corgi. It was customary to ask friends who were there to go to the scrap bin and pull out the cars of your choice, and then have them painted and assembled. Pete obtained 5 Mini Mostest models this way. He then bought 50 original shelf stock boxes for the Mini Mostest, and other rally cars.

However, once the factory had suffered its fire, much was lost. This was the beginning of the end for Corgi, and Pete's contract finished. Business was not so good, but he turned to many different ventures. He linked up with Dave Gilbert (DG) who wanted to use some of Pete's old Dinkys as patterns for white metal replicas. Barry Lester moved on to other things.

During 1965, Pete began working with Peter Roberts, who had made the patterns for the Skybirds range of military identification models, all in HO scale. He gave many of the originals to Pete, who cast replicas of both the figures, and vehicles such as Scammell and anti-aircraft gun, together with planes.

Pete had a basic lead casting machine, with which he produced an engine for a Morgan 3-wheeler. He made the complete car in 1965, using Dinky wheels, but was very unhappy with the result. He resorted to using the London Soldier Company to cast them for him, and had 100 made, costing £5.00 each.

By 1968, Pete had sold his shop to Les Turner, who continued to trade as a model railway shop and club.

The skateboard boom hit the streets in 1977, and this re-kindled Pete's interest in bikes. Through Peter Roberts again, he set about making a 1:32 model of a Greeves scrambler, as his son was now into scrambling. This led him to contemplate creating a model of the Brough Superior as used by T.E Lawrence. To achieve a better result, he approached Brian Lawrence, an experienced and high quality pattern maker, who obtained the original bike from the Brough Owners Club, and was able to use accurate measurements to produce a fine brass master. Pete had 500 cast from this and the Scale Models magazine gave the bike a very good review. The run sold out, mostly through the Brough Owners Club.

Pete planned to launch a range known as MiBikes, and sell them from his current premises, the Acorn Skateboard shop. He was put in touch with Brian Field, who was to cast them for him. These would be replicas of Britains' bikes such as the Norton 500 and the Greaves. However, there were many delivery delays, and then when he was visiting Leeds toy fair, he saw Brian Field, trading at a table, selling them! In his own way, Pete ensured that this range did not continue.

A Motor Cycle News competition in 1986 featured an invitation to readers to name their dream motor bike ride. The winner was for a race between a Brough Superior and a Bristol Bulldog fighter. As a result of the ensuing interest, the Brough Owners club contacted Pete again, asking if he had any more of his models left? He had six sets of castings, so he found a caster in Newcastle, David Lesley, and a further 2,500 were produced in a reduced detail form, with the rider fixed to the bike. These sold very well.

Pete attended the first ModeleX show in 1990, and no sooner had he walked in than he observed Richard Hutchins of SAMS models displaying his models of the Brough Superior. He challenged Richard about the ownership of these, and rights to sell, and an altercation ensued. Pete is convinced he is not a violent man, but on that occasion he was thrown out of the exhibition!

During this period from 1989 to 1991, Pete was living and working in New York, but returning regularly on business to the UK. At one point due to unfortunate circumstances, he found himself with $5 in his pocket, and had not eaten for 7 days. He had to pawn his passport as guarantee for his apartment. He had no ticket back to the UK, was alone and totally without resources. He walked 20 streets away to a toy dealer he had left some old toys with on a sale or return basis, and he was offered $3,600. Pete then took a taxi back to the antique mall on 5th Avenue and went to another toy dealer who gave him $4000. He never looked back! He was known in the New York toy trade as 'Peter the picker'!

By 1991, Pete was in his third marriage, and was attending a car boot sale on a Sunday morning in Swansea. He came across a man with a van in which there were buckets of old toys. After a couple of beers, Pete had purchased the contents of the van for £25, and had persuaded the man to take him to where these were found. He found himself looking

across the levelled site of the new Morfa Stadium, which had previously been a landfill. This had been the graveyard for the burnt remnants of Corgi's stock! He hired a JCB and excavated the area, removing three truck loads of Corgi Toys, mostly with fire damage, but including 12 Mini Poparts, white Man from Uncle cars, Chitty Chitty Bang Bangs, and James Bond Astons!

Pete's attendance at local boot fairs as a trader suddenly increased, and with adverts in local papers, he was able to sell the entire haul within a month.

During late 1994/5, Pete became involved with Swansea born Peter Bailey who set up Retro Scooters, selling scooters of any size from 1:1 to 1:84 scale. He used all his old models, and he recast and remade a wide range for sale. Colin Flannery undertook all the fettling, and Peter Comben the casting. Both worked well together. Pete Atkinson built all the models that Peter Bailey sold. However, due to firstly his personal difficulties, then Pete moving to Spain, the venture floundered. He believes that Peter Comben still has all the scooter moulds.

By 1996, Pete was living in Spain, still buying and selling old toys. He came across another TE Lawrence Brough, and this prompted him to continue making some more replicas of Britains motor bikes. On this occasion Dave Gilbert made the castings, and 5000 tyres were purchased from Britains to fit. Their agreement was that Dave Gilbert would not sell them for a certain period.

The brass master for Pete's Morgan 3-wheeler

The Morgan 3-wheeler was still nagging at Pete, as he always had wanted to make a really good model of it. He first approached Colin Flannery who agreed to build the models for £2000, and then Pete Comben in Lincoln, who used one of his remaining castings as a pattern to cast them, and tyres were sourced. It was made from 23 separate pieces, and over 3,500 were made and sold. The 1934 barrel-back with man and lady figure was first, followed by the 1935 Beetleback, and race versions of both. Spoked wheels and ribbed tyres featured, and colour schemes could be specified, and were sold from Spain, under the name Justa Espana. However, in due course financial dealings became difficult, but then Pete was approached by an American, representing Lilliput Executive Models. He wanted to market them as an executive toy, offering to pay £25.00 for each built model, and wanted 2000. Pete built them all, also under the Justa Espana name – the best in Spain. He regrets that he sold the brass master, which sold later on Ebay for £500.

Whilst Pete lived partly in Spain, between 1995 and 1997, he also recast some Britains tractors and parts, and the Britains four furrow plough. He also remade the Scamold cars, Era, Alta and Maserati, with correct suspension and drivers. The boxes for these were made by the company in Pembroke who made the original Corgi Toy boxes, in an old converted farm. Pete retains considerable information on the Scamold range, and hopes that they may be relaunched.

In all, 2,500 have been built by Pete, but more recently he diversified yet again, was involved in pubs and bars in Spain, and had little time for the models.

Now back in the UK, in Cornwall, Pete's mobility is somewhat restricted, but he has found his biking interest again! He has been creating 1:12 scale super-detailed racing bikes from Minichamps originals, complete with famous figures such as Barry Sheen and Valentino Rossi.

He is in contact with old friends in the business, with whom he is discussing further ventures, and it is quite possible that that Morgan may yet appear again!

Peter Cox &
Guy Harrison
Pirate Models

When two avid model bus collectors meet and find a synergy between them, there is bound to be exciting outcomes! Guy Harrison and Peter Cox met following a 'reader's query' that Guy wrote in the Meccano Magazine, asking if anyone knew of a small toy double deck trolleybus that he recalled from his childhood. Peter responded to this, as he had just visited the Taylor & Barrett factory, and had made some purchases.

Guy and Peter both lived in North West London, exchanged their knowledge on their prize possessions, including Guy's Charbens coach and a Keyser white metal half cab LMS road/rail bus, and a friendship was born which several years later led to Pirate models.

They both recall meeting on occasions at a model shop operated by Automodels at 70, Finsbury Pavement in the City, near where they worked. Automodels were the makers of Autokits, large scale white metal model car kits.

Some years later, Guy and Peter learned of a Blue Peter Appeal, on BBC TV, for viewers to send in brass light fittings and old toys. The aim was to melt down such items and raise money with the scrap metal obtained. The organisers of this appeal, had arranged a warehouse in Spittlefields, London, where the parcels were delivered. Guy and Peter approached the organiser and suggested that they believed that there would be numbers of valuable toys included in the parcels, and that they would be prepared to sort out as many as possible of these, so that they could be auctioned – that offer was gratefully received – but neither of them knew what they were letting themselves in for!

The appeal produced a total of 50 tons of both light fittings and toys. The parcels were opened by inmates of various prisons, who put the toys into paper sacks. These sacks had previously been used

*Pirate Models'
Interstation Special*

for chicken feed, and each of the sacks had to be opened onto the floor, to enable the sorters to see if there were any worthwhile toys. So, every day, after work, they and other helpers went to the warehouse, put on their oldest clothes, and set to work. The sorting was arduous and lengthy. In addition, all the contents had gathered a layer of chicken feed dust, as indeed did those shovelling the toys! The shovelling was to put the non valuable items back into the sacks for melting.

However, this later proved valuable, as several thousands of old toys were rescued from the furnace, and saved for the auction. These included many old Dinky Toys with broken parts, such as the 25 series trucks and 30, 36, 38 and 39 series cars, and some Tootsietoys. Following the auction, these helped raise many tens of thousands of pounds for the appeal. During the work Guy and Peter had realised that there was a captive market for replacement parts for these toys. However, what was then unknown was how to make them.

They met initially with Jack Alexander, who made 25mm soldiers, and he made masters for these, casting them using rubber moulds. This was a cottage industry process, a laborious procedure and so was not suitable for producing the spare parts that were needed in quantity.

Pirate Models' Greyhound Bus

Subsequently, they contacted Paddy Stanley, who was making a range of sports and racing car kits in white metal whilst also working as a military chaplain for the army, and he kindly introduced them to his casters, who incidently also produced the Marc Europa cars sold as built up models for Brian Jewell. So, they soon had the spare parts, but how to market them, and what to call them?

As these were mostly for old Dinky Toys, and they did not have permission to make them, the name chosen was Pirate Models. Later, as will be seen, the name was confirmed as a good choice, as when they produced models of buses, there was another connection with the name, as there were many buses in London in the 1920s, not operated by the London General Omnibus Company, which were popularly known as 'Pirate buses'.

At this time, they agreed there should be a third partner in the business, and initially David Pressland joined in a financial capacity, but as the work increased, he resigned and Graham Turrell joined Peter and Guy.

Before long all three partners became concerned about copyright issues with Meccano, the makers of Dinky Toys, but they need not have worried, as Meccano were pleased that they had embarked on this project, as they regularly received requests from readers asking for spares for their old toys, and indeed they agreed to refer collectors on to the trio. The first spares were radiators, and were originally plain white metal, but later they were cadmium plated, which offered a more realistic shiny effect, whilst strengthening the casting. Soon, the range of spare parts was increased, as headlights for the 38 and 39 series and steering wheels became sought after.

Pirate Models' charabanc

The spare parts were advertised mainly in model car magazines, and also in the Meccano magazine. At this time, Peter Cox designed the logo of the well-known skull and cross bones – but it is purely coincidence that it resembled Alec Douglas-Hume, the Prime Minister. Later they received a request for permission to use the logo, and as this was for labels for poisons, the request was approved!

Model Railway Constructor had an advertisement for a casting firm, based in Bristol, who had spare capacity, and thus was born the long association with Ron Charlton, who took on the spares manufacturing, of which the list increased, and included drivers, wheels, milk churns for the French Dinky Citroen Studebaker, and later, a folding type door made from part of a Dinky Atlantean bus, for scratch builders.

Many of the old toys rescued for the auction did not have tyres, and eventually a firm was found who made suitable rubber replacements, but not the correct profile for the Dinky 38 and 39 series,

Pirate Models' Greyhound 2

which had been found in large quantities at the auction, so a special tool was commissioned, and tyres in both black and white rubber were added to the range of spare parts. And, some makers of white metal cars, such as DG, bought tyres from Pirate for their models.

Ron Charlton had an association with a pattern maker, Mike Shepperd, and this prompted the next major development of Pirate models – into manufacturing original models, and the first was a kit of the most popular double decker contemporary bus, the Bristol VR. There were no toys or models of an up to date bus, just older Dinkies, although there was at that time a Yorkshire firm, Anbrico, which had issued one model in white metal, but this was a coach, so there was a significant gap in the market, which Pirate decided to exploit.

The patterns for this model were made by Mike Shepperd, using blueprints from the ECW, who made the body for the VR, showing the external details, together with photos, although being based in Bristol, which had large numbers of real VR buses, he could easily see any details that he wanted.

After the masters were approved, the partners made a really rash decision – which was to order 500 sets of castings for the new model, but at that time, they had no orders. These were made by Ron Charlton, whilst Guy and Peter did the packing up on their kitchen table. At this stage, the castings included separate sides, and so could be "flat packed" into a small shallow box. The upper deck seats were not castings, but were vac-formed plastic. The wheels and tyres were bought in from Anbrico.

The castings – 100 sets at a time – would arrive in containers resembling 7lb biscuit tins, from Bristol to the Red Star office at Paddington. When Peter collected them, the clerk would initially try and lift the container as though they did weigh 7lb, but would almost burst a hernia at the considerable weight of the box of castings!

The pattern maker, Mike Shepperd had always been interested in model railways, and through him Guy and Peter were introduced to Eames model railway shop of Kings Cross and obtained an initial order from Eames to take 100 of the kits. Others were sold by mail order, while the Model Bus Federation

also ordered a considerable quantity. Later, the London Transport Museum became stockists, a really prestigious retail outlet for Pirate, whose range included many London prototypes.

Guy and Peter used model railway magazines to advertise, and soon reached a stage when the editors were keen to receive a sample of their latest product for review. As demand grew, the work needed to be divided up in an efficient and business-like way. Graham handled the sales and distribution, and used his garage as a warehouse, and he also developed a relationship with the owner of How Model Shop, at 430 Hoe Street, Walthamstow, who acted as a stockist for Pirate products, and also as an accommodation address for postal enquiries for Pirate.

Peter produced all the instructions for each kit, testing them himself for ease of understanding, and handled the advertising and some development. Guy dealt with the accounting and administration but also with the major development of the kit side of the business, which included suggesting possible new items for the Pirate range, visiting the manufacturers and taking many photos of the various new bus projects.

Two very successful products were the London Transport Q trolleybus, and the Leyland National single deck bus – both of which sold well over 1000 units each.

As a result of the relationship with Leyland with

Pirate Models' hearse

Pirate Models' Paris Bus

the National, Pirate were commissioned by Leyland to make a model of their prototype new double decker bus, the B15, later further developed into the Titan.

Pirate began developing a range of buses in HO scale, of American prototypes, initially those made by General Motors, but also Grumman city buses, together with a Mack BK long distance coach, of which a preserved example is used by Greyhound for publicity purposes. Greyhound had a publicity leaflet for the coach showing the full livery – and a reference was put in the instruction, but as Greyhound did not wish to authorise the models, its name was not mentioned, but there was a reference to the livery details leaflet – 'available from the foremost US long distance coach company based in Phoenix'.

Arrangements to distribute the Pirate American range was arranged with the major US model railway mail order company, Walthers of Milwaukee, who agreed to stock the Pirate HO and later the N gauge ranges and Guy visited them to finalise the arrangements.

The Pirate range developed, and the models were, over the years, made in various scales – 4mm (00 gauge). H0 gauge – particularly for the American market) 7mm (0 gauge or 1:43 scale) and later, 2mm (N gauge, also for the American market) and one kit of a 1:50 scale bus, which coincided with the issue of the same model by Corgi. But a real diversification was the introduction of tube trains, of composite construction, white metal floor, bogies etc, and one piece brass sides and roof, in 00 scale.

The decision was made to form the partnership into a limited company called Pirate Models Limited, partly as a consequence of the American legal system.

The Department for Trade decided to object to the name possibly causing confusion to the public with another company called Pirate Craft Limited based in the Norfolk Broads, and the ensuing correspondence was very protracted. Guy met his MP to enlist his helping resolving this, as the boat operators did not object themselves, and did not see there could be any confusion to the public. This was, through the assistance of the MP, eventually sorted out, and an apology was forthcoming from the relevant minister of the government at the time, for the delay and

aggravation caused.

Due to the increase in the numbers of new kits being released, various other pattern makers were being used by Pirate in addition to Mike Shepperd, notably Brian Lawrence of LDM, and Adrian Swain for one model – the Bristol VRL double deck long distance coach. This latter arrangement was unique for Adrian, and only arose as Pirate agreed to place casting work with him for its model Paris buses, and, of course, the VRL itself, as well as including the HO Paris bus (which he acquired from Varney) in the Pirate range which was distributed in America.

One other pattern maker used was Martin Beacom, who made the masters of the Grumman city buses, and also a range of Plaxton coaches, which were also composite – using white metal for the ends, chassis and roof, but brass sides of various lengths and heights. Martin visited the Plaxton plant in Scarborough with Guy, and they were able to view the lovely new double decker coach, the prototype of which had been assembled inside the factory. They looked on with horror as the company attempted to wheel it out into the open, only to find that the doors to the factory were not high enough, and later the end of the factory had to be jacked up to allow the new bus safe egress!

Pirate Models' Lincoln Transport RT

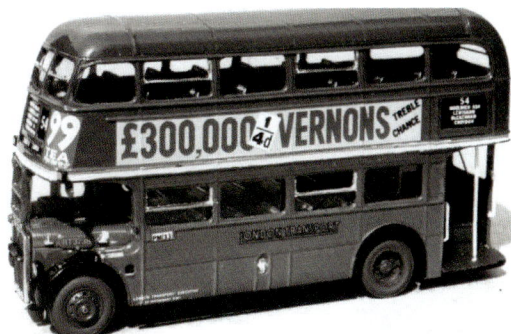

Ron Charlton's casting business relocated to Bonar Bridge in north Scotland, and was now called Sutherland Model Casters. He had also made his own range of model bus kits, called Cotswold, and Pirate agreed to purchase that range, and most were added to the Pirate line-up. Apart from Sutherland and Adrian Swain, Pirate also used Scale Model Technical Services (SMTS) to cast certain of the later American models, the baseplates from the spare parts range and also the Plaxton coaches.

A proud moment in the life of Pirate Models came when the London Transport Museum selected them to prepare two sets of the model tube trains to celebrate the extension of the tube to the (then) new Terminal 4 at London Heathrow. One set was to reside in the LT Museum, and the other was proudly presented to

Princess Diana at the opening of the line.

However, soon to come was a blow for Pirate, in that its main pattern maker, Mike Shepperd, a keen and enthusiastic motor cycle rider, had a major collision, leaving him unable to pursue his work any longer.

Times, they were changing, and the numbers of kits available from the various different manufacturers was really large, and production runs were reducing considerably, which together with the rise in the cost of white metal – mainly due to its tin content – meant that kits were now getting expensive. Also resin was now being developed for model bus construction – it was to deliver box shaped bodies in one, as opposed to separate sides, and could be produced more cheaply too.

Guy, Peter and Graham then made the decision to sell the company. The company was sold to Brian Emberton of Spilsby, Lincolnshire, who bought it for his son to run, but he lost interest as this was quite a big job for one, even if full time, so Brian then resold the business on to John Gay.

Later, of course, Corgi 00C and EFE diecast buses and also tube trains were introduced, and these did not require building or painting. These makes (and others too) virtually took over that market, as these models were considerably cheaper than the white metal kits, due to several factors – the cheap labour in China, economies in scale of production, and of course, the increasing price of tin, a constituent of white metal. However, it should be noted that several of these models were previously featured in the Pirate range.

Bill & Ted Friend
Graphic Designers Ltd

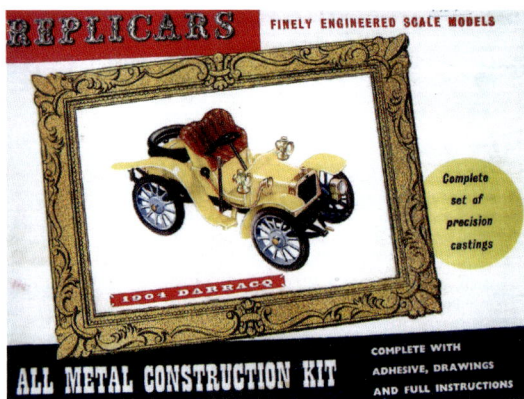

Could this be our first in white metal model cars? W. A. and C. H. Friend, known as Bill and Ted, founded a company known as Graphic Designers, at 4, Holly Park, Finchley, in 1951. It was a business involved in both designing and marketing many diverse items, all of which were automobile-related. These items included motor books, paintings, prints, scarves, place mats, coasters and motoring accessories.

They also designed and produced specialised Christmas cards as well as the race programmes for the Silverstone Race Track. Bill was the graphic artist and Ted was the engineer and sculptor. The company operated from its registered address and through various retail outlets, as well as having a mail order service for its products. Graphic Designers Limited ceased trading in 1994, upon the retirement of the surviving brother, Bill Friend.

During that 43 year period, the brothers produced quite a number of models, mainly cars, through ranges known as Replicars and Investment models.

The Replicars range was a small range of white metal kits manufactured between 1955 and 1960, consisting of four Edwardian cars and three racing cars. Although a little basic by today's standards of white metal casting, these pioneering models were undoubtedly the first white metal car kits ever to be marketed commercially in the UK, if not the world! They pre-date Bob Wills' Auto-kits range by eight years, and the Wills Finecast series by 10 years.

They decided to branch out into the model car manufacturing business in 1954 following the success of the classic film "Genevieve". This Rank Organisation film was a romantic comedy set around the annual London to Brighton run. Despite not being the first choice of the producer, a Darracq was the motoring star of the film, and models of the Darracq were produced by several companies, including Graphic Designers. Bill and Ted teamed up with Cyril Lewis, who ran a jewellery making business called the Exakta Casting Company Limited. Exakta specialised in the manufacture of high quality jewellery metalware by the lost wax and re-usable vulcanised rubber moulding and casting techniques.

The 1904 Darracq was destined to be the first in a range of four veteran car models and the late John Niblett was commissioned to design and create the brass masters. John was a freelance sculptor whose background was in fashioning scale model soldiers. At the time, John was particularly noted for his finely detailed 20mm and 54mm high medieval figure masterpieces sold at Hummel's model shop in Burlington Arcade, Piccadilly. John also made patterns of trackside figures and railway accessories for various manufacturers. The components were gravity cast into vulcanised rubber moulds by Exakta, using an alloy of tin, and some were lost wax cast.

The Darracq was initially publicised in the July 1985 issue of Model Maker magazine. H. A. Blunt

Graphic Designers' kit of a Darracq

& sons Ltd of London advertised it for 65 shillings (£3.25), assembled, painted and mounted on a plinth. The kit version was 21 shillings (£1.05). The scale was not referred to, nor was there any mention of the movie. However, at that time Genevieve, as both car and film, was a household name. In the same issue of model maker, Mersey Marine Models of Liverpool reported the Darracq available from stock at the same price as Blunts. The second model in the range was the 1907 Rolls Royce Silver Ghost.

Both models were advertised in the September 1955 Meccano Magazine. This time it was a Graphic Designers' advert, and stated that they were 1:36 scale. This was very odd, since all the range was designed to 1:24!

The range was packages in boxes with a picture frame design, inside which were pasted the illustration of each car. Bill Friend was responsible for design and artwork on the boxes, and the box sides illustrated methods of displaying the models, including mounting the cars on bookends, boxes, or lamps, some years before Lesney did with its Yesteryear plated range. Inside, each component was displayed separately, secured by a rubber band. A tube of special glue was supplied, and several pieces could be soldered. BA nuts and screws were also used. These models were a joint venture between Graphic Designers and Elektra Casting, and both names appeared on the boxes from time to time.

Airfix launched a Darracq around a year later than Graphic Designers, and it appears likely that it is a copy of the white metal design. The price differential was such that the damage to the sales of the Replicars Darracq must have been significant. Airfix was subsequently sued by Graphic

Designers for breach of copyright for both the model and the artwork.

A 1906 Rover, and a 1902 Peugeot followed the silver Ghost, and all the cars were personal preferences of the brothers. Patterns continued to be designed and mastered by John Niblett.

By June 1956, the brothers had introduced a Bugatti, also in 1:24 scale, and a 47 piece kit selling for 61 shillings. John Niblett again produced the master, but the white metal used was of a harder consistency, and therefore less prone to collapse as previous models. A removable bonnet provided access to under bonnet detail. November 1956 saw the launch of a Lotus XI, this time with its master sculpted by Ted Friend, followed by an Alfa Romeo P3 in December 1958, both in 1:24 scale.

Graphic Designers had by this time entered the lineside accessories and locomotive kit market, in a range of scales, all in white metal. The 1:24 car range appeared to decline, until in 1974, Bill joined Cyril Lewis to form Investment models based in Hatton Garden, creating prestige models, from sterling silver. The first was developed from the Replicars' patterns for the Silver Ghost. A second car, a Bentley, was patterned by a Hatton Garden silversmith, but Max Tomlinson suspects it was the work of Ray Watson, who mastered many of Bob Wills' range of Wills Finecast.

And so it was Genevieve that prompted Graphic Designers to go into white metal model car production, and there is little doubt that they were the first. Their process, however, was not economically viable to sustain further development. However, it was whilst they were enjoying success that Bob Wills was experimenting with new alloy mixes and centrifugal casting in rubber moulds for his railway accessories. His innovations enabled greater precision, and the Auto-kits and Wills Finecast ranges were born.

Graphic Designers' finished Darracq

Brian Jewell
Marc Europa

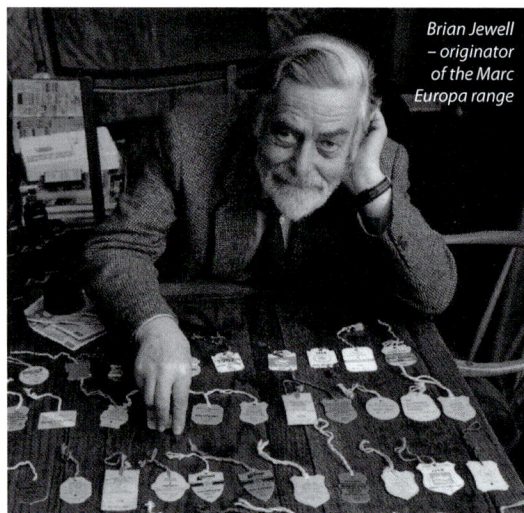

Brian Jewell – originator of the Marc Europa range

As with so many in this hobby, it was a natural progression for Brian from collecting Dinky Toys and Tootsietoys to the white metal scene. Brian's widow Pat recalls that they moved to Tunbridge Wells in 1964, and at the time Brian had been fascinated by how model cars that had once been children's toys had now become collectors' items. So much so that this became the main theme of his book, published in 1963, entitled Model Car Collecting, now collectible in its own right.

Brian had always had a keen interest in motor racing, and it was therefore not surprising that he spotted that there was no commercially available model of the Ferrari 250GTO. Despite being an amateur, he produced his own drawings and designed the model components himself. He then approached Denzil Skinner, who made both the master and castings for him, and his range Marc Europa was born. The Ferrari was launched in 1964 and was featured on the front cover of his book. By this time he had founded the Model Car Enthusiasts Club, and was receiving correspondence from as far away as Japan. It is understood that Brian had written to potential stockists offering a minimum order quantity of 100 models, and intimated that he hoped to progress to diecasting methods.

The next model, a Porsche 904 GTS coupe, came out in 1965 when a London jeweller undertook to make the pattern. Brian, perhaps not too wisely, decided to produce the castings himself. Both Ferrari and Porsche were stated as being available in fully finished form, but the 904 was issued in kit form. It is believed that at this stage Brian and Denzil Skinner parted company, with Skinner retaining the GTO

moulds and master. The 904 castings are said to be of superior quality by those who have seen examples. The diecast models never appeared, and whilst other models were intended, it is believed production ended with these two. It is doubtful that more than 100 Ferraris were made, and possibly even fewer of the Porsche. These two models can therefore be awarded the 1st in 1:43 scale for a handbuilt and a kit. It has been suggested that a 3rd model may have been made, a 1:32 scale 1964 Ford GT40 Mk I of which it is believed less than 10 were produced, and that it may have been based on a vacform slot racing body. This could not be substantiated by Brian's widow Pat. The models are illustrated in an article in the Vol 12 No. 1, October 1982 issue of the Modellers' World magazine, and these were from the collection of Cecil Gibson, which was eventually bought by Mike and Sue Richardson. As an already prolific writer, he was able to obtain publicity from the Cars & Car Conversions magazine.

Mysteriously, Brian also listed the production range of a Belgian manufacturer called Mabri, the existence of which has never been confirmed. This range was to cover cars of earlier periods, and 4 were listed in Brian's book as Duesenberg, Vauxhall TT, Sunbeam and Aston Martin Ulster, but none were produced. It is possible that Brian may have intended to produce this range, but when the name is compared with Brian's first range and his name – MArc BRIan – interesting conclusions might be reached! Pat confirms two helpful points to this puzzle, firstly that Brian had some Belgian connections earlier in his career. Secondly, and perhaps most importantly, that Brian enjoyed jokes, calling them his 'Ho hos'.

The answer to this intriguing puzzle is perhaps best consigned to history!

Continuing to write about and exhibit his own collection of model cars at the Racing Car Show, and other venues such as the Penshurst Place show, Brian

Marc Europa Ferrari 250 GTO

had made a speciality of 'chopping', that is adapting existing models to make variations on the theme with a special interest. In the domain of motor racing this was commonplace, but with the increasing numbers and diversity of standard production models seen, chopping became unnecessary.

From the late 1980s until shortly before he died Brian was closely associated with Lledo and Solido, designing liveries for their models with meticulously researched detail comprising themed advertising of all kinds as well as a very wide range of public service vehicles, military, fire fighting, ambulance, railway etc. For Lledo he collaborated with Paul Lumsden throughout the 1990s, whilst Solido's Tony Smith liaised with him in the production of innumerable model sets of which the series Cars of the Commanders (Staff cars of WWII Generals) realised a long cherished ambition.

As a writer, Brian had a very broad range of interests. His is still the standard work on the history of the sewing machine – Veteran Sewing Machines, with its sequel Antique Sewing Machines – and there were books on Motor Badges and Figureheads, Scales and Balances, Smoothing Irons and others, all published by Midas Books, who also brought out works of social history, another of Brian's enthusiasms represented by his Fairs and Revels, and Sports and Games. Collecting for Tomorrow is a useful guide for collectors of the orthodox as well as the distinctly off-beat. Allard to Zodiac appeared in 1985, an encyclopaedia cars of the 1960s. Later titles reflected Brian's experiences in the Second World War, such as Overlord, a handbook of the Normandy Landings, and Over the Rhine, recalling his involvement in the Rhine crossing as a very young

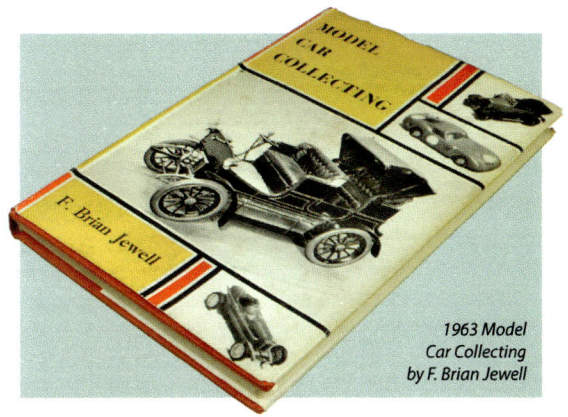
1963 Model Car Collecting by F. Brian Jewell

lance-corporal. Journalism continued with regular articles for Treasure Hunting and Soldier magazines, Antiques Weekly and Art and Antiques.

Brian found broadcasting particularly rewarding, especially the weekly programme with Radio Sussex, a 'phone-in' with the BBC's Dave Arscott. Brian answered listeners' questions on a variety of topics, including their mystery finds, a subject he treated with humour, intuition, great experience and enormous enthusiasm.

The annual collectors' meet also organised by the BBC with Dave, enabled him to meet the exhibitors and discuss their interests at their Brighton venue.

Having moved in 1987 to Harrogate in Yorkshire, Brian soon made himself at home in a new environment where he made many new friends. A projected publication entitled 'What Scale?' which he felt would prove useful to collectors was completed but never published at the time of Brian's death in April 2006.

Denzil Skinner

The Phoenix works

An army background brought this next pioneer into our story. Denzil Skinner was born in 1908, led a military childhood and career progressing through Sandhurst, and commissioned into the Royal Tank Corps. His interest in tanks began when he was employed designing them, and subsequently

specialised in tank track design.

After the war he became the first Chief Instructor at the School of Tank Technology. He left the Army in December 1948, and after spending his first three years working on selling Lloyd tractors, in 1951 he set up his company Denzil Skinner & Co Ltd, making scale models of a wide range of armoured fighting vehicles, together with regimental badges. The military model vehicles were mostly to a constant 1/100th scale, fully finished, and to our knowledge not on general sale to the public, as the primary outlet was the Ministry of Defence, for use as tactical and recognition training. An exception to this was at the Bovingdon Tank Museum.

His first premises were in London Road Camberley, and in 1957 he moved to the Phoenix Works, at Phoenix Green, Hartley Whitney. These were behind the Phoenix Public House which from 1934 had previously been the base for the Vintage Sports Car Club, and the premises at the rear, formally a

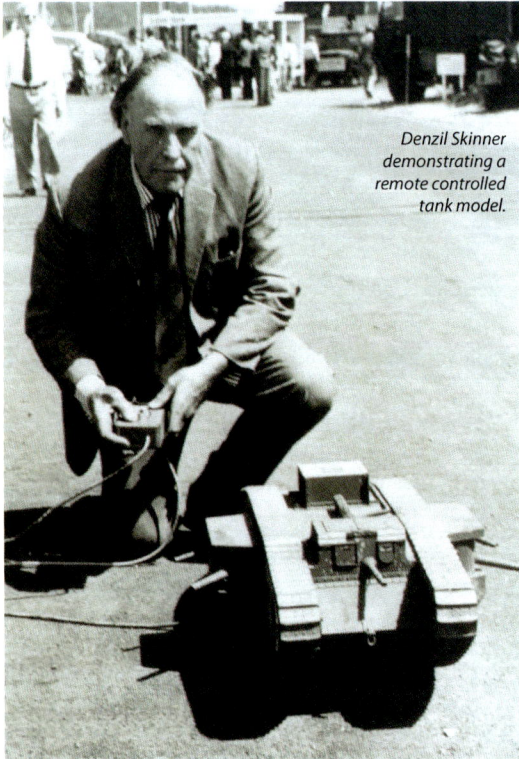

Denzil Skinner demonstrating a remote controlled tank model.

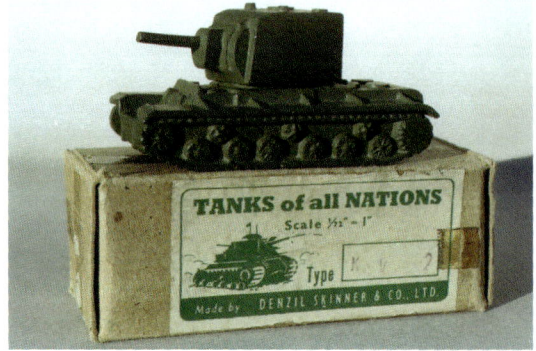

TANKS of all NATIONS
Scale ½" = 1"
Type K V 2
Made by DENZIL SKINNER & CO., LTD.

run-down garage, became a repair and maintenance business managed by some of its members. Such was its prowess in attending to many machines, that the pub became known as the "Home of the Vauxhall 30/98".

During this time Denzil Skinner took on David Shepherd as a part-time backdrop painter for his dioramas, and in due course David moved onto his own wonderful career as a successful artist.

Another of his employees, taken on as an assembler straight from school at 15 years of age, was Anthony Molay, who later went on to found Hart models. Tony recalls building the Vickers tractor

models, and undertaking finishing and casting too. The Phoenix Works was originally the paint shed for painting wooden horse-drawn coaches, and opposite stood the forge, where the wheels were made for the coaches. All Denzil Skinner's design work and the full manufacturing process were in house, and at the height of production, when tractors were a big part of the model output, he employed 30 people.

In addition to the model tractors, the portfolio of his production was very broad, encompassing, regimental and club badges, trophies, a small range of pre-war European sports cars, cast for the Rev. Paddy Stanley, a wide range of war games vehicles and scenery pieces of varying scales, aircraft, boats, figures, both military and civilian, and a comprehensive "tanks of all nations" range.

He was proud of his military life, and his two younger sons continued his links, both serving in the Royal Armoured Corps.

Single sheet leaflets were available for his products until at least 1980, but sadly, he died in September 1987. However, the ranges he produced were continued in the new name of Hart models, and the next chapter in that story was made available to us by Anthony Molay, who bought the company from Denzil Skinner's widow.

Paddy Stanley

Many collectors of a certain age will recall marvelling at the thought of an army chaplain making and sending out white metal kits from various places around the world, but it really happened.

Paddy's model making started with cut-out cardboard aero models in the Forties, moving on to SMEC and Scamold car kits and from there to Highway Pioneers and other plastic kits which followed in the 1950s. He then joined the Army as a Chaplain and the moving part began in ernest. Assembled plastic models did not travel well when

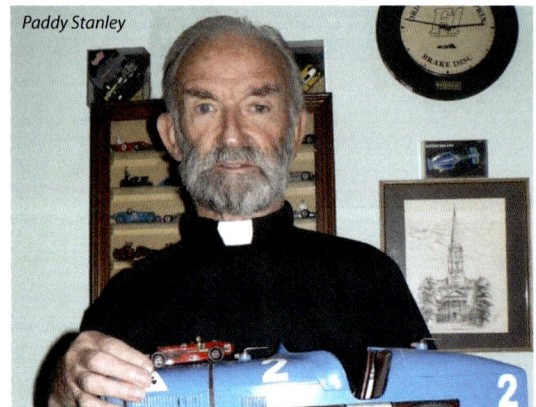

Paddy Stanley

subjected to the tender mercies of the Military Forwarding Organisation, besides which space became a problem, so much of his modelling moved to slot racing, and his collecting to Dinkies, Corgis and occasional Italian 'exotics' like Mebetoys, Mercurys, etc.

Paddy recalls building the Replicars 1:24 Silver Ghost kit in Ipoh, in Malaya, and believes these were the only kits before his range. He still has copies of the Model Maker magazine 1952 – onwards when it became 'Model Cars' and eventually went out of print, and some of the post 1966 ones did feature some w/m kits.

In 1964 Rex Hays produced a book of 1:24 scale plans entitled "Grand Prix and Sports Cars" and the stage was almost set. Paddy was on a posting in Cyprus at the time and scaled down the drawing of the 1924 P2 Alfa Romeo to 1:43 so that it would fit in with his Dinkies and Corgis. He picked this car because his elder brother had one of the large tinplate CIJ Alfas and also because its outline would be easy to cast since the rear springs were concealed inside the tail!

However, the moulding material was expensive and so, as a subscriber, he put an advertisement in Cecil Gibson's magazine telling of his intention and asking if anyone was interested in buying replicas in order that Paddy defray some of his costs. Cecil expressed an interest and so did some other pioneer collectors including Tony Kaye, now in Massachusetts, David Pressland and Derek Bannister, assistant organiser of ModeleX as well as collectors in the USA, Switzerland, Italy and New Zealand.

Paddy carved a master out of polystyrene sheet which he had cemented into a block and using a one-piece, open Silastomer mould he cast each body using gel coat, glass-fibre ribbon and casting resin – a very laborious process. The reactions of his first customers were favourable even though the P2 was one of Rex Hays' least correct plans. Paddy followed this with a 1924 GP Sunbeam, which he admits was rather narrower than life or the Hays drawing,

Having visited Bob Wills, founder of Wills Finecast in early 1968, he built his BRM kit, and also had a 1:43 kit of a Morgan 3–wheeler sold by Peter Atkinson of Swansea at about that time. It was poorly cast, and possibly an early attempt by Barry Lester. Peter Atkinson had previously marketed a vac-form ERA in 1:43 which was produced by Barry.

It therefore appears that it was a close run thing between Barry Lester and Paddy Stanley for who was 2nd with 1:43 kits after the Brian Jewell Ferrari.

Bob Wills told Paddy of Col. Denzil Skinner, whose works were about 5 miles from Bordon where Paddy was stationed, so Paddy met with Denzil Skinner, whose firm had made the masters for Brian Jewell's Ferrari, the candidate for accolade of the first 1:43

Paddy's own Alfa P2, the master for it, sitting on the big CIJ

kit. Denzil Skinner had produced the master of the Ferrari GTO for Jewell, and also the resulting kits for him. Paddy recalls it being rather 'clumpy' and very heavy with thick sidewalls.

Paddy Stanley was using fibre-glass reinforced resin for his scratchbuilt models but this would not stand the heat and pressure of the vulcanising process by which the commercial casting moulds were made. He then experimented with adding metal filling powder into the fibre-glass. This allowed commercial, vulcanised rubber moulds to be made, but the improvement was marginal and only worked as long as little bending stress was placed on the pieces. Bodies could not be cast in one piece but only in a number of thin pieces. Denzil Skinner made the moulds and Paddy Stanley did his casting on Skinner's machines, paying for the hire of the machine and the metal used.

After this first metal-filled GRP, Paddy then used lead as a medium for the 'commercial' masters which he found could be cast in the Silastomer, a cold-cure or RTV rubber.

As before, his patterns were made using polystyrene sheets, glued together to make a block, and carved to create the first master, from which a mould was taken using Silastomer. Once this was cured, lead or pewter could be poured into this mould, and a solid master made for casting purposes. White metal could not be used as a master, as it would melt or at least deform.

Paddy recalls John Day had written an article in the 1966/7 Model Cars magazine, announcing that he was launching a range of models much better than any other. He began this whilst awaiting his son's birth, and at this time he had been modifying Dinky Toys.

John Day told Paddy that he had enjoyed making Paddy's kits, as they were unusual. However, he was a brash man, and Paddy remembers, that he sought to build his business quickly, resulting in over reaching himself. This left his customers without models, having taken advance payment.

Around this time, Paddy recommended Denzil Skinner to Guy Harrison, founder of Pirate Models, when he was seeking a master maker and caster for

The Paddy Stanley range of models

his range of spares for Dinkies.

Paddy was based in Cyprus during 1965/6, followed by a return to Bordon from 1966/7 until 1970. From Hampshire, he was then posted to the Gulf at the end of 1970, followed by various postings in Germany.

At this time he passed his masters to Mike and Sue Richardson who acted as his agent, and went on to distribute and market white metal kits, using another caster. Through the 1970s Paddy then returned to Wales, from there to Gibraltar, back to Aldershot and after that to Cyprus for a second time, finally returning to Bulford near Salisbury. His first wife died in the British Military Hospital in Aldershot in 1981.

In 1983, Paddy retired from the Army, remarried and he and his new wife Pat began a 6 month honeymoon tour around Canada and the USA with a car and travel trailer. So successful was this that they extended it to a year, and Paddy was offered a part time job as an assistant in a church in Arizona. Here they then spent winters for four years, prior to taking a full time parish in Iowa for another six years, before finally retiring again.

However, half way through the honeymoon, in 1983, they returned to the UK and visited the Windsor Swapmeet. Whilst commenting on some models on a stallholders table, Paddy recalls being asked "Are you THE Paddy Stanley?" Pat was startled not knowing of Paddy's fame! The stallholder was making notes so he could write the encounter up in his column.

A while later he was contacted by a doctor in South Africa who had told him that he had collected all his models but one. Paddy told him he would make one of the Black Hawk Stutz that was missing from his collection, and to send him a cheque to cover postage only. A blank cheque arrived, offering all kinds of opportunities!! In 1998 Paddy and his wife took a cruise and when the ship arrived at Durban, he checked the phone book, found the doctor's name, and as a result obtained a very individual tour

of Durban.

Visiting Malta in spring of 2008, he found an old customer from the late 1960s era, a Dr Xuereb, who was delighted to meet him at last, and still has a wonderful collection of models from the 1960s and 1970s to the present day.

Paddy found that developing models was a solitary occupation as he moved around the world in his role as chaplain. However, it was very relaxing to focus intensely on something miniscule rather than dwell on the various full scale pastoral duties and issues people raised. He then enjoyed a "quick fix" at local swapmeets whilst on a return to the UK.

His current collection includes a tinplate CIJ Alfa Romeo P2 made in 1927 in 1:8 scale, a Pocher Monza Alfa and 1907 Fiat. Many Casadio Revival kits have also been built and are on display. Britains LSR cars such as the Silver Bullet, Bluebirds and Railton Mobil complete the range.

The widow of a friend who had sadly passed away gave him a full series of Marklin LSR models bought in 1937, such as Auto Union and Mercedes. This continued the theme of European record breakers that have been Paddy's favourites for so many years.

Unusually remaining an enthusiast and collector throughout, storage space eventually became an issue. Paddy has therefore sold his collection of Corgis whilst he was in the USA, together with his Matchbox Yesteryears. Other items that he no longer needs are now being sold on ebay, as he has no room left, having returned from the USA to a small flat in Frome, Somerset.

Paddy was regularly in touch with Barry Lester, founder of Auto Replicas, who moved to France. Not long ago, Barry had made some 1:13 scale Bugattis, of which photos were forwarded to Paddy. Many of his own masters still remain in Paddy's loft.

Paddy's very mobile career travelling the world has meant that the desire for travel is now deep seated. Now retired, he has continued to satisfy this pursuit by visiting Malta, USA, Ireland, France, and Spain for his daughter's 50th birthday, and Venice and down the Danube during 2007/08!

When back in the UK, Paddy's interests are many and varied, enjoying the Goodwood Revival meetings, and travelling on the Orient Express, being good examples. He has also been round the world on a container ship, across the Atlantic on a five masted sailing ship, and snorkelled on the Great Barrier reef!

Motor cars have always been a central theme however, and Paddy owned and rebuilt a Lotus Elan toward the conclusion of his Army Ministry. While part/time chaplain in the USA he bought 2 MG Midgets, to build one good one. On returning to the UK, he visited a breakers yard for spares, and obtained a crankshaft, exhaust manifold and various other parts. These were all placed in his suitcase ready for return to the USA, and as a result the weight shown at departure was very excessive!! He has also owned and worked on two Porsche 914s.

Approximately 15 years ago, whilst in the USA, he bought a Lotus Europa Special, for sale some 400 miles away, in a total of 12 boxes, plus body, engine, chassis and wheels all separate. He rebuilt this and sold it, buying a 1976 Cadillac Eldorado convertible, with an 8 litre engine which appealed to his wife more than the Europa! On return to the UK, he has since downgraded to a Ford Escort, and now runs a Renault 1.5 convertible coupe as his everyday car.

Paddy considers himself lucky he has never had to make a living from the model business. He therefore was able to indulge in his own views as to what were interesting cars and be happy if other people agreed. He aimed to produce kits that were correct in basic shape and detail but easy to assemble. Feedback seemed to confirm that this concept fitted in with what people wanted in those early days, since they were more likely to be collectors rather than builders by preference. On reflection, he takes the view that if the early enthusiasts had been faced with the multiplicity of photo-etched parts that we face at present, most would have thrown up their hands in horror and put the kit back in the box!

Paddy remains enthusiastic about all things motoring, in fact, he is contemplating making a model of the HWM, as he is concerned that apart from the Dinky Toys model, there is not an accurate model of this important British racing car.

Frank Vescoe
BEC Models

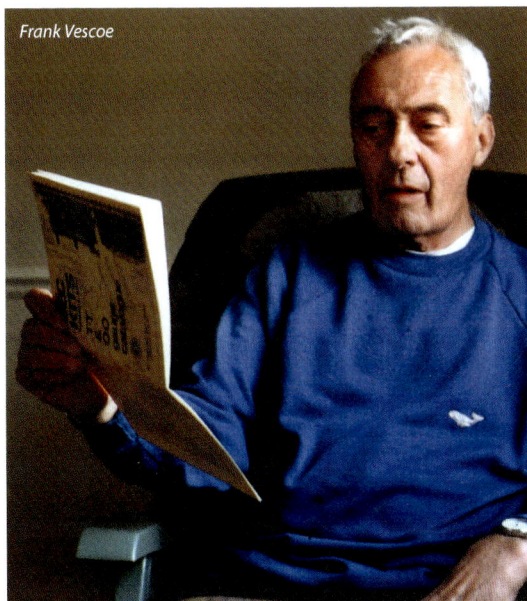
Frank Vescoe

A number of contributors to this book found encouragement and stimulation in the shop at 10, Tooting Bec Road, known as Bec Models. Both Brian Salter and Adrian Swain found model making as a hobby there, and it is thought the shop was first opened by Frank Vescoe in 1953. Known then as Bec Model Stores, the shop was handily placed just down the road from Bec School, thus appealing to all the school boys who sought an alternative to athletics. Brian recalls that he then discovered Micromodels at the shop, card model kits of various architectural and railway themes, together with maritime subjects, vehicles and aircraft. Frank sold a lot of these, but then the plastic kit appeared. A new Frog plastic aeroplanes kit range arrived in 1955, and were then were joined by Highway Pioneers from the US, and also Airfix arrived. Frank was at the forefront in stocking all of these ranges.

Frank made a point of having made up examples available to illustrate the end result. Railways, however, were the main emphasis at Bec Models, and such was the service that enthusiasts could bring their railway equipment and have it converted to two rail system, or fit scale wheels. The shop sported a traditional counter, and Frank would produce whatever was asked for, and explain its workings.

Brian recalls weekday lunchtimes and again at 5.00pm being busy, and on Saturdays extra staff were called in. Frank was always a Tri-ang stockist, and when they took the bold step of introducing the TT scale, Frank embraced the new scale and encouraged it.

However, in the room at the back, another activity entirely was taking place. Low volume white metal moulding had by 1957 begun to appear, at first with accessories and conversion kits. Complete kits then soon followed, and one of these was Bec Kits. Frank had met a retired Navy commodore, who had acquired the drawings of a centrifugal

Minding the shop at BEC models

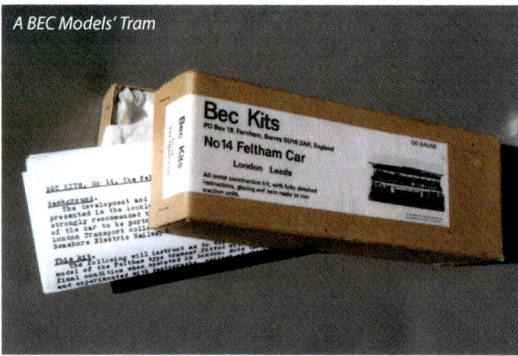
A BEC Models' Tram

casting machine from American businessmen in South America. He had returned home at the end of the war, and had surmised that by the use of this machine, he could produce artificial jewellery in volume. He set up in business, using Ron Southern and Bill Lines as his staff. These two went on to establish S&L kits, initially of wagons which Frank stocked in his shop. Frank produced his first brass master of a LSWR class G6 loco, and sent it to the Captain, for casting. It was so perfect, requiring no cleaning up, that Frank went to visit him in his cottage in Devon, and began using the casting machine and vulcanising press himself. Having taken measurements, Frank then had a replica of the machine made, and it too produced first class results.

That first loco body kit came along in March 1961, made to fit the well received Jinty chassis. Two years later, in 1963, came the first 00 gauge item, and in early 1966, the first tram.

Bec's series of trams reflected Frank's passion for them, and Adrian Swain recalls elsewhere his delight at being able to convert these for Frank's customers as well as some of his own. All this white metal casting was still taking place in the back room of the shop! By 1973, this industry was popular enough to stand alone, and the shop was sold in May to Bob Howes. Frank and Mary were married in January 1974, and moved to Ash Green in Surrey later that year. Mary had been getting concerned at the number of hours Frank was putting in, managing the shop by day, and the casting by night! The shop continued trading under the same name for some years, and was the London agent for Bec kits.

Frank and Mary had bought an old farmhouse, and Frank re-roofed an old barn to house his casting facilities, and created his patterns in the house. Their accountant was pleased that Mary had left her job with Wandsworth Council, and took on responsibility for the accounts, and also the packing of the kits, whilst Frank undertook the casting.

Frank and Adrian Swain were working closely together at this time, often purchasing white metal and electric motors jointly, and when a German collector contacted Frank, and due to an inaccuracy in a German tram kit, offered to supply Frank with scale drawings, another opportunity opened up. Adrian did the castings of a succession of German tram kits, and Frank supplied a number of German shops as a result.

By 1978 the trams were the whole output, and Frank developed the Tram range, until it totalled 45 different models. His 00 and TT gauge railway kits had been sold on to Adrian Swain, trading as ABS Models, who had been pressing him to pass it on for some time.

They moved again to Tilford in March 1983, as Frank was becoming concerned at the volume of traffic and the dangers for their family cats. Here they had an ironstone cottage, with a wooden garage and log store that became the casting centre. Four acres of woodland and grassland enabled them to enjoy life, and Mary was looking forward to Frank retiring. Through a contact in the BBC, they were introduced to Graham Cormick of the Hydestile Wildlife Hospital, with whom they worked returning many animals back to the wild.

The Aladdin Cave – BEC Models

Retirement was achieved in 1994, at age 65, and the remainder of the Bec Trams business was sold to Brian Robinson who is now believed to be in the Phillipines. Frank's health was declining, and a final move to Frimley in March 2004 brought them close to Mary's brother, and his wife proved supportive to her. Frank passed away peacefully on October 3rd 2006.

A selection of BEC kits are still available. Frank's shop can still be seen in Tooting Bec Road, now used as an office for chartered accountants, and the only shopfront to remain unaltered from Frank's era.

Bob Wills
Wills Finecast

Bob at home

After the Second World War, Bob Wills' first job was rebuilding bicycles in his bedroom, but there had to be something else. A friend had talked about getting a shop, and Bob too, thought this might be a good idea!

He found suitable premises in 1946, establishing his credentials with the name 'R. Wills Scientific Hobbies' at 92A Brighton Road, Coulsdon. Ron Chipping came to help with the shop-fitting, and on completion he asked Bob if he had any other work, as he had nothing else to go to. Bob was doubtful of finding any further work for him, but suggested he stayed around for a couple more weeks to see what might be available. Fourteen years later, Ron was still Bob's right-hand man in the shop! By then they were specialising in buying and selling all types of new and second hand models, also gradually acquiring agencies for well known brands.

Thus was built up a very successful model shop, something fairly new at the time. It became a favourite meeting place for modellers and was always jammed full on a Saturday, with many folk coming long distances! Prices were fortunately static for years and Bob still remembers that a tin of Humbrol enamel cost 4d. Having heard of a new technique for making moulds using vulcanised neoprene rather than steel dies, Bob undertook some experiments in the back of the shop during the early 1950s. No information was available at that time in the form of leaflets, brochures or books on this subject as the few people in the country who knew the technique were very anxious to keep it to themselves.

Not having heard of centrifugal casting, Bob decided to make up a unit himself enabling the metal to be pumped into the mould. Surprisingly this turned out to work well. The drawbacks were

that it was a rather slow process involving an element of danger!

The next discovery was spinning the mould to fill it. Bob already owned a machine used for cutting away the surface of the wax cylinders used on old-fashioned dictaphone machines. With a fair amount of 'butchery' he turned it into a fairly basic centrifugal casting machine, initially casting components for model railways, followed by small wagon kits. In 1958, now having acquired a proper casting machine, Bob made his first model loco kit. At the time he believed he was one of the first people to do so.

During these early days of manufacturing they continued to do the casting at the back of the shop, which meant that Bob could meet the people who were going to build the models, show them the latest castings and obtain their views. In due course the feedback from those customers was also very helpful in encouraging Bob to produce more models to a higher standard. The manufacturing side soon became an all-absorbing interest and in the early 1960s the shop was sold. Bob concentrated on manufacturing only with a small works at the back of a garage in Thornton Heath. They were very unsatisfactory premises, constructed mainly of corrugated iron, in which the temperature in the winter caused the thermometer to go off the end of the scale on the cold side and in the summer off the end of the scale on the hot side. However, despite the difficulties the business prospered and the sales of the loco kits increased.

On the strength of this it was decided that a stand should be taken at the Model Railway Exhibition in London. In 1961 at one of the first of these exhibitions that Bob exhibited at, he had a chance meeting with Ian Smith, an old friend. Ian who was one of the founder members of the British Racing and Sports Car Club. He asked if it would be possible to make a range of plastic car kits on the lines of the

Finecast Austin Seven Ulster

Merit models. This was of great interest to Bob who suggested not plastic, but using metal as this had already been at the back of his mind. Following this meeting, Ian set up a company called Auto-kits at Finsbury Pavement in London to market the range. He introduced Bob to Ron Platt, who produced the master patterns in nickel silver. All the manufacturing and some design work was by Wills Finecast.

Bob's shop, R. Wills Scientific Hobbies, 92A Brighton Road, Coulsdon

As far as can be ascertained, with the launch of the 'stack pipe' BRM in 1962, price 49/6d (£2.50)! Wills Finecast was the first company in the world to produce metal car kits, centrifugally cast in 1:24 scale in significant numbers to a quality that is still acceptable nearly 50 years later. The response from the public was amazing, and the quantities sold far exceeded their expectations.

By 1964 Wills Finecast had grown out of its premises in Thornton Heath and decided to move out. After initially considering Crawley, but finding factory space there was only leasehold, Bob finally found suitable premises in Forest Row, Sussex. He had been keen to have freehold premises, having suffered in the past with landlords. The Forest Row building had originally been built as a bus or coach garage and was licensed for coach building, which meant that it was a simple matter to change it to light industrial work. This was fortunate as it was extremely difficult to have a factory of any sort in such pleasant surroundings. Straightaway the premises were turned into a modern factory with

Graham Hill receiving his Wills BRM model for Christmas 1963, with Damon and sister Brigitte.

all the advantages of more space, including an attractive showroom.

Towards the end of the 1960s the Auto-kits company ran into grave difficulties finally seeking bankruptcy. Bob purchased the Auto-kits name and master patterns, which then became part of the Wills Finecast range. Bob had already introduced a range of 1:24 kits to an even higher standard of details, complete with engine and transmission, the first being the 4½ litre Bentley, which was reviewed in Miniature Auto of May 1968.

The Bentley was a great success and undoubtedly one of the finest models that had ever been put on the market.

W. O. Bentley himself gave the model his unqualified approval, and was so interested in the quality of the finished product that he particularly wanted to visit the factory. Unfortunately, however, he was never well enough to do so, and died without achieving this wish.

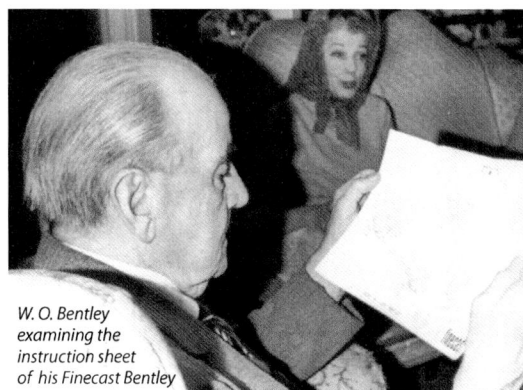

W. O. Bentley examining the instruction sheet of his Finecast Bentley

After the success of the Bentley, the Bugatti Type 59 was introduced, followed by the Vauxhall 30/98, the SS Jaguar 100 and the Rolls Royce Silver Ghost. Gradually, more were introduced, the last being an M.G. TF. In 1973/4, 1:43 scale kits were introduced. In addition Wills released a unique etched nickel silver spoked wheel which no-one had made before, as on such a small scale it had previously been impossible to cast the spokes.

However, some time before this they chose to embark on something else that no-one had done before, and with the ever growing interest in steam road vehicles they decided to develop a high quality 1:43 model of a Traction Engine, sparing no expense, trying not to omit any detail. Fortunately with many other models in production, they had plenty of time to develop this idea, and were not too concerned about the cost of development as it was financed by the regular sales of the other models. They finally picked on the Alchin Agricultural Engine as it was easy to get to see an original example at

Mass Production – the launch of Auto-kits

Horsmonden in Kent.

As there was no precedent the pattern making was very difficult. They were unable to examine how anybody had tackled this field before, so each difficulty had to be worked out as it arose, including the spokes which took a long time to perfect, before they found the right way to achieve the best result. When the model came on the market it was, to their knowledge, the very first of its kind in the world. They followed this with a Road Engine, a Showman's Engine, Foden Steam Wagon and Road Roller.

In 1987, H.M. Queen Elizabeth spent a day at Rolls Royce in Derby. She had a ride in the Silver Ghost and evidently enjoyed her time there very much. For Bob, the highlight of her visit was the presentation of his model Silver Ghost as she left.

Rolls Royce was also very pleased and wrote and thanked Wills Finecast. Rolls Royce had been very particular about the model, making sure it was accurate in every respect. For example, the valve push rods, which are visible on the engine, are seen to be in the correct firing order and the Dunlop lettering on the tyres in the correct type face. The patterns had taken nearly two years to complete.

That same year, when Philip Gibbs retired after 25 years with the company, the time had come for Bob to part with the cast metal side. Good links existed with Dave Ellis, a toy and model retailer in nearby Felbridge, who already stocked the Wills Finecast range. As a result, the entire business was passed over to Dave, with the birth of the new name of South Eastern Finecast. To this day Dave produces all Wills models and many more, in another location in Forest Row.

One of the most important considerations with this type of work is the people involved in the preparation of master patterns, and casting, with their particular skills and abilities. It was extremely difficult to find such craftsmen in the early days as there were very few around who had the skills, knowledge, and the artistic talent that was required when reducing from the full size example to creating a realistic model. Bob says that he has always been extremely fortunate in this respect.

In the early days many of the models for the Auto-kits range were made by Ron Platt, who later, with his wife Shirley joined Bob in Forest Row, staying for many years. A great asset to the firm, Ron's skills and design abilities were quite exceptional and thus started a friendship continuing to this day.

He also employed Ray Watson who was a particularly fine pattern maker, and the kind of dedicated person who would chase all over the country getting information on the models.

On one occasion, he travelled to London to check once again on details for the Rolls Royce Silver Ghost, but found that the original had been taken back to Derby the day before. He set off from London straight away in his car, arriving at Derby in the middle of the night. He slept in the car, in the morning visiting the factory to get the details he wanted and then returning to his home to continue with his work on the pattern making.

Not all the pattern making was done in the factory, as Bob had found from experience that the craftsmen with these skills and abilities often like to work in their own workshops.

Philip Gibbs joined the company in 1962 at the Thornton Heath premises. He ran the casting side, paying great attention to the quality of the product and was renowned for giving a good service to the customers.

Bob had always had the ambition in life to support his staff in enjoying and achieving in their chosen work. In addition, bearing in mind that the customer making the model would find it very frustrating if a part

The Finecast 1:24
4.5 litre Blower Bentley

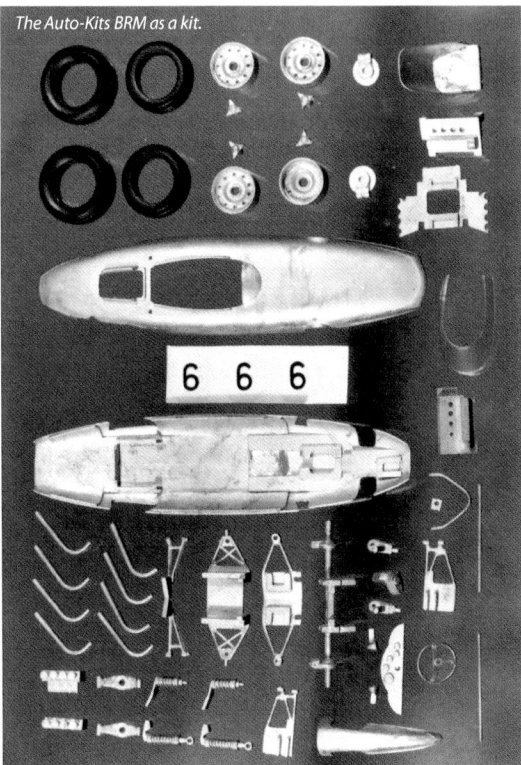

The Auto-Kits BRM as a kit.

6 6 6

and satisfaction, and worked well. Bob recalls hearing his staff often singing whilst they worked!

Bob was very fortunate in finding agents throughout the world, including Spielwaren Danhausen in Germany, and the 'Make Up Company' in Japan, the owner of which, Mr Uemoto, wrote many articles in magazines showing the construction of the kits. He even said that the Japanese should look to their laurels as the quality of work coming from England was superior at that time to anything being produced in Japan. Mr Gerd Winkelman, an enthusiastic builder of the Wills kits, wrote on one occasion to compliment the firm's craftsmen, saying, 'Your kits are absolutely the best white metal kits all over the world.'

The completed 1962 BRM 'Stackpipe'.

was missing or deformed, he instigated a production process whereby the person casting the parts also did the packing, taking the finished item to the store. This produced a feeling of personal responsibility

CHAPTER TWO
MAKING MODELS FROM WHITE METAL

Before we proceed further down the road of white metal history, let's stop for a moment and consider how white metal models are made – and before anything can begin, a master, pattern or buck has to be created by a master model maker. Making a master pattern to a fine standard is an extremely skilled task and the work of the best is akin to that of a quality silversmith or gunsmith. These days, this will usually be crafted in brass, and hold every detail to be cast, but it wasn't always the case. Early patterns were made from a mixture of putty, balsa wood or even polystyrene sheet. Wood became more regularly used, until brass was needed to withstand the higher molten metal temperatures. Rubber moulds are then taken from this master.

PART OF DOMESTIC IRON

NEOPRENE TO BE VULCANSED IN HERE.

Bob Wills drawings of a mould making fly press

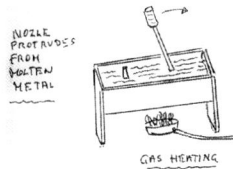

NOZLE PROTRUDES FROM MOLTEN METAL

GAS HEATING

RUBBER MOULD HELD OVER NOZLE BY HAND (GLOVE ON)!

ORIGINAL PRESSURE CASTING MACHINE USED IN BACK OF SHOP IN COULSDON EARLY 1950s

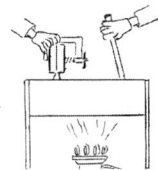

VIEW IN MOULD

Currently, the pattern is still most often made of hard brass to withstand the heat and pressure of vulcanising the rubber mould, though the more recent introduction of room-temperature vulcanising rubber can allow masters to be made of much softer materials such as Perspex, wood or plastic. However, when used with metal this can result in a much inferior product.

The use of room temperature rubber can offer scope for intricate, controlled mould design and manufacture, but does not allow for volume production, and mould life is reduced.

The whole business of creating such an original is a matter of calculator, callipers, lathe, files and a trained eye - and a dash of artistry. This cottage industry method is thus still far removed from the computer generated masters and dies of the major 21st century factory toy and model makers using the diecasting process.

Use of centrifugal casting machines utilises a circular mould, which can be spun, thus ensuring

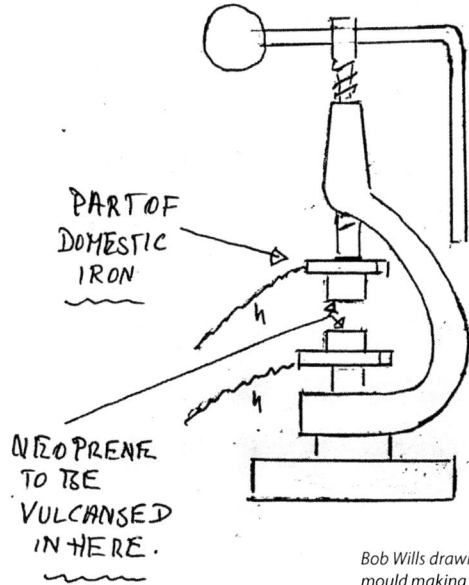

that the flow of hot white metal gets to all the small parts equally, and fills all areas of the mould.

When silicone rubbers became available, it was possible to manipulate the silicone material by hand, to ensure hollow areas of the patterns are filled.

Using a circular base made of card, a number of parts that will act as masters, perhaps of different materials, can be positioned around the circular base. This positioning is crucial, to ensure that the weight is balanced across the circle at any point, to ensure even distribution of the hot metal.

An early example of flash needing removal from the casting of Sanger Engineering's Humber

The silicone rubber can then be manually sculpted around the various patterns, being cut into small blocks where necessary to fill body sections whilst in a solid yet flexible state. It must be an exact fit to the shape of the pattern, and the art with one piece body pieces is to ensure that the join or split line of the top and bottom parts of the mould will create as insignificant a fault line as possible, thus reducing the fettling time once the casting has been completed.

The mould is effectively built up, upside down, and so the next step is to dust the first half with a light coat of talcum powder to stop the two halves of the mould from vulcanising together. The other half is then placed over the top.

The complete mould is then placed in a metal frame, which enters a vulcanising press, is heated to approximately 80 degrees C, whilst being compressed. Vulcanising turns the rubber into a harder substance, and the pressure must be maintained at a constant level. The length of time taken will depend on the thickness of the mould.

The mould is then opened, using a screwdriver, until the two halves can be peeled apart by hand, revealing all the brass pieces, which can then be removed. It should then be left open to the air for a week, after which the metal feeds and air bleeds must be cut, creating channels for metal to enter, and air to escape. The positioning of these is critical, together with their angle and size, to ensure the flow is even.

At this stage the biggest enemy of the caster is air, as with metal flowing at 350 degrees C, air bubbles out of the bleeds, but as the metal solidifies, it traps air. The whole mould is now placed into a centrifugal casting machine, spun at 300 – 600 revs, depending on the contents, for 45 seconds to 3 1/2 minutes, again depending on the contents, cooling down whilst spinning, solidifying the castings.

The castings are taken from the moulds as soon as they have solidified - often seconds. Chalk dust is used to ease the castings away from the mould. Operatives wear thick gloves and goggles for this!

Each time a mould is re-used, it needs a further dust down of talcum powder, to provide further lubricant. This also gives a far superior surface finish. The whole process, together with the fumes produced, requires extraction equipment to comply with Health & Safety requirements. Generally, if well cared for, moulds will last up to 20 years, but occasionally can split or break. Heat will also degrade them.

The whole process requires complete understanding, as to produce perfect castings is quite complex. It is often known in the business as a black art!

The white metal used is a mixture of lead and tin, whilst some companies use pewter, such as DG Models and Western and this makes the castings harder. Brooklin use different combinations of lead and tin for the bodies and small parts. There is less lead nowadays than was used 15 or 20 years ago in the early days.

There are relatively few people who have specialised in the casting and moulding process, but here we can tell the stories of three such businesses.

Seba Vulcanising Press

Tiranti - Casting Machine

John Allen
Scale Model Technical Services

John always has a mould close to hand

John Allen's first plastic kit was a Frog Vickers Viscount, and he still has the instruction sheet for it, plus many more instruction sheets for just about every kit he's made since! Kits were his mother's idea, and she helped him make the first ones.

John attended Carshalton College, and after leaving he went to work for a Ford dealership in Epsom, in their stores. After two weeks in the stores, he then became their warranty Administrator. After another 4¹/₂ years John joined the AA as a patrolman, and from there entered the Territorial Army and the Military Police.

John's model-making career kicked off in September 1976 when a friend at the Ford dealership recommended him to Western models. He became responsible for the casting shop, and mould making. Once John was shown how to make a mould, he found

he had a flair for it, and began developing different techniques for improving the casting, for instance, by controlling where the joint in the body was made, he would ensure the casting line did not show.

When the representatives from Northern Rubber visited the works, and introduced a new silicone rubber material to them, John was able to achieve different mixes, and improve quality much further. The industry had previously been using neoprene rubber, which had very little flexibility, and could not be sculpted.

After 7 years, in 1983, Keith Williams and John decided to set up on their own, and were fettling and building in Keith's front bedroom! Their first job was for Minimarque43, building and painting a Hudson. The breakthrough came when Keith found their first premises in Billingshurst, and 6 months later John went full time. They employed one other person then, and soon outgrew the new premises. A move to Hastings resulted, and by the 1990s they had 6000 square feet of factory area, and employed 34 staff. John remained responsible for the mould making and casting, whilst Keith oversaw the painting and building. Between them they handled the administration together. As the business progressed, Keith took on more of the administration, whilst John became the shop floor manager.

With the many specialist contracts that SMTS now handle, John's skills in mould making are still very much in demand, and this knowledge and his insight into the casting process ensures high quality every time.

John's interests outside model making are classic cars, owning and driving a Triumph Vitesse 2-litre convertible and a Rover SD1 Vitesse. The Rover attends a number of shows in south east England each year. John hasn't any plans for retirement yet, but can see a time when fewer days per week may be the order of the day.

Maurice Bozward
White Metal Assemblies

Val Bozward working on castings

It is not often that we come across someone who has made a major impact on the white metal model car field, yet has had no interest in model cars, but Maurice Bozward is one such person.

Maurice had been sheet metal worker by trade, but around 1976, when he was working for the Metal Box Company, work became short, and Maurice went onto a 4 day week. It so happened that a neighbour, Colin Tyler was using a centrifugal casting machine and Maurice did a little part time work for him. This was none other than Tyler Casting, which was the caster for John Day, pioneer of early white metal kits.

Colin and his brother were both toolmakers, and had begun plastic injection moulding, as well as the white metal casting. Maurice found that he had a flair for making moulds, and together he and Colin produced moulds and castings of cars and trucks, for John Day and Mikansue, for a period of 8 years. Maurice would take the completed castings home, and when required, his wife Val would pack them in their boxes for a little extra money.

The work expanded, and commissions came in from the USA from Franklin and Danbury Mint, casting in American pewter such items as animals as well as 1:24 scale cars. The Tyler Company made the masters, Maurice made the moulds, and then the items were soldered up, painted and sent back to the USA fully finished. Over this time materials improved dramatically, especially the properties of the rubber for the moulds.

By 1984 Maurice decided to become self-employed and work from home, making the moulds, and casting small items in pewter, such as the twigs or other parts for porcelain animals to perch on. To begin with his one and only customer was Tyler Casting. Maurice then bought a casting machine, and began casting model cars. His first customer was K&R Replicas. He would be sent the master, not knowing who had made it, and these may be either in brass pewter or sometimes plastic or resin. Thus was born White Metal Assemblies.

Since those early days, Maurice's customer base has grown considerably to include Crossway, J&M Classics, Kenna Models, ASAM, Illustra, and Motor City USA, together with European makers such as AMR, from France, Belgium and Sweden. Whilst the business grew and provided a fulltime income for Maurice and Val, at its height Maurice just took on one more young man who stayed with him for 4 years, until his family move took him away. At that time, working in two workshops, Maurice took the decision to give these up and return to working at home, and this he has done since 2002.

Currently, business is booming, despite the recession, which Maurice puts down to the secure financial position that many white metal collectors enjoy. His order book is full, and he continues to have a wide customer base in the trade. This now includes a significant contract with Armopax, makers of 1 metre long radio controlled tanks. All the tools such as spades and hammers attached to these fighting vehicles are made by Maurice.

Maurice is finding that he is casting ever bigger runs, with 160 as a first run for a European maker, of a Jaguar XJ series. The work is divided evenly between Maurice and Val now, with Maurice making the moulds, and then sitting back and watching Val do the casting!

Maurice has no plans for retirement, and continues to get very positive feedback from all his trade customers. It is good to know that quality casting is still being produced in the UK!

Dave Buttress & Chris Arnott
CMA Moldform

Chris Arnott at the ModeleX stand

The story of one of the most successful white metal and resin manufacturing businesses has humble beginnings.

Back in 1988, Dave Buttress was a Farm Manager working on a large farm in Newark, and as a hobby he built 1:72 scale model aircraft. Dave became the director of the Newark Aircraft Museum, and launched a model aircraft club there.

The museum had just moved to its current site on the ex RAF base at Winthorpe near Newark, and with the club being part of the museum, it wasn't long before the club was commissioned to build a diorama of the site for promotional purposes.

It was then that John Adams joined the club, and as he had just left the RAF, he was looking for something to occupy his time. John had a passion for model trains, and had just bought Millholme Models, a producer of high quality model railway white metal castings.

Meanwhile, Dave had mastered a resin nose cone as a conversion kit to create a Griffin Spitfire out of a standard kit. One dark rainy night at the Museum, John and Dave decided that they should begin producing conversion kits for model aeroplanes. As John's interest was jets, he worked on creating an ejector seat out of white-metal, which had the secondary effect of making a completed plastic kit much more stable, given its three wheel undercarriage.

3 or 4 months later, 4 or 5 different conversion kits had been created. Dave was approached by Ed Deeley, of ED models in Shirley, Birmingham, who was seeking a caster to make 1:72 and 1:48 scale

Dorothy & Dave Buttress at the ModeleX stand

figurines of RAF figures from masters that he had had made. A deal was struck, involving Ed selling Dave's white metal kits and parts, and Dave would cast the figurines.

By 1989, Dave had bought his first casting machine. At this time, Chris Arnott was running a business in Birmingham producing resin parts for a number of model vehicle and railway manufacturers, and Dave approached him for some resin casting.

Chris's resin production was bulging at the seams, and a happy marriage became obvious; Chris asked Dave to join him in Birmingham, with Dave leading on white metal, and Chris on resin. Together they formed CMA Mouldcast as a partnership in 1991.

Dave's wife Dorothy assisted Chris on the resin side of the business, and demand continued to grow with significant regular orders for 'trade' casting coming from as far afield as Australia and the United States. In 1992, Dave mastered some 1:43 resin and white-metal kits of classic Riley cars, which were sold under CMA's own name, and at around the same time Dave's own DB range of aircraft conversions became a direct licence made product of the company. Other large contracts at that time included providing the white metal 'super-detail' parts for Airfix and Heller kits.

With yet more casting work coming in, they made the decision to buy another 2 casting machines, making 3 in all. The white metal side of the business was proving very profitable, with resin production running along side by side. Over the years, Dave recalls providing a casting service to many of the well-known names in the market, such as Marsh Models, Modelauto, Promod, Fire Brigade Models, Crossway Models, Ralph Horton (RSH), Pegasus and many others.

Business direction was becoming more focussed, and in 1996 the rights to the Riley kits were sold to Roger Tennyson of Crossway Models, for whom they have since cast many other models. Contract casting remained throughout the core

business of the company, and the aircraft accessories side was sold to E.D. Models. By this time Dave's son Kevin had joined the company to strengthen the growing production white metal and resin production teams

In parallel with the scale model manufacturing side of the business, now a Limited Company under the name CMA Moldform Limited (the omission of the 'u' in 'Moldform' was deliberate!), had expanded into resin production of prototype and industrial components, early orders including automotive dashboards and components for full-size instructional and display aircraft engines.

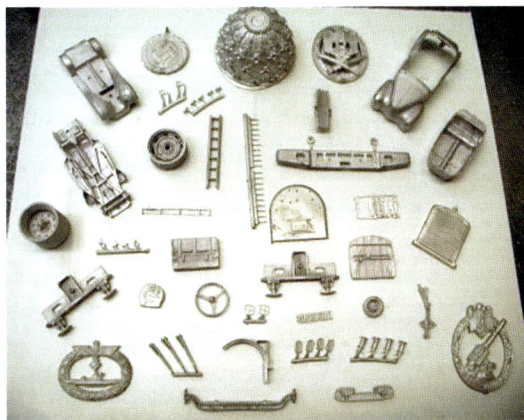
Range of white metal cast products

By 2000, Chris had become interested in exploring the potential of 3D CAD as a means of producing master patterns, this including the use of a 3D scanner to 'capture' the shape of an existing model to allow it to be re-scaled larger or smaller. Dave was in a position to buy out Chris's share of the business. Yet another white metal casting machine was purchased to cope with rising demand, and contracts were successfully obtained with diverse customers such as artistic promotion companies, the RNLI for lifeboats, and White Ensign Accessories making miniature accessories for 1:200 scale ships.

Riley drophead

Riley saloon

More recently, CMA have completed a commission to produce a medical presentation of an encapsulated hospital bed and wheelchair in 1:20 scale, CAD design work being undertaken by Chris. Dave now has a Head of Department overseeing the white metal services, with 4 casting machines and the staff to operate them. The masters for all the contract work are now created by pattern makers selected by the client. However, masters have recently been produced for Corgi for their range of large scale figurines of popular TV programmes, and these are then produced in China.

Today, Dave feels that about 1/6th of the business is white metal, and the overall amount has reduced by some 20% since the earlier days. This is partly due to the versatility of resin, and also due to popular imperatives. Model kit producers find that the 1-piece resin body is much more popular now than flat-sided white metal kits for buses. Postage costs are much lower on resin kits too, and the detailed obtained in the moulding process can be higher.

Dave foresees a continuing decline in white metal transport models, although the resurgence of kits is proving a popular choice. Promod, a long term client, have recently commissioned CMA to create new moulds from the original Somerville masters, in order that the Somerville range can be re-launched as kits.

Dave and his team at CMA Moldform are surely ensuring that white metal continues to be available to high standards of casting for collectors, whilst evolving to suit a changing market.

CHAPTER THREE
PATTERN MAKERS
THE HEART OF THE BUSINESS

The genesis of the white metal model is the pattern, or master, which whilst now is mostly made from brass or a fibre board called Sikablock, was originally made from other materials, including wood and fibreglass.

Softer materials such as this will not withstand the vulcanising process to create the silicon mould rubber, and so the industry standard is brass.

For those who copy diecast models, of course the original model is the master. When adapting an existing white metal model such as a saloon into a convertible, the white metal base model duly adapted becomes the master.

Brass master for Morris J Van

Brass pattern for Vauxhall Cresta Friary estate

The cost of the pattern maker's time in laboriously carving a piece of brass using hand tools results in that pattern often now being worth £2K-£3K. The ownership of this original pattern can take many forms. For some, a gentleman's agreement is all that is necessary. Some pattern makers and their customers agree stage payments, with a brass block of a general shape, complete with wheels being shown to the customer at an early stage. For others, the only way is to complete the task, show the customer the finished product, and make any further changes required, then submit the final account when the customer is happy.

For brass however, there is also a residual value in the pattern, and when we explore the history of different ranges, we discover that an original pattern may be sold on to another caster or assembler/distributor, perhaps be modified, say, from saloon to drophead, and thus have its life extended.

Sometimes, there is further definition achieved to render an old pattern usable by modern standards.

Adrian Swain described how in his early days of creating patterns, he would begin armed with a ladies nail file, 2 needle files, 3 drills and a soldering iron, and when this was found wanting a blowtorch. He was living in digs at the time, and would come home from work, have his meal at 6.00pm, then retire to his room and spend 3-4 hours, 'filing brass' and listening to Radio 3 on a very early pocket transistor radio.

Just occasionally, a model maker will use an existing white metal casting as a basis for a conversion to a different model. In creating a new model of a rare prototype Austin A70 Hereford

Kenna Models - conversion of A70 Hereford into a countryman, stages 1 and 2

countryman, Pete Kenna describes how he started with an existing Hereford saloon body casting, and a Standard Vanguard van body and then with a lot of sawing, soldering and filling with pewter he ended up with the piece of shrapnel pictured below! (A70 countryman pics)

All the brass pieces, window frames, roof panels, were soft soldered on, and then once the pattern was finished it was sent to the caster and a silicone mould produced. The subsequent castings were then centrifugally cast using white metal.

In the early days, most pattern makers worked in much the same way, in that if they wanted a quantity of castings from a pattern, they would give it to a caster who supplied a quantity free and then kept the pattern for their own use! This was obviously no great incentive to enthusiastic pattern makers. As a result, some pattern makers would have clearly agreed arrangements for the ownership of the pattern, whilst others may have diversified by obtaining their own casting machines.

We have interviewed most of the regular and consistent pattern makers in the UK, and here are some of their stories –

Kenna Models - conversion of A70 Hereford into a countryman, stages 3 and 4

Steve Bates
Pattern maker to John Day

Steve Bates - early pattern maker for John Day

For Steve, it all started in Hackney in the 1960s, when he saw his first motor race on a black and white TV. He was inspired!

He had been working as a plumber's mate, and picked up a copy of Autosport, and read a report on a non-championship race, and the name Innes Ireland struck a chord. Steve found out about the London Trophy race at Crystal Palace, went by London

Transport, and watched his new hero come from the back of the grid to win the race.

Steve had been brought up on Airfix and Revell kits, but with racing cars the priority, he hunted for models, but apart from the Merit kits, there was nothing until he found the Solido Lotus 18. He painted it in UDT colours, with Innes Ireland's colours on the driver's helmet, and was well pleased.

Once he could drive, he got a job driving vans, and then moving on to HGVs. He also enjoyed camping with friends in Europe, visiting model shops, and buying Mebetoys, Politoys, and Mercury racing cars not available in the UK. The next stage was to alter these models to a style he felt they should look like, using Plastic Padding he had discovered in his plumbing job.

Corgi then produced the Lotus 25, a passable model in 1964, and he bought lots in order to use the suspension and wheels to convert them to Cooper Maseratis and Ferrari, and the rest of the grid. For research, Steve spent a lot of time at the Motor Books & Accessories shop, and one day took in his conversions. They were impressed, and put them on show in the shop.

Not so long after this, Steve got a call from a Roger Moray from Lucerne, who had seen the models in the shop, and asked for a set to be made for him. A professional commission secured!

Whilst reading a model Cars magazine, he saw the first John Day advert for a Ferrari 375, and a 1904

Mercedes. He phoned John, who also had seen the Motor Books display. John was in Solihull at the time, so Steve visited John to explore building his kits for advertising purposes. When John then moved to Malvern, he asked Steve if would make a master of the March 701, and the Tyrell 001.

At this time Steve had been applying for jobs in motor racing, and landed a driving job with Firestone Tyres. Sensing the loss of a pattern maker, John Day offered him a full-time job in Malvern. Not an easy choice, but he chose Malvern. Steve moved up to Malvern, found himself working in a porta-kabin in a haulage yard. Rodney Henley was also working there, and Steve learnt how to spray paint. Steve made the pattern for John's Mercedes Streamliner, and Rodney was working on the Auto Union for Danhausen. John's pattern makers were making kits for the Mikansue range and others at this time. At this stage, most of his patterns were sculpted in Plastic Padding, then placed into a liquid silicone rubber mould, white metal then poured in, then into a centrifugal mould. The business then moved into the Morgan Cars complex. More patterns followed, but John had plans for a 'Motor Racing in Miniature' Museum, which Steve built cars for, but never materialised.

Steve was living the high life, with a sports car, attending race meetings at weekends, taking pictures. Other makers were beginning to appear, such as AMR, Teneriv, and Danhausen. John Day was heavily into the motor racing scene, sponsoring Alain de Cadenet's car, and on one occasion he hired a plane to take his team to Le Mans, armed with Press passes, and Steve met VIPs and was able to visit the Lola pit.

However, this was not to last, as Steve and John fell out when John wanted to make a ready built diecast March, so Steve went back to his driving work for two years. He had been working for the RSRE research facility in Pershore, but the airfield closed down, and he was transferred to Malvern. Out of the blue he received a call from John again, asking him to return to help turn out a range known as E2000, all simple 1½ litre cars. John was by now in serious financial difficulties, and he wanted Steve to make a pattern a week. Orders were not coming in, and it seemed that the business was running to stand still. Steve realised that they were not moving with the times, and by 1979, he had married, and moved away to Ledbury.

Steve then trained as an ambulance driver, but had an accident injuring his back, and by this time had two children. He took the bold step of contacting his old customers from previous work, and began building kits for them. This led to writing articles in magazines, and his name got around. Tony Bellm contacted Steve, wanting to develop a comprehensive collection of racing car models, and Steve reckons that literally thousands of kits were bought through Grand Prix Models, which Steve then built for Tony. This continued for 5-6 years, during which Steve was able to enjoy the corporate hospitality at Brands Hatch through his association with Tony.

When Tony sadly died, Steve packed up all his collection and transported them to Silverstone, where they now reside in the British Racing Drivers Club.

The last master Steve made was for a Maserati 3011, driven by Prince Bira. He was asked to produce this from scratch, and it incorporated the latest high quality parts, including wheels from Italy. The customer was so pleased with it, that he ordered more for his friends, and in the end a run of 125 models were made, fully financed by the customer.

With the passing of Tony Bellm, it wasn't long before Steve became aware of the appearance of quality diecast and resin models from Spark, Minichamps and Ixo, and he considered an alternative way of remaining involved with model cars. He toured the Toy Fairs, buying and selling, and to his surprise, met John Day again, who this time had just launched his 1:76 scale white metal kits. They came to an agreement that John would supply Steve, who would then build and sell the models at Toy Fairs. Perhaps not surprisingly, this arrangement lasted six months only.

Over the last 10 years, Steve has diversified into model plant, trading in the quality models produced by NZG and others. He was approached by Chuck Sword, who was involved with TWH Models in the US. He was seeking a distributor in the UK, and so Steve became the sole outlet in the UK for this range. As Steve says, he has moved from the smallest and fastest, to the biggest and slowest!

These 1:50 scale trucks are very high quality, and Steve is finding this market is both developing, and consistent. He now has his own home, two children one of whom has presented him with a granddaughter, a nice car, two horses and a dog which they all love dearly, and is considering when the right moment might be to retire!

Neil Bollen

It seems that a cluster of pattern makers and builders sprung up around Max Kernick in the Exeter area, and a perhaps lesser known pattern maker from the West Country is Neil Bollen.

Neil recalls the 00 gauge railway modelling scene developing for him an interest in detail, not so much for Neil the obsession with cars. By age 13 he was making his own jewellery at home, and in the

Neil Bollen in his workshop

Soon after this he moved to Devon, and began working for a clock making company, followed by setting up in business himself, undertaking repair and restoration work local antique dealers.

In the late 1970s Neil designed and manufactured decanting machines in silver or brass for vintage wine bottles. These were based on a Victorian design, and involved the use of both artistic and mechanical skills.

In the early 1980s Neil provided training in fine metalwork for a number of people who had incurred a disability. He was asked if he could focus the training for a trainee who wanted to retrain as a patternmaker for Max Kernick, and when the employee moved on, Neil took over.

Around the same time he had commissions from the armed forces to make table centrepieces. One, for the Royal Engineers, was a silver model of a Hong Kong junk, to commemorate the British departure from Hong Kong. This was followed by two Rolls Royces, the first being a 20/25 Landaulet, which Neil created in two versions, rear hood up or down. It was very complicated in design, and as a result, difficult to assemble.

More commissions for modern classics were to follow, and Neil remembers a 1950s Aston Martin for an American company. Whilst Neil usually uses brass or other non-ferrous metals for his patterns, the Aston was first created in Perspex as a shape, and then electro-formed in metal, with finer definition added later.

This working relationship with Max Kernick continued for 5 years or so, but Max had other pattern makers working for him, and Neil was developing restoration side of his business, working for museums collectors and dealers. As a result, the model car side of the business came to a natural end. Neil no longer has any connection with the white metal model car industry, but remembers his links with it with pride.

fullness of time studied art at his Technical College. Which way to go when you have an interest in both design and creation presented a challenge, and in Neil's case he was keen on ceramics, jewellery making and musical instrument making!

Neil progressed to the John Cass School of Art in Whitechapel, part of the City of London Polytechnic. It was regarded as the trade school for jewellery and silversmiths. 4 years later, Neil had been equipped with a good technical grounding in fine metal work. He began working with small boxes in silver, complete with fittings, and still there was no thought for model making.

Martin Feldwick

Martin Feldwick was born in Essex. His father made models and Martin's first memory of this was seeing his father making an Airfix Ferguson tractor kit for a friend. Apparently plastic cement was not yet invented, so his father used chloroform!

At technical school Martin was always making models, with a useful sideline in casting plaster garden gnomes, painting them and selling them to neighbours. His street was infested with decaying plaster gnomes by the time Rock and Roll, guitars and girls mercifully entered his life and the gnome making stopped.

When his Technical school initiated a course selection process, Martin was advised to take engineering instead of art; probably the worst advice ever given to him though the engineering did come in handy in the future.

Later, it wasn't until he tripped over some Historex models that his interest in models took off again, painting wargame figures and model soldiers. Being in the usual cycle of find right girl, get married, buy house, have baby, sell motorbike and buy car, he usually sold his painted models to supplement his income from being a line supervisor in the electronics industry.

He was into wargaming a bit, with his first figure being a German machine gun team made from

wire, barbola and a soldered up MG 42 on a tripod, all in 20mm size. He also painted figures and made dioramas for Edwarn Suren and Under Two Flags in London and eventually worked in Seagull Models of Exhibition Road SW7, after seeing how the electronics industry was shaping up and endless strikes. Concluding that sculpting the human form let alone horses was a black art he could never aspire to, he continued painting figures, winning awards and also got interested in painting the zinnfiguren flats that still inspire him for their action and freedom of movement.

Major Russ Salberg, an American customer who also became a friend gave Martin some epoxy putty called A+B and told him to try it out. A 54 mm master pattern of a Wachmeister of the Imperial German Army resulted, and was sold straightaway to Seagull models. Martin was on his way to becoming a figure sculptor. It wasn't that easy and some failures never saw the light of day.

Around the mid 1970s he became interested in 1:43 model racing cars. A subject that was to greatly influence his life .He began by building a few kits he had bought from the recently opened Lamberts of Ley Street in Ilford. As before he sold them back to the shop and began making more model car kits in his spare time. Martin had always been interested in motor racing. As a kid Motorsport and Hot Rod magazines, Beano and NME were standard buys with newspaper round earnings.

He was often appalled by the low quality of the models, mainly John Day but was encouraged by some of the foreign manufacturers coming into the market Later, Martin took an offer from one of his customers and started working for him in the record industry exporting singles by the tens of thousands. Using the money earned he moved to Norfolk with his family.

He also bought a brass US model railroad locomotive, which he had long dreamed of and now could afford to buy one. He painted and weathered it, and took it back to the shop to show them. They asked him to paint more for their customers and he was amazed when they presented him with an Escort van full. Painting US brass, making model car patterns from brass, sculpting figures and sometimes brass master patterns of cars and train fittings are not pursuits he really takes to, though the end result, as he puts it, is anything but proper work.

During the eighties he made railroad figures for Pacific Fast Mail in the US in all the main US scales. A hundred or so were made, and were well received and Martin was amazed that collectors in the UK and the US actually collected them as well as use them on their railroads. He also made railway figures for the highly respected Phoenix Model Developments. It was soon the small scale figure that Martin was making his own province, not the larger sized soldiers. His work for Phoenix and PFM meant sculpting men, horses, wild animals, good looking girls and ladies. He also made some figures in 30mm for Tradition Scandanavia. Most accredit the figures to Charlie Stadden which Martin considers the highest of all compliments.

In the nineties Dick Ward, pattern maker, decided to make some model railway figures in 00 gauge. Most 00 figures were pretty poor, and so Martin was contacted to work on a project called Montys Model Railway that continues to this day. He also worked for Omen Miniatures mainly making 1:43 racing driver figures and also very nubile women. He also launched his own Trackpass Miniatures, a series for 1:43 motorsport with figures like Gendarmes and photographers rather than just drivers, but of course some nubile women much loved by diorama builders.

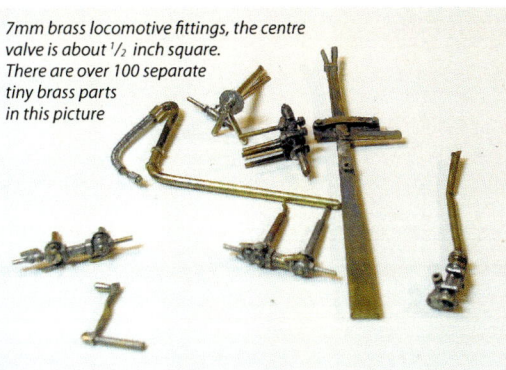

7mm brass locomotive fittings, the centre valve is about $1/2$ inch square. There are over 100 separate tiny brass parts in this picture

While gathering information on racing driver details like suits and seat belt harness he contacted Team Lotus and was invited to see the factory. It was addiction at first sight, sitting in Senna's JPS 97T which he was still racing, and having a private tour of the team factory. This led to attending an F1 test, and some full 3 day tyre test passes for Silverstone. Being in the pit lane with no speed restrictions and a full set of F1 cars testing all day for 3 days, he was totally hooked. He made models for quite a few teams and influential people who all helped feed the addiction

Later in the late nineties seeking a subscription from a Japanese Model Car magazine led to becoming a freelance Motorsport photographer and journalist for the group, interviewing f1 drivers and attending launches and functions and a halcyon day at Snetterton circuit photographing the Bentley Le Mans car from a moving car and being wined and dined royally. All that and he got paid for it too!

While motorsport was taking up a lot of time and money, he still had to work and make models and patterns. There seemed to be a time when work was drying up and he even thought of getting a proper job. This would have interfered with going at the drop of a hat to motor sport events. A chance telephone call led to him being asked to paint little plastic and diecast toy trucks for promotion companies. This was boring, erratic but also very well paid and enabled him to continue sculpting figures

and attending race meetings, and F1 team launches.

Currently, Martin is still making model railway figures, mainly for Dart castings, spraying plastic trucks in lurid colours and chopping up bits of brass, and his fingers, to make locomotive fittings .He has several new lines to launch for his own range and is returning to 30mm figures.

Over the years Martin has made figures for Monarch Miniatures, Carthage Miniatures, Omen Barton Miniatures, Phoenix Model Developments, Real Model, Montys Model Railways, Junes Small World (PFM), SMTS, Tradition Scandinavia, K+R Replicas, Grand Prix Models, Tameo Kits and and many others he has forgotten about. He is a little sad that some of his best work was for companies not so well known that seem to have disappeared into thin air.

Martin always jokes that it's a great way to starve but it also got him to places and meeting people that a factory supervisor would never have had the chance to do.

Rodney Fox
Concours Auto Models

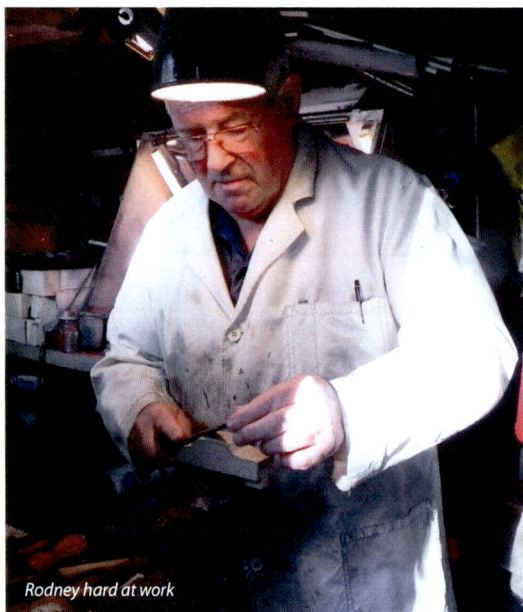
Rodney hard at work

After the end of WW2 in 1945, Rodney started collecting Dinky Toys, then Corgis and some of the diecasts from the continent. He became interested in model making and built several aircraft carved out of solid balsa wood, progressing to carving some 1:43rd car bodies also in balsa, then moved on to plastic kits. When white metal and resin kits came onto the

market he began building and collecting these too.

After leaving school he went straight into an apprenticeship as a Marine Fitter & Turner, then moved to Southampton in 1965 when he went into the aircraft manufacturing industry and eventually became a Tool Maker. However, he was made redundant in 1985, and being in his mid 40s found it impossible to get another job.

Within a few weeks of this happening Rodney was exhibiting models at the Classic Car Show in Birmingham and whilst there got talking to Ralph Foster of Pandora Models. Ralph suggested than he combine his model making and tool making skills and go into Pattern Making. He offered Rodney a commission, and so Concours Auto Models was born.

From those beginnings, over the years, Rodney has produced many patterns for different people, including the 1929 Arrol Aster Bluebird Land Speed Record Car, and the Gyronaught twin - engined L.S.R. Motorcycle, both in 1:43 scale, for Pandora Models.

Commissions for masters also came for the Piccolino range, in 1:76 scale, including the Sunbeam 1000 HP L.S.R. car, Golden Arrow, Porsche 908 Bergspyder, and the MG 'Old Number One'. 1:24 scale featured with the Jaguar XK140 D.H.C. for Small Wheels, and Jaguar 'E' type V12 Roadster for Highlander Models. Four wheel Models wanted an Alvis TA21 Graber in 1:43, and Electra, in Sweden commissioned two Volvos the PV445 Pick-up, and PV544 Rally car. Midland Racing Models used Rodney's skills to convert a number of Aston Martins, and he has also undertaken several military models in 1:87 scale, for Military Figurines.

*Rodney's pattern
for Pandora's Bluebird*

Rodney took on a number of special commissions, amongst which, was one for Richard Briggs of Minimarque43, to build and paint 100 only Ford Edsels in 1:43 scale, in bronze and white, all to be supplied to the Harrah Motor Museum in Nevada.

In creating his patterns, wherever possible he would gain access to the full size vehicle to photograph and measure. Most photos would be taken in black and white as that shows up body contours much more effectively. He made a small ruler out of aluminium strip, painted it black with white lines, and would attach this to the vehicle being modelled using Blue-Tack, thus transferring the measurement into the photo.

His photographic method was to lay down a tape rule parallel to the side, front and rear of the car and a few feet away, and then mount his camera on a tripod at a height at about half way up the car. The feet of the tripod would then be placed against the tape rule, so that all photos were taken at the same height and distance from the vehicle

Rodney's next step would be to take the first shot in line with the front bumper, then at the front wheel centre line, door shut lines etc. thus eliminating the parallax effect when photographing the complete car in one go.

From these photos Rodney would create scale working drawings, taking into account the percentage of oversize to allow for shrinkage of the white metal after casting. This in not required for models to be cast in resin as they come out of the mould size for size.

Rodney would always start by marking out the position of the wheel centres on each side as a reference point, then start panel beating the sides of the model in sheet brass. All the other body parts would be similarly completed, followed by silver soldering them together, using the highest melting point solder first, then gradually using lower grades so that the heat needed would not un-solder the previously soldered parts. Rodney is indebted to Peter Comben of Enco Models for his help and advice in the steps required at the design stage, to ensure that the parts would come out of the mould easily and construction of the model would be as straightforward as possible. One very valuable tip

Pete gave Rodney was to insert metal pins into the mould to form location pins in solid metal instead of white metal, which rarely come out perfectly round and are prone to breaking off.

The reason for patterns being made of brass and silver soldered rather than soft soldered is that the pattern needs to withstand the immense temperatures and pressures involved in creating a vulcanised rubber mould. This method was later made easier by the moulds having room temperature vulcanising silicone rubber inserts that do not require the same heat and pressure. This material is what is used for the moulds that resin cast models are made in, so that the actual pattern can be made of almost everything.

*Rodney's pattern for a
3 litre Alvis for Four
Wheel Models*

Rodney's favourite material for this method was a composition resin called Model-Lab. He found it is easy to machine, carve, rub-down and polish to a high gloss finish. Rodney also found Plasticard useful in various thicknesses, which he used to great effect when making the chassis and rear bodywork of the Volvo PV445 Pick-up truck for Electra.

During the 10 years until 1995, that Rodney was full-time pattern making, he also undertook wedding chauffeur duties on the weekends driving a range of classic wedding car such as Rolls Royce Silver Ghosts and Phantom IIIs. As the pattern making soon turned out to be insufficient for a full-time income, Rodney took on some individual commissions. The first was from the Photographic Librarian of the National Motor Museum at Beaulieu, who wanted a full restoration of a three feet long model of a Fiat made by a prisoner of war, in many different materials. Rodney had to remake many individual parts, using plastic steel and metal, so that once again its engine and gearbox would fully operate.

Rodney has been a founder member of the South Hants Model Auto Club since 1981, and through his use of resin to cast certain components, he has made spare parts, firstly for members and then on a wider basis, to convert or detail existing models.

Model shops would also seek his skills in building

and converting kits for customers, and these would often be Aston Martins. Around 1993, Rodney took on some tool making work to cover part of the working week, which he continued with after he retired from his pattern making in 1999. His pattern making work has all been undertaken in a workshop at the rear of his 20 feet garage at home.

He finally retired in October 2009, and has at last a little time to focus on building all the many kits that he has of his own. His role as Chair of the Southampton club has meant that he gets to construct and attend, with fellow members, their club displays at prestigious events such as the Aston Martin Owners club annual meeting at Silverstone. For the display there, in 2010, he created a scale model of the Jock Horsfall's 2 litre "black car".

Lawrence Gibson

Lawerence Gibson

It was not easy to catch up with Lawrence Gibson, as he had been preparing for an important exhibition of Cornish craft businesses in the house of St. Barnabas in Soho in early 2010, in company with traders representing fashion and lifestyle, clothing, skincare and 2 other jewellery and accessories specialists with an eco them as well as himself.

He has been building up his jewellery business over time, and is currently working on models to provide a steady financial base. He enjoys the variety, and hopes it will continue.

Unlike some pattern makers, Lawrence didn't begin in the jewellery line. After completing his university

Rolls Royce Aerocar for Max Kernick

course in industrial product design, and having made models of the concepts required as part of the course, he returned to Cornwall.

There was no work available in that specific field, but the Job centre was offering a post as model Maker for Gems & Cobwebs. Their previous pattern maker had left, and they wanted to keep that specialism in house. The process of then casting and spraying was all new to Lawrence, and here he was able to view the whole sequence.

Lawrence was 22 years old when he started with Gems & Cobwebs in 1995, and worked with Bernie and Graham Du Cros for 4 years until the business became Milestone Miniatures in 1999. Lawrence was keen to work independently, but continued to work for them on a freelance basis. He was responsible for the Brooklands range, and acknowledges that if the subject matter was particularly interesting, he put extra effort into the accuracy. He was also responsible for the Jaguar XK8 and several of their American range, amongst others.

Sometimes Graham would give Lawrence a model which he wanted

Alvis TA14 Woodie for Mike Rogers

modifying into something new. Graham knew of Max Kernick, and it was through this link that Lawrence was recommended to Max, who was developing his Top Marques range. Lawrence's first pattern for Top Marques was the Delage, and Max was pleased with the result, so Lawrence was promoted to Rolls Royces and also some modifications. Lawrence recalls with pleasure his time with Max, and between 2000 and 2008 he would regularly drive to Honiton where Max had his workshop. Where he also began taking on the new Alvis range. He did all the Alvis patterns, including the woodie, continuing to make them for Mike Rogers. During this time Roger Tennyson contacted Lawrence to ask him to do a pattern for Crossway, and as a result he continued working for Carl Merz when Roger retired.

The jewellery connection began to develop whilst Lawrence was still working in Exeter with Max. It was considerably boosted when Max decided to move to France and sold his casting and moulding equipment to Lawrence. Lawrence obtained a loan from the Prince's Trust, and a grant from the local business start-up scheme, and since then Lawrence has been able to use these for both jewellery and model making.

Other lines of interest for Lawrence include making patterns for resin slot car bodies for Classic Slot, owned by John Haywood. Currently, the jewellery side has grown as Lawrence has regarded it as having greater business potential. It has included a wide range of necklaces, pendants and ear-rings, and Lawrence has been focussing on getting these into high street stores.

The Trade Exhibition in 2010 was the springboard for this new venture, and Lawrence hopes to be selling to retailers very soon. At 37 years of age, Lawrence feels that the lines of interest complement each other, the one rising to support the other as markets rise and fall. The future looks bright for Lawrence!

Gerald Gilbert

It was a Matchbox Snocat that inspired Gerald Gilbert to make models, and although his brother was into Airfix plastic kits, Gerald preferred bits of cardboard and Sellotape rather than glue.

Not only Snocats but even working slot machines were created, but it wasn't until metal work at secondary school, and the compulsory bowls and adjustable spanners were created to a precise standard, that the bug set in.

Around 1974/76, Gerald signed up for a Adult Education jewellery class after school. This was followed up by a one year pre-apprentice course at the Sir John Cass School of Art in London, the intention being to continue into an Apprenticeship in diamond mounting / jewellery.

However, during the process of applying for jobs, somehow Gerald walked through the wrong door, and found himself being offered a part-time job in his home town of Sevenoaks, Kent. This enabled him to continue his studies at college, and between the two experiences, he learnt the crafts of diamond setting, and enamelling. He had begun to develop an interest in design and technical challenges, and as an experiment, he made his brother a model of Pentax camera in silver. A small scale Unimog followed, which was a gift to his wife, but was allowed to reappear on a display Gerald presented at a Goldsmiths Fair in London.

The turning point had been reached in respect of model cars, as Rolls Royce owner and model collector John Donner saw the Unimog, and commissioned a model of his Rolls Royce Phantom II.

By 1987, Gerald had left the Sevenoaks jewellers, and become a freelance designer and pattern maker. John then suggested to him that he should make a 1:43 scale model of the Phantom II, and to check out the market and viability of this scale, Gerald visited St Martin's Accessories in St. Martin's Lane, London. John then introduced him to Max Kernick, who at that time was producing vintage Rolls Royce models under the Top Marques brand.

Gerald made a few more patterns, including one for Top Marques of an Abbott bodied Bentley. After moving to Somerset in 1989, he undertook

Austin Seven

HRH Duke of Gloucester's Rolls Royce

some commissions for Les Andrews of Milestone Miniatures, the first of which was a Sentinel Steam lorry. A Vauxhall Velox for GTA Models followed, together with a Triumph Dolomite Sprint for a Norwegian client. A model of the Steyr-Puch Haflinger (of which he was an owner) was also made.

Gerald feels that his forte is with the older vintage cars, but in the early 1990s he was proud to be commissioned by the Duke of Gloucester to produce a model of his car, a Rolls Royce Phantom V. Gerald recalls being escorted into Kensington Palace by plain clothes policemen, and being privileged to

Brass patterns by Gerald

view the Duke's collection of models.

Gerald toyed with launching his own range, Recollections, which began with a 1:43 scale white metal model of the Hillman Imp, and the Californian variant. Having made the pattern himself, the initial castings were completed by Graham Price of GTA and latterly by SMTS. Graham and SMTS also cast his range of approximately 12 1:32 scale scooters, which were very detailed, and successful with scooter fanatics.

A Rolls Royce Phantom II of 1932 and the real thing!

Currently Gerald will take on a wide range of commissions, but has not produced any patterns for white metal model cars for some years, since the demand seemed to decline around 2000. Pattern work in non-ferrous and precious metals is the order of the day, and his order books are full.

Gerald's website has a wealth of illustrations of his work, highlighting his special talents in precious models, commissioned jewellery and pattern work. Other examples of his work have involved making items for TV adverts, awards, presentations and Hologram production. He has also undertaken commissions for Churches, Cathedrals and Societies.

Brian Lawrence

Brian Lawrence

One of the logos that appears on so many early white metal models is that of Brian Lawrence. Brian was made redundant from the aircraft industry in the early seventies, and set up his own business, Lawrence Designs & Models (LDM), working from the spare room of the family home in Worcester Park.

He had intended to establish a proper workshop in the garage, but that idea never came to anything. Indeed when he moved to Warlingham in 1984, the spare room was again used as the workroom.

Although he meant from the outset to be a pattern maker, having modelled for a hobby since childhood, it is unclear whether he made a conscious decision to concentrate on work in brass for the white metal market, or if this was just the way things developed.

It is almost certain that Pirate Models were his first clients, and although Brian never liked buses, he continued to supply them until Peter Cox and Guy Harrison sold out to John Gay. Other early customers included Transport Replicas, by Jim Varney, Western Models by Mike Stevens, Langley Miniatures by Tony McClellan, and Motorkits from Bryan Garfield Jones.

Although primarily known as a pattern maker,

Brass Patterns

Brian was a skilled draughtsman, and would produce artwork for photo-etching and decals, as well as drawing kit assembly instruction diagrams. He had a healthy distrust for published plans and dimensions, and would seek to physically measure and photograph a prototype himself whenever possible. Luckily he was quite adept at blagging access to museums and factories.

His repertoire was not confined to transport subjects and he produced patterns for everything from battleships to dolls house furniture. The only area he stayed away from was figures, which he sub-contracted to Ian Playfoot of Streatham. He also sub-contracted some railway subjects to Ian Pickering of Tenterden.

Brian's first love was aircraft, and to satisfy his own whims he produced a range of kits, and later some small desk top models. In later years, as he began to price himself out of the market for patterns, these received more of his attention.

Unfortunately, by the late nineties Brian suffered the onset of dementia and became unable to work. He died in a nursing home in April 2003 aged 64. It is with particular thanks to his son Clive that we are able to recount his story here.

On completion of his work on a pattern, Brian usually requested a sample casting from each master, and his widow has kept the display cabinet which reveals the wide variety of his work and serves as a small tribute to a great talent.

Pete Kenna

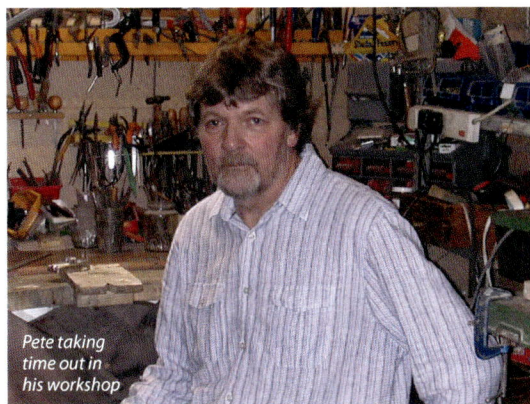

Pete taking time out in his workshop

Pete Kenna is an excellent example of a pattern maker first and foremost. Pete is 64, born in 1946, and is a toolmaker and pattern maker by trade. He has not collected model cars at any time. His first job as a model pattern maker was with Mr K.C. Keyser, the founder of K's model kits He was with them for 6 years, and remembers that they produced their first white metal item – a coal carrier in the 1950s.

Pete recalls that Keyser made some masters for Richard Briggs, of Minimarque 43 fame, but this ended in an acrimonious court case, which cost many thousands of pounds.

His first pattern was a 1:24 scale Ferrari Dino. He assembled 3, and they made about 40 – 50 kits, and he had made a pattern for a Daytona too. These were then purchased by SMTS. K's kits used to make the tools, and whilst Pete was working for them, he also made the tooling for Keilkraft plastic kits of trams and traction engines for them.

To earn his living in those early days, Pete was a member of a folk band until 1986, and when on tour, would often be 'whittling' away at a brass pattern on his bedside cabinet!

Pete teamed up with Alan Novak of Motor City USA in 1986, making patterns for the range and stayed with Alan in the USA regularly. However, when he launched his own Kenna models range he had to withdraw for a while. Later, Alan asked Pete to join him again, after which he made many patterns for

Kenna Models' Austin A40 van for the Netherlands

the range, including all the woodies, hearses, and some 1:24 scale models.

Pete's skills and experience have meant that over the years in business as a toolmaker, he has made patterns for a wide range of makers, some of whom are listed below –

- Conquest/Madison – the Rover P5B, now re-mastered; 300C Chrysler, Buick, and Jaguar 420.
- Belgium Trucks/Jupiter models
- Gear Andreason of Norway
- SMTS
- K&R Replicas
- Western Models
- Brooklin Models – and still working for them today.
- Motor City – most of their better ones, over the last 20 years! Pete has been a partner with Alan Novac in this business.
- IMP of Birmingham – a pewter range of Land Rovers, Triumph Stag etc.
- Vulcan models– his first pattern as an independent maker was a Rover.This company became CMA Mouldcast.
- Crossway Models – the first patterns to launch the range
- Spa croft – the first two patterns of Austin Goodwood and Hampshire woodie to launch Spa croft
- Pathfinder Models– Austin Devons and Herefords, and then took the patterns back and made convertibles, complete with added detail. He then took on the Standard Vanguards and made over 5000 of

Kenna Models' AC Greyhound brass pattern

these, and has now sold over 3000 vans and pickups. Pete has now settled into a business model in which he undertakes most of the processes himself, including having his own eBay shop, from which he sells direct to his customers.

Some of his range have a history, for instance, his Wolseley 9 is an ex-Motorkits model. Western patterns are now done in house, and so that long held association has finished. Pete helped Roger Tennyson by making his first few patterns when he started in business. He had a stand at Modele once, and then shared a stand with Sun Models, run by Geoff Moorhouse, who traded as Pit Stop models, now Heavy Goods.

Kenna models' Austin A70 Hampshire Woodie

Doug McHard approached Pete to buy Somerville from him when he decided it was time to retire, as he was keen to ensure his business and its goodwill would be in good hands. Pete had previously made the pattern for the Hillman Minx and the Sunbeam Talbot models in that range. He was offered the Somerville business, which was integral with Doug's own home, just for the price of his property. At one point, Doug had asked Pete to improve on the Allegro pattern, as he didn't think it was an accurate model. Pete declined as he felt there may unfortunate comparisons, and so Doug remade it himself!

Eventually, after Doug died Graham Ward of Promod bought all the patterns, and they are now owned by his company.

Motor Pro was a company set up for ex-miners with a government grant, and Pete made their patterns for them, including Ford Escort and Sierra castings. These subsequently went to K&R Replicas. Dinkum Models of Birmingham were a casting company of excellent quality, run by Peter Mulder, and still going.

It was John Haynes of Historic Replicars who showed Pete how to spray models. John died of emphysema, and was an agoraphobic; he did all his work, including spraying in a converted bedroom. Pete made one pattern for him of a Mercedes 300SL. His only outing was to go to Silverstone with Ernie Knott.

Recently, Pete has been re-mastering old patterns, such as the Allard P1 of Auto Replicas, that had previously been passed to Adrian Swain by Barry Lester. Once Pete has produced a master that is up to current day standards, then he will make the model for his range, and then pass the pattern back to Adrian Swain, who may use it himself again in the future.

Such is the quality of Pete's models, that owners of 1:1 scale cars use them as a basis for restoration! A re-creation of the Standard Vanguard transporter is being made using a Standard Vanguard van chassis and body, and using Pete's model as a guide!

Similarly, a European owner of an Allard K1, who had suffered a bad rear end collision, sought Pete's help in crafting a new rear body section. Pete sent him a casting of the rear body section of the model,

Kenna Models' Austin Pathfinders

and again, the real bodywork was formed using this as a guide!

Pete continues to achieve a full time living from his craft, and his models are a regular feature at fairs and in auctions, as well as on his website on eBay.

Ian Pickering

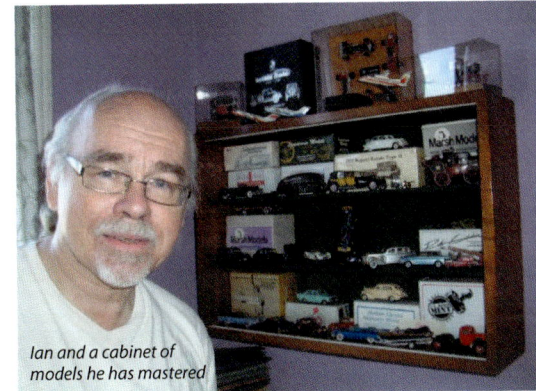

Ian and a cabinet of models he has mastered

If one pattern maker were to be regarded as being consistently at the top of his profession for over 40 years, then Ian Pickering would be amongst the likely contenders.

Ian was born in 1948 in Derby and moved to Leigh on sea in Essex as a baby. He spent his childhood making any model kits he could find. At the age of twelve he became diabetic and consequently missed a lot of schooling, leaving with few qualifications. He feels it was this that pushed him into working for himself. He says he's never had a proper job!

In 1964 he joined his local slot car racing club, Estuary Equipe. There he met organiser Reg Chapman who collected 1:43. scale model cars. As a result, he did some repaints and conversions for him. Occasionally Ian went to swapmeets somewhere near Liberty's in London. There he was introduced to people such as Guy Harrison. Reg introduced him to David Pressland, a well known collector from Poole for whom he did some one-offs in balsa wood. He passed Ian's name

to a couple of American collectors, for whom Ian produced more one-offs. One of these models held special attraction for Dr. Clint Seeley as he had made a road trip across U.S. with some friends which included a young Elizabeth Taylor in the car.

Ian also did some work for Neil Eason Gibson who at the time ran the RAC Competition Dept. About this time, Ian was buying and building the range of 1:24 scale Auto-Kits, as his father worked close to Auto-Models in Finsbury Pavement. He was asked if he was interested in building kits for them at £2 a time. He remembers building an ERA for them which was presented to Billy Cotton (Sometime racing driver and bandleader), by Eamonn Andrews on 'This Is Your Life'. Ian also made 14 Lotus Indy cars in a week for the Racing Car Show, in the late 1960's.

Ian had continued slot car racing and became a member of Team Russkit, An American slot car manufacturer, which ran a works slot car in endurance races, (12 and 24 hours) on commercial tracks. They also did a 500 mile race at Westcliff-on-Sea, close to his home, the first commercial track, which lasted about three days. The team came third of sixteen. They might have done better, but replacement tyres from the U.S. were held up in Customs and they had to scrounge worn tyres from other teams, which were luckily larger diameter than their own. (sounds like F1!)

At this time Ian met Mike Karslake, a local commercial model maker, and joined him on a freelance basis, helping with all sorts of projects, from planning models to dioramas, to a six feet high pneumatic drill. This was where he learnt the importance of deadlines. Mike would struggle with these by leaving everything to the last minute. None were missed, but Ian remembers several all-nighters! He particularly remembers one architectural model subject to a tight deadline. Ian was at the workshop at 8.00am to finish a model for that day, waiting for Mike who had the necessary drawings. Ian finally cajoled Mike into the workshop at about 2.00pm. Ian was not impressed finishing work at about 4.00am the following morning. Mike had four children and Ian remembers well his daughter Jo, who grew up to be a model and marry Ronnie Wood (the Rolling Stones Guitarist) and be a celebrity on 'Strictly Come Dancing'.

In 1970 John Day called Ian and commissioned him to produce the first of his range of white metal models on a commission basis, the first being an Alfa P2, 1954 Ferrrari, and a range of Lotus were favourites. The models were still made in wood and plastic. The problems with John Day are well documented and Ian did have trouble getting paid many times. John Day was a man before his time who took on too much.

Later in the mid 1970s, Ian was called by Marcel Van Cleemput, chief designer at Corgi Toys, in Nottingham and began a very fruitful working relationship with him, producing prototypes and patterns for Corgi for the next 10 years or so. Most of these were on-offs, but he did produce short production runs for toy fairs of the Spidercopter, Buck Rogers Star fighter and Superman in large and small sizes. Ian was responsible for the complete production on these. Through this connection Ian met Roy Fisher who was working for John Pipers Models in Kingston upon-Thames and Roy produced the castings. Roy later formed Mastercraft and thirty years on, Ian and Roy still work together. Ian had been working for John Piper making military patterns for him in 1:100 scale and Roy was his caster.

Over the years Ian worked with John Piper who produced military models and 00 scale model cars. Ian also produced a working model in August 1980 of a Dan Dare vehicle for a TV series that never materialised. Marcel Van Cleemput suffered from insomnia and Ian would often meet him somewhere between

Hockley where Ian was living and the Corgi base at Northampton at about 6.00am, so they could both do a full days work afterwards. When South Mimms Services on the M25 was built, it became a favoured meeting place. Ian and Marcel worked well together and Ian found Marcel a fine and honourable gentleman. When Corgi Toys went bankrupt, Marcel Van Cleemput set up a company called Acorn Technical Design and Ian made various models for him and found himself producing a run of BAE 146 aircraft models, in various liveries, one of which was for the commercial launch for Dan Air. These were approx. 5" wingspan. In May 1983 Ian recalls the decals for these being supplied without any clear backing, just the colours. As there was no time before the deadline to re-do them, Ian managed to deliver them by working through several nights, putting on each colour one at a time! He succeeded in delivering 100 models just in time. He also made a De Havilland Dash for Marcel Van Cleemput.

Marcel had introduced Ian to Phoenix Model Development based at Earls Barton, for whom Ian produced a series of Victorian hand carts and coaches, including a Royal Mail Coach. However, his favourite pattern was a model of the Cosworth DVF racing car engine, produced in 1978, to celebrate its 100th Grand Prix win. The full size engine was delivered to Ian to copy. The following year he produced a model Opel engine that Cosworth were developing. Both these models were cast and finished by Phoenix.

In the mid to late 1970s production of white metal cars boomed and various manufacturers approached Ian, one of the first being Jim Varney of Transport Replicas. Ian remembers producing an early fire engine for Jim and later, vans, lorries and buses. Bryan Garfield Jones of Motokits also commissioned Ian to produce an Austin 7 for him and this was one of the first brass patterns. Ian went on to produce 3-4 patterns for Bryan.

In 1978 Abingdon Classics commissioned Ian to

make an MGA and this started a long association with John Roff and Max Kernick. By this time Ian was working for Western Models. In the early 1980s John Hall returned from Canada and Ian met him when he set up in England. Ian's first pattern for John was a Lincoln Continental.

Richard Briggs of MiniMarque43 approached Ian in 1983 and which led to a long association with Richard on a wide range of models until his death. Ian remembers making the pattern for the Bugatti Royale that was auctioned in the U.S. and became the most expensive car in the world. This was done to a very tight deadline, requiring only 2 or 3 weeks to make the pattern. Then it had to be cast and finished before Richard took the models to the auction. Ian remembers the information he had to work on was numerous professionally taken photographs. Richard was outraged to find that the photos cost him more than Ian's pattern, clear evidence that pattern making has never been a well paid job!

From the early days of Ian's career as a pattern maker he has worked for people in the U.S, from the early days of one-offs to brass patterns. John Roff, of K&R Replicas put Ian in touch with Auto Buff in 1979 and he worked for American companies such as Great American Dream Machine, Legendary Motorcars Inc., Highway Travellers, Motor City, Durham Classics and Franklin Mint.

In 1984 Ian produced a 1:32 Buick Reatta for Hawtal Whiting, a company who had designed and developed prototypes for General Motors of the full size car. He made 100 or so models to be produced and presented to various people involved in the development of this car. These were mounted on a base with the name of the recipient on them. Ian recalls the names changing as various people were sacked and others replaced them. It was of interest that joins in the brass body pattern mirrored those on the full size car; a point pointed out to me by their engineering director. In 1984 he began his association with Marsh Models.

In the early 1980s, a friend of Ian's who worked as a public relations officer at a local airline, British Air Ferries based in Southend Airport, approached him to produce a gilt lapel pin approx. 1" wingspan, of one of their aircraft. This led to a very fruitful association of 10 years or so. The first pin led to contracts with British Aerospace, both military and civil and others such as the Battle of Britain Memorial Flight. Airlines round the world also were supplied. Exports went to some 13 countries. Ian actually exported to China, to a BAE representative who found it easier to source pins from Ian than BAE itself! He also supplied larger scale aircraft, encapsulated in acrylic for the El Yamamah Project in Saudi Arabia. Some 40 different aircraft were produced, the BAE 146 being the most successful. Ian

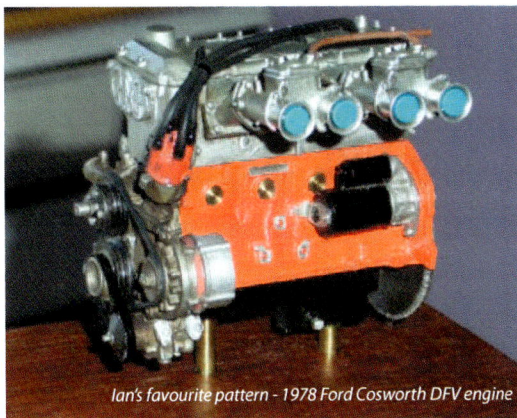

Ian's favourite pattern - 1978 Ford Cosworth DFV engine

stopped counting after some 350,000 were produced! Unfortunately, come the mid 1990s, the Chinese started using Ian's pins and patterns, producing their own product for a price he could not compete with. Ian did, however, also produce some in precious metals, gold and silver, hallmarked.

In the 1980s and 1990s he created a range of ship models approx 6" long, comprising container ships, tugs, a Viking long boat and oil rig supply boats for a company called Castco, run by an American named James McMillan and his wife Jenny. James later learnt to cast himself and went on to develop an improved casting machine. Ian recalls the first pattern he made for James was returned for some repairs, damaged. When Ian asked how it was damaged he said he had used it to learn how to make moulds and some had to be levered out of the moulds with a screwdriver when they became locked in the rubber. He used approximately 50 moulds. However, it was a steep learning curve and he went on to produce really good castings, and an innovative new way to cast. Ian found it amusing to hear that a Swedish museum had praised James on the accuracy of a Viking long boat. They obviously did not realise that a large scale plastic model kit had been used for a copy. While he was a hard task master to work for, Ian delivered patterns to him in London. Ian recalls that James always treated him to a good lunch somewhere, and many times he helped Ian on to the train back home, both of them very much the worse for wear! James became a very good friend and is now living back in the U.S.

It was at this time Ian realised his patterns would need to be bullet proof, as he was never sure who would be casting them and certainly did not want them returned for repair. To date, Ian confirms that he has only ever seen his patterns back for conversions, for example, a saloon into a convertible.

Over the years Ian has worked for virtually all the manufactures in the white metal car scene. Scales have varied from 1:144 – 1:8, and subjects ranging from oil rigs, engines, to motorcycles, lorries and of course cars, in fact anything mechanical. Ian's current clients include Brooklin Models, Illustra, Mastercast, Fire Brigade Models, Spacroft, J & M Classics and Wargames South.

In 1989 John Simons of Marsh Models was approached by a film company to make a video on making model cars as part of a range of hobby films. There were 2 videos, one featuring making a Marsh model from a kit and the other featuring the process of production from the beginning. Ian was filmed for a day in his tiny workshop, which became very crowded with director, cameraman and soundman. Ian is unsure if the video was very successful, and his dreams of becoming the next Tom Cruise receded. It is possible it was shown on an obscure Belgian TV Channel at some unearthly hour of the morning.

As a lifelong motorsport enthusiast, Ian enjoyed working with Mike Stephens of Western Models, particularly when he was producing F1 cars. Ian was able to visit the McLaren and Tyrell factories to see cars to be modelled, as well as various test days at Silverstone. He also occasionally reproduced obsolete car parts, such as door handles, badges, and light fittings for an old friend who had a company selling, restoring and building old Alfa Romeos. Ian's own classic motoring interest includes 3 Alfa Romeos, and a Ginetta G15 that he has owned since it was 6 months old. It is now 37 years old and in need of its second rebuild. Ian used this car for Hill Climbs and Sprints in the 1970s.

Through his many work contacts, Ian got to know a dealer, Steve Mattero, in New York and in 1990, with John Simons, of Marsh Models and Colin Fraser, Formula Models they visited Steve in New York and then flew to Indianapolis for the 500 race. As motor racing enthusiasts they had a great time, although the comparison of a model of an Indy car Ian had done for Colin from photos and a few dimensions with the full size car in the museum was a little challenging, he thought. This was ostensibly a working trip, although Ian cannot remember much work being done. A couple of years later Steve was touring with the rock band ZZ Top. Their drummer, Frank Beard, (the only one of the band without a long beard!) was a keen model collector and had invited Steve to tour Europe with them. Ian, his girlfriend, Suzie, John and Colin met him backstage at the Milton Keynes Bowl after watching the performance from the sound stage in the company of Brian May, of Queen and his wife Anita Dobson, the East Enders actress. When he introduced himself, his first words were "Hi, Ian. I recognise your face" Ian hadn't a clue who he was until he said "I'm Frank". Apparently he had watched the video Ian had appeared in. Sex, Drugs and Rock 'n Roll, Ian can now add Model Cars!

In 1994, Ian was asked by an old friend, who was living in Holland, to produce a 1:12 scale model of a Lola racing car to be used for raising sponsorship. These were to be in resin and he supplied some 20 models in white on acrylic bases. Ian had been to Silverstone to see the car testing, where something in the suspension broke and the driver, Cor Euser, managed to stop the car from 180mph. without crashing. When the car was brought back to the pits the driver was still in the car, wide-eyed, red-faced and looking as if he had stared death in the face. Shortly after this, when Ian had the last 6 to deliver he could not contact his friend in Holland, and no information was forthcoming. A few weeks later, Ian read in Autosport magazine that the team owner had been stopped with his car transporter and many kilos of drugs and guns had been found hidden.

Ian is philosophical about the white metal model car business, which he recognises has been seriously challenged by the Chinese in the last few years. For Ian personally, they arrived on the scene ten years too soon as he had hoped to reach retirement age before they flooded the market. As a result, Ian now seems to be working harder than ever just to pay the bills. Over the years he has also painted in oils or acrylics, and has sold quite a few of his paintings. They are mainly motor racing scenes and Ian is looking forward to painting more as the model car scene fades. Retirement continues to be just a dream.

Greg Roberts
Thoroughbred Models

When an enthusiast is keen to have a model of a car no-one else has modelled, then sometimes he has to do it all himself! That's the answer that Greg Roberts found after decades of collecting. Greg had collected Dinky Toys and other diecasts for many years from the time his mother gave him some pocket money to go and spend at his local toy shop.

He was 9 years old then, and also became

down on
ess you
them up

*Thoroughbred Models'
Jensen Healey*

interested in Airfix kits, many of which remain unmade in his collection at home. He continued to build his collection, mainly of models of BMW, Porsche, Alfa Romeo and rally cars through the 1970s to date, and took up a career in teaching, where he specialised in woodwork and metalwork.

In 1981, he entered the Model Engineering Exhibition in London, with a super-detailed plastic model of a Shearwater 3, a hydrofoil that ran from Southampton to the Isle of Wight.

Greg's first attempt at model making in brass was for Thameshead Models, for whom he created patterns for an N gauge Bedford OWB utility bus. After that, he made patterns for a 1:50 scale eight wheel AEC flatbed truck which was to be launched as the first of the new range of Highway models.

Becoming a little disenchanted with teaching, Greg bought the Highway Models white metal range of 4mm railway vehicles, including all the moulds and patterns, in 1982. That same year, he was contacted by Danbury Mint who were seeking a pattern maker for a new range of 1:57 scale model cars depicting the history of the motor car, in conjunction with the National Motor Museum at Beaulieu. Greg made them a brass pattern as a sample, and this was accepted. This was so successful they contracted with him to make a further 20 models. This was the shot in the arm that Greg needed, and he left his post in teaching to become self employed.

Greg continued working for Danbury to complete that series of 20 models. These spanned an 1898 Benz, through to 1950s and 60s Aston Martins and MGs. Now working regularly for Danbury, Greg was offered a contract to make the patterns for a series of

1:43 Jaguars, in association with Jaguar cars.

Following this, 2 years later, Greg had heard that Brooklin may be looking for another pattern maker, arranged an introduction with John Hall, and obtained a contract to produce a pattern for the Edsel Citation in the Brooklin range of American cars. The market for white metal then became less buoyant for a while, and Greg's personal circumstances changed, which left finances a little tight, despite a small but regular turnover of highway kits being purchased. Greg then landed work with Tony Bellm producing patterns for the Bellini range of 1:76 scale racing cars, these eventually were taken over by RAE models.

Come 1999, a turning point was reached at which Greg felt he really wanted to make that model that no-one else had made. This was the Jensen Healey Mk I. He created the master, now using resin workboard, a new material which can be drilled, shaped and cut with a knife. Greg sub-contracted the mould making, casting, painting and plating out to another producer. He then assembled the models and created the number plates. 175 pieces of each of 2 colours have been made of this model, and the success of the Healey spurred him on to make two further models. In 2003 he created the Vauxhall Firenza, and in 2007 launched the 2 door Vauxhall Magnum, both with similarly limited production runs.

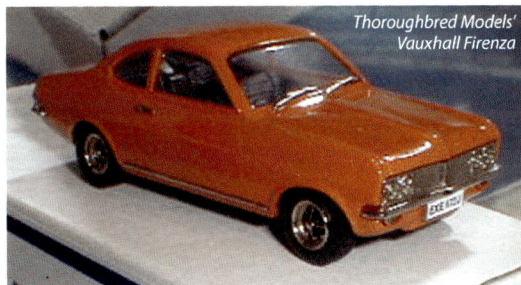
*Thoroughbred Models'
Vauxhall Firenza*

Greg is assessing the demand and viability for further models of cars not modelled to date, and will be announcing these in due course, but the next may well be available by the time this book is published, so watch this space!

Christian Sargant

As with so many of our builders of handbuilt models, Chris Sargant fondly remembers building Airfix Red Arrows Gnats in the 1970s, and he was hooked! Progressing on to his teens with Tamiya kits of Tornado GR1s and F14 Tomcats mainly, he made modifications to satisfy his requirements.

At aged 18 Christian took up a post in the MOD,

Chris Sargant

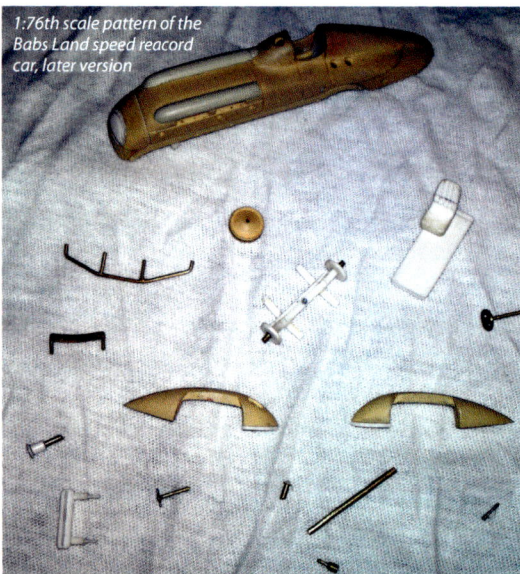

1:76th scale pattern of the Babs Land speed reacord car, later version

working in production for 1½ yrs until then moving on to being a production planner. He then moved to a post of materials controller working there for a total of 6 years, until in 1992 redundancy arrived. He was still building for his own amusement, mainly larger 1:48 scale Tomcats and a Spitfire. Whilst he was still keen to attend air shows, life without a job was hard, and for 18 months Christian trimmed his model expenditure by building a 3 feet long model of the Titanic entirely from scratch from card. By this time he had a young family to support, and one day whilst leafing through a scrap book he had kept of news cuttings in March 1994, a piece on the film Jurassic Park fell to the floor.

He turned it over, and saw a piece reporting Keith Williams showing a 1:10 scale Jaguar XJ220 in Yorkshire Police livery. Christian took the number, called Keith and asked if he could call by. They talked, about Christian's hobby, and he left his details in case Keith had any vacancies in the future.

Christian had barely got to the end of the road when he got a call from Keith inviting him to an interview the following day. This resulted in Christian working for Scale Model Technical Services for the next 18 months. He joined the team building handbuilt models, but was interested in how the pattern makers worked. He asked Keith if he could have a go with a body of an Aston Martin DB2/4 body, and was given the green light. He used resin tooling board, called sika block, which is like

wood, but has no grain.

Christian was given the drawings, full measurements track etc, and found he had to add a little to cater for shrinkage. The resultant shaped buck was rubbed down, and a mould taken from the sika block, using lost wax casting, then cast into a brass or resin master depending on the customer. As a result, Christian was keen to develop pattern making, but instead he was asked to take over the supervision of the building team.

By 1995 John Simons of Marsh Models had already contacted Christian asking him to make patterns for them, and he left SMTS to work with Pat Land at Model Assemblies on the same site. There he also undertook work for K&R Replicas, and John Simons of Marsh Models, which included a 1:10 scale model of an Aston Martin for Dunhill. Further work for Dunhill included metre diameter watch bezels for promotion of the Millenium Dunhill International at St. Andrews.

It wasn't until 1996 that Christian finally became self employed, and was pleased to be undertaking work for K&R Replicas, Marsh models, Scale Auto Bodies, Milestone Miniatures, South Eastern Finecast, and David Ferguson.

Unfortunately, his self employed career having taken off, Christian suffered personal difficulties after a few years, and in 2006 returned to Keith Williams to work for SMTS. He continued to do some work for both K&R and Marsh Models. At SMTS he would build and spray, and then take the completed parts back to his Battle workshop for assembly. At 39 years of age, Christian enjoys the challenge of improving the level of quality and detail in his models. Through Pat Land he has worked on 1:10 scale Aston Martin Vantage and Bentley Arnage models, followed by a Aston Martin Vanquish, all to be cast in aluminium.

Detail is certainly a key to the more recent work he has done for Tim Dyke of MPH Models, renowned for their miniature accuracy. Whilst working currently at SMTS, Christian has also developed his own range of aircraft models with John Simons under the banner of Aerotech.

Christian feels that the future with a combination of Keith Williams and John Simons looks bright, as he feels an affinity for these two model entrepreneurs. When we located Richard with assistance from Ian Pickering, it soon became clear that here was a man born to be a pattern maker!

Richard Stokes

Richard is a cockney, born in Bow, and his family subsequently moved to Crystal Palace, South East London. As a child he remembers an aunt's

employer who provided catering facilities for Fords at Dagenham. Through this connection, he regularly received copies of the Meccano Magazine. The latest Dinky Toy adverts inside inspired Richard to begin building models, but not for Richard the kits! At aged 7 and 8 years of age, he took his parents' discarded

cigarette packets, and by cutting and folding, created his own scratchbuilt models!

In the 1960s Richard started collecting Dinky Toys, Corgi Toys and Solido model cars, and then in about 1972 Model Cars Magazine advertised some model kits made by John Day. At this time Richard was working in London for the renowned firm of gun makers, James Purdey & Sons. The guns produced lasted a lifetime, and its reputation meant that the firm had strong historical associations with the Royal Family. While an apprentice, Richard met Prince Charles, Duke of Edinburgh, Earl Mountbatten and the Duke of Kent when they visited the factory. Incidentally an apprenticeship lasted six years. Latterly he also met the Duke of Gloucester, well known for his enthusiasm and support for classic motoring and model cars.

After seeing the Model Cars advert Richard bought some model car kits from John Day and after many telephone conversations, John suggested Richard might like to try building a set of patterns for a F1 Car.

Richard moved to Orpington in 1974, and established a workshop in a spare room,

He started to work full time for John Day in 1976. About this time John was becoming interested in producing 1:43 scale diecast model racing cars and as he was sponsoring a March F1 car these seemed an obvious choice. The models were not particularly successful. After working for John for about two years John found he could no longer afford to employ Richard so he became a self-employed model maker.

Richard first began making patterns in resin, but after establishing links with Mike Stephens of Western Models, switched to brass, which was more familiar to him from his experience in his previous profession. He also came into contact with Brian Harvey of Grand Prix Models while he was producing the patterns for John Day, who was supplying both Mike Stephens and Brian Harvey. Richard recalls that first brass master was the Mercedes C-111 record breaking car for Western models.

About this time through Lamberts of Ley Street Richard made contact with two Yorkshire enthusiasts who wanted to produce a F1 white metal kit better than any other. They had started a company called Scale Racing Cars and wanted to produce a model of Graham Hills F1 Embassy Shadow. This was a success and was followed by a Yardley BRM. Then in 1980 Richard was invited to join the company as an equal partner and really enjoyed making master patterns for them.

The hall of fame, for whom Richard has produced patterns is almost endless, but a few of the customers' ranges are:

John Day, Mikansue, Grand Prix Models, Scale Racing Cars, Western Models, Danhausen, Abingdon Classics, K&R Replicas, John Hall – Brooklin, FM Automini, Pat Shrimpton, Ralph Foster, Gems & Cobwebs, The Make Up Co, Japan, Pathfinder, Illustra, SMTS, Simon Jones.

Richard fondly recalls being commissioned by the Make Up Co in Japan to produce three 1:43 models, one of which was a Bugatti Atlantic, with opening doors and engine detail, including a removable dipstick!. The other two in this commission were a Supercharged Bentley and a 1948 Ferrari. All these patterns were dispatched and paid for, but sadly they were never used to produce what would have been wonderfully detailed models. Richard suspects they sit in a private collection in Japan.

He made the brass patterns for the Jowett Javelin and Ford Zephyr police car in the Pathfinder range, and also did considerable work for Richard Briggs at Minimarque43. He recalls how he would always insist on his payment at the time of delivery of the brass pattern, as it was his salary for the duration of time taken to produce it. However, with Richard Briggs, somehow this did not seem to apply! Two months later was the norm with Mr Briggs! Richard also built a lot of master patterns for Brooklin Models and has always received payment by return of post.

Richard clearly set a high standard in the quality of his brass patterns, but in addition to his model car work, as a pattern maker he would occasionally take on other business, such as a model of a North Sea oil rig and also patterns for model aircraft.

This style of life continued consistently until 2002 when Richard felt that the white metal model car market had significantly declined. He speculates that

F1 Embassy Shadow

this may have been due to there being too many models available. He feels that some makers particularly the French seemed to be turning out significantly higher quantities of handbuilt models each month and in his view if there are too many new models to purchase and collect then collectors just get bored.

Richard made his last set of patterns in 2002 which was his last commission. He had made master patterns for approximately 23 companies and only one company, an American never paid for the work done, or the pattern received. Richard's approach to clients was always that if the client didn't like the model then he didn't have to take it. No-one ever said they didn't wish to take delivery. He feels that he met some interesting people especially his good friends at Scale Racing Cars.

He is now enjoying his well earned retirement, and surprise, surprise for a born pattern maker, he is now scratch building 'O' Gauge Locos for his own amusement!

Adrian Swain

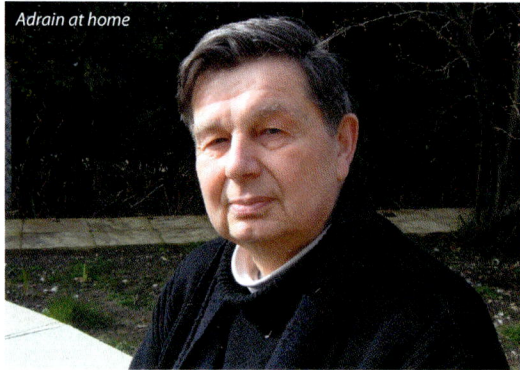
Adrain at home

There are few artisans, who include both pattern making and casting in their portfolio, who have remained in business through 40 years, but Adrian Swain stands out as one who has achieved this, and without fanfares of publicity.

Adrian was working for the British Aircraft Corporation (BAC), at Weybridge dealing with production problems for non-metallic parts used on Concorde, when he met John Day and Barry Lester in the late 1960s at an early Maidenhead swapmeet. John was carrying a wooden plinth with models of his Lotus 49 GP racing cars.

Prior to this in the mid 1960s Adrian had become involved with Frank Vescoe of BEC Models (Tooting Bec) through a work colleague, Eric, wanting a model railway layout but lacking the space to display it. He had decided on the new BEC Kits "Horsfield Tram" to feature on a tram layout as the only practical alternative.

At the time the only tram kit available was a Keyser's kit (K's), but the new BEC kit bore a resemblance to Hull trams where Adrian's colleague had come from.

Adrian build one for Eric, it was shown to Frank Vescoe who then asked for more to be built for his customers. The next tram produced was the BEC E1 class tram, which Adrian found would not run once motorised. Frank took Adrian's advice and changed the design which was then incorporated into the next model, the Feltham Tram.

Adrian really wanted to build early LCC London trams, but Frank told him he would have to make his own patterns, so armed with a ladies nail file, 2 needle files, 3 drills, a soldering iron, and when this was found wanting a blowtorch, he began. He was living in digs at the time, and would come home from work, have his meal at 6.00pm, then retire to his room and spend 3-4 hours, "filing brass" and listening to Radio 3 on a very early pocket transistor radio.

Brass pattern for 1926 Amilcar Italiana, for Auto Replicas, sold as chassis only or complete kit

1938 Packard 12 for Auto Replicas, as owned by Count Caluzzi

Having made a better job than the Frank Vescoe models, Frank eagerly took the patterns, made moulds and produced the six different kits Adrian had designed using many common parts. He gave Adrian a few sets of castings in payment – that's how it was done in those days, and thus was born in 1968 the BEC-ABS tramcar range, the very first of Adrian's kits.

ABS Models' Streetscene RTL in wartime livery, built by Colin Flannery

Adrian continued making model tram kits for Eric and, through Frank Vescoe, other customers. He obtained more information on Hull trams, bought himself a casting machine, and began production. Unfortunately, at this time, the supply of Tri-ang electric motors was drying up and apart from 4 models for Eric and about some variations Adrian made for himself the project lay dormant for over 20 years. He now had a casting machine but nothing to cast. Then fortuitously he met John Day, Barry Lester and two or three other budding entrepreneurs who all wanted castings and in most cases pattern making, without requiring the pattern to be donated to the caster.

Adrian was a lifelong Dinky enthusiast, and so was intrigued by John's models, having never seen white metal car kits in 1:43 scale.

The outcome of the encounter was that John asked if Adrian would cast for him, a timely event as it transpired. John's patterns were not made of metal but mainly carved wood and filler with a few bits of wire etc. and originated from Barry Lester.

For many years Barry had been making superb wooden model cars in various scales, and his models were highly sought after both in the UK and abroad. He had also made masters for vac-form slot racing car bodies and had tried the same method for mass producing 1:43 static models. However, the lack of definition, especially for louvres and similar detail made the process unsuitable. His skill with wood had caught John Day's attention, and as a result, Barry among others, had been making masters for him. These wood masters were turned into metal sub masters, usable in the white metal mould making process, by making cold cure silicone moulds and hand pouring lead alloy into them. The definition was not nearly as good as using brass or metal primary masters but was acceptable in those days.

Adrian's main interest lay in 4mm model railways but at this point he was making masters and castings of 4mm buses for GS Models, cars for John Day, Chris Leigh, MOPOK 4mm railway parts, and later Jim Varney of Transport Replicas, Westward Models and Pirate Models. The last three all being 4mm buses, all

3 commencing at the same time, typical of buses! By the beginning of 1971 it had become Adrian's practice to drive to his parents' home in Poole on alternate Friday nights, cast furiously Saturday, Sunday and Monday, taking a day's annual leave from BAC, and drive back Monday evening for work. The following two weeks would see the castings sorted, despatched and some more pattern making before the sequence was repeated.

Following the cancellation of the Concorde project, he had hoped to be made redundant, but his involvement in carbon fibre projects meant BAC was not keen to lose his services, in spite of the Monday absences. Adrian then made the decision to gamble on going full time as a model maker which he had always hoped to do. Moving back to his parents in Poole he soon had a nasty shock when two of his main trade customers closed down. This precipitated some new patterns for 4mm railway items of his own, which were the start of the ABS Models "Fourmost Models" range.

John Day was beginning to ask for more models but Adrian was very disappointed with the standard of his patterns and began making improvements mainly to the finer details and to aid casting. John was quite happy with this as he was not being charged separately although Adrian was charging a bit more for the castings.

Soon after this two policemen arrived in Poole enquiring about Adrian's connection with John Day who had apparently taken significant advance payments for supplies of kits which had not materialised. It seemed that the previous casters had not supplied John, possibly because of payment disputes. Having been told how to contact John the police went on their way. Adrian was of course rather alarmed by this situation but the work continued,

Brass pattern for a Castrol Oil Bin and jug, to compliment the Classic Commercials series

LCC "C" class tram in 1:76 scale - Adrian's first model kit

with the patterns remaining in Poole as insurance. John wanted more and more models but Adrian found car patterns very time consuming if made to his standards and in some cases the John Day patterns were almost completely replaced.

Adrian still has some John Day metal masters he made which were never paid for and when John's business failed around 1980 nobody wanted them. In the 1970s car kit sales were extraordinary, an initial run of 200 to 300 was often followed by a further 50 more at regular intervals, at least once a year.

About the time he moved to Poole, Barry Lester approached Adrian as they met at various swapmeets where Barry was selling his one-off cars. Barry had found there were many customers wanting them but as he was only working part time he could never make enough. He was now trying to get masters made for white metal kits as he realised how well John Day was doing, but wanted to produce something even better if possible.

So the Auto Replicas range was born with Adrian casting and Barry getting other pattern makers to do the masters in brass. The first 3 or 4 pattern sets turned up at more or less the same time but the quality was not really that good, and both Barry and Adrian felt something better was needed if success was to be achieved. Adrian agreed to rework some of them but the biggest stumbling block was the lack of really good drawings, dimensions and photos. Needing the work

Barry and Adrian were soon hot-footing it to Beaulieu to measure and photograph the ERA which became No 1 in the new range with its pattern largely made by Adrian. The Maserati 8C, AC Cobra, Brescia Bugatti and Healey Silverstone all followed with substantial upgrades by Adrian and with, at that time, Barry's unique selling point, the kits were pre-assembled but unpainted. The idea was that the buyer did not just get a bag of parts but an apparently complete model that only needed painting. Barry soon moved to Poole as well, having been living in Salisbury, and also decided to go full time.

Barry, Adrian, Barry's wife, June, and brother then went on the first of their autumn continental trips to the first 'International Model Swapmeet' in Poitiers, France where Barry met some of his customers. Adrian used the takings to buy French Dinky Toys and a good time was had by all in spite of the mosquitoes!

On their return Adrian made more castings to make good the Dinky expenditure.

Barry's 'built kits' were very popular and the designs were sufficiently good that Barry could make fully finished models in double quick time to satisfy the demand from those who had the extra money. Eventually with practice Barry himself was able to make most of the patterns with Adrian occasionally making a model such as the Amilcar. They were able to see this real car at the owner's home and to get authentic chassis detail the owner insisted that the car be turned on its side on the lawn to get good photos! Fortunately the car weighed very little and no damage was done. The car itself had spent the war years on a balcony at Harrods Repository alongside the Thames and after the war the previous owner returned to find the car in a sorry state, covered in pigeon droppings dirt and rust. Harrods agreed to reimburse him with its full value and he promptly sold it to a collector and bought a much newer car.

In 1980 with Mrs Thatcher in power many of the small kit manufacturers found difficulties surviving. Westward and GS models decided to call it a day promptly followed by Jim Varney. This was very worrying as about 50% of Adrian's business looked like disappearing within months. He was able to fund the purchase of the first two from savings but Transport Replicas was as much again. Fortunately he was only doing a few kits for Jim so this would not have been a financial disaster. The Transport Replicas range was very attractive however and with his mother's backing Adrian took the risk, driving up to Worcester to the Tyler Casting Company to collect most of Jim's moulds. At Worcester he discovered that they were holding many of John Days' masters. They asked if he wanted to buy them as John had gone out of business. Knowing from the past what sort of patterns they were likely to be he declined rapidly when he discovered

they were
not brass. They
returned to Jim's
house to collect all the rest
and pay the first instalment.
Adrian's 'Streetscene Series' range subsequently
incorporated all these acquisitions and others.

The Motorkits range had previously been bought
from Bryan Garfield Jones when Barry had told him he
thought it was for sale but was not himself interested.
Adrian had always liked commercial vehicles, and
met with Bryan with the intention of buying just the
commercials as long as the patterns were up to his
standard. For Adrian, buying a business such as this
all depends on the quality of the patterns, after all,
the moulds and castings can be re-made. As it turned
out, the commercial brass masters were good, and
the price was right to buy most of the cars as well,
so Adrian became the new owner. Motorkits original
patterns were often made by Brian Lawrence, known
in the trade as Lawrence Designs and Models, or LDM,
and were of a consistently good standard for the era.
The casting had been undertaken by Western Models
who had already had the pick of some of the cars for
their own range.

Barry Lester, June, Barry's wife and Adrian
continued their trips to Europe each autumn for
some years except when the pair hosted the event
in Bournemouth. It was customary after these
events to organise a dinner and a trip for some of
those attending and Adrian recalls that at the Italian
'International Swapmeet' the food was not to Barry's
liking and Adrian had to return home with an unhappy
Barry halfway through the meal.

As the years passed Adrian was consolidating
his railway interests by purchasing various other
businesses including model ranges for 0 gauge, 4mm
and buses. More recently, when Western Models
closed down, Adrian bought some of the English
car range, but found they were not of the quality he
had expected despite being some of the most recent
Western Models.

The story turned full circle some years ago when
Frank Vescoe, who had semi-retired and persuaded
Adrian to do most of his casting, decided to give up
altogether and sold all the English trams to Adrian who
thus received back all his original LCC tram patterns.

Adrian has known Pete Kenna, owner of Kenna
Models for many years, as they had both worked for
K's, and was able to pass on some of their patterns
when they shut down. Pete asked Adrian if he could
use some of the Motorkits patterns and Adrian
supplied him with the Wolseley Wasp and Austin
Goodwood, which Pete has improved for current
market standards, and introduced into his ready built
range. The patterns then revert to Adrian to sell as kits
when Pete has finished with them.

Adrian's plan was to retire when he reached 65,
continuing to make and sell batches of castings as
kits to supplement his pension. However his mother's
health deteriorated before this and in order to look
after her he decided to semi retire in 2004. His
colleague and friend Kay Butler (Wrightlines Narrow
gauge and IKB Models owner) had been handling the
mail order side of the business for some years and in
2006 created a website for him, and began selling his
ranges on the internet. The result has been that some
of his back-up stock has disappeared and he has had
to work hard to build the stock up again.

Adrian believes that his high standards derive
from his roots in railway modelling, in which many
modellers are fastidious about accuracy – "every rivet
has to be right". Adrian has now reduced his sales to
mail order and exhibitions only and generally wound
down his business, with recent health problems
slowing things still further. He is literally a one
man band now but hopefully, with small supplies
of Streetscene Series, Motorkits and all the other
ranges, there are over 2000 items in the current
catalogues.

Surely occasional new models based on Adrian's
patterns will still continue to impress us for some
time to come.

Glenn Thomas

Unlike the majority of people involved in this
industry, Glenn Thomas had no real interest in cars
as a child and young person. After he left school, he
obtained a job with a firm providing an architectural
and aviation model making service. This included the
construction of cut-away models to display detailed
interior and mechanical workings.

This experience gave Glenn a sound grounding
in all the techniques used in model making, and the
range of materials needed. After 5 years in this role as
a model maker, he decided in 1980 to become self-
employed as a model maker.

Although his main experience was in aircraft and

Armstrong Siddeley Whitley brass pattern for Crossway Models

dioramas, Glenn's first commission was from a friend, Dave Jones, whose partner wanted him to produce the patterns for a range of Fire Engines in 1:60 scale.

This was followed by work from Alan Smith, undertaking patterns for 1:48 scale commercial vehicles, mostly for the American market, and including big earth moving and industrial plant equipment. Hart models then came on the scene, followed by Brian Salter, who Glenn always found to be a stickler for detail.

Roger Tennyson, creator of Jemini and Crossway Models asked Glenn to convert some existing patterns to create different versions of the same vehicle, and Glenn always found Roger very helpful and knowledgeable.

More recently, a major change in Glenn's life occurred when his father asked him to take over his landscape gardening business on his retirement. Glenn had found that the pattern-making business had declined somewhat, and was insufficient to sustain an income to support his growing family.

Having accepted this challenge, he has been working long hours, and indeed he was very hard to track down for this profile! Glenn still wanted to keep his skills up to date, and found that there was more

call for producing resin patterns for resin models. He has therefore been designing resin patterns from acrylic block, (better known as Perspex) for a number of proprietors, including Paul Slade of Fire Brigade Models, and Steve of Traffic Model Cars. With Steve, Glenn has formed a sound friendship, as he says that both are somewhat 'odd balls'

Glenn reflected on the developments on manufacture of low volume models, commenting that when it can take many hours of work to produce a brass master for a relatively small production run, it is not surprising that those who commission such work are hesitant to pay the £2.5K-£3K that the pattern making process costs. Alternatively, he can fettle an acrylic pattern during his winter evenings, when the landscape gardening work is at an ebb, and achieve a result in a shorter and more cost effective timescale.

Glenn's main interest now is gardening, but his love of model making remains a challenge that he's never likely to lose completely.

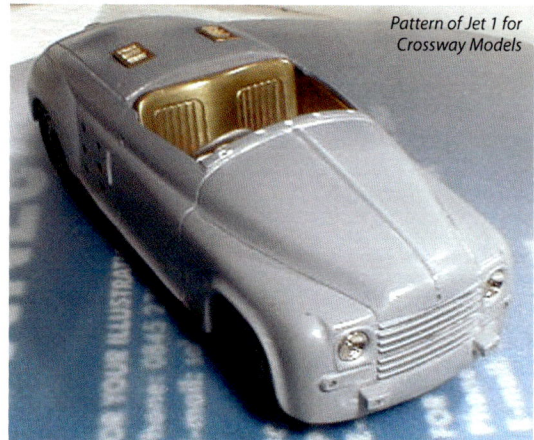

Pattern of Jet 1 for Crossway Models

Max Tomlinson

Some serious yet amateur model makers have developed considerable skills in producing patterns for their own use. Max Tomlinson is one such person, describing himself as a hobbyist pattern maker. He is essentially self taught, but with the advantage of having received an engineering apprenticeship, and thus having a good grounding in use of machine lathes, welding albeit not in 1:43 scale. He began in his youth chopping Dinky Toys, and from this began to create new wheels, radiators, lamps seats and some body components using aluminium and brass. On the suggestion of a friend, he progressed to making complete model cars.

His enthusiasm for all things Bugatti has enabled

Die press made from car bottle jack

Brass patterns for a Bugatti

him to research unusual examples of the marque not modelled by other makers. Max uses steel dies, on which he can press or form brass components, and where necessary he uses a press made from a car bottle jack and two heavy duty plates.

The illustrations show the dies, brass panels and components he is able to create, and some of the tools used.

Arthur Trendall

Arthur Trendall, pattern maker

It is uncommon to be able to hear the story of a pattern maker who came to the hobby via military connections, but Arthur Trendall is such a person.

Arthur began his career in 1949, serving an apprenticeship with Handley Page, which was followed in 1954 by 2 years National Service with R.E.M.E. By 1957, he returned to his former employers, to work in their wind tunnel testing using models.

Arthur then held various positions as draughtsman and machine designer working on special purpose machines for the machine tool and car industries. Arthur moved on to freelance design, working on high speed wrapping machines.

Arthur is at one with machines, always having a comprehensive workshop at home, and building and repairing live steam locomotives and other mechanical challenges in his limited spare time.

His first glimpse of the possibilities models might offer came in 1983 when he was asked by a manager at his workplace for a lift. Knowing of his modelling interests, he asked Arthur if he had ever made brass patterns. This was a new field to him, but he thought Arthur should meet a friend, Ken Targett of Buckingham Pewter, based in Twickenham. Buckingham Pewter specialised in highly detailed model soldiers in pewter, and they were keen to branch out into military vehicles. Ken must have been impressed with the examples of Arthur's hobby he was shown, as he asked him to make a pattern for an Austin 1 ton truck for him. This working link began in 1983, and was the start of a long association with Ken, during which time Arthur made patterns for a Challenger I tank, Warrior, Abbot S.P Gun, and a combat engineer tractor. Ken Targett had good connections with a number of Regiments, and Arthur believes that his models were being made for that market. These white metal models were being supplied for display purposes, and so various scales were used, the priority being that each model needed to be a certain size to fit the display setting.

Later, Arthur had been commissioned to repair some mechanical parts for a car restorer, and on a visit to his works he learnt of a customer to the local shot blasting company, who was undertaking some vapour blasting to some white metal castings.

This connection led to Arthur's introduction to Tony Molay, of Hart Models. On visiting Tony's premises, he soon spotted an old school friend, Bob Herridge, who had worked with Tony for some time at Denzil Skinner, and had jointly taken over that

Fire engine made for Paul Slade

business on Skinner's retirement.

The patterns Arthur had made for Buckingham Pewter had impressed Tony, and resulted in a long and fruitful association with Hart Models. Hart Models had a wide range of commercial, military and Land Rover models, and would also take commissions to build for other ranges. Arthur would be called to quote for making the patterns, and took over from Bob Herridge who had previously produced the patterns.

Arthur has never found it hard to create patterns, more it is the obtaining sound, accurate information of the subject that is the challenge. He recalls spending many an hour photographing and measuring the full size vehicle. Sometimes luck is on your side, and when Arthur was making a Range Rover pattern, he persuaded his local Rover dealer to put a Range Rover on his hydraulic lift, in order that Arthur could photograph and measure the underside details.

Throughout this period, Arthur continued with his work for car and motorcycle restorers, re-creating lost or broken parts such as catches, locks, con-rods, and similar sized parts, sometimes undertaking this work for museums.

Other ranges that Arthur has made patterns for include early days of Alan Smith models, J. Parker's range of Land Rovers, A&H Models' Thames Trader, Transport of Delight's Land Rovers, Mays Motors, and Brian Norman's Farm Models' range of tractors. Apart from these tractors, being in 1:32 scale, almost all his commercial vehicles and Land Rovers were 1:48 scale.

Paul Slade's Fire Brigade Models have had the benefit of Arthur's touch, as have SMTS, John Winnett's heavy haulage range, and John Fisher's Kingfisher Models.

Whilst strictly speaking a little beyond employment age now, Arthur continues to keep his hand in by currently working on patterns for both John Fisher and Brian Norman, and also undertaking work for vintage car and motor cycle restorers.

Half track made for Hart Models

Richard 'Dick' Ward

It was Auto Models of London's Finsbury Pavement that took Dick Ward into the model business. Dick discovered Auto Models as a source of 1:24 scale car kits as well as the Merit ones. He was soon commissioned by them to build their display and customer models.

When they introduced their 1:43 scale range, Dick was asked to make a brass pattern of the Morgan Plus 4. After Bob Wills took over the range, Dick continued to build the display and customer models of cars and traction engines, as well as helping his uncle with his antiques business.

In his twenties Dick became involved in motor racing, driving a variety of machines including an E-Type Jaguar and a Porsche 911, competing at most UK circuits and in Italy at the circuit of Mugello.

Then for many years Dick worked for John Piper making architectural models and helping to develop their model warship kits.

For a brief period he went to Thorp Models and then back to John Piper, now Scale Link, to develop

and make patterns for their 4mm (00gauge) model railway and the 1:32 scale military ranges. He also made many of the 'Clivedon Collection' patterns for their aviation jewellery and corporate giftware ranges.

Dick has made patterns from 1:12 scale cars to 1:200 scale aircraft and has worked and been a design consultant for SMTS; Brooklin; Illustra; Marsh Models; Aerotech 1:32 scale aircraft kits; Motor City USA; K&R Replicas; Minimarque43; Formula Models; Bellini 1:20 scale cars; Develotech's NASCAR range; Promod; Scaledown 1:32 scale tractor kits; Ted Webber; Miltra 1:100 scale military vehicles, Wargames South 1:144

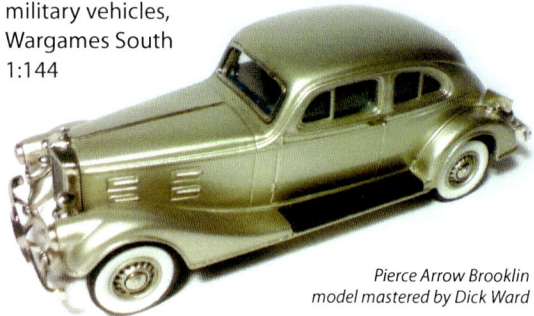

Pierce Arrow Brooklin model mastered by Dick Ward

military vehicles, Phil Alderman; Peter Wingfield, and many others.

At the time of writing, January 2011, Dick was working on several 1:43 scale racing car and road car patterns, 1:32 scale aircraft, 1:200 scale aircraft and other interesting projects.

Dick feels there will always be collectors and kit builders, but producers will be focussing on more obscure subjects as well as the traditional ones.

It's good to get a positive outlook from someone at the beginning of the hobby.

Aston Martin DBR/1 by SMTS mastered by Dick Ward

John Wright & Dave Weaver
John Wright Model Makers

Wallace's A35 van

John Wright was born the son of a Sheffield cutler, and thus was very familiar with the sight and smell of metal! His interest in miniature transport was born from building aeroplane kits, which then led to scratch built radio controlled aeroplanes.

Unlike many pattern makers in this industry, John went to college in St. Albans to study model making. From this excellent grounding, straight from college, John gained a position with a model making company called Master Models, where he was employed as a model maker and tool maker, creating commissioned models of aeroplanes.

When this company was approached by SMTS to produce patterns of model cars, this work was handed over to John. This in due course spurred him on to set up his own workshop in London.

Three years later, John moved to Bristol to establish his current workshop, which to begin with was very small, approximately 7 feet by 17 feet. It was equipped with one lathe and one pattern drill.

John began working with Brooklin Models in 1993,

starting with the new Lansdowne range. John's first pattern for Brooklin was in fact the Austin Healey Sprite LDM 1. He also obtained other commissions from SMTS, making a Lamborghini Miura and a Lamborghini Espada. Dave saw John working on the Lamborghinis for SMTS, and as a result John involved him in making model car patterns too.

Along parallel tracks, Dave Weaver had been making scratch built military vehicles out of plasticard whilst still at school. And the school often got in the way! He attended art college, but left as he was too distracted by other activities, including the essential work required on his father's farm. This entailed repair and re-manufacture of parts to keep tractors working, which also took him into motor bikes. Dave worked for three years in the motor trade and engineering, with a period of working in ceramics in bew plus a little in the building trade, but eventually realised that a regular job was not for him.

He had been working on small parts for some jewellery work, and needed some brass parts cast, and he was recommended to go to see john. Once installed in a corner of John's workshop, using his machines, he spotted John working on tie pins for a range known as the Cliveden Collection. These included 1:200 scale cars. John saw Dave's interest and in view of the quantity required, involved him in the job.

Dave's method of working lent itself to the way John Wright's workshop operated, together with an

Checker cab master and finished model for Brooklin Models

understanding of engineering, and Dave has been there ever since.

Dave arrived on the scene in 1991, and ever since John and Dave have regularly expanded their capability, constantly adding more tooling and skills. Dave's first pattern making job was a Jaguar Mk II for SMTS. Patterns for a range of Minis, as part of a collection, came soon after. By this time he had begun to work for Brooklin, and the pattern was then taken on by them, and used for their LDM 4, the Minivan. Dave continued to undertake various commissions under John's guidance initially. He has worked for SMTS, and also Henk van Asten, of Conquest/Madison Models in Netherlands. He made the pattern for their Buick Electra and the Packard Mayfair. Now Dave has made patterns for a number of Brooklin, Lansdowne and US Model Mint models.

However, more recently the market has changed dramatically for John and Dave.

About this time John's company was discovered by the animation industry, in particular Aardman Animation, also based in Bristol. This has resulted in them securing the contract to provide most of the machinery used in the Wallace & Gromit films, including the cars and motorbikes. Whilst John has taken on the overall management of the business, and negotiation with new customers, Dave's responsibility in the team is towards the running of the workshop, with 6 people in the team overall.

They have refined their pattern making process, using sikkaboard for the initial pattern, then using the lost wax casting process to cast the body and large parts, whilst the detailed parts are fabricated in brass.

Both John and Dave have now been in the same building in the centre of Bristol for some time, but techniques continue to change. Dave sees a secure future as long as Brooklin continue to use their skills, but he is exploring other techniques such as computer aided design to embrace the very latest technology.

CHAPTER FOUR

THE EARLY PIONEERS

By the late 1960s and early 1970s, the process of white metal casting had become known to more enthusiasts with a desire to fill gaps in their collections, and a number of entrepreneurs came forward keen to capitalise on this 'new' technology. The potential market for such models was huge, as those boys born in the baby boom years immediately after the war were now young adults, earning a wage, with money to spend to 'feed' their 'habit' of enthusiasm for motoring in miniature.

Mike Richardson wrote in the editorial of the July 1976 edition of Modellers' World: "Pioneered by Paddy Stanley, John Day and others, the white metal kit is now well established and forming the base of many contemporary collections. The existence of these manufacturers has enabled collectors to fill gaps left by the toy manufacturers, who are increasingly moving away from collectable models into toys, except for a few notable exceptions"

The number of businesses being launched during the 1970s was enormous, as can be seen by the timeline at Appendix 2, and the bulk of our research efforts have gone into tracking down as many of the owners of these companies as possible. The stories they have told us are many and varied and provide the most colourful chapter of this book –

Graham Bridges
Milikits

For many years a staunch member of the Maidenhead Static Model Club, Graham Bridges recalls that even as early as 9 years of age, in 1955, he was familiar with the pre-war and immediately post war Dinky Toy ranges such as the American 39 series.

So it was not surprising that when he spotted another pupil with a Lincoln Zephyr, he promptly offered to swap it for a current issue Austin Somerset

– Graham knew that the Lincolns were hard to find then!

By 13 years he had progressed into Airfix and Revell kits, model railways, and by 24 slot car racing. But in 1970, after returning from 3 years in Canada, his world was about to change, when through a friend he met Len Nash, a fellow enthusiast.

Len introduced Graham to the MSMC monthly meet at The Rose Pub in Maidenhead where he found tables full of old Dinky Toys and met Mike and Sue Richardson. Graham immediately joined the club and became an active committee member. The club was planning its second swapmeet at Monkey Island Hotel, Bray (the first swapmeet had been held in the Jack of Both Sides pub in Queen Street during 1969).

The 'MSMC Group' went on to form the hobby's first glossy magazine, a quarterly journal named Modellers' World (frequently referred to as Meddler's World by Jim Varney!). 8 committee members each stumped up £30 to total £240 which was the cost of producing 250 copies of the first issue. Mike and Sue Richardson had come up with the original idea and roped in Graham, Len and 4 other members, Tony Gleave, Alan Millington, Ted Manzocci and Barry Blight.

At this time Graham had been working in Canada, for the Dupont Corporation, operating computers for them when computers would fill a room. On his return to the UK, Graham sought out a different career path, entered the field of work study and factory planning, and finally a long career in

Milikits' Ford WOA 2 Utility

marketing consultancy.

All along he had continued his childhood hobby of collecting Dinky Toys of the 1950s, but had added to his collection the 1:60 scale models made by France Jouets. These sat alongside the Dinky military vehicles well. He recalls that he and his big brother had an army of around 120 military vehicles, known as 'army dinks' and these would be subjected to fierce battles in the garden, regularly being hit by dirt bombs.

From this position, it was a logical step to realise that there were some military vehicles not made by the mass producers, and perhaps Graham could make his own. He particularly wanted to see models of the Dodge ³/₄ ton ambulance and the Ford WOA2 utility vehicles. The range was to be called Milikits. He had become friendly with Mike and Sue Richardson, who were already selling models made by John Day, as well as their own Mikansue range. Graham had funds to invest in a model venture, and they introduced him to Dave Gilbert. He supplied Dave with pictures and line drawings, and the masters were completed. Graham commissioned a first run, and Dave cast 110 of the ambulance and 85 of the Ford Utility, both with solid metal wheels to achieve accuracy.

Graham launched the models through Modellers World magazine, and also advertised for 3 consecutive months in the military modelling magazines. Overall, the results were not good. About 60% were sold via mail order and by attending a few shows, and then Graham decided to finance the new proposed Americana range by Mikansue. However, Graham expected a swifter turnover of stock than actually occurred with the Milikits, and soon realised that the Americana range, along with many other white metal ranges, would require stocks to be held

for some time. After the 6th model in the Americana range had been released, Graham agreed with Mike and Sue that they would buy the remaining stock of Milikits, and take over the Americana range as well.

Graham had pulled out of producing white metal models 18 months later, and resumed his long term collecting passion, which to this day still embraces both 1:60 scale military models by both the mass producers, France Jouets and Buller & Barnes, and more recently Vintage propeller airliner models which include 1:200 scale diecast and white metal aircraft and period travel agency models in any scale.

Graham can still be seen regularly searching for these models at swapmeets around southern England, and looks back on his experience of white metal manufacture as a brief interlude in the life of a collector.

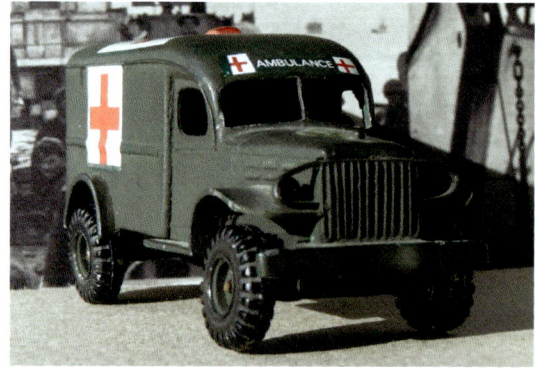
3/4 ton Dodge Ambulance

Peter Comben
Enco Models

Peter Comben's story is intriguing, and dovetails with that of Ernie Knott, model and classic car enthusiast. In the 1950s, when he was little, Peter's parents couldn't afford to buy him a pedal car, which set him on a path of building his own vehicles. He started with

soapboxes on pram wheels, then bicycles; later, it was cars and motorbikes, most of which were customized or restyled (both body and mechanics). After leaving art and design school in the late 1960s, Peter worked at Lola Cars. In the early 1970s he worked in computer programming and management, but realized that he missed the craft side of things.

Later, Peter worked for a model making firm in Lincoln for a while; a family firm, one of whose

Peter in his workshop

members had worked at Bassett Lowke in the 1930s. Peter's father in law, Tom Chapman, saw some of the work that he was making there and told him about a vacancy at Mettoy Ltd. Northampton, in the development section of Corgi Toys. Tom was the exhibition and display manager at Mettoy from 1956 to 1984 and had been the artist responsible for the artwork on the Corgi boxes from 1956 until the early 1970s. Tom had also developed inexpensive but very successful kites for Mettoy, including the Barnstormer stunt kite, often giving flying displays with huge numbers of stunt kites mounted on a single set of lines, becoming the world champion. He was frequently involved by the Mettoy Playcraft toy development department in solving their design problems.

Peter took some samples of his work along to Mettoy, was accepted, and joined the pattern making department in 1974. The section that he worked in was called the Proving Section. From the first dyeline drawings for new models, components were fabricated by hand, using brass for the metal parts and styrene for the plastic parts. It was accurate work and, provided that all the parts fitted together correctly, this 'proved' the drawings to be correct, and these could then be finalised and passed to the pattern makers and toolmakers. The hand made proving models ended up gathering dust in a cupboard.

During his few years at Mettoy, Peter learnt many new skills and also came across cold cure silicone rubber moulding, used by Corgi's sculptor, Steve Farmer, when developing masters for figures and animals. Steve had been trained at Mettoy by Les Higgins, and the silicone moulding had been an offshoot from the work of dental technicians. Peter could see the potential of casting low melt alloys

1:50 scale buses

centrifugally and asked the marketing staff if they would like authentic, working samples of 'next year's' new Corgi models for promotion at the world toy fairs. Hitherto, they'd only been able to show the buyers rudimentary wooden block models with painted windows and lights, because the new production models were yet to be tooled. Their enthusiasm was tremendous. Peter's plan was to use the hand made proving models, to take silicone moulds off their component parts and to reproduce short runs in pewter to be painted and assembled.

One such brass body and chassis for the forthcoming James Bond Lotus Esprit was sent to a centrifugal casting firm. Although slightly squashed in the process, the pewter castings produced were salvageable and Peter worked on the mechanisms for the retracting wings and rear bumper fins, together with pantograph machined nylon rocket launcher systems for the rear end. Vac form windows were also made. They assembled six working prototypes for the six toy fairs. The marketing guys were ecstatic. Peter went to his own management and told them about the reaction of the marketing department and asked them for permission to develop this process. They drearily declined on the basis that, "We've always managed alright in the past."

Tin Wizard Jensen Interceptor Convertible

Peter thought, "So be it, I'll do it for myself." At this stage, he knew little about the white metal models market, but Geoff Moorhouse, who worked in the drawing office, showed him some of the models on the market. Geoff, who runs Heavy Goods model trucks, had previously worked at Dinky Toys/Meccano and had some original dyelines of trucks that were never made owing to the firm's closure. He suggested that Peter could make brass masters for these trucks. Aware of the likely demise of Mettoy, Peter spent the next year or so of lunch breaks at work and in his own workshop at home building hand tools, a height gauge, a sander, a compressor, his first casting machine and many other useful items. With pattern work from Geoff and a few contacts in the field, Peter went self employed in March 1979 in the basement of his house in Northampton doing brass and plastic pattern making, white metal casting and ready built models for his first few customers. He also did industrial prototyping and pattern work, copper spark erosion

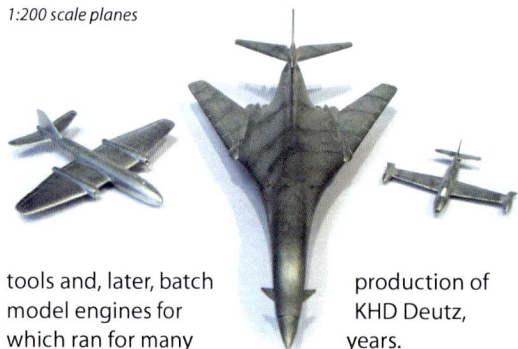

tools and, later, batch model engines for which ran for many

production of KHD Deutz, years.

Peter's philosophy was that the mould is the most important component in the production chain, and he aimed to produce white metal castings that were almost as good as diecast ones. He saw so many people produce beautiful brass masters, only to end up with somewhat inferior castings that needed a lot of fettling prior to assembly. Cold cure silicone rubber moulds allow predictable joint lines and do not need brass masters. Though not as durable as vulcanized rubber, they are repairable, and Peter could see that this process had potential.

Back in 1969, just before Peter joined Lola Cars, he had met Jim Keeble, co-founder of the Gordon Keeble Car company, at the Keewest factory in Southampton for a job interview. Peter had always been a fan of the Gordon Keeble GT, but car production had finished and the factory was by then making specialist furniture. Naturally, the first car in Peter's own model range was to be the Gordon Keeble in 1:43 scale. He decided to make it in the style of a Corgi Toy, with Swarovski crystal headlights, and his aim was that it should also assemble like a Corgi Toy: body, window, seat unit, bumpers and assembled chassis dropped in that order into a resin nest, then two screws to secure.

He visited Ernie Knott at the Gordon Keeble Car Centre in Brackley, Northants, in spring 1979 to get photos and measurements. It transpired that Ernie had always wanted a model of the Keeble, but there were none on the market. In autumn 1979 Peter completed the Keeble master and moulds and built a couple of prototypes (he still has the only surviving one). Having no expertise in marketing, he considered an offer from Ernie to buy the Keeble master, moulds and tooling, with Peter producing future masters, moulds and production casting for Ernie who planned to start his own model car business called EnCo Models (Ernie Knott's Company). In December 1979 Peter sold Ernie 100 Keeble kits.

In early 1980 Ernie was asked by a local Skoda distributor to produce a run of 1:43 Skoda Estelle models. Peter produced the master, moulds and castings and Ernie built them at the Keeble Car

Centre. When, in later years, the occasional Skoda surfaced on the market, Ernie tended to distance himself from his involvement in the project, but perhaps the jewelled headlights were a giveaway as to who had made it!

In June 1980 Ernie and his wife, Ann, bought the Keeble moulds and master from Peter and launched EnCo Models. For the next few years they commissioned from him the tooling and casting for the rest of their range: Sunbeam Tiger MkI & II and Alpine Mk4/5; Jensen Interceptor Saloon MkII & III, Convertible and Coupé; Facel Vega Facel II Saloon and Convertible; Ferrari 308GT4 European; Jensen FF. They painted and assembled the models at the Keeble Car Centre.

In due course, many other jobs came Peter's way. One interesting job early on was to produce a set of masters for 12 English chairs in 1:12 scale, ranging in period from Elizabethan to Victorian. Peter researched several at the Victoria and Albert Museum and accessed the rest with the assistance of Arthur Negus who was the adviser for the project, visiting all sorts of interesting old houses and castles. The model chairs were owned and produced by Mark Models Ltd. Another customer saw these chairs and needed a certain model chair making for acrylic encapsulation. It was to be a 1:12 scale model of Steve McQueen's chair from which he directed the film, Bullitt. This was, as far as Peter could see, a standard, folding director's chair with canvas back and seat. However, the customer insisted that it must be from the actual chair used by McQueen and it duly arrived from California by Securicor at Peter's cottage in the Lincolnshire Fens. He recalls sleeping with the chair at the foot of his bed for safety's sake until the master was finished and Securicor collected it.

By 1987, Ernie was so

Historic Replicas' 1:24 Jaguar and Mercedes

busy with his full size Gordon Keeble Car Centre work that he and Ann sold the EnCo Models name and business to Peter, together with all the tooling that he had made, plus the stock. Thereafter, Peter traded all his work under the Enco Models name, dropping the capital 'C'. He had developed many techniques in his casting work by this period and was able to produce castings as complex as the one piece bodies in 1:24 scale as for example, John Haynes' Historic Replicars range. He also produced pewter badges, lamp assemblies, mascots and other components for classic car restoration. He produced many castings and models for acrylic encapsulation, for example, trophies, presentations or executive paperweights. The encapsulation process, subcontracted out, was under heat and 10 atmospheres of pressure, and was very demanding on paints and materials.

Jensen FF body parts

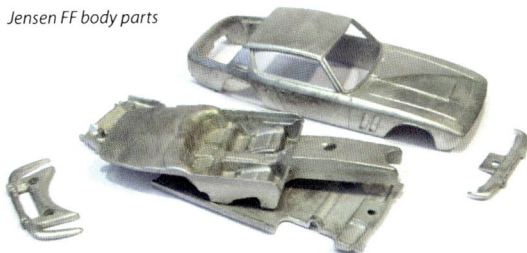

All this work was demanding on space, equipment and skilled labour. Steve Farmer, the Corgi sculptor, had joined Peter, combining his freelance sculpting work with Enco assembly work. Peter moved the business into industrial premises in November 1990 following the first ModeleX, which had brought him a great deal of work, especially in casting. He was also joined by John Fox who did most of the casting and helped him man their ModeleX stands, and by John Bennett, a retired toolmaker, who did pattern making and much of the mould making. Peter concentrated on patterns, mould making, admin. and some casting. Family and friends joined in when extra help was needed. The turnover had been increasing over the decade on a classic parabolic curve.

Two months later, in early 1991, Peter's wife was severely injured in what he calls 'the final blunder in a series of medical misdiagnoses,' and he has been her carer ever since. This was almost the death knell for the Enco Models range and for much of his other work. For the next four years, they concentrated at the factory mostly on Enco kits and subcontract casting, which was more lucrative. Peter divided his time between work and caring over an average 12 hour day. By 1995 the strain was too great. He closed the factory and kept only a small number of his customers, working once again from sheds at

Jaguar XJ6 parts

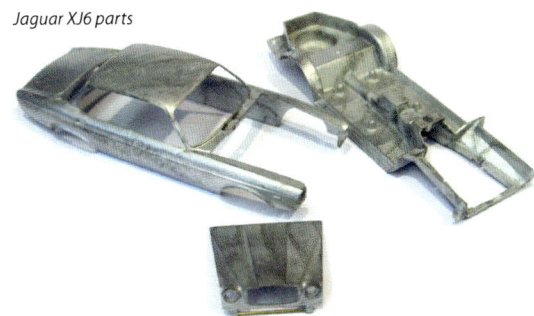

home where he could be of more help to his wife. The parabolic curve reversed.

At ModeleX 96 Peter was introduced to Thomas Wolter of Tin Wizard Model Cars in Germany. They had both started up in business in 1979 and they shared the same outlook technically. As with Peter's castings, Thomas's also had no shrinkage from the master size. Thomas asked Peter to mould and cast his bodies for him. A few years later, Peter made the complex and expensive decision to move to Germany. There were many reasons, but one was to secure the future for the Enco Models range. Another was to introduce Tin Wizard to his mould system so that his subcontract customers could be assured continuity of supply in the future should he be unable, for any reason, to work. On the technical side, Thomas and Peter planned to pool their many years of expertise in order to take moulding to a higher level.

So it was, that in late 2002, Peter and his wife moved with seven and a half tons of workshop, moulds, masters, materials, furniture to Germany. He registered a new business, Encotechnik, in Germany, which continued the manufacture and despatch of the casting work while their son, Tom, ran the admin side of Enco Models back in England, giving the UK casting customers the luxury of Sterling billing. Assembly of the Enco Models range was set up at the Tin Wizard factory, guaranteeing its survival, with a free hand given to Thomas Wolter to refine and market the models in kit   and built form.

1:24 scale Porsche and Healey

In 2007 Peter closed Encotechnik and he and his wife moved back to the UK, to sunny Norfolk, with the moulds, masters and most of the machinery. Peter retains ownership of the Enco Models name, masters and moulds, and produces batches of castings, shipping them to Tin Wizard. He has gradually made small improvements to his masters and moulds, but to date the Sunbeams and Ferrari are still waiting for re-tooling. His recent addition to the range has been the Jensen SP.

Today, most of Tin Wizard's own master work is done by CAD/CAM in Germany. The more complex moulds and castings are made by Peter in England and all assembly work is done in Germany. Peter continues to provide subcontract castings for his existing customers. Since 1997, he has also been involved in moulding and casting 1:200 scale aircraft, which is often more difficult than model vehicles. He is astonished how much the aircraft vary in size, the smallest so far being about 1cm wingspan and the largest around 25cm.

Peter says it never ceases to amaze him how every moulding job is different. Having made well over 1000 moulds since 1979, with individual components as large and deep as a 1:24 scale Jaguar XJ6 body, or the replacement rear lamp unit for the real Gordon Keeble at 33cm long, to some castings as small as pin heads, the challenge is always fresh. Very few items have ever defeated him. Some customers have remained with Peter since the beginning; some

Tin Wizard Gordon Keeble GT

came along in the meantime and are still with him. Some came and went, some went out of business. Some, sadly, are now deceased. Peter is due to retire in 2012, but wants to continue working beyond that date, health and family circumstances permitting. Whether he will add further models to the Enco range, he says, "it remains to be seen".

John Day
John Day Model Cars

Jaguar C-Type

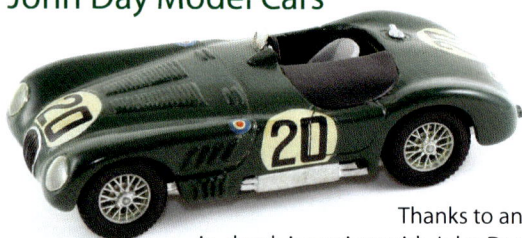

Thanks to an in-depth interview with John Day by Motor Sport magazine in October 1995, we can understand how John became involved in both model cars and sponsorship of the Grand Prix world. It was Christmas 1957 when as a result of a cancelled cocktail party, and the need to clear away all his son's toys, that he amused himself considering how to improve the authenticity of a Dinky Toys Cunningham racing car. He filed away, and repainted it, until for him it looked like a Cunningham.

John began swapping Solido models with a French journalist friend, and modified them to improve their authenticity. This was just a hobby, but when in 1969 he was able to set up in business himself, as a result of his employer being taken over, he decided to make 1:43 cars in kit form. After experimenting with the modifications for his existing centrifugal casting processes, in April 1970 he was ready to launch his first two models. These were a 1914 Mercedes, and the 1954 Ferrari Le Mans winner.

His journalist friend Christian Moity covered this event with 2 colour pages in L'Automobile magazine. John recounted burning the midnight oil making the kits ready for taking by aeroplane to Le Mans for the 1970 race.

For the following 4 years John found himself running a successful new venture. In 1974 he was asked by Alain de Cadenet if he would sponsor his Lola in the Le Mans race. Two years later, and now

employing 26 people, his company moved further into sponsorship by funding the Ensign team to run Chris Amon. Regrettably this deal didn't work out. However, on a trip to the USA in 1976, he reached agreement with Max Mosley to sponsor the March team. This resulted in 'John Day Model Cars' being displayed in large letters on the nose cone of Hans Stuck's March. Sponsorship in the 1970s was still in its infancy, yet John recalled that his relationship with Mosley and March was always very congenial.

John had always felt that sponsorship in motor sport had not adversely affected the sport, rather the bright colours had brought the cars alive, and provided a means of financing a very expensive game. His heroes were Hans Stuck, Ronnie Peterson and Jackie Stewart.

Birdcage Maserati

In order to re-create the spirit of the racing cars he modelled, John believed more emphasis should be placed on photographs than engineering drawings. He proudly told Motor Sport of the day his son Crispin presented Graham Hill with a set of Lotus 49s, with which Graham was truly pleased.

In June 1976 Ray Ashworth, a regular builder of John Day kits, had hopes of building his own model from patterns, and knew a Ferrari 330LMB in France which fitted the bill. He asked John for advice, and was invited to John's workshops in Pickerslea Road,

1921 Le Mans winning Duesenberg

Malvern. Ray was impressed with the comprehensive set-up of library, office, canteen workshop and casting facilities. This was not a cottage industry. He became aware that John was casting for other producers, such as Mikansue. Ray was engaged to build models for the Ferrari museum and the Laguna Seca Raceway owner. After completing the first batch at a rate of 2-3 models per week, Ray was again invited to the works, and a proposal made for Ray to be the front man for a new range called Le Mans Replicas. John already had other ranges including Mini Auto, and Equipe. A company was established, with John's wife, his manager Alan and Ray as directors. John wanted Ray to run this line from his home to keep overheads down and maximise profit. It was to be mail order, cutting out the retail trade.

Ray produced the masters from both
Stirling Moss's 'Mille Miglia' Mercedes

fibre material and brass, but along the way there was a dispute with the French maker, and former Le Mans shop owner Manou in Le Mans over the name, which was subsequently changed to V de C – Vainqueurs de Course. The formula was simple castings, reasonable quality, and a wide range of models. However, as other makers improved their quality, Ray tried in vain to persuade John to respond. John then decided to invest in equipment to produce a diecast F1 March. Thousands were sold, via retail outlets such as Beatties, but this project was also about expansion and volume sales.

During this time, John had been enjoying the buzz of success and the Grand Prix circus, but in 1980 John Day Model Cars crashed, with debts that couldn't be paid. Overstretched plans and budgets, pattern makers not paid for their work, and collectors submitting payment for kits that did not arrive, these

were some of the issues that then became more widely known. He recognised that he had expanded the business too quickly, and felt personally responsible when his staff were out of a job. His pattern maker, Richard Stokes had left a secure job at Purdy the gunmakers, but became self employed from then on. The Pickerslea Road factory was closed, and Ray moved on to work for John Simons of Marsh Models.

From that point, John left the world of model cars and turned to public relations. However, in the mid 1990s, he decided to return. He first experimented with pewter sculptures of famous motor racing scenes. However, he soon turned back to white metal, and 1:76 scale kits.

Known as the John Day Vehicle Scenics range they consisted of 1:76 white metal kits available by mail order from John Day or via an agent (Woodpecker) in Australia. He was also advertising the ability to supply made up kits from time to time, partly through meeting up with Steve Bates, who had originally made patterns for his earlier ranges. He re-appeared on the scene later on and focused on vehicles to accompany popular railway modelling eras in the UK. After John passed away in the summer of 2006 the models seemed to have disappeared from the market.

However, all was not lost. John's son Crispin and partner Caroline endeavoured to carry on the John Day model business in an attempt to continue supplying this range of models. Equally important, Crispin realised it would be a sad loss for modellers around the world if the model range which was his fathers' legacy were to slip away. Unfortunately as Crispin and Caroline were both professionals with young children and already lived very busy lives, they realised that to carry on with the models was too all consuming.

Daryle Toney, a time served engineer for the last 30 years had been a self employed antique furniture restorer. His passion for making models, like so many others, began as a child running up to the newsagents with his 1/6d pocket money on a Saturday morning to buy an Airfix kit. Daryle was finding it difficult to obtain sufficient work, and was

1953 Le Mans Nash Healey in French team colours

00 gauge Austin pick up by Daryl Toney

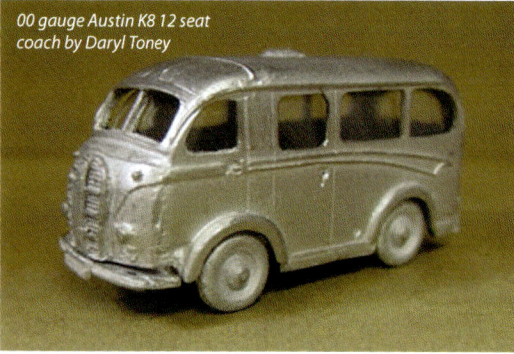
00 gauge Austin K8 12 seat coach by Daryl Toney

dismantling the N gauge model railway that he had built up, with a view to its sale. He found that the white metal model vehicles sold particularly well, so he bought some more from eBay, built the kits and sold them as handbuilts to a high standard.

Many of these kits were the JDM series that Crispin Day was selling, and through this he got to know Crispin. They talked about how to progress the business, and Crispin realized that Daryle had a real passion for small scale white metal kits. As a result, in order to continue the range of models and his father's name Crispin passed the business over to Daryle Toney in August 2009, knowing that Daryle would ensure John Day's name and work would continue.

Daryle's aspirations for the JDM range are firstly, to re-master wherever possible with improvements, notably the wheels, to enable collectors to paint them more easily. New masters in brass will be made and wheels will be available for kit builders to upgrade models. His vision now is that, with the power of the internet, he may be able to tempt at least some of the younger generation away from their computers and electronic games and re-kindle the art of model making. Daryle sees this as a pastime that will last a lifetime, otherwise these skills will be lost forever.

Daryle will be concentrating on the heavy commercials, railway vehicles, related items and machining of brass masters for the wheels. He is a pattern maker as well as a modeller, and is using the skills of Rod Parker to refurbish some of the cars, especially those he mastered in the first place, John Day used as many as five different pattern makers but Daryle considers Rod to be one of the finest.

Daryle feels that there is still a place for the small manufacturer, and whilst manufacturers such as Oxford Diecast and Classix are undoubtedly affecting the market, he intends to produce items they are not likely to, such as animals, figures and sundry items for the railway modeller. He produces kits for people who like to model and gain satisfaction in making something. He feels that with mass produced items, once these are removed from their packaging the magic evaporates. He says that Oxford Diecast and Classix are for those who would buy a print and hang it on the wall, whilst his customers would rather create that picture by completing a jig-saw puzzle and gaining much pleasure in doing so.

00 gauge Morris Commercial C11-40F

Bryan Garfield Jones
Motorkits

Another of the true early enthusiasts who began by trading in obsolete diecasts was Bryan Garfield Jones. Bryan has had a long-term interest in both model and classic cars, like many other white metal manufacturers of the 1960s and 1970s.

He had travelled Europe on business, working for IPC Technical Press, and had begun acquiring diecast toys for dealing from home in the late 1960s. With his business role touring Europe, he was able to seek out French dealers with whom he could trade, and thus build a part-time income and regularly replenish his stock.

He built up a select list of discerning clients, amongst which was Graham Pilgrim, enthusiastic purveyor of classic car sales brochures. Graham recalls receiving a telephone call from Brian after a foray into France, and visiting his home in Horsham to be shown his latest mint/boxed acquisitions. Graham would then select the next model for his growing collection of French Dinky Toys, and, as

Bryan Garfield Jones

a favoured client, place the cost on account, not paying until his next visit.

It was in this role that Bryan first met Mike & Sue Richardson, Brian and Rachel Harvey, and Mike Stephens. They all shared a common interest, met up socially, and swapped notes with each other over models they wished to see made. By then, Bryan recalls, Bob Wills had bought the 1:24 scale range of cars from Automodels, trading at Finsbury Pavement.

From trading in obsolete diecasts, Bryan began in the white metal world by joining Mike Stephens and Ken Wootton, who were then making spare radiators for Dinky cars and trucks, to form Western Models. Mike provided the technical expertise, Ken the enthusiasm, and Bryan the distribution network in France.

They explored 'lost wax' processes with a number of different metals, including mazak, with North London firms of jewellers, including BAC Castings, but found it too expensive. Typically, a caster in one part of Clerkenwell would produce 40 wax 'castings' which would form the stock of duplicate 'masters', and these would be transported to another part of Clerkenwell, where one at a time they would be placed in a large mould filled with sand, into which molten metal would be poured. The hot metal melted the wax, which drained through drainage holes, the rough castings were then removed from

Motorkits MG SA drophead

the sand, and passed to another worker to clean up.

Mike was the engineer, and their first casting machine was home built, using a washing machine motor to drive the centrifugal motion. Both Mike and Bryan carried out casting in Mike's garage in Epsom, until neighbours 'shopped' him to the Local authority – fair cop, so they were given 6 months to re-locate. This they did to Salfords near Redhill, in premises behind a butchers shop. Here they cast, prepared, sprayed and built their models.

Motorkits 1933 Austin Heavy 12 taxi

The first Western model was the Mercedes 540K, launched at the Montem Leisure Centre in 1972, where German dealers ordered 100 items.

Bryan wanted to explore the kit market, so Mike bought out his share in Western, in May 1974, and Motorkits was born. Mike Stephens moved to Kings Mill in Redhill Aerodrome, where Western did the casting for Bryan, and his master model builders were Brian Lawrence, Ian Pickering, Adrian Swain, and others for less complicated ranges such as the Circuit Series. Bryan also used Bewdley Leisure, as did Mikansue and John Day, for casting. Bryan's aim was always to get a one piece body casting, which was a big step forward.

Motorkits Morris delivery van in John Barker livery

Bryan had plating done by Redhill Plating, and then the castings and chrome pieces were delivered to his home in Heath Way for boxing up. Gilly and Bryan remember boxing up 100 MGTDs for a German

Motor Models Dennis Tanker

dealer one night.

After that, Bryan obtained rented premises in London Road Horsham, sharing a flat and basement with a rat! Autoroute, their shop, opened in September 1976, and was able to sell both diecast and his Motorkits range there. Keith Williams, of SMTS, produced the shop sign for Bryan. Keith had been building kits, and of each new Motorkit released, Keith would build approximately 15 into handbuilt finished models, for sale to customers who preferred their Motorkits ready built.

The first to be released was the Morris 8, followed by two Austins. Of the Motorkits range, the MG TD was a runaway success, and the Wolseley Wasp was the slowest seller, with only about 100 being made in a single run.

Following the cars, the commercials came along, including the Carter Paterson van, John Barker Ford Model Y, then 3 European racing cars.

The Advertising Manager at Shell/BP approached Bryan for a special model of the Dennis Tanker, and this was announced in April 1979 in Modellers World. Brian Lawrence made the pattern, and travelled down to Beaulieu National Motor Museum where the real vehicle was housed, to take photographs and measurements. With just 100 handbuilts being made, Shell/BP was not happy with the tanker being labelled as part of the kit ranges, and so the Motor Models range was born. MM1 being the tanker, and MM2 being a little Morris Z van in Robertson's Jam livery. The same van was available in kit form in Royal

Mail livery. Whilst other models, including a Dennis fire engine were considered, Bryan found the handbuilt project difficult to finance, and so there were only two Motor Models in the range, both being built by model maker Keith Williams.

Most of the Circuit Series of racing cars, designed to be of less detail and simple construction, were mastered by RPH models, working in association with Bewdley Castings. Each production run was about 100, using best quality white metal, whilst successes like the MGTD may have sold up to 1000 in total.

Bryan still has a Dennis Tanker, a Ferrari 246 from the Circuit Series, and a prototype of a Ford Model Y made by Keith Williams as a street rod, but the view was that this would not sell in England. The last delivery of castings for Motorkits was made in January 1980, and the last supply was passed to dealers in April 1980.

Motor Models Z Van

Bryan says the reasons for closing the range down were partly that diecast manufacturers were producing cars for collectors far cheaper, and sales therefore were slowing. Also he wanted to expand the wholesale side, and to do this he needed investment funds.

Bryan now enjoys his retirement, still living in Sussex, and spending time visiting areas of France for which he and his wife Gilly have fond memories.

Dave Gilbert
DG Models / Autocraft

Dave Gilbert was born in 1941, and always built models as a boy, mostly balsa wood and card, and remembers the Micromodels range of printed card models.

Dave made a model of the coronation coach for school, and as a result he was featured in the Birmingham Mail in 1952. His mum was very proud!

At the age of 15, Dave was offered a place at Moseley College of Art, but chose instead to take up an apprenticeship at The Birmingham Guild.

A succession of very short term jobs followed, professional model making remaining his ultimate

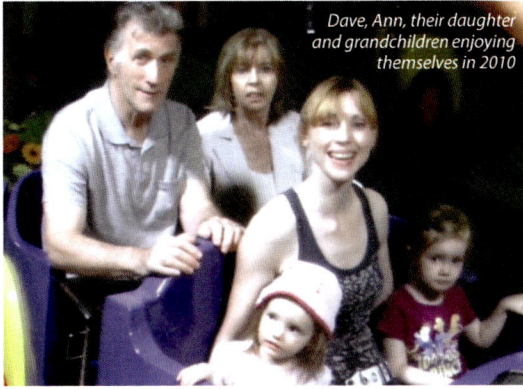

Dave, Ann, their daughter and grandchildren enjoying themselves in 2010

goal. In 1968 Dave entered and won two categories in an international scale modelling competition in 1:32 and 1:24 scales. John Day saw the winning built models featured in an article locally and contacted Dave with a view to producing masters for a new venture he was undertaking concerning 1:43 scale racing cars. It was this meeting with John Day that changed his life.

Model Cars magazine of March 1971 described John's ideas, confirming that Dinky Toys were made for children, not collectors, a belief confirmed by the late Doug McHard, and so John Day asked Dave to make him a brass master for his planned 1914 Mercedes GP and 1954 Ferrari 375. Dave was paid £15 for creating the master for the Mercedes.

At this point, Dave felt it seemed like John Day, Ian Pickering, Barry Lester (Auto Replicas) and himself were the sole producers in the industry. He remembers Barry Lester producing the Lotus racing car, and stating that the spaghetti shaped exhaust pipes should be made of wire and bent by the model maker. Dave took the view that modellers may not have the patience to do this, and so cast a complete set of 'spaghetti' pipes. Similarly, on a Bugatti, Dave was asked to add 120 louvres on to the bonnet.

In the beginning of his model making career, Dave employed vulcanised rubber moulds, using jewellery manufacturer Karl Zissman for casting, and made Austin Seven vans, tourers, and a Duesenberg.

Morestone GWR Tricycle dilivery box

The definition was poor so he decided to build his own centrifugal casting machine, which he did using an old Hoover electric drill. He fitted the chuck with a disc, and with clamps and slots in a piece of attached wood, he created fixings for the moulds, for pouring the metal whilst the machine was spinning. The system is now pneumatically powered, and can produce up to 100 castings per hour.

In 1971 Dave registered his company as D.G Models, at the same time he began experimenting with silicone compound moulding and centrifugal casting. He perfected this system, and it is still in use today, undertaking the whole process from generating the prototype through to the finished article.

Duesenberg

In the early days Dave was selling his kits by word of mouth and reputation, but had regular sales through supplying shops such as Grand Prix Models, originally known as Pit & Paddock, and Lamberts of Ley Street.

Dave's first models were what the market was craving for; accurate representations of real cars, such as the MG TC, an American Duesenberg racer, and various Jaguars and Bentleys.

In due course Dave developed the Dinky Style or DS range, which were simpler to make and sold well. Dave approached Meccano Dinky Toys for permission to reproduce the 28, 1st series vans and the 24 series cars, with the Dinky Toys trade mark scored through to distinguish the reproductions from originals. Doug McHard, who was their Marketing Director, asked for a sample to be sent and was so impressed with the quality produced in white metal that he ordered a full set of the vans and cars with the Dinky Toys trade mark to be left intact, to be displayed in the Dinky Toys Museum. One wonders what happened to these examples when Dinky Toys was closed down?

With complete one-piece bodies now available, Dave made for Milikits, Len Buller, and Pirate models. He has developed a way of making masters and casting from any material, even plastic.

After having produced the artwork for his own transfers for the Dinky vans, he found a company in Birmingham which specialised in transfers, and had made the transfers for Dinky Toys using a system called stone engraving. These are now on display in the Science Museum. By the early 1980s, Dave had

Riley Lynx drophead

begun his motor bike models, and obtained orders from the RAC for 1,500 models.

He was selling mostly to the USA, Japan and Canada. There was keen interest from overseas customers for popular marques such as Rolls Royce, Jaguar, Packard, but the lesser known English makes such as Riley were less popular. At its peak, D.G Models/Autocraft was employing up to 5 staff.

During the 1980s Dave teamed up with Brian Evans from Church Stretton, and formed Gemini Diecast International, first developing white metal bodies to attach to proprietary diecast models, such as Yesteryears. A contract was agreed with Creaks of Camberley, to create their Alternative Collection, which were not just new liveries but completely different van and truck bodies. Brian obtained the base models, Dave made the conversions, and so the Code 3 industry took off!

Dave's 28/1 Series Dinky Van approved by Doug McHard

He knew Jack Odell quite well, and when Days Gone started in 1984, Dave and Brian mortgaged their two houses, met with Jack, who always referred to Dave as "that Brummy bastard", but in a very affectionate way, and became wholesalers for Lledo! They attended the Harrogate toy fair, got rates agreed with Corgi, and soon found themselves shipping out wholesale supplies of W. Britains, Corgi, Matchbox and Lledo to retailers in Australia and America by chartered aircraft. 40,000 Lledo Coca-Cola and Hershey sets passed through their hands on the way across the Atlantic. At one dinner engagement with Jack Odell, Dave recalls suggesting that he made a Morris Minor in the Days Gone range, but he didn't think it would sell, and gave horse

drawn vehicles higher priority.

However, the big time wheeling and dealing was not to Dave's taste, and in due course he and Brian closed down the Gemini wholesaling business. Dave bought Budgie, Modern Products and Morestone, and after the original dies were tested (they were made in the 1940s and 50s), Dave adapted them for use on modern machinery and produced 2000 of each of the larger Budgie castings, such as the fire engine, V.W. and Wolseley police car, also printing the boxes - the models were offered for sale through Graham Ward's business Promod, often for promotional purposes.

By now the Chinese writing was on the wall, and diecasts were arriving from China cheaper than they could ever be produced in England. As a result, many shelves full of Budgie boxes, tyres and transfers were emptied and destroyed.

Since then several other Budgie dies have been tested for future releases, including Sam's Horse Drawn Café and Early English Stagecoach. Recent releases are the Morestone Tandem Cycle with Sidecar and the Ice Cream Salesman. The original art work and printing plates for Micromodels card cut-out models have also been added to his portfolio which he continues to develop and produce. Still the main interest in Dave's modelling life is the design and manufacture of white metal models.

Throughout his working life, Dave has viewed his business as a family, and has borrowed and re-mortgaged in order to keep his staff together and production rolling. As such it is promoted as a very small, mainly family run affair based for the past 23 years in a rural South Staffordshire village in the heart of England.

Currently, Dave employs one helper, while his wife undertakes all the secretarial work, his daughter helps with packing, and is training to hopefully take over the business. He is using the same machinery producing a few new models, but some of the old favourites continue to generate a demand. He says it's in his blood, and now in his late 60s he plans to continue as long as there is a demand out there.

At the time of writing Dave's latest creation is the 1928 Morgan Aero in 1:32 scale and 1:43 scale, the first of a planned series of Morgan 3 wheelers.

Long may Dave's energy and depth of experience enable him to bring out new models in the whole field of transport.

Press cutting aged 11 - his Coronation model

Brian Harvey
Grand Prix Models

Buccaneer Models Dinky Toys replica Streamlined Rover

And now we have one of the cornerstones of this industry. Grand Prix Models have for many years been the model world's best known model car specialists, but few realize that they were one of the industry's pioneers.

Brian Harvey, the company's co-founder believes that they were the first specialist model racing car shop in Europe. He and his wife Rachael first opened the doors of what was then a shop, in Hertfordshire's pretty Radlett village in 1972.

It all began when Brian decided to take a year off from motoring journalism, where he was Managing Editor of Cars and Car Conversions magazine. He had been building plastic kits for review and came to the conclusion that no one was offering selected high quality scale models of great cars direct to motoring enthusiasts. At the time he and Rachael were both racing a wide range of British club racing cars such as Lotus Cortina, Unipower GT, Ginetta G12 Lotus, Allard Ford, works Hillman Imp etc

Through attending continental toy fairs and swapmeets, he found models made by makers such as RAMI and Dugu, not imported into the UK, and would bring them back to the UK. These were at first sold from home alongside the plastic kits and when this business was sufficiently strong it was moved to the Radlett premises.

They had found that within that scene, fellow race drivers were unaware of good scale models. The Radlett premises were intended as a dual-purpose business, starting a motoring magazine from the rear and selling model cars from the front. From day one they were inundated with enthusiasts looking for just the kind of models they had located. From there on it was self generating but driven by their own enthusiasm to scour the world and find the best new models. At first they had to deal in ready made diecast models as there was little else. Then the first specialist metal kits came along and they began to offer models of Jaguar C and D types.

The range of models on offer was enlarged to include the likes of Airfix, Revell kits and obsolete Dinky Toys, Corgi Toys, and Matchbox. Auto Replicas, Dave Gilbert, John Day and Western Models, soon followed and then Brian began his own range of GPM classics.

Brian felt it was a means to an end as they wanted to encourage others to make obscure subjects like the J2 Allard Cadillac Le Mans, famous rally cars like those of Roger Clark, the Brooklands Chitty Chitty Bang Bang and the first Corvette - but at first other makers were reluctant. Soon however, many others followed their lead and from those small beginnings emerged the industry we know today. However, there was still nobody making many of the models they felt needed to be made. From that conclusion it was only a short step for GPM, as it became known, to start producing its own models.

Brian's first model car kits in white metal were marketed as the Classic Car range, were 1:43 scale and launched in 1974. They were manufactured for GPM by John Day Models.

Two years later, Brian bought his own casting and moulding machinery and began releasing kits created by a team of pattern makers including Richard Stokes, Ken Whetton, Bob Hine and Reg Bishop. This development resulted in the release that year of a series of modern racing cars models under the title 'Serie 76'. This subsequently became 'Serie 77' and so on for some years.

Come 1977 Grand Prix Models began releasing a series of hand built models under the range name "Classic 43" made for them initially by Brooklin Models and then Western Models but from their own masters crafted by Richard Stokes.

With the rise in the prices of the very early Dinky Toys, there was an emerging market for copies. A number of people in the trade moved into this field, and in 1978, Brian was particularly horrified by the very high prices being demanded for first series Modelled Miniatures. So he responded with a new series of models, replicas of those early Dinky Toys,

Buccaneer Models Dinky Toys replica 1939 Chrysler Royal Sedan

Buccaneer Models Dinky Toys replica Chrysler Royal Sedan

called Buccaneer to replicate both old Dinky Toys and Tootsietoys. These were sold as both kits and hand built models. The master patterns were created by Colin Flannery.

Grand Prix Models have always majored on sports and racing cars, and with the increasing values of the original series of Solido models, another market opportunity opened up. So it was that in 1979 Grand Prix Models launched another new series, entitled Dannini Modelli using old Solido and Spot On range models as patterns.

Increasing links with European producers, through selling their ranges, led in 1980 to GPM releasing their kit of the MG Metro rally car in resin made for them by Starter of Marseille with metal parts produced by Grand Prix Models.

Around 1982, the overall white metal and handbuilt market had changed somewhat, and Brian made the decision to cease manufacture of models in order to concentrate on importing and exporting from all over the world. The manufacturing legacy left by Grand Prix Models amounted to around 230 models being released by them, having been made by or for the Grand Prix Models label.

An interesting anecdote came our way, that in an Autosport magazine, in the 1960s/70s, innovative Castrol adverts began appearing, displaying a sheet of Castrol notepaper. This was crumpled and at an angle, with the word Castrol crossed out, and giving the impression of being typed on an old typewriter, complete with manual crossings out. They were different in each issue, but always appearing written as a letter, to 'Dear Auntie Flo' and signed off from 'your loving nephew Edgar' Occasionally the text would refer to 'us Jessops'

Our informant, Paul Crowther, subscribed to Four Small Wheels, the GPM in-house magazine, and noticed that Edgar Jessop was the editor. Later Brian was heard to relate a story of when he was at an Isle of Man TT Motor Cycle event, talking with a number of friends. They were at the bar, and getting irritated by a lady journalist from the USA, working for Harpers Bazaar, who said she was 'looking for some human interest'.

Pointing out a shabbily dressed man in plimsolls, who in fact was Dunlop's motor cycle tyre expert, they told her this man was Edgar Jessop, and recounted a heroic story of how he had won a motor cycle race, after his footrests had both sheared off, which was why he had to wear plimsolls. However, she was warned not to approach him as he was very sensitive about the whole affair! In due course the story was published in full in Harpers Bazaar! The myth of Edgar Jessop was alive and well.

Today GPM has gone from strength to strength. The same basic principles drive the services they provide, a desire to provide enthusiasts with the very best in accurate scale modelling and to spread the word that good models are being made.

GPM now stocks every worthwhile 1:43, 1:20 and 1:24 model range and produce their own successful model car magazine, Four Small Wheels, which operates as a rolling catalogue, as the industry changes at such an alarming rate that any comprehensive 'catalogue' would be out of date before it was even published. Therefore, the GPM website and the magazine are all that collectors need to keep up to date with all the recent developments and releases within the industry.

Ever popular are collections of cars driven by the likes of Ayrton Senna, Michael Schumacher, Damon Hill and Nigel Mansell. GPM holds a database with a search facility to enable collectors to develop their own themes.

In the early 1990s GPM had outgrown the original Radlett shop and moved to new premises in St. Albans, remaining there for 15 years or so. In the past few years there have been a lot of changes to the market, with a significant increase in the number of higher volume diecast models produced in the far east. The quality of these has also improved drastically and the embracing of resin casting technology, most notably by Spark, means that they are able to produce runs of a few hundred rather than the thousands of examples needed to make a traditional

Buccaneer Models Dinky Toys replica Series 28/2 van kit in Yorkshire evening post Livery

steel diecasting pattern viable. GPM have also noticed a drop off in the number of kit manufacturers as many of the pioneers in the field have retired. Those kit manufacturers still active are, for the most part, enjoying good sales with single seater racing cars of the 1960s, 70s & 80s remaining particularly popular. GPM have also seen an increase in higher quality large scale resin and metal kits and also transkits to convert plastic kits into alternative race versions.

Brian and Rachael joined the retirees in 2004 and the company is now in the hands of their daughter, Justina, and son in law André, the latter having worked for the company since Radlett days. Another big change at Grand Prix Models came over the Christmas and New Year of 2006/7 when they finally left Hertfordshire after over 30 years and moved some 70 miles to Banbury in Oxfordshire, right at the heart of the British motorsport industries. GPM seems set to continue to hold its corner of the market for years to come.

Max Kernick
Top Marques and Autotorque

David and Max Kernick at home in France

Classic British motor cars can engender enthusiasm in many. Being an avid MG enthusiast, Max Kernick started collecting literature and models of anything MG during the late 60s. He recalls buying 3 Dinky Gardner Record Cars at a toy fair which started him off exchanging and selling.

Max worked for Lesneys for a couple of years testing new products but having to cross London every day became rather tedious.

Through an advert, he came in contact with an American, Dick Knudson, who has put together several books on the MG marque. Dick asked Max whether he would be interested in producing a proper model of the MG TC and TD. He said he would give it some thought.

Max had been buying metal kits from Brian Harvey's Grand Prix Models at Radlett. Most were quite acceptable for the time, although, a lot of work was required to produce a decent finished product. However, he baulked at Mikansue's MG L Type Magna kit which was not up to his standard. In the meantime, he had seen some extremely well cast and detailed models of early buses and horse drawn carriages produced by Jim Varney, in his Transport Replicas series. On contacting him, he felt that Jim had tried to discourage him by saying that whatever model he wanted, Max would have to guarantee to take 300 sets of castings of which 200 would be taken straight away. The cost would then be £2000 or more – a great deal of money for 1974.

However, Max was not put off and went ahead with the MG TC. He remembers that these initially sold assembled for around £6.50 each. To start with, production and sales were quite slow but an advert in the MG magazine Safety Fast for the annual Silverstone MG weekend in 1975 produced a lot of interest. Max had booked a very small stand at the event and had a couple of dozen TCs ready to take. The night before leaving, he received a visit from a Dutch MG enthusiast who wanted to buy all 24. He sold him 18 and kept the others for the event.

Max had been living in Finchley, North London since he started of Abingdon Classics in 1975 and it was towards the end of the decade that he was involved with John Roff (K & R Replicas – Kernick & Roff) but split up with him in 1979. The Abingdon Classics range were very popular, and to assist in meeting demand, around 1980 John Simons, of Marsh Models began making some MG PB airlines for Max as Abingdon Classics. At the time, Max was looking for someone to help with production. Most of those he approached were not up to the standard required, but John sprayed & assembled the models to a very high standard.

FM Autominis Bentley Continental

Rolls Royce Phantom IV
Queen Elizabeth II

Max's patterns up until this time had mostly been made by Ian Pickering. Richard Stokes had made an MG C type Montlhery Midget, MGB/MGC & Midget, also a Bentley Continental. Brian Lawrence made the unusual MG High Speed Van.

Max was then approached by Frank Wong who wanted to produce a Bentley and Rolls Royce model. Under the name FM Autominis (FM – Frank/Max) he made an R type Continental & Rolls Royce Silver Cloud 1/Bentley S Saloon (not many of these were made). Later they produced a Mercedes-Benz 450 SLC. Production stopped when Top Marques started in 1984.

It was during the period Max was producing FM models that he received a phone call from Richard Briggs who placed a large order. Unfortunately Max did not take his call seriously. A friend had a habit of phoning him fairly regularly pretending to be different people and Max assumed it was him. It was a few weeks later when Richard rang again asking about his order that he realised he was genuine! Richard was a nightmare to deal with as far as business was concerned but otherwise a very likeable and gentle man. Max was in contact with him right up until the time that he very sadly died. He sold most of the Abingdon Classics range to Richard in the early eighties and later on the Alvis range to Mike Rogers of J & M Classics.

The first Rolls Royce in the Top Marques range was a four door Silver Cloud Convertible for which Max applied to Rolls Royce at Crewe for a licence. This was not a good start as they agreed to license Top Marques for future Rolls Royce and Bentley models but turned down the Silver Cloud. On examination of the model they had found it to be a 4 door short chassis. It should have been a 2 door short chassis or 4 door long chassis. After this mistake they employed the help of a local jeweller, Neil Bollen who produced their first main Rolls Royce under the name Top Marques, this being RR1 (Rolls Royce 20 hp Barker Landaulette). Later he made RR3 (Rolls Royce 20/25 hp Mulliner).

Max and his wife Julie were working in their workshop in Max's brother in-law Barry Gowthorpe's premises near Exeter along with Ralph Savill who worked for Richard Briggs, Peter Richards and Philip Peall. It was around 1986/7 when Julie, who was friendly with Mike Roger's sister heard that he was looking for some different work. The outcome was that Mike cast for them for several months, and then went independent in a different line of work.

By 1989 they had moved to West Hill near Ottery St Mary, and Mike extended their shed/workshop around 1991. At this time, Top Marques personnel consisted of Max, his wife, Julie, Philip and part-time, Julie's sister Jan Gowthorpe who is a successful artist. Philip was an excellent model builder and his input with Max was important to the success of Top Marques. This is when they brought out the Gold Series (a very limited edition. GS1 to GS18). The patterns for this series were made by a friend and jeweller, Gerald Gilbert. Max & Gerald introduced the small accessories to go with the models e.g. various picnic baskets some with champagne bottle & glasses inside, umbrellas, golf set, croquet set, and suit cases.

The business was mainly operated from the workshop at their home in West Hill with their pattern maker at that time being Gerald Gilbert. In 1996/97 Rolls Royce were tightening up their licensing arrangements and wanted all manufacturers of Rolls Royce and Bentley models to visit Crewe with samples of their production. The company really approved of Top Marques' work and they received a verbal contract to make models for the company. As this would mean a considerable increase in production, in 1997 they moved to a unit in Honiton and took on another member of staff, Steve Todd.

Abingdon Classics
MG Speed van

It was several months later that Rolls Royce was sold to BMW and VW took over Bentley and the factory at Crewe, thus negating the contract. Top Marques had put a lot into the factory unit and had taken on a partner to help financially. He had insisted that the company be a limited one so they became Top Marques Miniatures Limited. However, having expanded the business there were not enough orders to continue in this type of structure, and also Max and Julie wished to return to a family run business. During this time at Honiton they met Lawrence Gibson who produced several good patterns for them and remains a good friend.

Around 1999 Max sold some of his Alvis patterns to Mike Rogers, who finished off the limited numbers & then began producing his own. Max got him off to a good start by giving him details of suppliers and retailers, and making available some of their tools.

In 2001 Max and Julie decided to move to France, with their sons who were 11 and 9 years of age. This was something they had wanted to do for years. In France, they started Autotorque for a sports car range and continued later with Top Marques. Lawrence Gibson has made most of the patterns but they are now starting to make their own. As well as doing their own casting & spraying they used Graham Price of GTA Models, who has done excellent work for them for more than 20 years.

On moving to France, Max's good friend Chris Linnell built the Marqueart website as a platform to market Autotorque and later Top Marques, and Mike Roger's range of J&M Classics were also added. Chris still runs the Marqueart website successfully for Max & Julie.

Mention should be made of Max and Julie's son David, who had been 'doing his own thing' for 18 months, since their move to France. Firstly, he began by re-building & detailing old Western models, and more recently starting his own range based on some of the Top Marques patterns under the name of Manoir Miniatures. Max and Julie hope he will not do this full time, but only as a hobby, as university beckons!

Barry Lester
Auto Replicas

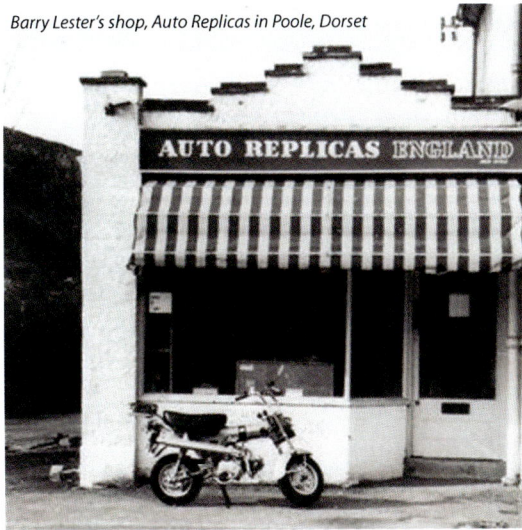

Barry Lester's shop, Auto Replicas in Poole, Dorset

Founder of the Auto Replicas range, Barry Lester began making 1:43 wooden car models for collectors. These developed from his other modelling activities, which included the publication of various articles, model car and boat plans, and other similar projects.

In the mid 1960s collectors started to become aware of these models and, in addition, specialist model shop owners such as Jacques Greilsamer in Paris and Jacques Simonet in Le Mans started to order Barry's wooden 1:43 models in small batches. Also, at around this time, Barry began working with Peter Atkinson of Acorn Models in Swansea, producing the master patterns for vacuum-formed 1:43 kits which were developed from his range of vac-formed bodies for slot cars. After a while, they began producing plastic and white metal kits such as a 3-wheeler Morgan. However, the joint venture halted when Peter suddenly developed other interests.

Elsewhere, John Day was developing his plans for a big range of white metal kits and asked Dave Gilbert and Barry to make some patterns. Unfortunately, as they were not paid, work stopped!!!

One of Barry's regular customers for his wooden models, Leslie Hurle Bath, was already importing various diecast models from around the world, such as the Diapet range from Japan, as a sideline from his main business of importing fabrics into Holland. To assist in the promotion and sales, Reg Miles helped the new business with his regular column in Model Cars magazine. Reg died in December 2004 at 93 yrs, and had kept in touch with Barry throughout his later life.

Leslie and Barry decided that they could produce their own range of white metal kits and thus Auto Replicas Ltd. was formed in Salisbury, England at the end of 1971. Following on from this Auto Replicars

Promotional desktop model made for Barry Lester's Auto Replicas

Barry, second from right at official presentation in France

was formed in Amsterdam.

Their first kit, an ERA was premiered at a swapmeet organised by Paul Gallotti and his friends in Poitiers in the autumn of 1972, and following on from this, they toured Europe for several years to promote their products at swapmeets, even organising an International swapmeet in Bournemouth!

They aimed at introducing a new model every 3 months, and Mike Karslake did some of the pattern work for them, together with Adrian Swain, who made the ERA, their first model. However, most was done, along with casting, by Adrian Swain known as ABS Models, and without him, they would not have got far.

Soon a range and network of agents through Western Europe, Scandinavia, USA, Canada, Japan, South Africa, Australia, New Zealand had been established, and in recognition of these efforts, Barry received the Quattroroutine Diploma Speciale at an exhibition in Italy. He always found that his models were more popular overseas, although Grand Prix Models did retail some.

This level of sales and production continued for some years until Barry bought his own casting and mould making equipment and began making his own patterns. Adrian continued to cast all the earlier models, and Barry shared equipment with Adrian since they were then both living in Poole!

With his own machinery, Barry was able to get outside sub-contract work for pattern-making and/or casting, from such names as J & M Models, Pirate Models, Bellini, Walldorf and Model International. This work was mainly casting railway items and soldiers, including a lot of work for J & M, followed by pattern making and casting for Lowland Model Buses, which subsequently went into administration. John Gay took the patterns over to add to the Pirate range he had already bought.

Award presented to Barry by the Automobile Club of France

Barry then continued to make bus patterns for him, with casting done elsewhere. A vulcanising press and later, an injection moulding machine to make tyres were added to the portfolio of equipment available to Barry.

However, the casting equipment was solely used for sub-contract work, leaving the in-house ranges of models to continue to be cast by pattern maker Adrian Swain. Following the move to Poole, they bought premises in Sandbanks Road, but once Leslie left the company to concentrate on other business matters, Barry returned home.

At this time, the business became BKL Developments, although the range was still Auto Replicas. It grew, firstly into 1:24 scale then 1:76 and 1:86 ranges. The latter was created for Otto Duve of Model International but when he went over to plastic models, his range was incorporated into Auto Replicas. Over the years, Auto Replicas and BKL Developments have made models in many scales, including 1:24, 1:32, 1:50, 1:86, 1:76 & the BLK series which was H0 & 00 as well as 1:43.

Bernd Schultz and Otto Duve of Model International were strong customers, and this helped spread the risk and costs, for patterns and casting work for both Adrian Swain and Barry.

Around 1990, Geneviève appeared on the Auto Replicas scene! She enjoyed sorting and packing castings and undertaking the administrative side of the business. In 1993, the couple moved to Lanhelin in Brittany taking the business with them. At that point the changed circumstances meant that it was no longer possible for Adrian to continue casting, so Barry and Genevieve took it all over.

Sales had always been mainly abroad, beginning with France. The second catalogue listed agents in Australia, Belgium, Germany, France, Italy, Holland, New Zealand, Portugal, South Africa, and the USA. From there, expansion took them to sales in Switzerland, Sweden and particularly high sales in Japan. Originally, models had been selling in their thousands, but sales had reduced to hundreds by 2000.

Auto Replicas always produced illustrated catalogues, which were on sale at one of the first Retromobile shows but, not at the specialist toy fairs, although they were seen at the ModeleX Fair in 1990.

In France, Barry and Geneviève began to realize that it was almost impossible to run a small business with the many bureaucratic regulations, and also at that

AUTO REPLICAS

auto replicas have been awarded the 1974 Quattroroutine special diploma, the first british firm to be so recognised and the first white metal kit manufacturer in the world to receive the award.

club delle quattroructine

DIPLOMA SPECIALE

al sixner

Barry Lester ⋆ Autoreplicas

per la sua partecinazione al XIII° salone delle quattroructine
cateneria
fabbricanti di modelli

data. 16.11.1974.   *Il Presidente della Giuria*

AUTO REPLICAS LIMITED,
56A, SANDBANKS ROAD,
PARKSTONE,
POOLE,
DORSET,
BH14 8BJ
telephone castle hill 2104

1974 - the first white metal maker to be presented with the Quottroroutine Special Diploma

time, the Chinese were beginning to copy their new designs and mass produce them at lower prices. They continued to produce for a few years but decided that 31st December 1999 would be the final curtain.

The following advert appeared in the Model Auto Review magazine in January 2000 –

AUTO REPLICAS FOR SALE

"Barry Lester is one of the pioneers of the specialist model vehicle business, and his work has been described many times in MAR, notably a feature on

his life's work by Max Tomlinson. Now, with almost 30 years under his white metal belt buckle, and looking forward to his retirement in France, Barry has decided to put the range up for sale. Any interested parties can contact him direct at the advertisement in this issue. Barry will continue to make patterns for other people, to restore models, and will continue to develop his activities with his wife Genevieve. They draw and paint, and both are involved in language teaching. Genevieve teaches French to expatriate Brits, whilst Barry teaches English to the native French in Brittany. So, if you fancy the manufacturing equipment and/or patterns, moulds etc for the many Auto Replicas 1:43, 1:24, 1:87, 1:50 and 1:32 white metal ranges, get in touch soon. "

Adrian purchased all their equipment, stock and patterns, except the Bugatti ones which Barry has kept. In 2001 Barry and Genevieve moved to the South of France to enjoy the sun and local wines. Geneviève is an artist and shows at an annual exhibition, locally in Port Leucate.

Barry's affection for France is clear, and so it seems appropriate that his own model collection is now under the care of the Automobile Club de France at Place de la Concorde, in Paris.

Sadly, Barry died in July 2010, so we were privileged to have obtained his story direct from him the year before. By all who knew him, he remains regarded in high esteem, as the pleasant Mr. Nice Guy.

Auto Replicas ERA

Mike & Sue Richardson
Mikansue

In a memorable article in Model Collector in July 2005, Mike Richardson describes himself as an almost cured collector! He recalls being given his first Dinky toy, a 22c Motor Truck, at the beginning of the war by his father, who regarded it as an investment. It is repainted and repaired, but Mike still has it. When Mike was an engineering student in Glasgow, he had a flat in which he kept a glass fronted cocktail cabinet, which was ideal for displaying his 60 or so Dinky Toys that he had repatriated from his parents' house. He bought new Corgis and Dinkys to help

fill the cabinet, and then bought more cabinets. Exchanges followed with a Japanese student, whilst 1963 saw a visit to London where Mike discovered Auto Models of 70, Finsbury Pavement. Here he stocked up on French Dinky Toys, and at around the same time first met Sue. A present of a Tekno E-Type confirmed to Mike that Sue was of like mind, and by 1965 they had moved together to Bracknell.

Mike recalls the availability of models being very limited in the early days. Paddy Stanley, a British Forces chaplain, was producing simple kits cast by Denzil Skinner, who lived near to him when he was stationed in Aldershot.

Auto-kits 1:24 scale metal racing car kits were available from Auto Models, but they were notorious

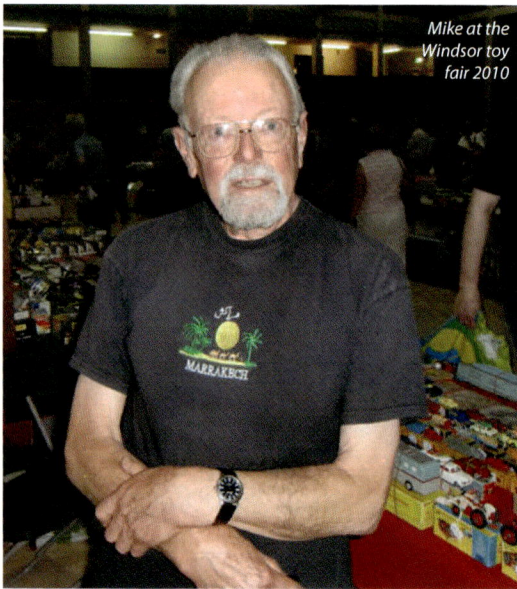

Mike at the Windsor toy fair 2010

non payers, and the range was taken on by Bob Wills, of Wills Finecast, which was instrumental in their production. From information Mike obtained from other collectors, it appears that another maker, known as Replicars or Graphic Designers, manufactured by Exacta Castings, made three 1:24 scale kits between 1956 and 1962. It was Auto Models that sponsored a collectors club, which in due course led to the founding of the Maidenhead Static Model Club.

Mike remembers John Day's first 5 models, which included a Jaguar C type, and Mike had owned the real car – chassis number XKC021, registration no. PUG 676, which is still running and even now may have a mileage of not much more than 40,000 miles.

Mike just had to have the model, so he wrote off to John Day, sent the cheque, but the kit failed to arrive. Fortunately, John Day was trading at the new Windsor swapmeet in June 1971, and Mike obtained his kit through this channel. There were beginning to be other concerns about John Day not delivering at this stage, as readers may have or will discover.

1971 also heralded the arrival of the Modellers' World magazine, a step in which Mike and Sue were instrumental. The magazine ran for 14 years, by

Mikeansue Austin Healey Frogeye Sprite

which time it was wholly owned by Mikansue.

By 1972 Sue, having given up part time teaching to give birth to their son, was looking for a new direction in her career. After having begun trading at swapmeets, they decided that running a mail order business from home, specialising in white metal kits would be a good idea. By October 1972 they had become an official distributor for John Day kits, and P models, made for Peter Oppenheimer, a Swiss collector / dealer in old toys.

At this point, Barry Lester arrived on the scene, with his own creation of an ERA, mastered and cast by himself, and the first in his range of Auto Replicas. This set a new standard in white metal, and showed up the John Day kits as somewhat crude.

Dave Gilbert had also entered the arena in 1971, and is fondly remembered by Mike as the first dealer to bring a supply of Kestrel lager to the Windsor swapmeet! His first model was the Austin chummy. By April 1973, John Day, now living in Ledbury, Gloucestershire, had re-cast Paddy Stanley's range, and seemed to be the sole caster for many ranges.

Mikansue Marcos

To distribute his finished castings to those who would then stock them, a regular meet would be arranged at the Aust Services on the M4, now known as the Severn View Services. The tried and tested regular routine entailed Mike and Bryan Garfield Jones taking turns to drive there, meeting with John Day, Brian Harvey of Grand Prix Models, and sometimes other traders. Initially they met in the restaurant, for a basic meal such as sausage, egg and chips, and discuss future models for their ranges. Sometimes relations between dealers may have been a bit strained and to avoid 'industrial espionage' and the theft of trade secrets, they would each take a different corner of the cafe for their meeting with John!

Following this, all would retire to the car park to their cars, all parked alongside each other away from prying eyes, open up their boots, and exchange shoe boxes full of castings. The kits at this time were packed by John's family and supplied in plain plastic bags. The traders fitted their own header cards or boxes. A shadier looking group of people you could not wish to meet on a dark night in a car park. Happily the police never became interested!

Mikansue Triumph Dolomite Roadster

And so the Mikansue range was born with No. 1, the Jowett Jupiter in October 1973, with a casting made by John Day, and patterns made by either Steve Bates or Rodney Henley who then worked for John.

In 1973 Paddy Stanley's range had been re-introduced, with John Day continuing to do all the casting. John had bought a bulk supply of French Mini Auto magazine back numbers, as it had ceased publishing, and decided to use the Mini-Auto name to make a new range of kits to a slightly higher quality. This would effectively raise the price of his kits from £2.00 to £4.50 to be produced with a Limited Edition status, only 200 of each being made. The reality was that this was a regular production run for such kits in those days.

Needless to say, of the 8 models listed in Modellers' World in 1973, all were sold. 1974 heralded the arrival of Danhausen in Germany, and Classic Car kits by Brian Harvey, the founder of Grand Prix Models. Both of these ranges were made by John Day.

The production of a number of model ranges cast by John Day begun to have an effect on the visual impact of those models for customers, in that they all appeared similarly crude. Yet the M4 traders group, Mike Richardson, Bryan Garfield Jones, and Brian Harvey all still regularly attended the Aust Services to meet John Day and collect their shoe boxes. John Day was by now announcing that he would be releasing a new range known as S. B. Models, which may have referred to the pattern maker Steve Bates, or in some people's views, 'Special B******s'! With another price rise to £5.00 each, this range was sold exclusively by Mikansue, although they had no influence on the choice of subjects. The advantage for Mikansue was that they did not pay John until the kits had been sold.

Western Models appeared in the market place in 1974, offering ready built models, whilst FDS, run by Francesco De Stasio of Naples, produced his models with what to Mike felt like ex-church lead! Walldorf Models run by Otto Duve, the owner of Model International, a German model shop, were one of the few ranges not using John Day, their castings being made in Germany.

Mikansue's Americana and Grand Tourisme ranges were released in 1975, initially by John Day, and then taken over by Mikansue. October 1975 also saw the launch of yet another John Day range, the Museum Series. These were supposed to coincide with the opening of a museum of 1:43 scale racing cars by John in his factory which was then in part of the Morgan car factory. These Museum kits had far greater detail than the previous models. They featured engine detail which could be seen by taking off the removable bonnet. Mike cannot remember the actual museum being created.

Come 1977 a number of factors led to Mikansue and John Day parting company. Mikansue were appointed distributors for the French market, but unbeknown to them, French outlets had already been established by John Day, and they were not best pleased by this move.

The quality of John Day's castings was not really improving, and so Mike Richardson approached Rodney Henley, John's pattern maker, who decided to go self-employed, and began making master patterns for both Mike and Sue Richardson and Bryan Garfield Jones. The final straw came when on visiting John Day's factory in Malvern, to make the break, Mike found no evidence of any kits being made. It turned out that they were in fact being made by Colin Tyler of Bewdley Leisure Products, who were making both the moulds and the castings.

A meeting was held by Colin, Rodney and Mike, and possibly Bryan Garfield Jones, to cut John out of the loop. Colin was able to offer them a significant quality improvement, namely, plated small parts for the kits. He had wanted to do this for John but he turned the idea down on grounds of cost. Having removed John's percentage from the trade prices the group were able to offer the improved kits at the old price for some years.

Pattern for Rover Jet 1

During 1977 Mike began working with Martin Field as a pattern maker who liked working in brass; hitherto patterns had been made in metal. The very first Mikansue model created using a brass master was a Triumph 1800 Roadster, their No.10. This model's body was an innovation, in that it was all one piece. Martin had obtained a steel wing from a Triumph Roadster, and used it throughout the creation of the brass master, in order to get the measurements right. This master had been kept by Mike for years, but was recently handed back to Martin in thanks for his work done.

Around this time, in 1976, unbeknown to most people apart from friend Bryan Garfield Jones, Mike and Sue had purchased the Dinky Toys collection of the late Cecil Gibson. This included a massive archive which Mike viewed one Sunday when invited to lunch, and although there were other offers it is likely that the collection came to Mike and Sue due to their deep commitment to the hobby, and their plan to use the collection and archive to record for posterity the details it contained. The collection was collected in an ancient Morris J4 van, driven by Bryan Garfield Jones all the way to Leicester, complete with a load of cash. The collection occupied over half a double garage for some years, and it provided subject matter for many articles in Modellers' World, and of course the books that Mike and Sue subsequently published

Pattern for V16 BRM

After October 1977, Mike had no more contact with John Day, and introduced a further range known as Mikansue Competition kits, consisting of mostly European competition and racing cars, the first being an Alta –Jaguar. There were 69 in this range, and the other ranges made by Mike reached 36 for the mainstream Mikansue, 27 for Grand Tourisme, and 18 for Americana.

Production runs for most of these ranges were approximately 200 on average, but some of the best sellers, such as the Austin Healey rally car, sold at least 2,500. This model was so successful that it was re-moulded 4-5 times, and the Jaguar XK150 was of a similar order. These two are excellent examples of popular cars that had not been modelled by any of the big diecast manufacturers. Rodney Henley launched his own range of kits at this time, C Scale, this being a pun as he also made waterline ship models.

Mike and Sue first began to place their, by now, extensive knowledge into print in 1981 with the publication of Sue's book Minic – Lines Bros Tinplate Toys. From this came a commission from New Cavendish to write their Dinky Toys Book. This remained in print until in 2000 when it was superceded by their volume The Great Book of Dinky Toys, but only after selling about 20,000 copies.

By September 1983, Mike and Sue had obtained a shop in Eton Wick, near Windsor and used the name Modellers' World for the new venture. After 5 years they decided to sell it as a going concern as it was taking up too much time. They did keep their personal ranges for themselves and returned to trading from home.

However, 1988 brought forth a wide range of superlative white metal models, and Mike was then feeling that they had reached the limit of their own technology, and were being overtaken. They either had to invest a lot of money to embrace the new standards, or sell out. First to go was the shop, which brought great relief at no longer being tied to shop hours, and was celebrated by a cruise on the Nile.

After that, the next decision was to sell the kit business. After, 'putting the word around' a deal was struck with a couple named Morrison from North London. Mike took them to Bewdley Leisure Products where the moulds were kept, and all the moulds, patterns and remaining castings were passed into the new owners' hands.

Since then, Mike saw the Morrisons at a Sandown Park toy fair with a pewter TVR Coupe, which had been made with their pattern, but without glazing. Strangely, the Morrisons have not been seen again, although some castings have surfaced which appear to be from Mikansue moulds. Some masters also reached Keith Edney of RAE models, in Chertsey, and re-appeared slightly modified.

And so Mike and Sue turned their experienced hands to buying and selling on the toy fair circuit again. They also returned to writing books which they started in 1981 publishing Sue's book on Tri-ang Minic Toys themselves. Dinky Toys and Modelled Miniatures for New Cavendish Books followed in 1986. Sue's Diecast Toy Aircraft was in 1997, also with New Cavendish. Next was Christie's World of Automotive Toys in 1998 and they returned to New Cavendish with The Great Book of Dinky in 2000. Mike did produce two short paperbacks for Francis Joseph;

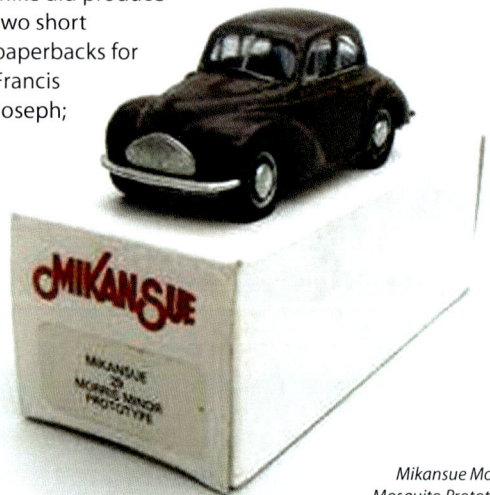

Mikansue Morris Mosquito Prototype

Collecting Dinky Toys in 2001 and a similar book on Corgi in 2004. Mike and Sue wrote regularly for Model Collector from its launch in 1985 until 2004.

In 2000, the Director of the National Motor Museum at Beaulieu, Michael Ware, proposed to put on an exhibition showing the history of motoring through toys and models. The exhibition, entitled Motoring Through Childhood, showcased the collection of Ian Cummins of Sydney, who was trading as Model Cars (Australia) some years before and stocked Mikansue kits. Mike and Sue have both enjoyed their involvement in writing and publishing, although Mike admits that it is Sue who is the more accomplished!

Since then they have spent much time travelling to satisfy their joint interest in archaeology, particularly around the Mediterranean region.

In 2004 Mike and Sue made a major decision to move to France, where they have enjoyed a healthy and rural way of life, unencumbered by the ever changing and hustling world of toy cars. A year later, they decided to sell their collection and books, apart from the 20 or so favourite pieces that remain in a cabinet in their home in France.

Their reputation travelled before them, even in the large Departmental city of Angers in the Loire valley, when in December 2007 they decided to visit a toy fair. They found traders and members of the public whispering, "Is it them?" "It is isn't it?" Needless to say one, a Modellers' World reader, finally sought confirmation of their identity. They found a trader selling a white metal MG PB Airline, one of Bryan Garfield Jones' Motorkits range, an example of why they came into the hobby in the first place, and a model no one had modelled. The vendor had originally bought the kit from Mikansue and found that it started him in the kit building business. In gratitude for getting him started he gave Mike the built model, which is now in the cabinet with their own models.

Sadly, Sue died in January 2010, somewhat unexpectedly. Sue was an acknowledged expert in a number of toy collecting fields, but the Tri-ang tinplate was her first love. Sue's keen interest in photography complemented her love of travel in many countries, and with her love of cooking, their home in France enabled her to explore both food and wine in depth. Her knowledge and wisdom across the world of collecting will be sorely missed.

Mike & Joyce Stephens
Western Models Ltd

Joyce and Mike at the Nuremberg Fair

Following a move from the West Country, Mike Stephens in conjunction with a friend, Bryan Garfield Jones, and Ken Wooton, both of whom had been dabbling in the supply of replacement parts for Dinky Toys, founded Western Models Ltd in 1974.

At that time Mike had 1500 – 2000 diecast toys, Corgis, Dinkies, etc.; a truly amazing collection for that period. However, wanting to have a business of his own, he could see a good possibility to make quality models which would appeal to collectors and which were not obtainable from any other source. Whilst it was not long before a small factory was set up near Redhill, Surrey, the foundation and formulation of objectives, etc. were carried out in Mike's house in Epsom, Surrey.

Western's first models, announced early in the same year, were a 1938 Mercedes-Benz and a 1937 4.5 litre Lagonda Rapide, both of which were very fine replicas and examples of the standards Mike had set himself. As new fully finished models they were soon discovered by enthusiastic collectors who had for so long been building their own from kits or scratch.

Indeed, the Mercedes-Benz was launched at a Windsor swapmeet after a hectic few days and late nights completing the 100 models they planned to show there. Sales success was unbelievable in that all the models sold very quickly, and, they received a large order from the Lang brothers, proprietors of the Danhausen shop in Aachen, Germany

Their range of 1:43 scale models expanded rapidly and 1975 saw a 1951 Jaguar XK 120 fixed head coupe and a 1937 3.5 litre Bentley announced, to the joy of British collectors. Kits of all their models were available and the period saw the commencement of 1:24 scale models. It was about this time that Mike and Bryan split the company and with Ken already gone Mike assumed sole control.

Mercedes 300SLR made for Plumbies

To achieve all this, Mike had the support of a strong team behind him to be able to offer a complete service to any organisation commissioning models from the company. Keith Williams was responsible for producing the drawings and for 28 years, Robin Housego was their sole 'in house' pattern maker. Others, including Brian Lawrence, Ian Pickering, Ian Playfoot and Richard Stokes took on some of this work as the company grew and more and more models were being produced. Mike designed the moulds and John Allen had the responsibility of making them. The casting was largely down to Mike.

Such was the quality of their models that the skills of their employees were sought by others, including Jim Varney's Transport Replicas, Richard Briggs' MiniMarque43 and, of course, Bryan's Motorkits series. Danhausen, with their large Minichamps, Metal 43, Metal 24, Plumbies, and Plumbies Inter ranges were Western's most prolific customer and together, this volume necessitated a significant increase in staffing. At the peak of their production for them, nearly 40 people were employed in the Redhill factory.

Mercedes 540k - the first one

Such was Danhausen's involvement that Gunter Lang sought a partnership with Mike, his brother Peter having gone his own way, but this did not meet with Mike's agreement and the existing arrangement continued until the Minichamps range was re-launched as a 1:43 diecast range made in China in 1984.

As a result of this, Western Models' Redhill premises were closed and the business was moved to Taunton, there with a staff of 20, some moving with the

company. Thus they continued, concentrating on their own ranges and other contract work. During all this time, Mike was ably supported by his wife Joyce who took the responsibility of overseeing assembly and packing of the models as well as looking after the administration. Also involved were his three children, Tim, Lynn and Nicola. Tim made moulds for many years, after John Allen and Keith Williams left Western to set up their own company, Scale Model Technical Services, whilst Lynn handled the book keeping and Nicola gave assistance in all departments as and when necessary.

The ranges then established were Western Models - 1:43 Classic cars, including many American examples and Record breakers, Western Racing – 1:43 F1 and other Competition cars, Western Prestige – modern 1:43 and Western Formula 1 – 1:24 F1 cars. Small Wheels was a separate company bought into Western's ranges in the early '90s.

Jaguar XK150 made for Metal 43

Mike's involvement with Formula 1 in 1979/80 was significant, the high standard of the 1:24 models taking him to the highest level of involvement with the F1 fraternity. This started with Frank Williams and the Saudia Williams FW06, being given full factory access to measure and photograph it together with other potential model subjects of his and many others who sought Western's services, Brabham, Lotus, McLaren, Wolf and Aston Martin/Lagonda to name a few. They all resulted in 1:24, scale models being produced.

The Formula 1 connection led Mike into 1:8 and 1:4 scale vac-form plastic models for exhibition and show stands, hundreds of these being made for that purpose. Two hundred 1:8 scale Porsche Le Mans being a good example.

In 1995, a 1:200 scale aircraft range was launched (or took off !), eventually rising to 30 or so models, including a Silver City Airways Bristol Freighter, their first, and a Super Constellation, which was very popular and resulted in various liveries being produced. Surprisingly, perhaps, this was the first collection of aircraft models to be issued since those from Dinky Toys, many years before.

Much later the Taunton factory was closed and re-

Western models Aston Martin V8 Volante

located next to the Stephens' home in Devon, using the building that served as a hangar for the Cessna that they had operated earlier. This location saw the introduction of British cars of the 1930s, including a 1938 Morris 8 series E saloon and tourer, and a 1938 Vauxhall 14/6 DX saloon.

As the new century unfolded, Mike began to think about retirement. Sadly, it was not realistic to expect to sell the business as a going concern, so as 2008, his planned retirement year, approached Mike sought buyers for his various ranges, to include the patterns, moulds and all associated items such as

drawings, decals, vac-forms, etc.. He found a buyer for the aircraft in China, American cars in the USA and the English cars were sold to pattern maker Adrian Swain.

This hobby has a significant record for retirees not actually retiring and Mike is no exception to that following, still maintaining a keen interest in the handbuilt model world and keeping his hand in with a few development ideas that interest him.

Bristol Super Freighter 'Silver City'

Jim Varney
Transport Replicas

Days out on a bus with a bus pass

Probably one of the best known characters around the south of England fairs and steam show circuits, Jim Varney has been for many years an enthusiastic visitor to these shows with his faithful dog by his side.

He recalls that as a child he always had a fascination for buses, and at aged 8 he would take particular note of the different shapes in London. Not for him the bus numbers pursuit, but toy buses

became a regular favourite to indulge his love of transport.

Jim was a pipe fitter and welder by trade, but got browned off with the work, and one day found himself attending the old Windsor swapmeet at a local school. He then began chatting to his local shopkeepers who allowed him to check out their storerooms, where he was able to buy quantities which he then used as stock for trading at the fairs.

As toy fairs began to take off, he recalls in 1972 attending the Gloucester swapmeet run then by Mike Rooum, and meeting Adrian Swain, a collector of toys who also was a white metal caster. After some discussion, Adrian offered to make a master for him for no charge as long as he agreed to use him as his caster of the kit.

Adrian Swain was the originator of ABS Models. Jim settled on the Shillibeers horse drawn bus

Black Country Models Midland Red, built by Colin Flannery

No 36 AEC kit

as one of his favourites, and went to the London Transport museum at Clapham and took numerous photos and measurements, and despatched these to Adrian. 200 castings were made, and the Shillibeers was launched in 1973. But regrettably this No1 in the Transport Replicas range did not sell well (like a feather falling from the moon – JV!) Jim's next most vivid childhood memory was an STL double decker running through Godstone in Surrey, so this became the next made, numbered 4 due to renumbering of others.

Jim recalls that Prince Marshall, once an employee of Ian Allan Publishing and a long time writer and publisher of bus related material, was the first to bring open top tourist buses to any European city. He found a derelict Thomas Tilling STL, and gained finances to fund its restoration, prior to it being introduced to the streets of London. Marshall talked Jim into making a model of his STL.

Marshall persuaded London Transport to grant him rights to the number 100 tourist bus route on a 3 year contract, and also put ex-Midland Red D9 buses converted to open top on tourist routes. However, once the 3 years were up, his profile took a knock as he was allocated much less lucrative routes. Jim sees Marshall as an eccentric visionary who paved the way, but did not have a good head for business

No 35 Hastings Trollybus, built by J. Elliott

when dealing with the big boys. They soon ousted him, and put their own buses on the streets. You only have to look at cities all over the country and the world for that matter, and you will see open toppers everywhere.

Jim continued to trade at local toy fairs, using the proceeds to assist in financing his white metal series, and used a number of casters including John Day. Colin Flannery was his model maker for handbuilt models.

After 2-3 years Jim diversified into cars as well. However, after a short period he sold that range on to Bryan Garfield Jones, who launched them in his Motorkits range.

Jim's Ford Model 'A' van had already been marketed in the livery of the Old Motor magazine when the Ford Motor Company heard of his work, and called him in to their factory. An amicable agreement was reached securing Ford's authorisation of his model, whilst confirming that Jim would use their factory colours.

London transport RT

The Pennine Chain tram car range included an E3 London Transport tram produced in a limited run of 50 only, the last items to be cast and made by T.R. Ltd. '0' gauge RT models came along in a batch of 50 as well, fully built, one off models for the Open University. Also, London Transport Advertising asked for 50 Routemasters to be made in two sets of the special Routemaster Shillibeer Omibuses and Paris buses in kit form to the same gauge.

The BBC approached Jim to produce a set of Shillibeers horse drawn buses in a limited run of 50 only, in which there would be 2 each of 25 different advertisers. This was to promote the Open University. To commission transfers for this job would have been financial ruin, so Jim sought out a model painter of railway locomotives living in Gloucestershire, who hand-painted each one. A single set was for advertising purposes, and the other was for a prestigious meeting of managing directors of companies in the Guildhall, London, where each example would be placed in front of each MD!

Jim's distribution of his kits included attendance at toy fairs, mail order, and advertising in Collectors Gazette and Exchange & Mart. He also attended many bus rallies and similar outdoor events. '00' gauge was served not only by buses, but also by a small range of cars similar to the larger 1:43 range, and these now, in the 21st century appear on eBay regularly at a premium.

From this solid business base Jim diversified into copies, having found a rare Dinky 22 series tractor, which was minus a wheel. Not content with creating replicas of both parts, he improved on the model by fabricating a radiator grille, and a baseplate. He gained permission from Dinky toys to sell this model.

This was the birth of a new range – CopyCat models. 14 more models entered service for Jim in this range, all copies of existing toys from Crescent, Dinky Toys and Morestone ranges. These were charming toys, being both copies and developments of the original. However, by 1980, recession was biting, and Jim was paying 21% for his bank loans to keep the business going. This would not last, and he obtained support from a family member to clear his debts, sold the CopyCat range to Colin Penn, and chose to take another direction in his life. Touring with a caravan meant freedom from business pressures, and he now looks back with pride on his career creating a range of models for the model railway enthusiast.

It is now clear that Jim was one of the pioneers in widening out the availability of model buses for bus and model railway enthusiasts, and thus paving the way for the arrival of the diecast manufacturers who, with the advent of Chinese production, were able to develop further the bus field.

Jim now lives alone, surviving on his state pension. Sometimes, however, he can still afford to get out for a few hours to bus rallies and toy fairs by train or bus, accompanied by his faithful hound. His first loves are always toys and models, and the real thing of course.

Keith Williams & John Allen
Scale Model Technical Services Ltd

Keith Williams and John Allen , the partners at SMTS

One of the most successful companies in this industry is SMTS, and its resilience is due mostly to Keith Williams, its co-founder.

Keith Williams was 18 when he finished school, and decided to take a year out before he went to university. He took a job at Caffyns in Horsham, then a local British Leyland dealership. It was there that he met Bryan Garfield Jones's wife Jill, who was working on the accounts there.

Keith had made models of cars, and worked in a shop before, so he was invited to build up models for Bryan's range, Motorkits. After he graduated, he was still making the Motorkits, and in 1976, Bryan recommended that he visit Mike Stephens, who at the time was running Western Models at the Watermill, near Redhill.

Keith was employee number 8, and commenced work on a 3 days per week basis building models. By this time Western Models had already released their Mercedes 540K roadster. Mike soon realised that Keith could draw too, so he began drawing designs as well. Whilst at Western he met John Allen, who was to be a strong influence in his life. Keith became a full-time employee, and at the time they had a contract to supply Minichamps, who were then producing ranges known as Plumbies, Metal 43, Metal 24 and Metal 87. Minichamps have come a long way since those days, and they have created a museum in Aachen to record their long history in model cars.

Western was expanding fast, and achieved approximately 60% of Minichamps' business. However, with casting facilities developing in China, Minichamps decided to move into the diecast model car field, and pulled the plug on a lucrative and critical contract with Western. By 1983, Keith and John were spending their lunch hours, eating their sandwiches, and planning how they might one day move out and start their own business. They

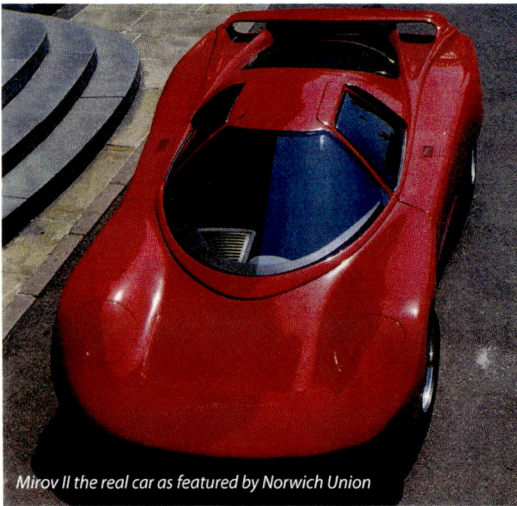

Mirov II the real car as featured by Norwich Union

made their decision, left Western and pursued their independent careers together. The departure of Keith and John from Western came at a bad time, but it did enable Mike Stephens to plan a down-sizing of the company.

Keith fondly remembers visiting Formula 1 teams and meeting Patrick Head and Gordon Murray in the course of research for models. At this time he commissioned Ian Pickering and Richard Stokes to make patterns for him. Whilst Keith and John were the two enthusiasts getting together, they were soon joined by Steve Overy, who was a catalyst in helping SMTS to obtain suitable premises.

The Arrows A6 was their first model and has happy memories for Keith as through it, he made the connection with Jackie Oliver. He used to make 1:4 scale presentation models of Jackie's F1 cars sign written in potential sponsors colours. Jackie was married to the lovely Lulu, who was a dancer with the Top of the Pops dance group Legs and Co at the time. The jobs were always hush, hush, and rush, rush, and Jackie was always flying all over the place trying to raise money, so Lulu would come to Keith's place to pick up the models.

Ian Pickering made the pattern, but the rest of the construction was in house. Keith commissioned Kaylee Transfers to do the decals, from artwork drawn by Keith.

Lotus 49 Jim Clark 1967 debut win for Cosworth DFV and Lotus 49

When he introduced the Arrows A6, SMTS sold about a dozen kits to one person. They speculated who would want 12 kits of the same car? The answer was that the 'ultimate' 1:43 race car collector Colin Frazer, later to become a good friend and the founder of Formula Models. The Arrows sold well, with 500 units being distributed to retailers who had agreed to take the new SMTS models.

Steve Overy arranged to move the factory to a unit in Hastings in 1986, but soon afterwards he left, leaving Keith and John as the two partners, as it remains to this day. Keith took on the business and development side, whilst John was the mould maker. Keith would commission a pattern, choosing the pattern maker according to the brief and design he was planning to achieve, and was therefore the 'front of house' man. John has been content to be the 'back office' supremo.

Mirov II promotional model car with literature for Norwich Union

Технология для Прогресса

Around this time, Keith recalls, one of his first commissions was a 1:43 Mirov II Russian supercar. Part of a world wide promotion by Norwich Union, it was intended that 200 certificated models be released, but Keith recalls only 50 or so being cast and built. The promotion began on 16 June 1989 and was aired in London and Norwich TV regions. It related to an imaginary Russian sports Turbo of the future which represented the kind of investment opportunity people could one day share through a Norwich Union savings and investment plan. Just two real cars were made, and the advertisement had a voice over from Ludovic Kennedy. One car remains in road worthy condition in private ownership.

In the late 1980s Henk van Asten, an experienced Dutch collector, asked Keith to produce a range of 1950s American cars, and from this beginning, Henk built up the range known as Conquest and Madison models, which included a number of British cars. Much later, Henk retired, and sold the patterns to American retailer, Dave (Buz) Kirkel, on the understanding that SMTS would continue the manufacture. Soon after, Buz also bought Western's

Jaguar E-Type lightweight low-drag coupe Linder/Nocker Le Mans 1694

US range of models when Mike Stephens retired. The deal included the patterns, some of which were then passed to SMTS. Keith and his team are now upgrading these patterns, and awaiting more from the same source.

In due course they outgrew their small factory unit, and bought a piece of land nearby, built a purpose built factory on it in 1992. At this point and in the early 1990s, there were 32 employees working with SMTS, delivering a consistent quality standard in all their models.

However, overhead costs were high, and with the arrival of more detailed diecast models, it was clear that the market was declining. As a means of diversifying, in 2000, Keith Edney, proprietor of RAE Models, found a buyer near Heathrow who wanted a range of aircraft, and Skylines were born. SMTS models have followed a number of thematic ranges, known as 'The Racing Line', 'Those Classic Lines' and 'Skyline'.

Soon after this, Keith had a visitor to the factory, Bruce Rolston, one of the world's foremost collectors of earth moving equipment, who had recently retired to Hastings. He was seeking some casting work to fill the remaining gaps in his collection. This enquiry led to the commissioning of some fully built models from SMTS, which became the launch of the Black Rat Mining Company, a range to meet the needs of this specialist market. As the Skylines aeroplane range

was overtaken by Chinese made diecasts of the same aircraft, SMTS switched to other lines and markets. The American customer base is particularly strong at present. This exemplifies the versatility of SMTS in responding to customer needs in many fields.

Over the years customers have sought 00 gauge locomotive bodies from Keith, others have ordered dolls house furniture and staircases, which still generate a twice yearly order. Wargaming tanks and other military vehicles have also featured in their portfolio. SMTS undertake the casting for the K&R Replicas range, developed by John and Stephen Roff.

Keith developed and introduced a new range of large scale motorcycles, in conjunction with David Baulch, but after a few hundred had been sold, the arrival of the Minichamps similar range rendered this venture unviable.

Both Keith and his partner John Allen are beginning to consider the future of SMTS, given the declining market, but it appears that the opportunistic approach to their work is continuing to draw out new customers. A small range of fantasy cars for Bridgestone Tyres has been a recent commission.

With a number of key customers relying on the range of skills that SMTS has to offer, let's hope they will have been able to ride the recession and continue to provide the industry with their valuable range of services.

Ford E83W van with works Cooper on trailer

By the end of the 1970s, a plethora of ranges made by many producers had appeared on the market. However, as this new and rapidly expanding hobby seemed to be insatiable, not only did these makers expand, but a new tranche of producers appeared in the 1980s, and later in the 1990s. Many of these sought to improve the detail, definition and features in the models they issued. Some delivered much broader ranges of cars.

Significantly, apart from a small minority, most up until this stage were in kit form. The 1980s were characterised by the arrival of a greater number of fully finished white metal handbuilt models, for which there was no kit equivalent. Signature ranges included EnCo Models and Minimarque43. Others such as Brooklin and Pathfinder Models developed a regular issue approach which is featured in Chapter 13, the Volume Producers. The hallmark seemed to be a more commercial, business like approach to their market. The following subjects are, however, an eclectic group of people who have continued the often colourful tradition amongst producers, giving us some fascinating stories to tell.

David Baulch
Classic Model Motorcycles

The brainchild of 'bike' enthusiast David Baulch, Classic Model Motorcycles commenced marketing 1:9 scale motorcycle kits in 1985 with a 1962 Triumph Bonneville.

Manufactured by SMTS and comprising up to 180 parts, including plated items and appropriate make/pattern real rubber tyres, more than 400 kits were soon sold to bike and model enthusiasts worldwide. Priced then at £65.00, each kit was supplied complete with extensive detailed instructions and 'exploded' drawings to help the builder.

The second model, of a 1961 BSA Gold Star in Clubman's trim followed soon after and achieved similar sales success.

The expanding range was still in production in 1989 and included more Triumphs including a Trophy, Tiger110 (Bathtub), Thunderbird(Bathtub) and a BSA Rocket Gold Star.

We understand that these models remained in production until Minichamps produced a similar range. Sadly, David died around the turn of the century.

Richard Briggs
Minimarque43

Daimler 420 limousine

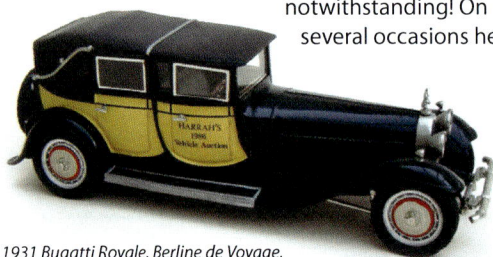
Richard outside the Montem Leisure Centre

Like so many small boys, Richard Briggs always loved cars and drove his father's Rover 12 well before his teens. After leaving school he had various jobs selling cars and had a long spell in South Africa in the motor trade and the restaurant business. He visited the USA many times, becoming a recognised authority on American cars and in 1980 formed his own company to produce models of the cars he so loved.

His first two models, a Riley RMB and a Packard Caribbean received rave reviews and were the forerunners of the many fine quality white metal models that established his reputation.

A lifelong batchelor, the last twenty years of his life were centred on his enthusiasm for all the models Minimarque43 produced and, indeed, the collection of classic cars he established at his home in Halsham, East Yorkshire. Packard was his favourite marque and many models of these cars were made.

He travelled to America again at this time mostly to deliver personally the orders from dealers and collectors, customs officials notwithstanding! On several occasions he purchased a car to make his deliveries and then despatched it to England to add to his collection. A lovely story tells of one occasion when, instead of buying a car, he hired one for the purpose with an unlimited mileage agreement and returned it three weeks later with nearly four thousand miles added! The hire company was not amused.

Over the years, new ranges were introduced, including Cars of the Stars, Commercial and Military vehicles, to name just a few. Richard's keen eye for detail, discerning choice of models and prolific range ensured his continued success right up to his passing on 27th July 2002.

He commissioned various pattern makers and companies to make his models and, indeed, independent specialist builders on some occasions. A true classic amongst the models that were produced for him and much sought after is the 1931 Bugatti Royale, Berline de Voyage, Type 41, finished in black and yellow, some with Harrah's 1986 Vehicle Auction logos on both front doors

Friends will remember Fido and Cilla the two dogs he was devoted to. Both pre-deceased him, but Cilla's memory lives on with her image or name on the base of all his models.

A big man in every sense of the word, Richard was always happy to talk and listen to those who befriended him. His presence is sorely missed in the scene he chose, but his models are still around. Not only that, many of the models are now available again, marketed as Minimarque models.

1931 Bugatti Royale, Berline de Voyage, Type 41, mastered by Ian Pickering

Boston-Nicholls
Gearbox Models

At the end of 1988, Birmingham based Boston-Nicholls, well founded in the use of pewter for general modelling, announced their first model car a 1:43 scale 1936 Austin Ruby.

Until that date pewter, the finest form of white metal, had not been used seriously for the construction of model cars. As such, Boston-Nicholls concentrated on producing models for sale as cast. They later planned to make them available painted, with all the usual finishing items.

The Ruby was followed by a Triumph Stag in three versions, a Rover P6 V8 and a Range Rover, with an Austin Pearl and Aston Martin DB4 in prospect.

Despite plenty of publicity, 'as cast' pewter models never made a breakthrough with specialist model collectors. However, Gearbox Models, an associate company, did succeed for a while with construction modified painted examples, complete with vac-form windows, plated parts, rolling wheels, rubber tyres, etc., but not in quantities that justified using the more expensive pewter castings. In due course they ceased production altogether.

Ian Burkinshaw

Ian Burkinshaw modelmaker

From building the inevitable Airfix kits as a child, whilst living in Wakefield, Ian Burkinshaw visited a swapmeet at York Racecourse in the mid 1980s, and spotted various white metal and early resin kits for sale on the stall of Ralph Foster of Pandora Models fame. Kits were purchased and a friendship developed with Ralph. Ian was bitten by the bug.

Following a motor cycle accident in 1979, Ian's career in the motor trade was affected by being unable to drive manual cars anymore. Ralph had heard on the grapevine that Minimarque43 were looking for model builders and suggested a trip down to see Richard Briggs. Ian came away from the

Triumph roadster for Minimarque43

meeting with a box of models to build. Thus followed a 17 year friendship with the big man!

Ian recalls his first impressions of Richard Briggs as a bit of an oddball, but they laid down the ground rules between them. From then on Ian felt that Richard would helpfully give him constructive criticism when he took his built models back to Richard, which was taken in good heart. Ian converted his garage into a workshop, and they were in business. To begin with Ian used aerosol cans, but soon progressed to using a compressor and spray guns, and automotive paints as his production line developed to 50 – 60 cars at a time.

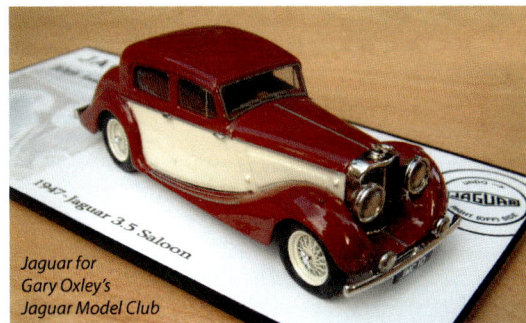
Jaguar for Gary Oxley's Jaguar Model Club

Ian built many of Minimarque43's models, including the $3^1/_2$ litre Mk IV Jaguar drophead, and in later years continued his association with Jaguar by building models for Gary Oxley, who founded the Jaguar Model Club. This also entailed modifying existing patterns to create a different version of the same car, such as racing MkII Jaguars of Stirling Moss, Graham Hill, Jack Sears, and on a few occasions even full patterns for models. Charles Barnett also features amongst his customers.

Whilst Ian made models for Richard Briggs for 17 years, he was one of a number of builders, including Graham Price, Steve Overy of Illustra and Colin Flannery. His memories of that period are often amusing, including falling victim to Richard Brigg's well known narcolepsy, particularly when Ian was talking to him! Ian also recalls driving to his house by appointment with a batch of completed models only to find him not at home! One white knuckle ride through the centre of Leeds to see Rod and Val Ward at Modelauto in a very large mid 1950s Cadillac definitely caused premature greyness. Richard is sadly missed.

Ian is now 53 years old, and has found that with the shrinking market for white metal handbuilt models, work is not so plentiful. He has therefore returned to the motor trade working for a company that specialises in the reconditioning of car parts. At home, he still has hundreds of unbuilt kits, which have now become a hobby again, his passion being Le Mans cars. His one regret is that neither of his sons show any interest in his hobby, so all the kits will have to be built - eventually!

Alistair Duncan
A & S Modelmakers

Towards the end of 1990, Grantham based pattern maker and model builder, Alistair Duncan, brought a new range of American cars to market with the launch of a 1958 Ford Thunderbird.

With experience of making American car models for others, it was not surprising that the first model of his own would also be of an American car.

With only his wife Sally working with him, it was remarkable that the two of them were able to carry out nearly everything necessary for production themselves. Alistair made the patterns himself, and together they carried out the rest of the process, including mould making, casting, painting, brass etching, artwork for decals, vac. forming, and assembly. Plating was probably done elsewhere.

Aiming for top quality, with many parts, their first model undoubtedly achieved. This large two door convertible looked every bit the part – the street machine of the day! At £85.00 including VAT, it was exceptionally good value.

The plan was to introduce a continental kit and a hardtop version as well as other models, but no record of further production has been available. Around 1995 production ceased, and the patterns were sold in due course to Minimarque43. This company continued to issue the Thunderbird.

A&S Model Makers - 1958 Ford Thunderbird

Keith Edney
RAE Models

This is a father and son story, with Keith Edney, always into motor cars and motor bikes, following his father into the family model making business just 4 years after he left school.

An aircraft cabin built by Keith

Keith's father had always worked on model boats for another company, but left to form his own business, RAE Models, in 1975. He used his own initials, Robert Alan Edney, to name the business, and began by working on specialist furniture and fittings for kitchens, some years before companies such as MFI came into being. However, it wasn't long before some of his previous customers came to him asking him to continue to work on boats and other models. Individual commissions also included model aircraft and model hovercraft.

Keith left school to join British Aerospace, working on Concorde. He served a four year apprenticeship, in which he moved around in every department of the works. This even included the guillotine shop, in which all unwanted metal was cut up. Keith learnt his welding and woodworking skills over this time, and then, apprenticeship over, he joined his father's business in 1975, shortly after it had been established.

At this time, neither Keith nor his father had any interest in model cars, but a number of factors came together to change all that. Firstly, they were using a white metal casting company to create the fittings for the display and promotional models they

1:24 Scale Ferrari 250 GTO

specialised in.

These included models of the hovercraft, the APT and HST trains, and Brush locomotive prototypes.

This white metal casting company decided to diversify into making printed circuit boards, which in a common production area, do not sit comfortably beside dusty white metal working! The result was that they decided to opt out of white metal casting, and offered the casting equipment to RAE.

Keith was then approached by an individual who was keen to make a Morgan pedal car, and also supplied Keith with a set of plans for an MGTF. His proposal was to make both from glass fibre. This project did not come to fruition, and the necessary equipment and plans for the project sat dormant in his loft for seven years.

He was then approached by Tony Bellm, a millionaire, who wanted to start a 1:20 scale range called Bellini Models. He owned a pharmaceutical factory in Guernsey, and firmly believed that his current workforce there could build the models! This was not a successful venture, not least because 1:20 was an unknown scale.

However, the Piccolino range, in 1:76 was more marketable. Tony chose the full range of cars that his son had driven in his racing career, right up to 2010 and the Ford GT40. Keith recalls that Tony Bellm had spent well over £1m on his model collection before he died, and was indeed a truly addicted collector.

Tony Bellm had commissioned Michael Wall and another pattern maker to produce the Bellini range, but Keith undertook the patterns for almost all of the Piccolino models, in brass. Each of these was costed at £400 to produce, but when Keith entered production, clearly economies of scale in tyres, wheels and other parts helped. These ranges enabled Keith to develop his experience and understanding of the world of white metal model cars. He realised that the racing cars in the Piccolino range did not suit model railways, and that 1:43 scale was achieving the most popularity amongst collectors.

It was with this realisation, that such models commanded prices of £75.00 upwards, that he decided to utilise the MG TF drawings, and go into 1:43 production. He was unable to give a lot of time to the first pattern of the MG TF, and

he acknowledges that he didn't fully understand the market, but the model was relatively popular, and kick started the range of RAE MG models. All the subsequent patterns were created in house, latterly by a friend of Keith's, Gary Sheldon, who had previously worked on stretched limousines and armoured cars. He also produced all of the patterns for a range of Jaguars, and became the full time pattern maker for RAE.

At the high spot in the buoyant market for white metal cars, Keith was employing 20 people, but this was never solely on model cars, as the industrial side was maintained as well. Production runs ranged from the usual 300 – 500 for an average run, to up to 2000 in all for the ever popular MGB roadster. A tour round the MG factory when the MG RV8 was being built resulted in unique assistance with the details of this car, for another MG in the range.

During his attendance at ModeleX, Keith always reserved the right to sell direct to the public, as he was wary of retailers buying his newest releases and then selling on to customers.

During the 1990s, the diecast makers began to have a big effect on his business, but Keith feels that the increasing demands by specialist retailers for more stock, followed by ceasing their repeat orders, due to over stocking, caused serious difficulties for the white metal industry.

As the market declined, Keith diversified into 1:8 scale models. The first model was the Jaguar XK120, of which 300 were made, and a similar number followed with the Porsche 356. An American collector then approached him to create a 1:5 scale range; a million dollar collection! This included the Ferrari pictured here. Keith continued with this project for 3 years, producing models that were costed at £5,000 each.

RAE Models Rolls Royce Corniche

Keith feels that this project could have been very successful, if it had been a fully developed product, a range carefully created, and the promotion and marketing undertaken. However, he found that wealthy customers require the product immediately, and he was not in a position to supply in any

RAE MG
SA 2-tone
saloon

quantity. Eventually, Keith offered the 1:8 scale line to two employees to take on as their own business, complete with free workshop facilities. They took it on, but wanted to set up on their own, and after three years, the range was closed. Keith agreed not to resume manufacture in 1:8 scale for 5 years, but this deadline will soon pass, and he has some ideas.

As for the future, Keith is still considering new models, and feels there is a market for a 1:8 scale AC Cobra. He would prefer to supply this in kit form, feeling that customers would be mostly kit car builders, well versed in building and customising. Keith still owns all his master patterns from the RAE range, and occasionally he will cast a few and sell them via eBay.

He fondly recalls the story of the Mikansue patterns. There had been advertisements in the trade press offering them for sale, for £12,000, and Tony Bellm came into Keith's workshop one day, having seen them. He gave Keith a signed open cheque for £10,000, and told him to go and view them. Keith took up the challenge, and although there was not every Mikansue master present, the lot comprised approximately 80 – 100 masters. Transfers, tyres,

and instruction sheets were all included, and so Keith's ceiling of £10,000 was agreed. Only later did he realise that there were some missing, but he found them in good repair and only 10 – 15 of them needed re-mastering.

Keith did some work on the Mikansue patterns, and used many in his range, including the Triumph GT6, Dolomite Roadster, and BMWs. Keith still owns them all. Other ventures have included expanding the Piccolino range to include 1:76 scale Land Speed Record cars, and then some in 1:43 scale in resin. There was a possibility of collaboration with SMTS on a motor cycle project, for John Hodder, called the Stratford Collection, but with the advent of the Minichamps range, this was not viable.

Keith built his own Cobra replica!

More recently, Keith has returned to his roots, to contracts for museums, such as interactive displays. A travelling exhibition for the Science Museum, involving an elephant clock and scenic dioramas are some of the work now undertaken.

RAE Models now resides in 2 workshops in Chertsey and it appears that thanks to Keith's emphasis on flexibility, according to the state of the market, business is brisk.

Dave Ellis
South Eastern Finecast

Dave Ellis lived in the Crawley/ Three Bridges area in the early 50s and had friends who were involved with railways. It was not surprising, perhaps, that like many youngsters of his time, he took up railway modelling. Along with this, he remembers saving up to buy a train set.

He started work as a trainee wireman at a factory in Crawley and then moved to Gatwick as a maintenance electrician. Later, seeking more reward he spent 'time on the road' for Ever Ready batteries and in

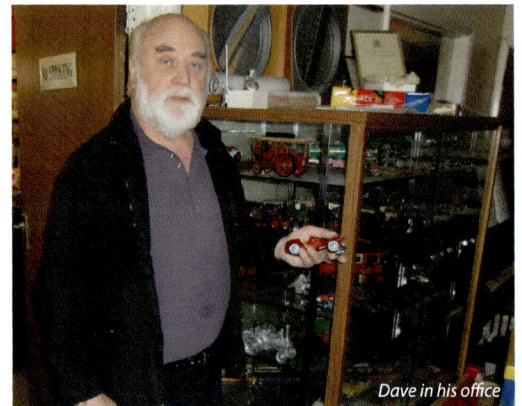
Dave in his office

the same capacity he became a representative for a cable company including two wire manufacturing companies.

His first involvement with toys was as a rep. for Tonka Toys, then Burbank, a subsidiary of Pedigree, with dolls and soft toys. A year with Eisenmann & Co, importers of Bburago and Lima model railways led David to take retail premises in Felbridge, East Grinstead in 1977 – the premise being that 'every town should have a model/toy shop.' During the period 1977-1988, South Eastern Models as it was called, had some very successful years selling a large cross section of toys and models and specialising in model railway. To a certain extent his business thrived as a result of many other similar shops in a 25 mile radius closing down.

Over the years, Dave had formed a good working relationship with Bob Wills / Wills Finecast in nearby Forest Row. So, in 1988, when Bob decided to retire, South Eastern Models was a natural successor. The decision was taken to close the shop, and Dave worked in Forest Row for a year or so, with Bob on hand to ensure a smooth transition. So, for Dave, it was a move from retailing to manufacturing.

Ian Playfoot, who had made patterns for Bob Wills carried on doing the same for Dave and continued Bob's established line with a 1:24 MGBGT and Tourer, followed by a same scale MGA, hard top and soft top. Austin, Morris and Cooper Minis were produced but were potentially unsaleable, because Tamiya had produced a many version plastic Mini. During this time, Mike Stephens of Western Models was involved with various projects, including producing vac. form

Foden K Steam Wagon

WHITE METAL
STEAM ROAD VEHICLE KIT
TO SCALE OF 3/8" to 1ft.
(1/32nd or Guage 1)

south eastern
finecast

windows for trains.

The time came for Bob's long-time workshop to be re-leased and Dave managed to find a nearby unit to continue the manufacturing work and this has been the centre of action for the last 20 years. Early in the life of the new premises, the 1992, recession hit hard and was a worrying time for Dave as sales fell away. However, he set himself a target of doubling the turnover in 3 years and just about achieved it.

The manufacturing now is predominately in railway, contract casting and vac forming which is now carried out in house. Model cars still have a following but production is currently quite low, most items being cast to order, rather than casting to maintain stocks.

Dave can be seen at various shows, nationwide, where he continues to keep in touch with existing customers and meet new collectors.

Martin Field
Guild Master Models

With the arrival of his Jaguar XJ13 in 1987, pattern maker Martin Field probably scored a number of 'firsts' – his first model in the name of Guild Master Models, the first 1:43 scale model of the Jaguar XJ13 and the first model to be produced using a combination of materials – white metal and resin, the Jaguar having a resin body.

Other models planned included a Piper GTR LM69, Ginetta G15, Austin Healeys, and a Mallock U2, in both built and kit form.

In 1988, he entrusted the production of his models to Diane and Clive Davies of Small World Distributors, and anticipated including aircraft kits and other miniature accessories under the Guild banner. A shop was planned in Nordelph, Norfolk, to be called The Albion Aerodrome, where enthusiasts could gather in a club type atmosphere. We have no knowledge of subsequent developments.

Brian Gildea
Mascot Models

Mascot Models arrived on the scene in 1985 with the first in a series of 1:43 scale Town and Country Station / Estate wagons of the period 1940 – 1960. The launch model was a 1949/50 Chrysler Town and

Country Newport in a first run of fifty built models, with kits available as well.

Brian Gildea from Gosport, Hants, was the man behind the proposed series, which were offered at £32.50. The owner's confidence in the range indicated that initial expenses would not be repeated and a 30% reduction in the retail cost was forecast.

At the time, Mascot were seeking information from collectors who had details of any other British or American Town and Country vehicles suitable for modelling and offered a free model for the right information received.

No more models are known to have been produced and sadly, Mascot Models disappeared from the scene as swiftly as they had arrived.

Pat Land
Model Assemblies

Pat Land

Many in this trade began their interest with Dinky Toys or kits, but Pat Land at Model Assemblies enjoyed taking toys apart as much as putting them together! At 7 years he remembers having an insatiable desire for toys to take apart, and he remembers being with his mum in Woolworths in Worthing, having a tantrum until he could obtain the next project!

Pat says that he did not excel at school academically, and recalls his junior school report in which his teacher, perhaps searching for words, stated "Patrick has made some very nice models" They must have been good to impress his teacher!

On leaving school Pat worked as a production assistant in a bakery, until he saw a card in the local Job Centre seeking a model maker in Billingshurst. He enquired, but the job had been filled. Undeterred, he visited the premises, speaking with John Allen and Keith Williams at Scale Model Technical Services, which had been established there for just 12 months. They had already taken on a young lad, but when Pat introduced himself, Keith handed him a Minimarque43 Packard Caribbean model, and was impressed by the way Pat handled it demonstrating his respect for the piece, and his care and potential skill.

This proved to be the start of his career at SMTS, working alongside Keith and John, the then and now owners of the company. After joining SMTS at Billingshurst where he was building and painting models, he then moved with them to larger premises in Hastings, where he assumed responsibility for both painting and running the production area.

After 12 years at SMTS, Pat felt that he wanted to apply some of his own ideas and in 1997 he established Model Assemblies. In the years that followed he launched his own range, Saxon Models, which comprised an Aston Martin Vantage, a Lunar Rover on a moonscape diorama, together with a Series I & II Land Rover.

A year later John Simons of Marsh Models invited Pat to join the Court Lodge Farm group, undertaking painting for him. Pat soon set up a casting machine, and his business grew. He now paints for J&M Classics, Spa Croft, Formula Models as well as Marsh Models. He has built up a valued customer base, which includes Bentley Motors, with whom he has a prestigious contract to make models for them, from pattern through to final assembly, and an exclusive licence to sell them himself.

Pat is currently working on new quotations for Bentley for a Limited Edition Mulliner S2 Continental, and then a Park Ward version. Production runs for these models may be as limited as 50, or up to 100 or more. Pat has just launched a Bentley Classic Models website, which has a link from the Bentley Motors site, in order to promote his models of this famous marque.

In addition to cars, Pat has made various items, including a Dunhill clock, displayed at St. Andrew's Golf Course, carved and detailed by Chris Sargant. He has also taken on some more exclusive commissions, which include a 1:12 scale Aston Martin Vanquish incrusted in jewels, from a wealthy client.

Pat works with his partner Wendy, together with other outworkers, and between them they are able to offer a flexible service, such as mould making, casting, fettling, painting & lacquering, to a professional finish for both large or small batches alike.

Pat and Wendy appear to have found their ideal work /life balance, in a quiet country barn workshop, with model making friends John Simons and Colin Fraser next door, and a full order book. Who could want for more!

1:12 scale Aston Martins

Mike Michelak
Cheshire Scale Models

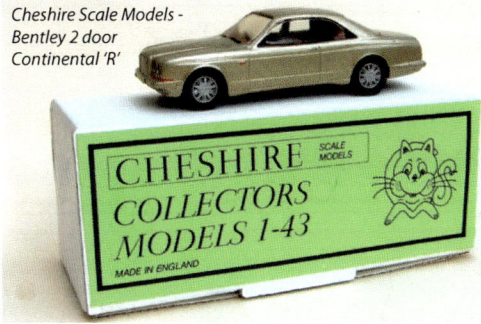

In 1992, a Bentley Continental 'R' type appeared from Cheshire Scale Models. Produced by Mike Michelak, it was available built only, finished in green or gold with left or right hand drive.

Licensed by Bentley Motors, it was a nicely made straight forward model with silver painted wheels, orange and red lights. The only plated parts being the headlights and radiator grille. Numbers made are unknown.

Bristols 401, 402 & 403 were also produced in a variety of colours as was a Daimler 420 saloon and hearse variant in late 1992/93. The latter models were cast for Mike by Peter Comben, but it is not known who cast the other models.

These appear to be the only models made and sold in the UK, before Mike emigrated to Australia and re-established as Premier Model Cars, but we have not been able to trace him there.

Steve Overy & Mike Murray
Illustra Models

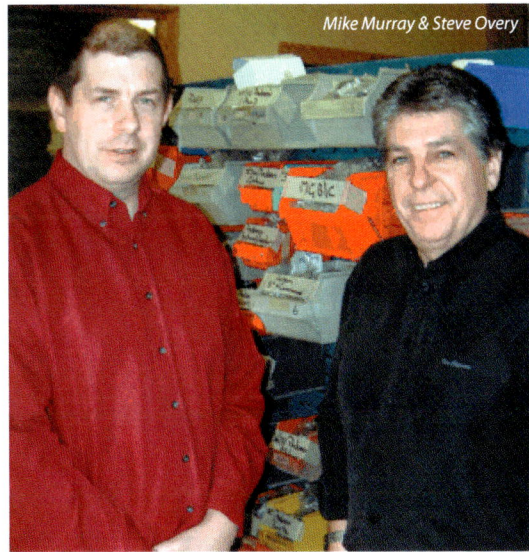

Mike Murray & Steve Overy

Illustra Lamborghini Miura P400

Steve Overy and Mike Murray are based in St. Leonards on Sea, on the second floor of an old character building just back from the seafront.

In 1983 Steve entered into a partnership and SMTS was born. The partnership was dissolved in 1986 and Steve acquired a plating business, which he installed in Hastings, in 1987. During this time Mike worked for SMTS, after leaving school to start work as a panel beater and paint sprayer, but left to join Steve when he moved his business from Bolney to Caves Road in St Leonards. The plating business was dispensed with as being too time consuming as the model manufacturing became more established.

In 1987, Illustra commenced making models for Minimarque43 and carried out other contract work. One such contract was for Jimmy Saville's TV programme – Jim'll Fix It. Yes, Steve fixed it for Jim, by making all the medals given to the people who appeared on his show. Over the years, many more models were built for the Minimarque43 range. Generally classic American cars were modelled, in keeping with Richard Briggs' wealth of knowledge in that field of interest, particularly with Packards and Cadillacs.

Most models were delivered personally by Steve to Richard at his home in Halsham, near Hull. On one occasion Steve had to return to base with all the models because of an incorrect colour or some other

Minimarque 1958 Edsel 4 door sedan

fault, such was Richard's insistence on perfection.

Mike's role encompasses every discipline in the business – pattern making, mould making, casting, building and painting – all self taught. The painting and finishing was especially important as they find that collectors are very particular.

Whilst getting itself established Illustra had a yearning to produce some models in their own name and it was not long before a Lamborghini Muira was produced as an Illustra model, followed by an Aston Martin DB5. The patterns for models were made by Richard Stokes and Dick Ward and a Ford GT70 and a King Cobra were other early cars in the Illustra range. A Porsche 962 was the first to be highly detailed. Then came their Midlantic range of sports racing cars, all made in resin.

Highway Travellers, and Legendary Motorcars, both based in the USA, were sub contract clients serviced by Illustra.

After Richard's death in 2002, a run of 100 1934 (Richard's birth year) 1107 Packard Twelve Convertible Coupes were issued as a Richard Briggs

Minimarque 1936 MG SA saloon

Memorial Model.

Steve took the decision to continue the legend of Minimarque but decided to drop the '43' as there would only be one MM43; that was G Richard Briggs. All the new Minimarque models carry the reference GRB in memory of a very good friend.

Most of their models are exported to the USA, where Illustra have several specialist dealer outlets. Grand Prix Models, Peregrine Model Cars and Crossway Models are a good source for their ranges in the UK.

Gary Oxley
Classic Jaguar Miniatures

Gary enjoying life in a XK180

Not many people in this business focus on one marque to specialise in, but that's exactly what Gary Oxley has done. His love of classic Jaguar cars really took off when he bought a Corgi Jaguar MKII to represent his real car. Gary soon realised that this Corgi Toy was not a good representation of the MKII so after searching for a better model he finally came across white metal kits and built models. Gary was totally convinced that the way forward was to build your own kit and collect a wider range for his future collection.

Gary launched his Classic Jaguar Miniatures (CJM) range in 1996, and by this time there were already rumblings about the model car trade suffering from ever better diecast models from the Far East. He was starting from scratch, and never planned for the

range to become so wide, but realised that whilst he would have never make a living in this field, it was important to make sure that he was well known to collectors. He did not plan for it to become a full time business.

Gary's first model was the 1928 Austin Swallow Sports 2 seater, an obvious choice to begin with, as this was Jaguar founder, Sir William Lyons' first car, is linked to Jaguar, and shown in every good Jaguar reference book. As such it is a very important little car in the history of Jaguar Cars. Gary's choice of pattern maker turned out to be not the best for this car, although they produced a very neat model that represented the Swallow exactly, thanks to Gary's research on the car. With the help of Gil Mond from the Swallow registry as well, Gary also supplied all the drawings they needed. The model had full underbody chassis detail exactly as the real car, but the weakness in the design of the master and castings meant that the model would not travel in the post without arriving

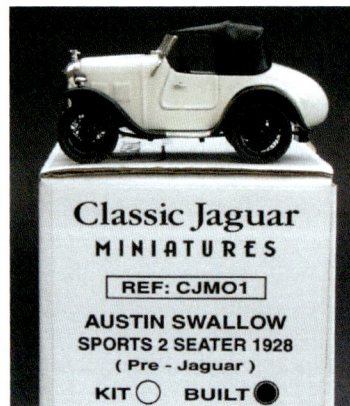

Classic Jaguar Miniatures - Austin Swallow

in painted pieces. In the end Gary passed the pattern over to SMTS which created a model he could safely post to arrive in one piece. Gary's second Jaguar was the 420, which was made using an up dated pattern from Conquest Models.

Other key people that made Classic Jaguar Miniatures possible included Ian Birkinshaw of Pro Models who built for CJM and the Jaguar Model Club which Gary founded in 1996, and in the later stages helped Gary make the patterns in house. Gary holds Dave Buttress of CMA Mold Form in high regard, as being the best in the business with white metal or resin castings. He had tried others to cast for him, but CMA provided a reliable service, delivering exactly to Gary's specification. Gary also gained much advice from Steve Overy and Mike Murray at Illustra Models in the later stages of CJM.

Because Gary had kits cast and models built for him, he has not had the need for premises although one room in his house became full of model related parts, kits, models and stock. From the very start the project was a challenge, with the pressures getting heavier as he progressed. Gary feels that without a sense of humour and an outlook of 'keep going no matter what' he would have given up a lot sooner.

Gary issued some resin models, and regards them as equally as important to him and the CJM range as the white metal releases and do include a mixture of both materials. As far as production quantities are concerned, His models were mostly limited to 200 castings, but some were much shorter runs, perhaps

Racing Jaguar MkIIs
built by Ian Burkinshaw

50 built up models only.

Gary mainly sold to his own customers of whom many were from overseas. He finds it very satisfying that many of his models are in collections all over the world as far as Argentina, Australia, Japan and the USA, as well as the UK. Apart from Grand Prix Models, who sold some of his models, He mainly sold them himself via the Internet.

Gary produced all his own packaging, boxes, labels, printed bases, instruction sheets and sourced all the signatures personally from each driver, and is proud that these are genuine hand signed items.

Although he has not produced anything since 2007, Gary feels that he may take up the trade again in the future. He suffered badly in the disastrous floods of June 2007, losing much of his private collection, CJM material and 98% of the contents of his house. As a result, he has never been able to regain his enthusiasm for models yet, but let's hope that this may blossom again.

Gerry Pettit
GP Mobilia

Gerry Pettit

When it comes to high quality 21st century resin and white metal kits of amazing detail, Gerry Pettit is up there in the top drawer. Gerry was a motor mechanic in the mid 1980s, previously having worked on Aston Martins for 15 years, and then going self employed

repairing Astons.

He began attending classic car auctions, and saw models and toys there too. He also had a shop selling automobilia, which included diecasts which he was buying and selling. Reading a copy of Collectors Gazette, Gerry saw toy fairs, attended the Sandown Park fair and bought a Corgi Aston Martin from Martin Uden, a collector and trader who emigrated to Australia.

At Kempton Park he met a dealer who specialised in handbuilt models. He then began trading himself, travelling to shows all over England. It was hard work, and the competition became sharp, with market traders bringing in cheap diecasts in bulk. He then began trading at classic car shows, over a full weekend which provided a more leisurely approach. These were in Belgium, France and Holland, and the best one being Essen at in Germany.

As his interest was specialist cars of the 1950s and 60s, and his shop was not reaching collectors, he decided to rent it out, and decided to go into manufacture. His materials of choice were both resin and white metal, with photo-etching for the finest detail. Gerry's 'raison d'etre' was that English collectors liked the weight they associated with white metal, but resin gave a better definition for the body.

He now has a range of 6 Aston Martin kits, which he sells on eBay, or passes to Pat Land of Model Assemblies for completion and sale as handbuilts. Some masters have been done for him by Keith Edney of RAE Models, but others by David Hamilton. Gerry sells a total of 60 – 75 of each model, and CMA produces the moulds for him. He has done other scales – a 1:8 Ferrari SP196 Dino mastered by David Hamilton, in wood, of which about 30 sold.

Gerry is also working with John Shinton to produce a 1:32 Aston Martin V8 1977 Le Mans car. He attended ModeleX a few times, but the Japanese and US traders and buyers that came to start with no longer came.

Now he finds the classic car shows are too

Aston Martin Atom

expensive, and the growth of eBay into the most sophisticated global market means he can sell the kits on it to Australia, Japan, Kuwait, Malawi and many other countries besides.

He treats this as a small income and a hobby, and has returned to his former role as part time restorer and mechanic for Aston Martin specialists.

Graham Price
GTA Models

A man of many hats - moulder, caster, fettler, sprayer, builder, polisher

Graham Price was a 1980s entrant into this white metal world of ours. He returned home from Heng in Saudi Arabia in 1980, and took a job at a local paper mill. In 6 months, due to the 'Last In First Out' principle, he was made redundant.

Together with a colleague who also had a fibreglass car – Graham had a Lotus Europa, and Terry had a Marcos 3 litre – they set up a business repairing fibreglass cars. Sadly, Terry found he was allergic to the fibreglass dust, and so Graham bought him out.

Not long after, another ex-colleague arrived

and asked him if he would spray some models for him. These were white metal MGs, probably of the Abingdon Classics range, and Graham charged him £2.00 each. Amazed at the standard of finish, the satisfied customer happened to be working with Max Kernick, who hearing about the standard achieved, asked Graham if he would spray for Max.

The MGs were destined for Richard Briggs of Minimarque43, and in turn Richard Briggs also wanted some of this standard of finish for his range. So Graham found himself spraying a variety of bodyshells for both Max Kernick and Richard Briggs.

For the next 2 years, Richard was sending more and more, and had taken on 2 staff of his own. By this time the fibreglass repair work was in decline, as the requirements of the motor insurance industry precluded small businesses from getting repair work.

With potential for a full-time market in white metal casting and assembly, Graham found himself a suitable unit in Broadclyst near Exeter, and, in 1987, bought a casting machine. The bulk of his work was for Minimarque43, but with bigger orders coming in, he began to find that Richard Briggs would delay payment for a wide range of reasons. Graham's staff needed paying, and when Jeff Sharrock of Pathfinder Models approached him, having had problems with his previous painter, Graham took over the entire casting, painting and assembly work for his models. Patterns for the Pathfinder range were being made mostly by Ian Pickering and Pete Kenna, and once approved, would be sent to Graham for moulding and casting. He always kept the pattern for the duration of the production run, in case of mould failures, and would then return it to Jeff Sharrock once the next model was released.

This was full time employment, handling up to 600

1923 Duesenberg Model A

castings at a time, for 3 British car models per year, together with special issues, so whilst continuing to produce for Minimarque43, this became a lesser priority.

Arrangements were also made with John Martin of JM Toys to launch and make the Viscount range, as a spin off from Pathfinder, but this was short lived, as the models were less popular.

Sadly due to the retirement of Jeff and Sue Sharrock in 2002, largely due to Jeff's ill health, a major sector of the white metal market had lost a quality product. It was the Lansdowne range from Brooklin that filled the gap first established by Pathfinder.

In due course, the patterns for the Pathfinder range were finally polished up and mounted on a perspex plinth, and sold to a loyal customer Gregg Clay, on condition that they would not be sold on for an agreed period. Subsequently, some were sold on to Mike Rogers of J & M Classics, and Crossway Models, whilst Pete Kenna acquired the Austin Dorset and Hereford.

Around this time Richard Briggs died, and the Minimarque43 range was no more. There were four main makers for Minimarque43, Ian Birkinshaw, in Yorkshire, Steve Overy of Illustra Models, GTA Models, Western Models, and also latterly SMTS, who had manufactured for MM43 in the early days, along with Keysers.

Commissioned work from Minimarque43 was always on a verbal basis, and often, although Richard Briggs intended to produce up to 300 units of a new model, he would then only order 50 as a first batch. Mike Stephens at Western insured himself

against this by insisting on a minimum run of at least 200 sets of castings. Thus, on Richard's death, there were moulds and tooling work undertaken by these makers that had not been paid for. Regrettably, a submission to the executors of his estate brought forth no response.

It is worthy of note here, that the caster and assembler is a sub-contractor, and therefore in a difficult position, especially when a commissioned line stops. Does he own the pattern? He certainly has made the moulds, and until full funds are received, may be entitled to make further castings to recover his costs.

1923 Duesenberg Model A

Graham is contemplating resurrecting the Minimarque43 name again, qualified by a sub title of 'by GTA models', as he has a number of patterns of Cords, Auburns and Duesenbergs. He hopes that the first model will be an Austin Sheerline Belfast Telegraph van.

Over the years, Graham has cast for Crossway Models, operated by Amanda Redman and Karl Merz, J&M Classics, owned by Mike Rogers, and recalls his early days producing for Max Kernick. Max was one half of K&R Replicas, the other being John Roff.

Currently, Graham has a number of individual commissions, including an Austin A70 Hereford countryman from Pete Kenna, along with work for Autotorque, J&M Classics and Spa Croft, and having been a 'backroom boy' in the past, maybe launching into the retail market. Despite the consolidation of the Chinese manufacturing sector for all levels of quality in model cars, Graham believes there is still a cult following for white metal miniatures in the UK and elsewhere.

Mike Rogers
J&M Classics

Mike's story begins in his father's TV and radio shop in Guildford, where some early model plane kits were also sold. In the earliest days Mike remembers, in 1946, at 10 years old, forming a model aeroplane club at his boarding school in Purley, and building

kits from his father's shop.

The shop had a distinguished yet little known history, supplying wiring for RAF Spitfires built for the war effort. After finishing school, Mike worked with his father in the shop, until at 18 years he was called up into the RAF. Three years later, he returned to the shop, at the time that TV began to take off in a big way.

After having given 30 years to this trade, Mike fancied a change and moved to Exeter. He met Max

and Julie Kernick through his sister who knew Julie as a friend. Mike had some free time and joined Max and Julie, working for them for about 12 months on casting & preparation. At this time Max Kernick had a workshop in his brother-in-law's premises just outside Exeter.

It was 1984, and the Abingdon Classics range was becoming very popular amongst the emerging population of white metal collectors, being a range of iconic MGs, and Max needed the services of three men in preparation and casting to support the demand.

Mike recalls learning the trade from Max, developing the Top Marques range, and hopes that he may have given him some help with consolidating his business. He always felt that Max was brilliant as a model car maker.

Shortly after this period, Max decided to close the workshop and work from home in Ottery St. Mary, which prompted Mike to move out of model cars. He went into building and decorating, but kept in touch with Max, and met up again around 1991 when he extended their workshop.

Max had already started the range of Alvis models, but he was keen to put more time into the very popular Rolls Royce model range. Mike was interested in retiring from building work, and Max offered him the opportunity to be responsible for the Alvis line. For the first 18 months, Max continued

Alvis TA Drophead

to cast the components and complete the base spraying. Mike would then assemble and finish each model to customer requirements. After the initial joint venture, he became more interested in the business and in 1997 purchased the Alvis range from TMM Ltd, with the assistance of his bank. Mike recalls with amusement how his bank manager actually visited Max's workshop to inspect the product line. He was amazed at the standard and quality, and was pleased to agree Mike's loan – does this practice still happen these days?!

At this time, Max was using Lawrence Gibson as his pattern maker, whose patterns were also being used by Milestone Miniatures. Should Mike need to expand the range, Max recommended Lawrence, who at that time was working in his home town of Helston with his father. So Mike began using Lawrence as his pattern maker too. He was now the proud owner of the moulds for the Alvis range of three models, so these were then marketed by him in his new range; J&M Classics was born! To begin with, St. Martins Accessories took all the models Mike could build, and then after a year Mike began to supply other specialist outlets such as Crossway Models, JM Toys, Midas Models, PK Models, and Spa Croft.

Healey Abbotts

However, circumstances inevitably change, and a year later, Mike moved to Burgess Hill, and switched to using Graham Price of GTA Models to provide his castings. Graham was then living near Countess Wear.

Once Mike had developed his skills sufficiently, he decided to release a new model, the Alvis TA14. Following Max's advice, he continued to use Lawrence Gibson for his patterns, and GTA for the casting and spraying. More recently, Maurice Bozward of White Metal Assemblies has taken over the castings and Pat Land, Model Assemblies, has taken on the spraying, particularly specialising in the duo and triple tones so much a feature on Alvis cars.

After Carl Redman of Crossway bought a Daimler SP250 Pathfinder pattern from Greg Clay, who had acquired all the masters from Pathfinder, hel showed the sales list to Mike, who had already been interested in producing a Daimler Conquest convertible. He therefore purchased the patterns for the Daimler Conquest saloon and also the Jowett Jupiter Mk IA. These he has adapted to create a Daimler Conquest drophead, and a Jowett Jupiter MkI.

J&M Classics Alvis TD21 - a special version of th car owned by HRH Prince Philip, Duke of Edinburgh, and built to his own specification

To introduce a Healey range, he had hoped to use the Richard Briggs pattern for the Healey Silverstone, but this did not materialise, so he asked Lawrence Gibson who had already made the Elliott pattern to produce a pattern for a Westland as well.

Eventually, as the range increased, Mike developed a strong association with the Alvis Owners Club, which has many groups around the world, and he has become a member. As his ranges became more popular, his space in Burgess Hill became too confined.

As Mike had fond memories of Littlehampton as a child and teenager, in 2007 he moved to his current premises, and currently works on his own, using only a young person to assist in a part-time basis with casting preparation.

Mike has found that the year 2008/09 achieved the highest turnover yet in his ten years of operating as J&M Classics, but the first quarter of 2009/10 was quiet.

His production is sold through a limited range of outlets, predominantly those listed above, but also a new Web-based outlet, Marqueart, started up by a friend of Max Kernick, selling mainly Autotorque/Top Marques and J&M Classics.

In a similar way that the white metal model bus industry has paved the way and set the standards for the Chinese diecast trade to achieve, there is no doubt that white metal handbuilt model cars of the standard of J&M are setting the standards to beat for 1:43 diecast model cars.

However, Mike feels that his customers confirm that the solidity of his products offer a quality and endurance that the current Chinese diecast and resin models are unable to achieve, given the fragility of some of their fine photo-etched parts.

John & Pam Simons
Marsh Models

John and Pam Simons

John Simons, proprietor of Marsh Models, has built models since he was 6 years old. From this he moved to control line flying around 12 years and eventually to slot cars and at 17 had joined the Estuary Equipe slot car club. He recalls with pride taking part in a 500 scale miles endurance race that took a grand total of 63 hours! His racing team for this event was the US branch of Team Russkit, racing 1:24 scale sports cars.

Through the slot car scene he met Ian Pickering, a name that is synonymous with quality modelling, and Chris Paterson. It was through Chris that he was introduced to his wife Pam. They also became friends with Barry Foley, well known for his Demon Tweaks

cartoons in Autosport magazine and his St Bruno's Lotus 7.

In 1975, John and Pam had moved to the Bahamas but returned to the UK in 1977, where John began work on the building of the Dungeness 'B' Power station. His hobby never waned, and when he was finally made redundant on completion of the project, through the suggestion of Ian Pickering, began making models for Max Kernick, the mastermind behind Abingdon Classics, and more recently Top Marques.

Initially things were somewhat crude, working in a spare room, with a self made spray booth that used an old hair drier as an extractor linked to a hose from Pam's vacuum cleaner dangling out of the window! Not wanting to be dependant on only one supply of work, John approached Grand Prix Models, and Lamberts of Ley Street in Ilford, Essex about building white metal kits. This led to Marsh Models being formed in 1981 by John and Pam initially as a kit building agency. The company was originally set up in the Romney Marsh area of Southern England hence the Marsh name and frog logo.

In 1984, after becoming dissatisfied with the standard and detail in the kits he was building, John approached Ian Pickering to undertake the production of a pattern for a brand new model. They agreed that if Ian would make the pattern, for free, he would receive a royalty from the sales. This first model was the 1967 BOAC 500 winning Chaparral 2F.

Lola T70 Aston Martin

Scale Model Technical Services were commissioned to produce the castings, and altogether John reckons that 2000 units were made and sold. At this time there were very few manufacturers making endurance sports racing car models, apart from the French diecast firm of Solido.

It was a wide open market, and so the new range of historic sports racing cars in 1:43 scale, known as Thundersports, was born. The plan was to produce 2 models per year, all in white metal.

A range of Corvettes followed, together with other specialist big engined cars such as the Lola Aston Martin. Marsh was also the first company to seriously look at making models of Canam cars, as this area had been little explored and Marsh has since been synonymous with this class of car.

In 1988, John and Pam moved to East Sussex and now have their studio on an organic farm, with Formula Models and Model Assemblies on the same site. In 1996, John and Pam set up their own casting facility to give them more flexibility. By then, Marsh had started to use Christian Sargant as their main pattern maker, his work making up most of the current Marsh range. John says that it is crucial to know the individual skills and interests of the pattern maker, so that the 'feel' for the car being created is right, and the resultant model has added value. This confirms the view that the pattern can only be hand crafted, as the human eye is all important at this stage.

Whilst photo-etched parts were used when John started, he was the first to use it to make items such as rear wings and interior tubs on competition cars to replicate the real parts made in aluminium. This has been an example of the great advances achieved with the arrival of new technology and computer aided design. John feels that similar strides have been made in the drawing and creation of the most detailed of decals needed for accuracy, particularly in sports racing cars.

More recently, Marsh Models have been using resin as the medium, with bodies produced by CMA Moldform, to provide greater definition, and to respond to the smaller market.

Looking to the future, John acknowledges the advances made by companies such as Spark and Bizarre, using economical labour in China, to produce good quality in mass production. However, his view in the long term is that there will always be a niche market for hand crafted models, particularly of those cars not viable as a proposition for mass producers.

Another development has been into aeroplanes. Their range, known as Aerotech, was suggested to them by Chris Sargant, who proposed its launch with the Luft '46 aeroplane, in 1:72 scale. These were planes that were never built as they came too near to the end of the Second World War. They have then moved on to 1:32 scale, and average sales amount to 150 units each time, with the popular DH Comet now being sold out These models are made in resin, due to the size and weight considerations. Pam now has an increasingly important role in the business having varying functions including kit production.

John and Pam have realised the merits of diversifying their ranges, and have established another new line of DecoArt, which has taken their production back into the traditional material of white metal for the entire car. This range began with a 1930s Delage and will continue with this theme. John believes he is very lucky having the mixed talents of Pat Land of Model Assemblies and Colin Fraser of Formula Models at hand and a great deal of co-operation occurs between the three companies. In a world of bland uniformity, Marsh Models believe in producing true hand made models to the highest standards.

Currently, every model in their normal range is available in kit and built form with the built models being signed by John, and the newer releases now being limited to 100 built models only. They will also occasionally produce models that have been either signed by the designer or by the driver.

Having been the company that introduced such items as photo-etched interiors and wings, and resin tyres, Marsh Models will continue to bring innovation and quality to the world of model cars and aircraft modelling. At the time of writing they have a range of around 150 different models.

Jaguar D-Type

John Shinton
Model Maker

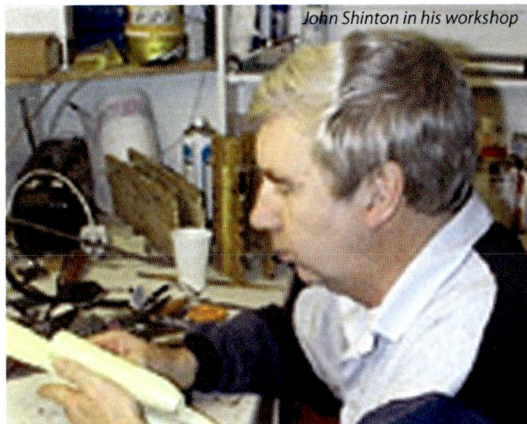
John Shinton in his workshop

John started John Shinton Models about 17 years ago following some time as the wind tunnel model maker for Tom Walkinshaw Racing on the Jaguar team.

Working with Ross Brawn, he produced the 1:4 scale models for the Jaguar XJR 14, that went on to win the World Sportscar Championship. John also did some development work on the Jaguar XJR 12 for the Le Mans 24 hour race which also proved a winner. Prior to this exciting period, John had worked as a pattern maker for 22 years, learning the trade from his father in Wolverhampton.

He started as a professional model maker with a range of Land Speed Record cars in 1:43 scale, selling them as kits and hand built models, and then progressed to a range of historic Grand Prix cars,

James Hunt's Hesketh 308

also as 1:43 scale kits or hand built models. His last 1:43 scale model was the Thrust SSC that set the first supersonic land speed record.

John was commissioned to produce a series of 1:8 scale models of the Austin Healey 100, including the 100M and the 100S, for Charles Matthews of Triple M. Most of the models built were customised replicas of the clients' own cars.

Along the way John has made many one off promotional models for sponsors and advertising, of both cars and boats. He is always available for commissions of a one off or a series of any subject, in any scale. John was involved for some time with Quicksilver, a jet powered boat project to attempt to break the World Water Speed Record. He worked on the wind tunnel and test tank work on the boat, and now produces 1:20 scale models for sponsors and collectors.

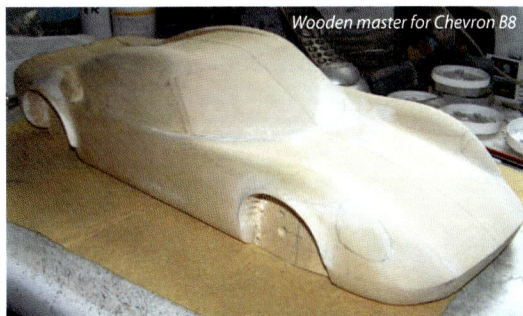
Wooden master for Chevron B8

Over the years he has made models for Sir Jack Brabham, Gina Campbell, Tom Green, Lord Hesketh, Jackie Oliver, Murray Walker and John Watson. Apart from his own products, he has produced master patterns and artwork for other manufacturers, such as G P Mobilia, Maxi Models and Javan Smith.

Currently he is in production with a 1:8 scale Lola T 70 Mk3B. His next 1:8 scale release will be the Chaparral 2F, and he is also working on the master pattern for a 1:8 scale Lotus 62 and Lotus Europa, that he will be producing for Europa Engineering.

John has also played with full sized racing cars in the past. He has raced Formula Ford and Formula 1300, and has run his son Jody in an Autograss Mini as a 16 year old in a junior class.

Ted Webber
Specialties International

Well known for many years around the Kent model scene, Ted Webber was born and raised in Bridgewater, Somerset. He was a collector from the word go, with his parents buying him models of cars, fire engines and trucks for Christmas and birthdays.

Ted continued adding to his collection, and never parted with those original toys. Indeed, his wife Joan remembers when she met him, in his early twenties in Scotland, he was enthusiastically attending local swapmeets and visiting collectors there. Right from these early days too, he had an affinity for stretched limousines.

Ted's trade was electrical and mechanical engineering, working for the Ministry of Defence in

Ted at ease

Portsmouth, and later for a year in Scotland where he met Joan. He returned to London and for a while worked for the Metropolitan Police, before leaving to work in the private sector.

It was Ted who teamed up with Jim Mills to become one of the founders of the Maidenhead Static Model Club, and Ted took part in the early meets at Monkey Island.

In the early 1990s, Ted and Joan set up a small wedding car hire business, acquiring 2 Daimler 420

Ted's Daimler 420 Limousine

limousines, which they operated at weekends. By 1993, establishing that no one had made a model of the Daimler 420, he decided to do it himself. He used the services of Dick Ward for the pattern, the casting facilities at Illustra in Hastings, and made 100 in total. 30 of these were distributed through the Ashford Model Collectors Club, which Ted had set up. Ted and Joan chose the name Specialties International for the model range.

Ted and Joan had been buying and selling at the Maidstone toy fair, and Joan remembers David Hatt the organiser in those days with great fondness. Ted felt it would be a good idea to create a toy fair at the Stour Centre in Ashford, to serve the Kent collectors, and this was very successful.

Ted's collecting continued, even taking in the USA when he and Joan would visit her sister in Texas, and when attending toy fairs, his main delight was to be able to chat with his fellow collectors, and tell them jokes from his considerable repertoire!

Ted's two tone Daimler

Despite plans Joan and Ted had for retirement, sadly, Ted's health declined, and after 4 years fighting cancer, he passed away in 2004, aged just 56 years.

Those who knew Ted will always remember his love of those Daimlers, and his Specialties International Daimler model stands proud amongst the more recent models of this car.

Phil Winslade

It has been really interesting to hear from some of the builders who work with the bigger players in this industry, and one such builder is Phil Winslade.

Phil's interest in building came from an unlikely source, assembling the Aurora kits of dinosaurs and other horror creatures! This was whilst at school, and armed with this very relevant background interest, he secured a job with RAE Models at the tender age of 17, fresh from school, building some of their models and assisting with exhibitions display work, the other side to RAE.

At that time the firm was still run by Bob Edney, Keith's father, and Phil was taught his trade by the other two builders Mike Broadbent, who subsequently moved to Australia, and Neville Smith. They were working mostly on the Piccolino and Bellini ranges of cars, and Phil remembers the Weybridge workshop as a true working assembly atmosphere. Building and painting were the key trades to be learnt, and Phil spent 3 years with RAE until he found that the wages were not sufficient to support his needs.

Dodge M4S for the film The Wraith 1986

from other suppliers, and he finds that the market always seems to produce work, even if the subject matter changes. Currently he is working on American sought products, such as the models that used to be in the Henk van Asten Conquest range, and the old Western models. These are all being re-launched by Route 66 Models.

Phil is content to have full time employment, but accepts that there may be changes necessitating another move some time.

Interiors for Cadillac de ville for SMTS

The building sites beckoned, and it wasn't until 1991 that his interest in the skills of model building awoke again, and he landed a full time post with the team at Scale Model Technical Services. Here he was working for Keith Williams and John Allen, and the initial demand was for 1:24 scale Cobras and E-Types.

For Phil, the work at SMTS has always been a mixture of in house lines and commissioned work

CHAPTER FIVE

THE MODELEX ERA

Ray Strutt, organiser of eleven successive annual shows from 1990 – 2000 in Birmingham, England describes the origins of ModeleX and its expansion and success during the 1990s.

The late 1980s in the UK was a time of big expansion and progression in the model collecting world, with the diecast manufacturers getting into full swing and producing more and more items for the ever growing number of collectors. At the same time, the more adventurous and discerning collectors, dare I say it, were becoming increasingly aware of a different range of collectables that were not available from their local model shop and were only occasionally to be seen at the swapmeets/toyfairs. These were the handbuilt white metal models that the artisans were bringing to the market place.

INTERNATIONAL SPECIALIST MODEL VEHICLE SHOW

THE COMPTON SUITE
NATIONAL MOTORCYCLE MUSEUM
SOLIHULL, WEST MIDLANDS

OCTOBER 13-14 1990

EXHIBITORS INCLUDE MANUFACTURERS BOTH LARGE AND SMALL SHOWING PATTERNS, CASTINGS, MOULDS, GRAPHICS, FINISHED MODELS ETC. AND SERVICE COMPANIES WITH CASTING MACHINES, DECALS, PHOTO-ETCHING, TYRES, VAC-FORMS ETC.

SPECIALIST RETAILERS.

INCLUDES THE 1ST NATIONAL KIT-BUILDING CHAMPIONSHIP

TROPHIES AWARDED TO BEST: FORMULA CAR · SPORTS CAR 1/50TH COMMERCIAL VEHICLE ETC.

SPECIAL LIMITED EDITION MODEL TO MARK THE OCCASION PRODUCED BY BROOKLIN MODELS

CATALOGUE £1

At that time, I was Deputy and Overseas Editor of Collectors Gazette, a monthly newspaper for toy and model collectors. Along with many other responsibilities, I was writing White Metal Miniatures,

a regular column for handbuilt model enthusiasts – mostly reviews of recently released models, together with any other news items of interest in that area of the hobby. My position, 'close to the action' led me to believe that a show, exclusive to handbuilt models, was fast becoming a necessity.

ModeleX 90 promotional van by Brooklin

A couple of moderately successful small shows for handbuilt models, staged as 'Model Auto Collectors Meets,' organised by Ferrari enthusiast Nathan Beehl, had been held in a community centre in Luton, north of London, in 1985 and 1986. But from every point of view, particularly those of the exhibitors, the scene was crying out for a professional presentation. Also, David Baulch of Classic Model Motorcycles sought to hold a show at the Leas Cliff Hall in Folkestone in 1989. However, the planned June event in the south coast location did not get off the ground on account of the place and the time. One potential exhibitor saying, 'great idea, but wrong place and wrong time, we'll all be at Le Mans!'

So, for me, early 1990 seemed the right time to explore other venues and locations. I sought support from the biggest manufacturers through to the 'one man bands' and all the indications were very positive. A lot of discussions took place and I made many telephone calls. Several venues were inspected and ultimately The National Motorcycle Museum, Solihull, Birmingham, was chosen for its central location and good facilities. As October had always suited the Society of Motor Manufacturers & Traders for their annual Motor Show, it seemed sensible to have The Scale Model Motor Show in the same month as well. The Solihull Moat House was the most popular and most used of the hotels as the show hotel for those who needed overnight accommodation during the course of the eleven shows.

For the first show, I hired one room at the Motorcycle Museum, and with a professional presentation in mind enquiries were made of stand manufacturers/hirers. Soon after that, I began talking with fellow collectors and enthusiasts to create a team of helpers. In due course, booking forms were sent out and not surprisingly, perhaps, the show was soon over subscribed and a waiting list formed. In the weeks and months that followed I held meetings with my helpers, started advertising the show in the collectors magazines and prepared a catalogue with company advertising, profiles of exhibitors, floor plan, etc.. Supplementary stand lighting was requested by a number of exhibitors and this was catered for. As the time drew near, anxiety set in for me and my small team of helpers, but as it got very close, a great sense of anticipation took over.

And so, on Saturday 13th October 1990, the big day arrived. For the first time a professional model show was about to launch, with a catalogue/programme, a show model by Brooklin Models and shell stands! The stand contractors commenced soon after 6.00am and exhibitors began to arrive well in time for their entry at 8.30am. The collectors began to arrive as well and the queue outside was soon very long, and we were overjoyed – and overwhelmed! So much so, that for several periods of time during the morning, we had to wait for some visitors to leave before we could let any more in!

Other memories of that first show include the relief that all the elements had come together and no major problems had occurred. I remember too, the tremendous enthusiasm generated by both participants and visitors, for a show that was markedly different from the normal swapmeets and toyfairs. That year it was very much a national show, but word of its success spread and in 1991, the show expanded into two rooms and we were to experience an influx of exhibitors and visitors from overseas.

Pier van Netten

1990 - Centre stands with Barry Lester, Auto Replicas

ModeleX was always a two day event, specifically to allow exhibitors to meet and socialise during the 'in between' evening. In the early years the whole of Saturday was given over to the Press and Trade visitors. All setting up was on the Saturday morning, with the stand contractors starting at 6.00am. As the years passed, with the Show now truly international and visitors coming from all over the world, a Friday

set up was established and everyone breathed more easily. Also, the exclusive entry for the Press and Trade was changed to Saturday morning only and the rest of the day was open to all. A popular move by all accounts, particularly for those coming from overseas, as this gave collectors a choice of day, or two days, to attend.

A National Kit Building Championship was part of the show from the start, in the capable hands of two leading model clubs. Ray Ashworth was the team leader of The Northern Model Car Club and Chris Derbyshire led The South Hants Model Auto Club. The competition entries and the Clubs' own themed displays were always a major attraction.

Dale Coleman was a triple Champion (1990, '91 & '92) as was Phil Meiners (1993, '96 & '99), Ray Guy was twice Champion (1995 & '97) and Richard Eley (1994), Roger Holden (1998) and Nicholas Hazelton (2000) were the Champions in the other years. At ModeleX 2000, Dale Coleman was voted the Champion of Champions and was awarded the spectacular

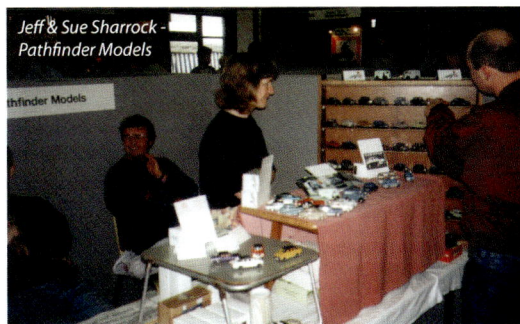

Jeff & Sue Sharrock - Pathfinder Models

Various trophies and cups, 1994

Samurai Helmet trophy by Hideyuke Uemoto of Make Up Co. Ltd. – Superior Models of Japan.

Collectors Gazette awarded a trophy for 'Best Stand' for all the shows, voted for by the exhibitors themselves. Brooklin Models Ltd and Durham Classics Inc. won three times, ABC snc di Brianza, CMA Moldform and SRC Models won twice, Compulsion Gallery, Model Masters and SMTS won once. Some years there were joint winners.

From 1994, Classic and Sports Car magazine awarded a trophy for 'Best Model'. Every year Editor Mick Walsh and Mike McCarthy came to the show and, often with great difficulty, selected the model of their choice. Winners included Aardvark Models, , ABC snc di Brianza, Crossway Models, Mach One Models, Make Up Co. Ltd., RAE Models Ltd. and Somerville Models. Generally, the winning model was featured on the cover of the following year's catalogue.

Not surprisingly, the majority of exhibitors were UK based, but they also came from many other countries around the world – America, Belgium, Canada, Denmark, France, Germany, Holland, Italy, Japan, Spain and Sweden. A dozen or so exhibitors from abroad came to every show, whilst others returned on a regular basis. The Italian manufacturers were particularly supportive with four or five normally attending every show.

Models of all scales could be seen at ModeleX. 1: 43 predominated, but there were always plenty of 1: 24 models about. The latter years saw participants with 1:18 and 1:12 models and on one

occasion a new exhibitor from Spain arrived with a magnificent 1:10 Bugatti. A 1:8 Vanwall was said to be in preparation, but never materialised. Resin construction became established, but white metal always seemed to be the favourite. Some other materials were acceptable, but plastic and diecast products were always excluded.

ModeleX generally provided for four categories of participant – the small manufacturer, the specialist retailer, the large manufacturer and the collectors. It undoubtedly provided a platform for many of the small manufacturers, for they were able to generate enough work to take them through the year. The specialist retailers who came, by the nature of their involvement, needed to show a good return on their presence and this they seemed to do, judging by the fact that the same ones returned each year.

Regrettably, the support from some of the larger organisations that were in business was not so good, despite their earlier enthusiasm. It was said that they needed to take big orders to justify their presence, but that was not the way of things and their absence only served to mystify the collectors, who after all, were those who bought their products. It was my view that, by their absence, they were doing a disservice to their customers and ultimately losing sales. There were a few companies that chose to ignore ModeleX altogether. Finally, the collectors......... well they came back year after year and I knew they enjoyed themselves, because so many of them told me so!

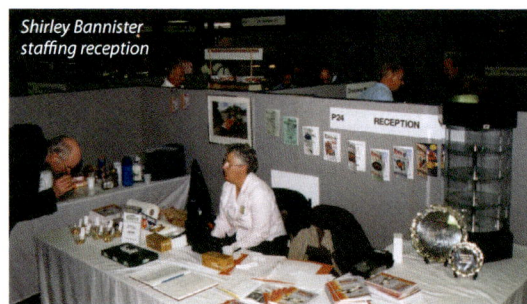
Shirley Bannister staffing reception

Many readers will be aware that HRH The Duke of Gloucester is a model collecting enthusiast, who was first seen at various toy fairs in the late 1980s and pursues his hobby to the present time. In 1992, I recorded his interests in a feature in Collectors Gazette, revealing his passion for Rolls Royces and other models that just appealed to him. It also told how much he enjoyed kit building and making models of his own choice from 'chops' of existing models and creating some of the many different bodied Rolls Royces of the 1930s. Besides the toy fairs, ModeleX became a regular destination for him and he came on many occasions, seldom leaving without more models to add to his collection. We are grateful to him for

Ray presenting Best Stand 1995 trophy to Chris Arnott and Dave Buttress of CMA Moldcast

ModeleX show models, 1990-1994, with Omen figures

agreeing to write the Foreword to our book.

As ModeleX grew in status, it was pleasing to see more and more people, prominent in the model collecting world, coming to see what it was all about. From Canada, George Maxwell, proprietor of Mini Grid in Unionville, Toronto paid a visit, as did Richard Stafferton, sadly no longer with us, who ran Autophile, a collectors' shop, also in Toronto. Another visitor who has passed away, was Frank Roodt, an eager collector from Birchleigh in South Africa, who attended on many occasions. Geoff Sear, known to many for his own range of English sporting cars only got to ModeleX towards the end and found he had a lot of catching up to do.

On one occasion one of my team crossed paths with John Surtees, waiting for a meeting, in the museum foyer. Seemingly, with some time to spare he was invited in and given a guided tour. Others seen, were Randolph Hurle-Bath, Replicars, Holland; Larry Dunn, Revere Auto Miniatures, USA; Eric Waiter, New Jersey, USA; Paddy Stanley travelled from the USA, living there at the time; Gerry Weight, Weico Models, Australia; Pier van Netten, Model Car Imports, Sydney, Australia, had a stand one year ; Mike Simpson, Premier Model Auto Services, Germany and so many others. They travelled from all over the world and, indeed, were all internationally recognised in their chosen field of work.

Whilst I remember many of the visitors and where they came from, I needed to trawl the Visitors Book to remind me just how many did come from overseas. David and I have been in contact with some of them

George Maxwell

and we believe their stories make interesting reading.

Every year saw a change of exhibitors, which was good for everyone. One difficulty for me as organiser was that the regulars always wanted the same position, which limited presentational changes. I understood that reasoning for when there are, say, three hundred exhibitors, but with seventy or so in two rooms ?...... oh, never mind, the customer is always right!

A catalogue/show guide was produced every year since the inaugural show and was eagerly acquired by exhibitors and visitors alike, for it contained a wealth of information about the handbuilt model hobby – names, addresses, tel/fax numbers, email, web sites, company profiles, advertising, etc. Over the years, they became a reference for many participants and, indeed, have assisted David and myself in recalling and tracking down many of the people featured in this book.

In 1993, the first ModeleX Prize Draw was held. From the generosity of exhibitors donating prizes and donations given for the draw tickets during the course of the later shows, approximately £10,000 ($14,000) was passed to charities and other organisations that care for disabled children and young adults.

ModeleX 99 was promoted as the 10th anniversary show, but in fact it was the 10th show and the 9th anniversary. Like the millennium, for some people, I was a year too soon! Whatever, like all the

John Hammick - Backing Britain and White Metal!

Ray presenting Ella Brianza with the Best Stand trophy, 1999

preceding shows, it was deemed a great success by most participants. As organiser, I had great pleasure bringing so many like minded enthusiasts together through eleven successful shows, ModeleX 2000 being the last show I organised. In the manufacturing field, the hobby used to be a very 'closed shop', cards were held very close to chests and there seemed to be little information exchange. Largely, ModeleX brought an end to that attitude and it was very rewarding to see so many people enjoying each others' company and exchanging ideas in the field of interest that brought them all together. Many were the times when former 'rival traders' were seen to be laughing and enjoying a pint or two together at the bar in the evening.

ModeleX 2002 and 2003 were organised by Mike Kennington of Greenwood Exhibitions at Warwick Hall, Stoneleigh Park, Coventry and I supported him on both occasions. However, whilst the enthusiasm was still present and the presentations were just as good as those of previous years, the numbers attending weren't. Apart from a very small show with the ModeleX name at Bentley Motor Museum in Sussex in 2006 on the occasion of a Classic Car Show, no other ModeleX shows have been held.

However, I did organise Modelexcellence in Lille, France in March 1998. The idea was

developed with the help of some of the Belgian and French ModeleX participants and, indeed, the choice of hotel venue was a joint one. As usual, it was a two day show and it was well supported by exhibitors and visitors. However, the closing time for Saturday, agreed by my continental helpers, was much too early and I was disappointedly aware that people were still arriving after the show had closed that day. For the record, I did try to organise ModeleXtra at a hotel in Maidstone in March 1999 and explored the possibility of another show in Lille in 2001, but neither made the start line!

1947 Ford V8 Station Wagon in ModeleX two-tone green, together with unique yellow and black version for closed bid charity fund at last show in 2000

The show catalogues always recorded my thanks to the small team, generally named, who assisted me with the running of the shows as they happened, in particular, Roger Bailey, Derek Bannister, Derek Hattersley, Ann Knott, Eric Lewis and Patricia Marchant. Valuable input was also given by Steve Overy, Ian Pickering, Will Roe, Rod Ward as well as my wife, Chris. There were others, mainly members of the local Coventry Diecast Model Club, whose members provided the necessary stewarding year after year. I would like to take this opportunity to put on permanent record the help they all gave over the years, for without it, ModeleX could not have happened.

Oh yes, the red trousers I wore on the very first occasion, so I could be identified amongst the new faces, served their purpose at every subsequent show, and still fit me 21 years on, but now are only seen on Christmas Day. For the same purpose the team and stewards wore ModeleX T and sweatshirts appropriate for every year.

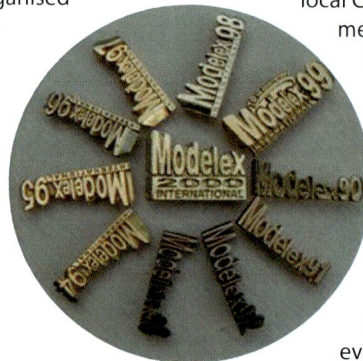

A pin for every show, 1990-2000

ModeleX International, The Scale Model Motor Show, was billed as 'the only show of its kind in the world – the show to be at and be seen at' and will be remembered as such by everyone who attended and, perhaps, mourned by those who never had or took the opportunity to be there.

It is to be hoped that by publishing this book, the excellence, experience and skills seen at ModeleX and during the years since, will be enshrined for ever.

1997/1999/2000 ModeleX programmes

CHAPTER SIX

INTERNATIONAL CONNECTION

There is no doubt that the arrival of ModeleX introduced an international element to the white metal car industry. Whilst the main driving forces were within the United Kingdom, a small number of enthusiastic artisans were pushing back the boundaries in their own countries. Australia, Canada, France, Germany, Italy and USA, were the main international pioneers. Each majored in its own national cars, typically filling in the gaps that the big diecast manufacturers had left out. In this chapter, we feature these

vanguards of the white metal art, and the stories do highlight how many came together through ModeleX, and were encouraged to expand their markets beyond their national boundaries. They are both producers, retailers, and in one example, an adapter or flatterer!

Internationally, retailers tend to be spread thinly across each major country that has white metal collectors, so those we have been able to contact have been few. However, here are a small number who have been in the business a long time, and some who are new arrivals -

Phil Alderman & Paul J. Burt
The Great American Dream Machine

Mako Shark x 2, Chrysler C-200 and 1954 Cadillac El Camino Show Car

Phil Alderman has been in this business since 1975, and model cars had been a hobby for him for over 10 years prior to this. Based in Brooklyn, New York, he was the first man behind this range of models of exceptional American concept cars through American history, and in addition he was responsible for the ranges Dust & Glory, QuarterMile and One43.

In 1989 during his short tenure of the range, Phil introduced, a 1:43 scale Buick Le Sabre, the showcar of 1951, finished in silver / blue metallic with plenty of plated parts and whitewall tyres. Given with this

Cadillac L'Espada and Buick Centurion

model was a reprint of the rare 1952 factory brochure describing the one of a kind classic.

Other models included a 1954 Corvette Nomad, a Buick 'Y' Job, and the Lincoln Futura. To these were added the Cadillac La Espada, Buick Centurion, Mako Shark, Chrysler C200 and the 1954 Cadillac El Camino Showcar. We believe that a total of 12 models were made before, at some stage, Phil retired.

However, Paul J Burt, a classic car enthusiast living in Lake Forest, Illinois, spotted a GADM Buick Centurion whilst exploring a local model hobby shop in 1995, and was besotted! He did not have sufficient funds, nor had he encountered model cars of that value before, so he walked away. However, the memory nagged him, and eventually he returned and bought the model. He asked the shop owner if there were others in the series, and he was shown a Lincoln Futura, already reserved for another collector.

Without the assistance of eBay, which had not yet developed, but through other collector friends, Paul located the remaining models in the range, and

Cadillac L'Espada, Packard and Lincoln Futura

then learnt that Phil Alderman still had the original patterns. He called Phil on a number of occasions to persuade him to sell, and finally Phil agreed. Paul bought the company, the patterns and the rights to build, and has set about rebuilding the brand. About 4 years ago he launched a white metal Batmobile, and has developed a new website to promote his range, www.GADM.com. He regards this as a non profit making hobby, making between 25 – 50 models of each car.

Paul has established a close working relationship with Keith Williams at SMTS, and through him, has used Ian Pickering for his new patterns. The result has been that casting, vac form and decal technology has shown much improved quality over the 1980s issues.

Paul is keen to make the Cadillac Cyclone, and declares on the current website that he used to have hopes of making over 100 dream cars of the 1950s and 1960s. He has resisted the idea of diecasting in China or Japan, as he personally loves the feeling of quality achieved in white metal, by the old world craftsmanship of SMTS.

On September 1st, 2010 Paul launched his Burt Collection of classic American cars, and offers restoration and servicing facilities to fellow enthusiasts. He sees GADM as the perfect complementary hobby, and is optimistic about the place of white metal models in the hands of dedicated collectors.

Henk van Asten
Conquest/Madison Models

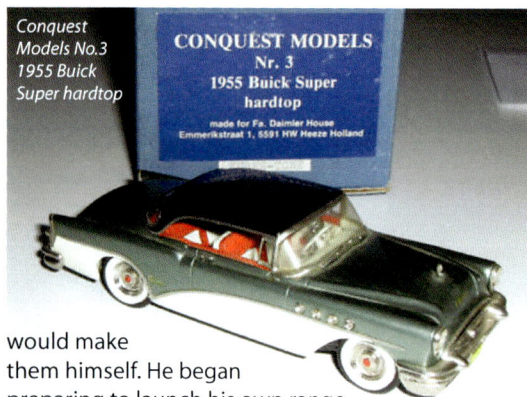

Conquest Models No.3 1955 Buick Super hardtop

Not many producers have emerged from the Netherlands, but one name that is well known is Henk van Asten. Henk was born in 1946, and received his first Dinky Toys at the age of 10. Eventually, he had about 20 to play with, and a few of these have survived, albeit in a poor state of repair.

After he left school he became a teacher, at a high school in economic science and trade science, including book keeping. However, his love of Dinky Toys was to be re-kindled when, one day in 1972, on his way home from school, he discovered a shop in a village which still had many old Dinky Toys from the 1960s. He bought about 25 of these, and this started his collection. Serious collecting came about 4 years later. The Dinky Toys range was limited, so he began to collect Corgi Toys, Spot-On, and other makes in 1:43 scale, and also visited swapmeets. This led to trading in these toys.

To enlarge his collection, he also started collecting handbuilt models. He soon realised that many real cars were not yet modelled, and concluded that he

Conquest Models AC Greyhound

would make them himself. He began preparing to launch his own range in 1983, and as he was drawn by the detailing on American cars, it was these that he chose to release.

He made contact with Scale Model Technical Services, who were able to supply him with the models in the quantity he wanted, and his first Madison release appeared in 1987. This was followed 4 months later by the first Conquest model. Henk founded his company Fa. Daimler House in order to have a trading name, and he found that sales soon increased to a point when he was able to stop teaching. His range continued to grow until 2002, when he restricted his production from SMTS to re-runs of existing models. Henk was always a keen classic car owner, all of which were British. Not surprisingly, one of his favourites was the Daimler Conquest that he owned from 1974 to 1992, which gave its names to the company and one range.

In 2005 Henk decided to retire and made arrangements to sell both the Conquest / Madison ranges to Buz Kirkel. SMTS continue to make the two ranges for him.

Carlo Brianza
ABC Brianza

The history of ABC Brianza goes back over 45 years, when in 1963 Carlo Brianza launched his first unique models. In the beginning he only made single models on a large scale, from brass. These early models were single pieces in 1:10 and 1:13 scale. They had opening doors and bonnets, with working locks and suspension. The steering wheels and engines were reproduced just as the real vehicles, and he won the Quattroruotine d'Oro, the highest award given in Italy.

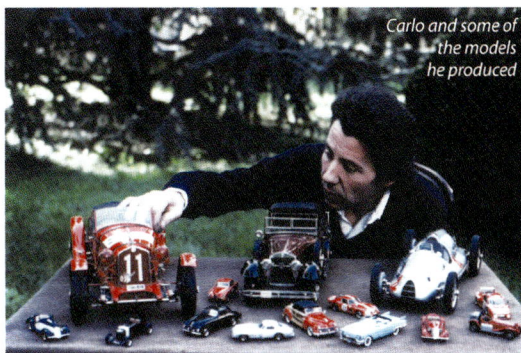
Carlo and some of the models he produced

Ferrari 512BB - an early brass 1:18 scale with many working features

The aim for perfection brought him together with two other great names in model car making: Michele Conti and Manuel Olivé Sans.

Carlo started working in the veranda at his house, together with his friend Giovanni Venegoni, with whom he built aeroplanes. Then Carlo decided to build cars for sale, and the first model he made was the Ferrari shark nose. There he also built models for the Porsche Museum and Alfa Romeo Museum in 1:10 scale, and also some 1:4 scale models for Mercedes Benz. All these models were in brass with full suspension, engine and opening doors.

As a special commission, he built an Alfa Romeo for the crime museum in Milan. With this model, the scale was 1:2 or ½ size! An alarm rang when the doors were opened. Carlo's main problem in creating this model was with the tyres, as he could not find them, and so and he made them in his garage.

The step from the production of single pieces to the production of high quality model car series was quite easy. In 1973, together with his wife Ella, he founded ABC. He produced model cars in 1:43 and 1:14 scales.

The first series he produced was limited to 300 pieces, then Carlo decided to extend the ranges to 400 pieces. Now they are limited to 500 pieces ready built and kits. The Autostile series was in white metal completely. All other models were made in resin with white metal parts. The Autostile range is still available.

ABC's co-operation with Fiat and Lancia became a partnership which lasted several years. In this period ABC produced various promotional series for these famous Italian makers. Today's co-operation with Stola in Turin is heading towards a similar success.

After Carlo Brianza passed away in 1994, his children took over his leading role within the company. Now his son Andrea takes care of the development of prototypes and his daughter Laura is running the Commercial Department, all still under Ella's approval and control.

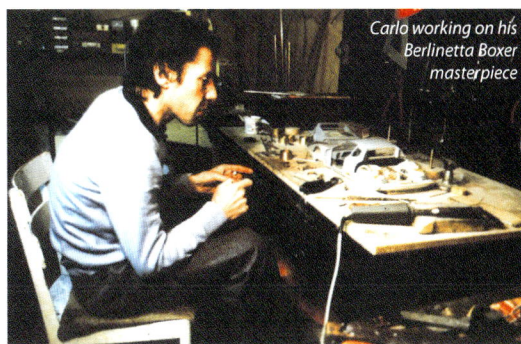
Carlo working on his Berlinetta Boxer masterpiece

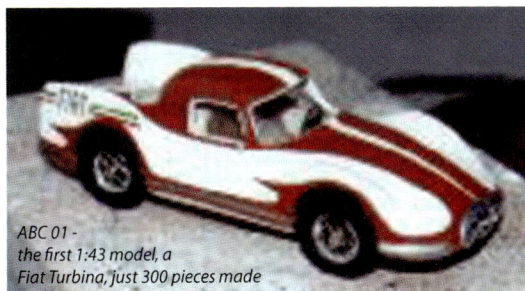
ABC 01 - the first 1:43 model, a Fiat Turbina, just 300 pieces made

ABC Brianza supplies directly all over the world, both to retailers and collectors. They sell directly to customers from their showroom and provide a mail order service. They exhibit at the Trade Toy Fair in Nuremberg, Retromobile in Paris, Technoclassica in Essen and Hobby Model in Milan. In the 1990s, they regularly exhibited at ModeleX in Birmingham.

The ABC Brianza colour catalogue is now printed

every year for the Toy Fair in Nuremberg. Brianza do not send samples to journalists, but supply detailed pictures of their models. Models can be mounted in a showcase, in any scale, and larger showcases for large scale models are of course tailored made in plexiglass.

ABC Brianza do not supply distributors preferring to deal directly. Instead it is a distributor for several Italian and other foreign brands. They produce both ready built models and kits. The patterns and moulding are made within the company. White metal suppliers and photo-etch producers supply to them.

Looking to the future, the Brianza family takes the view that collectors are always searching for unusual models, those marques not yet produced, and most of all, they require the highest quality. This is the path they intend to follow.

Ella and Carlo at home

Marshall Buck
Creative Miniature Associates

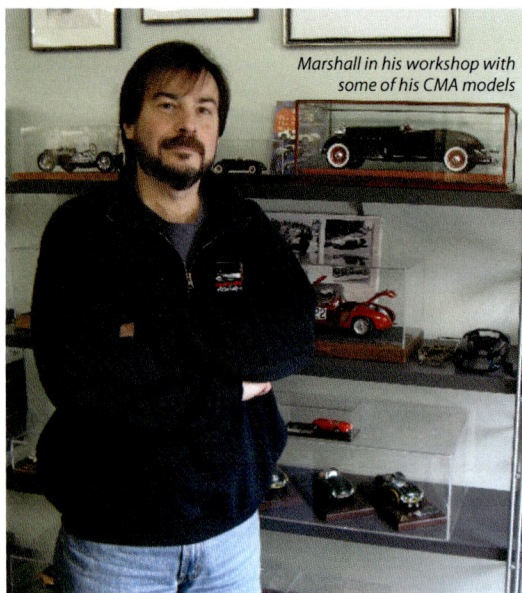
Marshall in his workshop with some of his CMA models

Marshall's childhood was steeped in culture, including regular visits with his parents to museums, antiques & art dealers around the world. Quality in both piece and its presentation became very important to him at an early age.

Always fascinated with all types of miniatures, Marshal had a very strong penchant for cars. As a child, he preferred car magazines to comics. He recalls many friends and family visiting, and enjoying rides in the latest Aston Martin, Porsche, Rolls Royce, or Corvette.

As a child he began his collecting with toys produced by Corgi, Dinky, Solido, and many others, but by 13, his quest for more accuracy and detail introduced him to building plastic kits of hot rods. At school, studying the French Revolution, Marshall became fascinated with the guillotine, constructing a scratch built miniature working model, about 1:12 scale, which caused some concern in the family!

In about 1973/74 he purchased his first 1:43rd white metal kit from Grand Prix Models. It was a 427 Cobra, and he recalls it was a very crude kit. Marshall was attending boarding school in Gloucestershire, at the time, and the kit looked better in built form in their adverts than in the box! He was disappointed and it never did get built, as he felt its details were no better than the mass produced Corgis & Dinkys.

After his family moved back to the States, and while still in high school, age 15, he had a keen interest in designing landscaped slot racing layouts. He produced his own scale drawings, and, encouraged by a close family friend, after much effort, Marshall got an appointment with the head of Research & Development at the Aurora Toy Corporation. From that meeting, he began to receive freelance work from them while still in school!

After a short spell working for a New York City audio/visual studio, Marshall moved into television production, but became dissatisfied with the 'cut throat' politics of T.V. Along the way, he was developing his model making skills and knowledge, reading car and model magazines, as well as meeting a few serious local collectors who taught him a lot. In his early twenties he started attending swap meets, buying and trading models, as well as building. By the time he was working in T.V. production he was selling some of the models he had built through two local model dealers, and to a few private collectors. This all helped supplement expenditure on collecting hand built models and kits in all scales, but primarily 1:43 and 1:24.

In 1982 he was unhappily working for Broadway Video in New York City, and continuing to build models for a few select clients, one of whom was a Greek shipping magnate. With his strong urging and help, Marshall unexpectedly went full time into the model making business. One day when delivering a couple of built models to one of his regular clients the Greek client asked "What do you do when you're not making models for me?" which progressed to .... "have you ever thought about doing it for a living?" and then finally to a point when he offered Marshall separate premises to work in, and funding for the business. The rest was history.

Tempted by his love of automobiles, in 1986 Marshall decided to take a break from model making, and went into sales of exotic cars in Greenwich, Connecticut, for a few years. Marshall had a lucky break in 1988, when his backer introduced him to the late Art Eastman who was the Editor of Vintage Motorsport magazine. Art asked Marshall to write a featured model column for the magazine which he did for 10 years. However, he was constantly getting drawn back to models by many insistent clients, including his original backer, and in 1989, Marshall moved back to model making full time. Marshall started custom-building models for collectors, and advertising his building services in various automotive magazines. He believes he was the first professional model builder to actively advertise such services. He then expanded into buying and selling high quality handbuilts, followed by representation of the great automotive model maker Manuel Olive Sans, to finally launching his own production lines of CMA Models in 1:43, 1:24, 1:14, and 1:12 scales. CMA limited edition models was born.

At this time Marshall had established separate space for his work in a large vintage race preparation and restoration business also owned by his backer, at

Ferrari 166 MM Barchetta, chassis no. 0064M, in 1:14 scale. Modelled as when in long tem ownership of Jacques Swaters

Aston Martin Vintage Racing in Connecticut. What a great place to have an office and work shop!

Later, when AMVR closed, and he moved back home, he began to realise that he was going to need more builders very soon, and a much larger space. He found both on Parker Ave. in Stamford, Connecticut. Once he had expanded his production facilities, he was able to produce his own patterns, artwork for photo-etch and decals, RTV moulds and resin castings in house.

Marshall had 9 people working there plus a few more freelancers and services. There were numerous production and personality problems with all but one of his employees. The two most talented guys were truly fantastic builders and pattern makers. That said, they were also two of the most unreliable people he had ever come across. Marshall relied heavily on these two, and subsequently found that his business had suffered considerable damage. After taking a review, he set about working from home once again, and occasionally taking on outside corporate contract such as for Honda Performance and Toyota.

His first CMA production run was of the 1955 Aston Martin DB3S in 1:24 scale. This was an all white metal model and was only produced as a hand built limited edition. Not knowing any better, he took his pattern and project to a well known British model production company who were producing their own lines of models as well as offering contract production services to many other specialists such as myself. However, there were numerous quality problems, including missing parts. Marshall finally decided to withdraw from the arrangement, and contracted with Graham Price of GTA models to continue to produce the Aston Martin DB3S models. Not only did GTA surpass the other company in terms of quality, fit and finish, but GTA even did it for slightly less cost!

He believes that really great pattern makers, like great independent model builders, are not easy to find. Indeed, one of his later 1:12 scale runs, the 1970 Ferrari 312B, went through the hands of 5 different pattern makers before Marshall found a reliable one.

Aston Martin DBR-1/3, 1958 Nurburgring 1000km winner, modelled - as driven by Stirling Moss and Jack Brabham

Andy Martin of Aardvark Models has done considerable work for Marshall over the years and was a key player in some of his projects, including the 1:14 scale Ferrari 166 MM Barchetta. Andy took this over in the early stages after the original pattern maker failed to deliver. After it had not been available for Marshall to show at the Ferrari Club of America's National meet, Marshall arranged to recover his pattern and all materials it from California. These were then sent to Andy Martin who came through with flying colours!

The Barchetta 1949 Le Mans winner model became a 'tour de force' in research, and detail, so much so that the collector who owned the real car used the model as reference for further corrections and updates in its additional restoration to ensure accuracy as it was at Le Mans in 1949.

Marshall was encouraged by others to make more than one Barchetta, which seemed a sensible business approach, incorporating all the detailed differences. However, he soon learnt that no two Barchettas were alike at all, and indeed there were huge differences! Marshall feels that he has learnt a lot from this, in terms of properly assessing the scope and potential of each model made.

He also recalls a difficulty with a batch of his 1:24 scale Ferrari 250 SWB, Rob Walker/Stirling Moss models being built by a French builder Marshall was working with at the time. On arrival, this batch was all painted the wrong shade of blue! All previous work from him had been fine, so what had happened? His explanation was that he had simply run out of the correct colour so had used another that he thought was close!! The colour he used was almost black, not the correct dark blue.

For a more recent CMA production run in 2009 under the Black Horse Collection label, Marshall was researching Ernie McAfee's 1953 Carrera Pan Americana Siata 208S Spider race car. He contacted a man who he had heard knew Siatas quite well. He explained what he was doing and asked specifically about the Pan Am car, asking what he might know about it and did he have any photos or know of where Marshall might locate some. He replied that, yes he knew the car very well, and thought he could be of help, going on to say that the car was sitting in his living room!

Creative Miniature Associates was the original manufacturer contracted by Legendary Motorcars to produce their line of 1:43 scale American Luxury cars. Marshall first produced the 1960 Lincoln Continental Coupe and Convertible, and later a short run of the Lincoln Mk II in both Coupe and Convertible form. Marshall commissioned Paul Fisher to make the patterns, and all other work was done in house.

However, the owner of Legendary wanted such a

Chrysler Imperial Speedster 1:14 scale. Walter P. Chrysler's personal car. Total of 28 models produced

high level of detail that each model took an excessive amount of time and high cost to produce and build. Since we were losing money on every model produced, after we had the third pattern completed of the 1967 Cadillac Eldorado, we ceased all work for Legendary. Marshall strongly suggested that the owner contact Illustra Models to take over all the work, which did happen. Marshall noticed that, though Illustra have made very good models, they may have reduced the detail level, which he himself would have liked to have been able to do.

Marshall is proud to have gained access to a number of race drivers and personalities, and to have achieved autograph deals with them for personally autographed plaques to go with many of his limited edition models. This began in 1990.

Commissions became a special part of Marshall's business, on one occasion being approached by The President of Chrysler Financial, who also happened to be a client at the time, to produce a very limited run of 1:14 scale high end models of Walter P. Chrysler's one-off 1932 Imperial Speedster for the Chrysler Corporation. These models were used as awards for their top ranking International distributors. Commissions from Steve Earle, the original founder and promoter of The Monterey Historic Automobile Races, to build special award models for them were quite prestigious too! Achieving such commissions requires the ability to produce top quality work in the first place, and creating a reputation for consistency.

The shortest time period would have been in production for just a few months to the longest being about 4 years.

CMA Models limited editions ranged from as few as 10 models to as many as 300, though Marshall's preference is for low numbers of 25 to 50 at a time. Sometimes, such as with the 1:14 scale Ferrari Barchetta, he has produced three versions - distinctly different cars offered in editions set at 250, 100, and 50 giving a projected grand total of 400 models. In reality he stopped production after a total of 130 of all 3 versions combined had been produced. This has often been the practice, stopping production before the entire run or projected run has been produced. This has caused some collectors to miss out on getting some models, but has also made them substantially more rare as well.

CMA Models have always been sold retail direct to collectors as well as wholesale to dealers/retailers around the world. Their direct sales to collectors were and are mostly via mail order, but also at various high end Concours and Vintage race events, as well as the occasional specialised automobilia show. CMA still displays and sells at two to four events each year. Toy Fairs are left for the retailers.

Originally, Marshall issued flyers with color photos to promote the model ranges, then in 1989 he offered a large, full colour catalogue which was available up until 2000 or 2001. Currently, it's primarily the web site. Occasionally he will put out a brochure or colour photo sheet on a specific model, depending on what marketing is required. No samples are ever sent to magazines, just high quality photos and detailed information. Often a journalist and or photographer will come to his shop, or to one of his clients for viewing and taking photos. He also sends out press releases. CMA and its models have been featured in numerous automobile magazines over the years, which has proved excellent for marketing and promotion.

For many years advertisements were also placed in various model car and real car magazines on a regular basis, but nowadays that is a rarity. Marshall considers that the market has changed greatly, in addition to the increasing amount of information available. He feels that the Internet has both helped and hindered the industry.

Marshall feels that he has worn most hats in this business. Model builder, pattern maker, writer, packaging and design, graphic artist, distributor, retailer, consultant, broker, manufacturer, project director, caretaker, shipping dept.., and more......

He has also had others manufacture for him. Some CMA issues were done completely in house and for others he has had parts or entire issues made for him. Marshall has worked with about 8 or 10 different pattern makers over the years. Some he feels were great, whilst others "couldn't glue two sticks together without the help of a good psychiatrist"! He holds the same view for some 'so-called professional model builders'

Reflecting on the future, Marshall sees this area of collectibles as constantly evolving, which is what he makes sure he does with his ranges. He's seen substantial changes in the industry during the past 30 years, and feels sure there are more to come.

Overall he is confident the future is bright for CMA. He has some great and very exciting projects in the works now as well as those planned for the future. As long as demand is there, which he believes it always will be, Marshall will keep producing high end, low volume hand built models and kits for serious collectors.

Jean Francois Consille
Imit'Toys

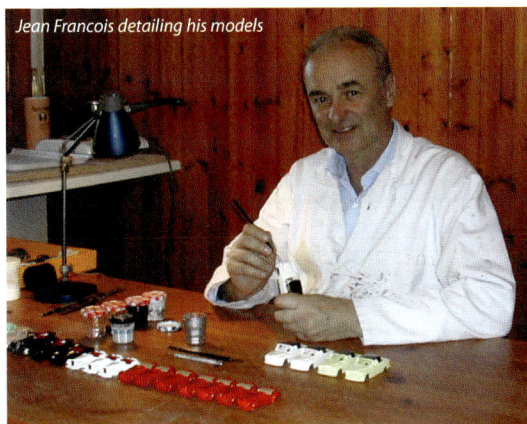
Jean Francois detailing his models

It is not every day that we hear about a model maker from Andorra, the sixth smallest nation in Europe, and a principality nestling in the Pyrennees, but Jean Francois Consille has been making his own versions of Dinky Toys there for 9 years.

As a child, Jean Francois' favourite toys were all small cars, but especially Dinky Toys. As Dinky Toys were made in metal they particularly appealed to him as they closely resembled the real cars. Years later, when he had married and had children, the desire to search for and collect Dinky Toys returned again. His collection of Dinky Toys soon grew in size.

However, he soon noticed that Dinky Toys had not created all the models that he had expected. The only answer was to make them for himself. He obtained some dental resin, and set about sculpturing two that particularly appealed to him. These were firstly a Renault 4CV, and then Jean Francois modified a Dinky Toys Citroën 11BL sedan to create a coupé. Having created a pattern, he then made the moulds in order to re-create the new model in metal. At this stage, he was just producing models for his own collection.

Soon after, in October 2001, Jean Francois presented the results of his labours to two friends, Joan Villasevil of the Basar Valira model shop in Andorra and Jean-Marie Gianni of 43ème RUE in

IMIT' Toys Citroen 11BL cabriolet

In March 2003, Guy Girod had reviewed Imit' Toys in the magazine of Club Dinky France, and Jean Francois launched his Peugeot 203 coupé. Flushed with success, Jean Francois has made numerous other models, details of which can be found on his website.

Most recently a Citroën DS 19 Chapron Coupé Le Paris was launched in November, 2009, followed by an MG TD in June, 2010. Shown here is the prototype in dental resin of a DS 19 convertible released at the end of 2010.

avec glaces

IMIT' Toys Citroen DS decapotable pattern

Paris. They were both impressed, and suggested that he make some models to sell in their shops.

This he did, and these sold like hot cakes! Then in November 2002, a French journalist, Stephane Guillou from Gazoline magazine, discovered the Renault 4CV in the Paris model shop, wrote about it, and as a result many collectors became regular customers.

Otto Duve
Walldorf Miniaturen

Christina Eckrich, Otto Duve, Wiltrud Duve

In 1975 Walldorf Miniaturen launched their range of German model cars in the Modellers' World magazine, and Otto Duve became known to many retailers and collectors in England. His story begins in Düsseldorf 77 years ago. Otto was born on 30th January 1933, the day Hitler took his first step to the Reichstag. He travelled to various regions of Germany as a child between 6 and 8 years, even as far as the Polish border. In 1942, he was evacuated

to Thüringen. At the end of the war, in 1945, he saw US troops entering the town. He knew that Russian troops would be coming next.

His first introduction to the model world was building a big sailing model within the 'Hitler Youth'.. xx He recalls friends of his parents visiting to show off their new 1936 Opel Olympia launched shortly after the Berlin Olympic Games hence its name

From his time in 1940 in Düsseldorf Otto remembers that a dentist friend of his father had a 1938 Horch in his garage, but without its wheels, which had been taken by the military authorities. Much later Otto returned to Düsseldorf and driving along that street, nothing except the nameplates had altered. It was then that he decided that the Horch was part of his life and was to be made! Other significant memories include the owner of a fruit shop in the main station in Hamburg in the 1950s who bought a Mercedes Cabriolet 170S in olive green. Many local people knew this car in the bombed city, as being the signal to better times, and to working towards a better future.

At that time Otto was an apprentice in a sweetshop and his boss had a DKW Meisterklasse, in which he learnt to drive. Later on he sold the DKW and bought a Mercedes 170 V and these were also memories of models he had to make. His father had begun his own business in restaurants and with the business came an old Ford Eifel 1937, which Otto also had to make.

At school aged 10 Otto recalls his father being at war, and moving to Thüringen in the centre of Germany. Here he lived near a car repair workshop, and in the yard there were old cars that had not been taken away by the "Wehrmacht". These included an old Wanderer, two different Horchs, DKWs, and also an old Adler Triumph Junior. Alongside were Hanomags, and a wonderful Maybach SW38. Otto was allowed to play there, and as most of those cars were without tyres, having been confiscated by the Wehrmacht, he was able to play driving these cars and making engine sounds. He imagined he was really driving along a highway.

About 40 years later, in 1974 Otto had left an automobile workshop, which a friend and he ran in the city of Frankfurt. Here, car owners could repair their cars on a DIY basis, assisted by mechanics who could provide hints and help. Owners would pay by the hour, including the use of various machines, such as drills, tools and all the tools necessary for working on cars.

He and his business partner had different views on the business, and so their 12 year partnership came to an end. Otto was expecting a fee for being "bought out" of this business, but sadly nothing ever materialised.

During his time at the workshop, Otto had met a young man, aged about 16, named Bernd Schultz, who came to the workshop as he too was very interested, like Otto was in motor cars, and so Otto gave him some work to do in the office, such as booking customers in and out. Otto later learnt that Bernd was a model car collector.

Later, Bernd Schultz asked Otto if he would be interested in supporting him financially in his new business. Otto was invited to his home and there saw his collection of model cars. He had established an international 'network' by writing to other collectors worldwide.

Estimates were discussed, and the pair then went

Horch in gold plated finish

by car to England, visiting various swapmeets around London, Birmingham, Poole, Bournemouth and others. Here they discovered old Dinky Toys, Spot-On and also many white metal models. Whilst they knew little about these, the diecasts were ideal for selling through their international 'network'. They bought as many models as they could carry.

At that time they got to know Mike and Sue Richardson in Eton Wick, John Day, Dave Gilbert and Barry Lester in Poole, and also a company in Worcester. Otto remembers one trip when they spent more than 12.000 DM, which was far beyond their limit set. On their return home, they made a list of the models they had bought, calculated their prices and sent the lists to their customers. They started a little model shop in Walldorf, naming it Model International Duve & Schultz GmbH (the equivalent of Ltd. in the UK)

The response was tremendous, and encouraged them to return to Heathrow by plane and buy more stock. The model shop had to be stocked with more and more items in the model field, as found at the annual Toy Fair in Nuremberg, where they went every year to visit.

So before long they had a stock worth more than 400.000 DM. Unfortunately, at this exciting time, Otto's settlement from his previous business never came. They had to try to find new areas to develop, such as external manufacturers for whom they could be agents in Germany. But this did not materialise. So they decided to investigate making their own range like John Day, Mikansue and Auto Replicas by Barry Lester.

But how to do this? They knew nothing about mouldings, patterns, or centrifugal casting. So, when visiting England next they met with Barry Lester, who was willing to do the moulding and casting. All paperwork and boxes they designed themselves in Germany and when the first shipment arrived, they began boxing and packing.

Once they knew the way forward, they looked for model makers or sculptors. That turned out to be not so difficult. At that time they had already started organizing their twice yearly swapmeet in Walldorf, which attracted many people interested in building for them. Of those who they saw, 85 % of the trial models offered were usable. They established some guidelines, and the price was to be agreed in advance.

1936 Opel Olympia in the Walldorf Miniaturen 1:43 range

BMW 327

On one occasion, one builder who made a model for them misunderstood the process, and used thin tin plates, formed them into the shape of the proposed car and then glued them together. There was no interior, and the wheels and base plate were all either glued or welded to the model. It looked good, but for their purpose it was absolutely unusable; but he was so proud of it!

At that time, their white metal kits were not very good quality. Due to the centrifugal casting process, the metal was always spun to the edges, resulting in the outer parts being thicker than those inside. The moulds were made from heat resistant silicone, and were soft, unlike steel moulds, which were more expensive. Another drawback was that by using metal heated to about 400 degrees centigrade, the moulds were worn out after about 50 or 100 pieces. The range of models they wanted to make was from Otto's memories of the backyard area of that workshop.

The Tempo three-wheeler was the first, as Otto was able to find old drawings of the 'VIDAL' company who made it. Whilst some of the German cars Otto recalled in his childhood were never made, a BMW 327 in both open and closed versions joined the Tempo. In addition to the main Walldorf kit line in 1:43 scale, they also created an Economy line, named after the "Economy class" in most airlines. This line was introduced because the prices for their kits seemed to be too high for widespread sales. The Economy line kits had only a few parts such as body, baseplate, wheels and some chromed parts, and inset panels for the vac-form windows.

Models in the Walldorf Economy line included a Toyota Celica 1600 GT, specially made for their Swiss agent, 1953 Mercedes Benz 180, 1958 Opel Rekord,

BMW Isetta, Goggomobil Coupé, Mercedes 190 SL, Borgward Isabella Coupé, 1950s Opel Record four door sedan, and a late Mercedes 220SE Sedan. The planned Opel Diplomat V8-Coupé, DKW-3=6, and the Lloyd 600 were never made.

They spent a lot of time producing and selling these models until the end of the 1970s, when Bernd Schultz decided to leave the company. Otto wanted to continue on his own, and started with the a diecast model of the Opel Manta in 1:43 scale, as he was able to buy the moulds from the former owner, with whom Bernd and Otto had some contacts from the Nürenberg Fair. Otto also considered making models in 1:87 scale, due to the cheaper price for the moulds. However, at that time, moulds for one model in 1:87 were around 100.000 DM. Therefore, at least 100,000 pieces would have to be produced and sold for 1 DM to regain the mould costs. It was a risky route, but when Bernd left, Otto was lucky in finding a very clever young man, who was familiar with business matters and at the same time a collector of 1:43 models. He was well known to Otto, and was duly engaged as his right hand man.

His name was Mr. Ruland but after 1978 when the company moved to St.Georgen, in the Black Forest area, they had to separate. Through his connections with Paul Gunter Lang of Danhausen in Aachen, Otto was able to arrange for him to obtain a job with Danhausen, where he still is to this day.

During his years in the toy field he became familiar with computers, acquiring his first in 1978. He became interested in programming them and when in 1992 the Microsoft programming tool, Visual Basic came on the market, he began programming with Windows. Otto has sold many models on eBay but this has recently reduced. Otto finally retired from his model car business in 1997.

Otto will be 78 in January 2011, and he plans to write a restaurant programme for managing the waiters and tables, in which automatically at a desk, all orders can be controlled and archived. He is currently, writing a book, in which his childhood in the Nazi era is reviewed, has already reached 280 pages, and is only part way. It should be an interesting read!

A colourful life indeed, of which Walldorf Miniaturen was a formative part!

Dave Eames
Automodelli Studio

Dave Eames is an experienced collector who lives in Australia, and author of a comprehensive website of ranges of low volume specialist model car makers. However, his story began in England. He was originally a screen printer by trade, so this later enabled him to produce his own decals in small quantities.

He was first hooked on limited edition specialist models in about 1973 when he was given a metal

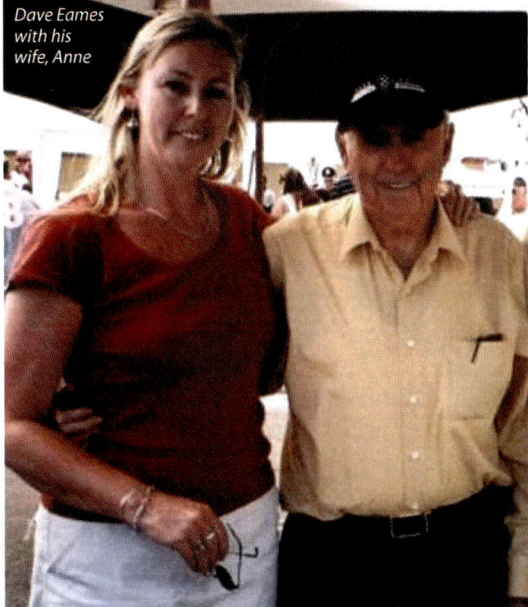

Dave Eames with his wife, Anne

model kit of an MG as a birthday present by his parents. He found it was very easy to become a convert, and thus started the slippery slope.

Many hours after that birthday, after shutting himself away in his bedroom, he remembers emerging with his creation in hand to applause and congratulations from his parents, and thus a long association began. In the months that followed, he sought out many more kits, both plastic and metal. A couple of years later, he found Grand Prix Models, then at Radlett, Hertfordshire. Dave recalls hearing that Brian Harvey and his wife Rachael had started GPM from their garage at home selling plastic kits.

In 1976 Dave began working in building maintenance, first as maintenance assistant and finally to become the building services manager for an international publishing company.

After emigrating to Australia, he and his wife Anne soon became established as a model making team, with Anne helping with the accounts and retail side. This has changed more recently as they use sub contractors to produce the metal or resin casting, the design and the photo-etching. This gives Dave more time to build, and to run the business.

He was very familiar with the legends of the early

1970s, such as John Day, Paddy Stanley and Barry Lester, who filled gaps in the ranges of model cars, and also those in mainland Europe such as Jacques Greilsamer, Carlo Brianza and Ugo Fadini.

And so, for Dave, began a relationship with 1:43 scale metal and more recently resin model car kits that has spanned over 30 years. Dave views this sometimes as a sad story of isolation, in his quest for achieving the definitive listing of all specialist model cars.

As a collector, there was a period when his full time job had to take over, in order to pay the mortgage. Now he has returned to what he really wanted to do all along, that is to create one off models of his favourite cars and, as a builder, to create one off models for his customers. He has built over a thousand models, not only for himself but for friends, car clubs and model shops. He has met many collectors in his years of building for others, from the man in the street to rock stars, famous movie makers and royalty, and they all share the same passion.

Grand Prix Models, one of the largest suppliers of model cars in the world, are still Dave's preferred supplier and he can get most models his customers need from them. For the remaining needs, Dave can often source kits even long after the manufacturers have stopped making them.

His on-going venture is the catalogue website. The original concept for this site was a discussion he had with Roger Dutemple, of Axel'R when he visited Roger at Cournonterral in France in the spring of 2008.

With regard to the current market, Dave believes that there will always be a niche place for the well researched handbuilt kit, and that the high end Chinese ready built models are very good, but they still have their faults, mainly a lack of attention to detail to make them true to the historic original vehicle.

Dave and Anne considered writing a book on the subject of the specialist 1:43 scale model car and its history, but felt that such a listing would not be an attractive proposition. However, the Internet offers a way to engage many other collectors and traders, and thus make such a record available to all. Dave hopes that the people who have been involved with the business from its conception in the early 1970s, will submit their information, and the web based catalogue can evolve as a definitive record long into the future.

Lee Elmes
American Automobile Miniatures

The brainchild and founder of American Automobile Miniatures, Canadian Lee Elmes, had a lifelong interest in cars and model cars. Starting from employment in mining and metal engineering with a Canadian firm of consultants, he first turned his hobby into a business in 1982 by opening Autophile, the first retail shop in Toronto, specialising in all motoring collectables, books, and models. Five years

Lee Elmes

interesting American car models which were to follow.

Three months later, their second model, a 1960 Chevrolet Impala 2 door Sport Coupe, numbered AAM 003 to allow for a variation later on their first model, was released. A tricky model to master, in several areas, it was ably completed by Alistair Duncan and as with the Packard, incorporated a wealth of detail and plated parts.

As it transpired, the Chevrolet was to be AAM's second and final model. Various difficulties confronted Lee and the business was closed down. Subsequently, Lee and his wife returned to Canada.

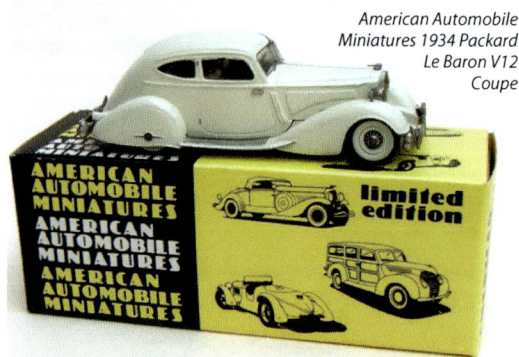
American Automobile Miniatures 1934 Packard Le Baron V12 Coupe

later, he sold the shop to Richard Stafferton and came to England with his English wife to pursue his desire to manufacture his own models.

So it was that in 1988, his first model, a 1934 Packard Twelve Le Baron was released. A distinctive, beautifully crafted and finished model, heavy with detail and plated parts, it was a credit to his expertise and that of Alistair Duncan, the pattern maker, who helped him in many other ways through the manufacturing process.

As a result of this, Alistair joined him in partnership as they moved on to produce other noteworthy and

Ged Fitzsimmons
Fimcar, and other white metal model car manufacturers in Australia - in his own words!

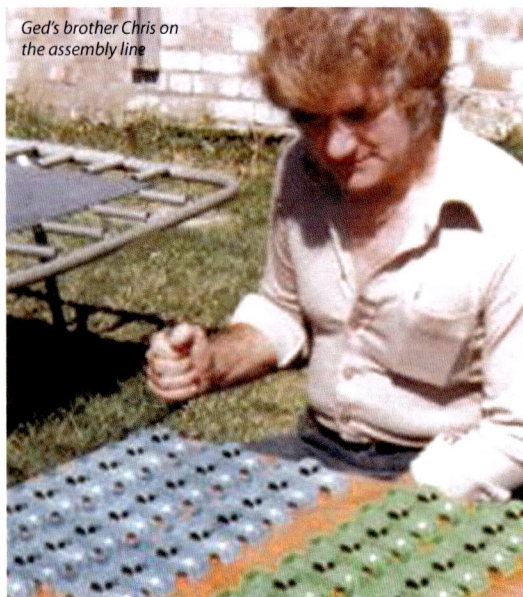
Ged's brother Chris on the assembly line

Ged Fitzsimmons ran a Sydney business in the 1980s called Twentieth Century Models, specialising in diecast metal model cars. Born in northern England, he was intrigued when old diecast model Australian Holden cars started to turn up. In fact, Micro Models had first produced toy Holdens around 1950. Having become one of the major Australian collectibles dealers, Ged listened to his customers closely, especially those wanting model Holden cars.

The only mass-produced diecast Holden available was the Matchbox HJ utility, along with some overseas General Motors clones like Vauxhalls and Opels. However, an older, highly sought after miniature Holden was the Dinky Toys 1962 EJ sedan. Ged was selling many Dinky Holdens and he began to think about manufacturing his own series of white metal Australian cars.

In 1981, there had been a successful run of 200 white metal FJ Holden sedans, made exclusively for Pier van Netten's Model Cars Of The World by Brooklin Models in England. The business like Dutchman had also acquired the rights for a failed diecast Streamlux 1958 FE Holden in 1:40 scale. Ged acquired several of these kits from Pier and they were fast sellers.

Ged's immediate inspiration was an enigmatic Londoner named Mike Stack, the first person in

A History of White Metal Transport Modelling

Australia to create a series of 1:43 scale white metal models. The earliest Dinkum Classics were an XK-Jaguar, a 1948 Holden sedan, and an MGB sports car. Mike's products were first promoted by Model Cars Australia, run by the wealthy auto enthusiast Ian Cummins. Amongst the toys, bottles, weapons and paraphernalia in Ian's shop, the Dinkum Classics debued, with the Holden being the fastest seller.

Impressed by Mike's success, Ged abandoned his secure government job to manufacture model cars. Disregarding the silicon rubber techniques used by other white metal model manufacturers, he would cast his products in multi-piece resin moulds. He turned a wrecked Dinky Holden into the master pattern for the 1963 EH Holden, and then created a six-piece mould. Inside the garden shed stood Ged's home made centrifugal casting machine, as described in his forthcoming book:

The basis of the machine was a wooden plank, bolted to a large fishing reel. At one end was a resin crucible, at the other end a counterbalancing weight. The crucible and the clamped-down mould, sitting on a separate pivoted piece of wood, were lined up so that molten metal would pour into the mould at the instant the machine began spinning.

Basically, he heated the metal, poured it into the crucible, pulled on a long rope that was wrapped around the fishing reel, and then ran like the clappers out of the shed, during which few micro-seconds the crucible and the mould swung into place. The hot metal then cooled, producing a perfect model car body. Well, that was the idea, but it was usually one hit and three misses. The castings were sometimes full of air bubbles, sometimes only half-formed.

On two occasions, when Ged hurtled out of the shed, the rope broke and he ended up spreadeagled

Home at last !!! The FIMCAR Morris Minor

Ged's daughter Mel packing up

on the concrete path. The first time this happened, he was unconscious for several minutes. "Sadly," says Ged, "nobody missed me and nobody came looking for me. The second time it happened, late at night, I lay there for quite a while, counting the stars in the heavens."

Naturally fearful of the molten metal flying through the air, Ged built a cardboard fence around the machine to protect his tender flesh. On hearing of Ged's travails, Mike Stack roared with laughter, being the only one who could empathise. Mike's own original casting machine was converted from a Simpson clothes washer. The beast would spray hot metal all over the workshop, so Mike took to wearing a home made cardboard suit of armour whenever he was casting. What a sight that must have been!

Ged's casting experience grew tenfold, but he knew he couldn't go ahead with the EH first up, as it required windows and suitable wheels, with no immediate sources for these items. So, the first Fimcar would be the 1950 Holden Utility. Ged had an original Micro Models version on hand. "It was a crude toy," says Ged, having been produced from what was called a jelly mould. This requires only two sections, so that the top and bottom pieces can be easily removed, leaving an intact casting in the same way that a jelly is produced.

Ged telephoned the manufacturers of a new range of 1:43 FJ Holden panel vans in Western Australia. In 1981, they owned the trademark Micro Models and their Holden van was identical to the original 1950s model, except that their product was made from plastic. "I had a pleasant conversation with Mrs Sue Williams," says Ged. "She and her husband Gordon came from Salford, the very place I was born. She assured me that they could supply the wheels and axles I needed."

Sixty-five castings of the Fimcar Holden forged ahead. Heavy ingots of lead, tin and antimony were produced by a western Sydney foundry. Three hundred rubber tyres were actually neoprene 'O' rings, made by a Sydney engineering company. The

Ged looking over his Holden Estates

cardboard boxes were manufactured in Hurstville. As far as paint went, Ged liked the smooth colours on the Dinkum Classics.

"What's the secret, Mike?" asked Ged. "How do you get that perfect finish?" "No secret at all," replied Mike, with a straight face. "I use Dulux outdoor enamel paint." With the castings strung across the yard, Ged loaded up his spray gun with Dulux Full-Gloss Exterior, then proceeded to paint the cars on the assembly line. "If you are walking along," says Ged, "painting small inanimate objects, you aren't really watching where you're going, and I tripped over a big rock. I lay there, legs waving upwards, spraying blue paint on the trees, the grass, and my backside, everything except the Fimcars . "And the castings, when they dried, were a bloody mess, with a terrible golf ball finish. I knew I had been had. I could picture Stacky, laughing his head off."

Those castings had decidedly inferior paint jobs. Nevertheless, Ged's July 1983 catalogue announced the release of FIMCAR, a fine new series of limited edition models. The Holden Utility was designated No. 100, available in three colours, and all units sold out within the fortnight.

Future Fimcars demanded a better paint finish, and this is where Chris Fitzsimmons, an experienced spray painter, came in. Ged's brother Chris was happy to sit in the sun, filing, sanding, and painting, fortified with the occasional beer. "Thanks to Chris, the new Holden castings and eighty Morris Minors made it into our 1983 Christmas catalogue," says Ged.

"The Morris was based on the old Spot-On toy."

In March of 1984, Ged released a highly-detailed 1953 FJ Holden utility, with all 110 units having a built-in black tonneau cover, the first ever model of this commercial vehicle. From now on, each new Fimcar would be a genuine first.

The next Holdens were the EK Sedan, EH Sedan and the FC Panel Van. Mike Stack would produce the necessary 300 plastic window sections at $2 apiece. In due course, Ged approached Mike with a wad of readies. Mike reached behind his counter and brought out the little window sections. Ged nodded his approval, then asked for a receipt for tax purposes, as you do. Mike blew his stack and tossed the bundle into a conveniently-placed basket.

"I don't give receipts," said Mike. "Look for your windows somewhere else…" "Don't be bloody silly," said Ged. "Take the money --- I've got to get them on the market! I've got a house to feed, and three children on a mortgage."

The Fimcar EK and EH Holdens, with windows and shiny five-stud wheels (courtesy of Dinky Toys), were released in October, 1985. Two months later, thirty FC panel vans appeared, ready for Christmas. In January, another forty vans were selling steadily, but slower than other Fimcars.

"I soon found out why," says Ged. "Pier van Netten had commissioned Weico Models to produce a range of cheap Micro Reproductions, which were simply white-metal copies of original Micro Models, except for their 'new' FC Holden panel van, based on the old Micro FC station wagon, but it was an inferior casting. When I explained the faults to Pier, he sent me a cheque for the more accurate Fimcar version."

It was not until July of 1987 that a new Fimcar was released, the 1966 HR Holden Premier Sedan, priced at $55, in metallic gold or silver. There were still parts left over for thirteen EK sedans, thirty FC panel vans and thirteen EH sedans. Twelve uniquely blue EK Holdens were sold to Automodels in Parramatta, whose flamboyant proprietor, Bob Rusconi, was happy to stock an exclusive Fimcar variation.

The FC Holdens had been slow sellers, so why not convert them into fire brigade vans? Fire-related models always sold well. Why not make them a numbered, limited edition? Geoff Sherriff, of Sherriff's Mini-Cars, was keen to have a batch of Fimcars that nobody else had, especially his arch-rival, Bob Rusconi. The castings were supplied with the legend Sherriffs Mini-Cars on the base plates instead of Fimcar, but Geoff was not impressed. He had wanted his own Fimcar, to be able to trade it with other dealers! Geoff consigned the thirty non-Fimcars to his store room, where they languished for more than three years.

Another local dealer, a cheery English chap named

Dave Barry, was always on the lookout for a money making proposition. Dave badgered Ged regularly about the potential market for white metal models. Dave commissioned Weico Models in Melbourne to run off some white metal copies of the Dinky Toys Morris J van, to be sold under the banner of Austra Models. A later production was the early Ford Zodiac, based on an old Micro Models toy.

Australia's bicentenary occurred in 1988, and Ged took the opportunity to market his last dozen EH Holdens as a contribution to the occasion, painted in metallic gold, and finally using up all spare castings.

Mike Stack - Dinkum Classics

It was time for a revolutionary new Fimcar. Mike Stack had left white metal behind, and Dinkum Classics were now made from resin, with windows and interiors. To compete, the new Fimcars would have chrome-plated parts, full interiors, and realistic wheels.

Gerry Weight, proprietor of Weico Models, had been casting the Micro Reproductions for Pier Van Netten, as well as the Austra Models for Dave Barry. Gerry had long been known for his white-metal HO/OO railway accessories. Ged contacted Gerry, who agreed to undertake the casting of all exterior and interior parts for one hundred HR Holden station wagons.

When the parcel of castings arrived, everything appeared OK, but there was an ugly hole in the roof of each model. During a heated telephone call, Gerry agreed to repair everything at his own expense. Two weeks later, an impatient Ged received a hundred body castings in intact condition, ready for finishing.

Les Hardaker, owner of the world's largest collection of Holden models and paraphernalia, brought his camera along and photographed the eagerly awaited wagons. Occasionally, the retired

Dinkum Classics
Holden F J Panel van

Les would do some casual labour for Mike Stack, cleaning flash from Dinkum Classics castings, and preparing them for painting. In fact, Les was occasionally heard to hint that he "helped to make Dinkum Classics", but that was probably stretching it a bit. Mike Stack himself appeared to be independently wealthy. Making Dinkum Classics was Stacky's hobby. Not only that, he was employing others, like the talented commercial artist Tony Hannah, to sculpt the master patterns, and Mike was happy to pay Les Hardaker a bit of pocket money.

The HR wagons sold rapidly, but Ged began to accept that the business of making Fimcar models was becoming extremely labour-intensive. He had already promoted the Fimcar 1970 HQ Holden sedan. The ever-reliable Les Hardaker provided an official HQ Holden engineering report, and Ged did his best work to make the first 1:43 scale miniature of this innovative design. But Fimcar was never going to be a money-making concern. A thousand units had been sold, with very little to show for it financially.

"Mike Stack, bless his dodgy heart," says Ged, "came to the rescue". He took over the HQ masters, and marketed them as Dinkum Fimcars, so Ged had no further obligations to his collecting clients.

In 1990, Ged went to work for his former competitor, Geoff Sherriff. In Geoff's store room, he discovered the Holden fire vans, the non Fimcar models he had made for Geoff some years earlier. Ged displayed one in the shop window, with a sign advertising them at $80 each. That was their only promotion, and yet all thirty units were gone within days.

Gerry Weight's Micro Reproductions were re-named Nostalgic Models, as a New Zealand company

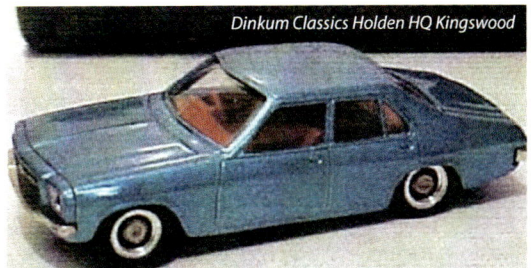
Dinkum Classics Holden HQ Kingswood

had bought the rights and the tooling, in the early 1990s, for the original Micro Models. Mike Stack went on to manufacture the resin Dinkum Classics Leyland P76, made from Ged's white metal master, but the Fimcar brand name was soon dropped, despite Mike saying he had great plans for it.

The name FIMCAR thus went into oblivion, but it still turns up on eBay now and then…..

Sergio Goldvarg
The Goldvarg Collection

Sergio in his special collection room

Parckard woodie

It was 26th January 1990 that Argentinian Sergio Goldvarg and his wife Mariana launched their very first 1:43 white metal model, the 1957 Oldsmobile, to herald a range of American 1940s and 1950s model cars, made in their home country.

Sergio had his own factory where the models were manufactured in Buenos Aires, Argentina, and this was the very first attempt to make white metal models in 1:43 scale, for the collector, in South America. All the brass masters were made, and the painting, casting and assembly, were all undertaken on site by either Sergio himself or his employees.

The models produced were strong and heavyweight, without the fragility of some contemporary examples of the time and certainly had a character of their own. The presentation of their models was a style not seen before, with leaflets included in the eye catching red and gold boxes promoting the models in comic style. Each model carried a tag signed by Sergio.

Their first model was an elegant 1951 Henry J Kaiser finished in a light metallic grey with maroon interior and an

The Henry J Kaiser - one of the first

abundance of plated parts. The base inscription included a tribute to their son Kevin, born in 1991.

The Goldvargs original plan was to produce sixteen models. However, on Sergio's move to Florida, USA, the 1958 Oldsmobile was made in England by SMTS, using his pattern. Sergio found the costs associated with production in England very high.

However, the story of The Goldvarg Collection continues as he currently has completed brass masters to produce the following:
1. Plymouth Fury 1960
2. Pontiac Bonneville 1959
3. Nash Golden Airflyte 1952 4 door Sedan
4. Mercury Park Lane 1960
5. Oldsmobile 1957 Convertible.
6. Pontiac Star Chief 1955 Hard Top w/Continental Kit
7. Mercury Montclair 1956 Hard Top.

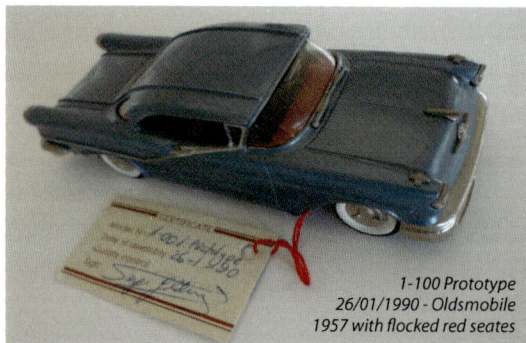
1-100 Prototype 26/01/1990 - Oldsmobile 1957 with flocked red seates

He also intends to produce a number of different variations from the old original brass masters. He is now looking for the right manufacturer. Sergio has a huge scale model car collection of his own, totalling nearly 14.000 models, in scales ranging from 1:43, 1:50 to 1:18. In 2007 and 2009 he achieved an entry in the Guinness World of Records, the first time with 7,000 models and in 2009 with 12,000.

Whilst his main collection is at home, Sergio has

Pontiac 1959 brass master

Sergio with his collection of 1:1 scale cars

many 1:18 scale models on display at the restaurant that he owns at 3285 Hollywood Boulevard, Hollywood, Florida, known as 'Waffleworks'. He also collects Batmobiles in all scales, from 1:87 to 1:1,

owning one of the original cars used by Adam West! So if you're in Hollywood, be sure to stop by and enjoy a meal in this fun restaurant, and soak up the model car ambience!

John Halcrow
Big River Models

John Halcrow

John Halcrow founded Big River Models in 1994 with a background in drafting and tool making and later styling models for luxury motor cruisers.

He had already enjoyed a lifelong interest in modelling, including ships, aircraft, trains, slot car bodies and of course road vehicles and so looking for a new direction with more challenges, creating hand-built model cars seemed like a good idea.

At the time, Somerville Models' quality was the benchmark to achieve, but the prominent players were of course Brooklin Models, Crossway Models,

Minimarque43 and Western Models in the UK, with accurate models also from Europe & USA.

Big River Models commenced with a range of Australian model utilities and later Holden Commodore road cars in 1:43 scale, and in 1:76 scale, double deck buses. These began to find their way overseas and then two interesting developments occurred:

Firstly, the Armstrong Siddeley Car Club approached BRM to produce a model of the Sapphire. These were produced and were immediately sought after world wide.

Secondly, a stand at ModeleX 2002, which had to be transported as airline luggage, proved extremely successful with four prominent UK, and some continental dealers ordering models. This relationship is ongoing.

Along with magazine advertising and editorials and, more recently, production of other makes, success has been assured. Production has not been easy. The data for each model has had to be sourced with photos and drawings produced. The masters for body shell, chassis, wheels etc all had to be hand made. Silicone moulds, and digital drawings for photo-etched window surrounds, had to be prepared

BRM Bristol 402

and sent to Hong Kong for manufacture.

For a one person operation, this is a huge undertaking and limits the model range. John produces all the patterns himself, together with the moulds, and then undertakes the casting. Photo-etching is outsourced, and the tyres are purchased from Italy. Attempts have been made to acquire assistance from other model makers but only the model train industry in Australia is really able to do this and that is mainly in the castings. As is well known, to find a pattern maker who can produce a convincing

body shape which can then be cast is a difficult task.

BRM models are not made in limited numbers. They can be purchased in almost any colour the buyer wishes. They can be customized (racing versions), fitted with white walls, two toned, whatever. John believes that their headlights are possibly the most convincing in the business. New models are added as time permits, some are expensive, some, in resin are less so. These include trucks and semi trailers of late 1930s to early 1950s and will have a good variety of body types.

Bob Hooper
Dominion Models

Bob Hooper of Dominion Models

Bob Hooper, an urban planner by background, founded Dominion Models on January 1, 1990 in Salem, Virginia. The emphasis was, and continues to be, on white metal models of American cars, although market conditions have required a somewhat broader scope in recent years.

Brooklin Models' products are the backbone of the business, although high end limited production offerings remain popular. His personal service and trademark "Free Shipping" have helped him become one of the largest 1:43 scale dealers in the country. Shows played a large part of Dominion's early history but have dwindled substantially with the coming of the Internet.

The website, founded in 2004, now accounts for about $1/4$ of the business with the remainder coming mostly from mail and telephone orders. Bob has has a small showroom and welcomes visitors by appointment. Their printed brochure, 'The Dominion Quarterly' is supplemented by seasonal extra brochures which highlight bargains from collections, which have become increasingly popular.

Buz Kirkel
Route 66 Model Car Store

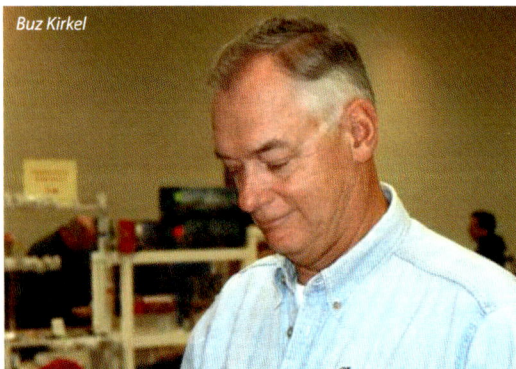
Buz Kirkel

Once an American collector enthusiast gets the buzz, it's amazing what they can achieve, as Buz Kirkel has shown!

Buz started collecting model cars around 1983 to use on his Lionel O-gauge train layout. The first white metal car he bought was a Brooklin Models 1948 Tucker which he still has to this day. He recalls that his family was very poor and $80 was a lot of money then, but he just had to have that car!

He progressed from being a collector to a Brooklin dealer ten years later, around 1993. Building his business, Buz has acquired the Highway Travellers range of ten models, originally by Paul Patterson. He later added Western Models and eventually all of the other major lines to his stock available.

In 2005 Henk van Asten, owner of Conquest/ Madison Models in the Netherlands, decided to retire

Conquest Mercury Montclair

and agreed to sell Buz his business. Buz continues to have the Conquest/Madison line manufactured for him by Scale Model Technical Services in England. In 2007 when Mike Stephens, owner of Western Models, decided to retire, Buz reached agreement with Mike to purchase the range of American cars from him, and these are now known as Western Models Collectors Editions. The production of this line including all pattern making and casting was then transferred to SMTS. At the time of writing, no. 104 was a very rare 1961 Plymouth Fury.

Buz feels that having been a collector before becoming a dealer gave him a unique perspective on what enthusiasts are looking for in terms of subject matter, quality and customer service. When he bought the two white metal lines, he planned to improve the quality, add more detailing, offer different body styles and develop new cars, rather than maintain the status quo.

Production runs are small, usually 30 units of a particular car and often in 2 or 3 colour choices. After a particular car is built, it may not be made again for 2-3 years and then generally in a new colour scheme.

Buz primarily sells directly to the enthusiast through his sales company Route 66 Model Car Store. His customers are evenly divided between the USA and Europe/rest of the world. Buz uses a number of major toy shows in the US to set up a stall and show his ranges each year.

He now has a web store and an eBay store known as Route 66 Model Car Store as well as providing a paper catalogue, and finds he only needs to do minimal advertising in hobby magazines. Depending on the season, Buz is located in the Chicago suburbs and Arizona. He sees the current market as remaining steady, and retirement does not feature in his plans as yet!

Paul Günter Lang
Danhausen and Minichamps

Paul Gunter Lang - now CEO of Minichamps

The company, originally known as Danhausen, was founded in 1921 and traded mostly in bicycles and motorcycles, but also as a sideline sold toys. In the following 50 years toys and model cars gradually took over.

In the early 1970s, the two brothers Hans Peter and Paul Günter Lang took over the company, finally acknowledging its principal customers by renaming it 'Spielwaren Danhausen', Aachen. They built up a record of addresses of every one of their model car collectors. In an interview recorded in Model Auto Review in 2004 Paul, now the CEO of Minichamps confirmed that he has never collected model cars. Since he was 14 years old his interest has been in two wheeled vehicles. However, he has always been interested in the design of all vehicles, and his preference is for those from the 1930s, 40s and 50s. He admitted to occasionally collecting models that excite him because of their construction, design and technical features.

On the brothers' initiative, an international model car swapmeet was established and held twice a year from 1972 in Aachen. These events were then, in addition to the swapmeets of Otto Duve's 'Model International' in Walldorf, the 'mecca' of the model car scene in Germany.

As avid model car collectors began to send their wants lists to the Lang brothers, in return, they were

Early Danhausen Mercedes models

offered help in finding the ones they wanted, not only in the Aachen shop, but also via mail order. From these lists of models, annually produced catalogues were published and sent all over the world.

The first Danhausen catalogue with 38 pages appeared in 1971, and was reproduced in the 1981 'Danhausen World Model Car Book'. This book was unique in that it provided values to all the model cars listed in one publication.

These annually published World Model Car books thus became indispensable reference books, indeed, almost a model car 'bible' for any serious collector. The last such book was published in 1993, had more than 350 pages and contained details of 15,000 models. Nowadays, there is no comparable tome to use for reference purposes.

By 1974 the brothers Lang had decided to launch their own model car ranges, in white metal kit form. This 1:43 scale range was named SD Models. In 1975, in co-operation with Western Models, they developed an additional series of 1:43 model cars known as Plumbies.

Much later, around 1987, Paul Günter Lang took over sole control of the Danhausen company.

Paul's roots have always been in the toy world and his family owned the toy shop in Aachen, known as Spielwaren Danhausen. Model cars became a large part of what was sold in their shop. From that base, kits and handbuilt models were developed, until they reached a point where they took over the AMR (André-Marie Ruf) company in Paris. Paul soon realised that the cost of production in Germany would not be viable for much longer, as it became apparent that a handbuilt model would soon cost 500 DM. Paul knew that at this price level he could not get the substantial sales obtained in the 1970s and 80s. As a seasoned producer and retailer of model cars for more than 20 years, He considered how he would get the same quality, but at significantly reduced costs. He had to find a low wage country capable of making this kind of product. In 1990 that was Hong Kong.

Danhausen Martini Porsches

At the Nuremberg Trade Toy Fair of 1991 they introduced their first model from there, the Audi V8 DTM (German Racing Championship), driven by Hans Stuck. The first production model from the DTM series was a BMW M3, Audi V8 and Mercedes EVO 1. The recommended retail price was 29.50 DM. A handbuilt model of the same car would have cost ten times as much. Before the Fair opened, Paul was already convinced that the price/quality ratio was acceptable. They were 90% satisfied with the quality, and were positive about the whole project and thus decided to go ahead with it. And so the new diecast, mass produced Minichamps range was born, and the white metal era closed. Paul Lang put a great deal of care into every aspect of model production at Minichamps, hence the slogan on the packaging, Paul's Model Art.

The Spielwaren Danhausen shop in Aachen in 1987.

Paul Günter Lang and his family

Inside the Spielwaren Danhausen shop

Germany, and exports go to 60 countries. Japan is the second biggest market, followed by Great Britain, the USA and France. They find that the American market is not so interested in 1:43 car models, preferring 1:24/1:25, 1:18 and 1:64 scales. As a result they are reluctant to produce models of American cars. A significant part of their business is supplying the car manufacturers with promotional models. To keep costs and prices down, whilst maintaining quality, Minichamps were the first to move all production to China and many other diecast manufacturers have followed since. Paul believes that whilst their sales have been affected by computer games and other new media, collecting is here to stay, and a new generation will be interested too.

Nowadays the hallmarks of Minichamps models are that the vehicles, whilst not having any moving parts, have very elaborate interiors, original paints, and accurate wheels. In the course of 10 years, the company has developed into one of the most successful model car manufacturers. In August 1999 the ten millionth car model was produced. It is good to know that the roots of this successful model car producer lay with artisans working in white metal!

In 2010 Minichamps celebrated their 20th anniversary.

In 1998 Paul Lang sold an 80% share of Minichamps to the American company Action Performance. Action Performance is a retailer of models of NASCAR and Indy race cars. However, he feels that his continuing influence on the content and quality of the range remains considerable. They are now global leaders in 1:43 scale. Paul and his wife Romy bought back the 80% interest from Action Performance in the year 2007, so that Paul's Model Art / Minichamps is again 100% owned from the Lang family.

In 2000 they started making 1:12 scale motor bikes and now these form an important part of the collection. Fifty per cent of their production goes to

Adler 2 ½ litre kit

BS McReynolds
Autobuff

The details surrounding Auto Buff models are a little unclear, but the information here is thanks to Wayne Moyer, model car enthusiast and regular contributor to Model Cars magazine in the USA. The models were not generally available from model shops in the USA. Now, apparently, they are most likely to be found at auctions, and garage sales. They were simple, and not always to 1:43 scale.

The leading light in the USA producing the Auto Buff range was B. S. 'Mac' McReynolds, who always used the slogan 'Fords R Us' with the R mirror-imaged.

The first kits were exact copies of the AMT 1:43

scale plastic kits but cast in white metal. In fact, the tyres and chrome plated parts from the AMT kits were included. Mac listed a total of 50 Auto Buff kits, of which according to Wayne Moyer of Model Cars magazine, 28 were produced. Masters were completed for the 1950 and 54 Fords but not produced until Herb Jackson bought them and produced them under the Oakland Models name. Mac also bought some John Day kits and had them built and sold.

Reviewers of the day say that the best Auto Buff models were his Model 'A' Fords. The Roadster pickup is reckoned to still hold its own today if built well. Probably the rarest are the '42 Ford Jeep and the '53 Stake Bed truck.

Apparently the models of Herb Jackson were made from the Auto Buff masters. A Mr. Baas was in charge

1940 Ford Pick-up
and 1940 Ford Coupe

of production for Oakland Models and told Wayne Moyer that Oakland had masters for 25 Auto Buff models, though only the 1950 and 1954 Fords were made under the Oakland name.

After Herb's death, a Mr. Wells purchased what he thought to be the 'remaining masters' from Herb's estate but only got eight. It is not known what became of the other 17. Mr Wells sent Wayne Moyer a box of parts but then sold the masters to another company who planned to use them as model railroad accessories. That was 15 years ago and they still haven't appeared.

Auto Buff produced hand made models as well as kits. However, the quality varied widely from the first ones, made by well known California modellers, to the later ones built by Asian immigrants. There is no means of distinguishing a factory built model from ones made by an individual model builder, except kit building instructions have been found in some boxes.

Several years after Mac told Wayne and others that he was dying, he was seen alive, and apparently well, in Los Angeles by people who knew him.

Mac is said to have stated in a letter to Wayne that he was dying of cancer and had left a legacy of 17,000 Auto Buff kits in Los Angeles!

Mike McNally
Model Auto Emporium

Originally from Sussex, England, Mike and Jacqui McNally established Model Auto Emporium (MAE) in Renfrew, Ontario, Canada after emigrating there in 1981.

Whilst it is believed that the business started in 1983 with a resin made 1929 BABS Land Speed Record car, it was Spring 1985 before their first white metal model, a Cadillac, top down (102), first appeared.

Mike was a tool maker by trade and made all the brass masters in their range. He also made their tyre moulds and produced the tyres in house. Together with his wife, they painted and assembled all their models themselves.

MAE 1939 McLaughlin Buick

In September 1988, A Racing Line was announced to include Grand Prix cars and Indy/North American cars, the first being a Lotus F1 (R03) and then a Chaparral.

In March 1989, a Record Car series of four models was announced and by November of that year their ranges were described as Grand Prix, Record and Road cars. A Green Monster on a plinth, signed R J McNally was being offered for a staggering £395 – indeed, most of MAE's models were expensive by comparison with other makes.

In October 1991, a few more models were announced, some for 1992, but how many of these were made is not known. Certainly, no other models were produced and, sad to relate, the business folded.

Whilst MAE were only making models for a relatively short time, it has to be recorded that the name is famous for their 1939 McLaughlin Buick Royal Tour car, not known to have been made by any other company. This was a very special limited edition model of one of two full size cars that they obtained permission to go and take photographs and measurements of in a museum in Ottawa. The tour cars were built for the King George VI's tour of Canada, and one was stationed on the East coast, and the other on the West coast, so that at all time a suitable car was available.

Measuring nearly 6" long and weighing just under 1lb, it is an open convertible (107) and it is believed that less than 500 were made. A top up example was listed (116), but is rare, numbers unknown.

This exquisite model is thought by discerning collectors to be MAE's finest and one which ranks with the best of other respected manufacturers.

Pier van Netten
Model Cars of the World

Pier and Hilary outside their shop

When proprietor Pier van Netten was 9 years old in 1955, he would spend his one shilling pocket money on lead farm animals. Every week he would walk to the local toy shop in Box Hill, near Burwood East, a suburb of Melbourne, Victoria about a mile away from home and come back with one or more lead farm animals. By the time he was 12, he had over 300 pieces in his collection and he still has them all today.

When he was 12 years old his pocket money went up to one shilling and six pence so he saved up to buy a Dinky toy and the one he bought was the Bedford articulated truck and it was going to cost him twelve shillings and six pence On arriving at the shop the lady serving said we are having a sale this week and all the Dinky Toys are on sale at half price, so he bought two identical trucks as he liked them so much, and he still has the one truck in his collection today, having swapped the other one 15 years after the original purchase.

At 14 he started working for his Dad as a carpenter's apprentice and earned the princely sum of three pounds, so that meant after he had paid his Mum for the board, he had a bit to buy tools and some to save up for more toys. He thought he was the only person collecting Dinky Toys and farm animals over those years.

When he met Hilary, his girl friend, over 45 years ago she knew the model cars came with him. They married over 40 years ago and in all that time Hilary has been a wonderful wife, supporting him in his collecting.

The 4 specially commissioned Holden models made by Brooklin Models

In the early 1970s Pier had the opportunity to start his own building business and it was at that time that he met up with a small group of collectors who met once a month and swap and buy models from each other. In the late '70s he heard of a collector who was selling his collection of over 1000 model cars. They negotiated a price and with the stock purchased he started the business, Model Cars of the World. This was a first in Australia as no one else was selling model cars as a business. Starting with mail order, Hilary would type a monthly catalogue and help him with the packing, as well as running the building business.

A short time later he found out about a swapmeet that was held in Gloucester and decided to come over to the U.K. and have a look. Wow, he bought more than 500 Dinky Toys and his customers were very happy, so he started to come over twice a year. So, it was to be for the next 30 years or so that he would go to the UK twice or 3 times a year to buy model cars

...and inside their shop

In the 1980s he bought a little shop in Burwood East about 5 miles from his home; retired from the building business and devoted all his time to buying and selling model cars. He looked forward to going to the swapmeets and bringing back lots more to sell. It was on one of these occasions that he first saw a hand built Brooklin model and a Western model and was most impressed with the weight and quality

So the next time he was in England he visited John Hall at Brooklin Models in Bath and Mike Stephens at Western Models in Taunton and thus began the launch of these makes into Australia. The collectors there were most impressed and he had many standing orders for the new releases. The more he came to the UK the more he learnt about the handbuilt model manufacturers

When Pier heard that Ray Strutt was having a ModeleX show for hand built models he signed up straightaway. It was there that he discovered models by Somerville, Pathfinder and MiniMarque 43 to name a few. What lovely people and what lovely models they made. He even had some special editions done exclusively for his company and again the Australian collectors were very impressed with the quality of these special models. One such was the Holden that Brooklin Models produced for Pier, a batch of 200 models in four different colours, 50 of each, now very sought after.

Over the years Model Cars of the World have commissioned handbuilt models made in Australia, from Dinkum Classics, Fimcar and Weico Models to name some of them. In the last few years the demand for handbuilt models has declined in Australia as the diecast models manufacturers are producing models of such high quality

As for the model car business, it seems to be moving more to the internet so Pier and Hilary have a website and they are now on eBay The internet is changing the way people buy and sell model models, and it gives collectors a huge choice, but Pier still loves going to the swapmeets. They have adapted to the changes with online working and this has become the major focus of their business, but they still trade from their shop on Thursday, Friday and Saturday mornings.

It has been a tremendous 30 plus years running their model cars business with Hilary and Pier having the opportunity to meet so many nice people with similar interests, from manufacturers to stall holders, fellow collectors and shop owners, and they look forward to meeting many more in the future.

Alan Novak, Gene Parrill & Jeff Thomas
Motor City USA

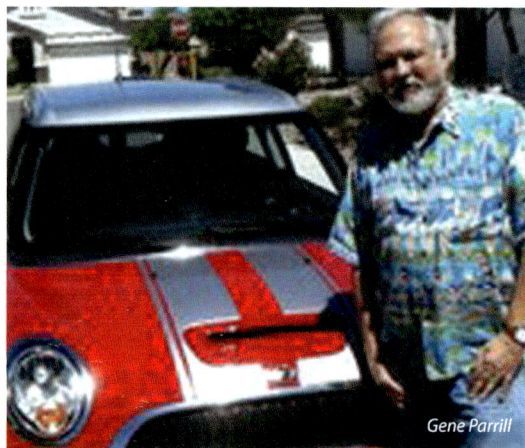
Gene Parrill

The longevity of Motor City USA is due to the efforts of three men, Alan Novak, Gene Parrill, and Jeff Thomas.

Gene met Alan Novak in 1990 after he had retired from Xerox. Alan was looking for a partner for Motor City and Gene fitted the bill. At that time Alan had three people working for him besides himself. He had just released the 1955 Chevy and was working on the shoebox Ford (1949 to 1951). The Chrysler Town and Country was already out and was the talk of the world.

Pete Kenna had joined Alan in 1986, made patterns for the range and stayed with Alan regularly. However, when he launched his own Kenna models range he had to withdraw for a while. Their pattern maker at the time was Don Loos who had just moved from Los Angeles to Las Vegas. Don was extremely skilled, especially in making the small parts such as rear view mirrors, and door handles. All his patterns were made out of brass. Latterly, in 1996, Alan asked Pete Kenna to join him again, and he made many patterns for the range, including all the woodies, hearses, and some 1:24 scale models.

They had a local firm that did all their casting up until 1997 when they brought in their own casting equipment and started doing their own casting. They gradually expanded to five people and added a second paint booth.

By the year 2000 Gene had grown tired of driving the 62 miles each way from Costa Mesa to North Hollywood and gave his 50% of the business back to Alan.

To create a truly international flavour to this story we need to look no further than Jeff Thomas. As a child Jeff lived in California, and recalls in particular visits from two elderly grey haired aunts from Germany. These ladies would regularly give Jeff presents of Matchbox 1-75 cars, and Jeff recalls with great fondness his first two, the 56 Trolleybus and 26 Cement Mixer. These and many other Matchbox vehicles still remain in Jeff's collection to this day. To this excellent base he added Tootsietoys, including a late 1950s Plymouth. Whilst the Tootsietoys became battered and were repainted, the Matchbox cars

Jeff Thomas relaxing in Canada

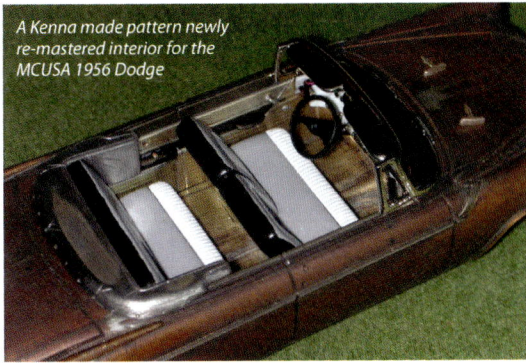

A Kenna made pattern newly re-mastered interior for the MCUSA 1956 Dodge

were revered.

Collecting model cars had cemented itself in Jeff's life, and, later aged 12 or 13, his family moved to New Jersey where he discovered that there were clubs for serious adult collectors of old toys. He chose to join these, and soon began writing articles about his collection and all aspects of his 'passion', the cars and the models themselves, for the clubs.

Such was his obsession with Matchbox that at age 15, Matchbox senior staff saw his articles, and not realising his age, invited him to visit the US facilities in Moonachie, NJ, and the factory in north London. Eventually he made the trip across the pond, also visiting Ray Bush, the editor of UK Matchbox Club. Before long he found himself working for Matchbox (US headquarters) in the summer holidays, and had become a member of three collectors clubs. Matchbox staff would at times encourage him to pass information to the clubs about upcoming products!

The 1942 Chrysler Windsor Town & Country, known as the 'Beetleback' - probably the best example of a MCUSA model

Now whilst the collecting of model cars has remained with him consistently, Jeff qualified as a pharmacist and has a passion for travel, as well. It was his travels around Europe which eventually led to his employment first at Schering and now Bayer, jobs which have allowed him to live in Germany, England, and France. He currently specialises in crop protection.

On one occasion Jeff recalls his ex-boss at Matchbox calling him and offering him a ticket to join him at the Nuremberg Trade Toy Fair. There he discovered serious model producers showing examples of 1:43 American cars, and fell in love with

a Collector's Classics DeSoto. With excitement he researched the market to find more information on dealers in the USA and came across Brooklin Models, Conquest, Motor City USA, and others.

He began collecting the white metal US models seriously, and developed a close link with Gene Parrill, one of the founders of Motor City. Gene supported his collection by assisting with the supply of models to Germany, where Jeff was based. It was the high quality of Motor City products that particularly fascinated Jeff.

1956 Dodge Custom Royal Lancer convertible - Jeff's first brand new model

Alongside his profession, in 2007-8 he began to consider an idea of developing a production facility in Germany to supply collectors with a product to fill the gap he recognized in the market: Durham Classics, Motor City USA, Victory Models and others had effectively stopped producing. However, when it became clear that Alan Novak was planning to retire, the idea began to take on a new and different form.

A financial difficulty he experienced then turned out to be an opportunity. Jeff was being taxed in both France and Germany due to the mobile requirements of his job, and after three years of this he changed the arrangement, seeking a refund. When this came through, it was, he said, a case of 'intaxication' (euphoria at getting a tax refund, which lasts until you realize it was your money to begin with), but it was sufficient to allow him the necessary 'plus' in liquidity to buy Motor City USA outright from Alan Novak. This was achieved in 2009.

The logistics of Motor City entailed many pattern makers, casters and builders in many different places, and Jeff has sought to rationalise this. He is very keen to not only maintain the high quality that Motor City was renowned for, but improve on it still further.

His first new release is to be the 1956 Dodge, already featured in the previous range. Jeff, however, has ensured that the pattern has been re-mastered to improve upon it still. An example of the new master is seen in the accompanying picture.

In an economic environment of world recession, it is immensely encouraging to find an enthusiast who is determined to uphold and even surpass the quality standards already reached by many white metal ranges, and to ensure discerning customers enjoy accurate miniatures of the golden years of motoring.

Gene Parrill
Precision Miniatures

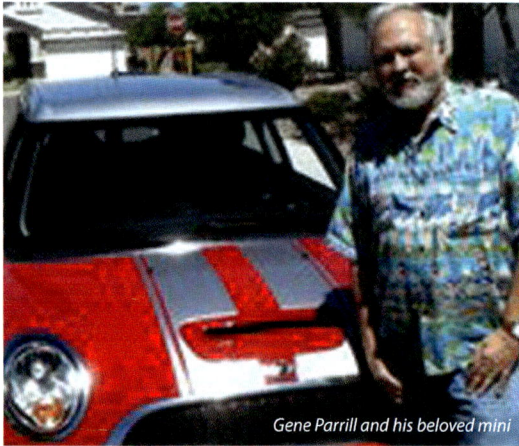

Gene Parrill and his beloved mini

Amongst the small band of American producers in the USA, Gene Parrill stands out as having been in business for some time.

Gene recalls that in 1964 he went into a toy store to buy a birthday present for his daughter. He saw a Solido 1:43 model of a Le Mans Porsche that he didn't know anything about, and as he was driving a 1959 Porsche 356A coupe at the time, he bought it. Later he thought it might be a fun hobby to collect Porsche models so he began ordering from Sinclair's Auto Miniatures.

A few years later Gene discovered Replicars in California and started ordering from them as well. In 1968 Gene was transferred to the Los Angeles area where Replicars was based and in due course he met the owner, Lynn Becker. Lynn told Gene he was going to sell the business. Since Gene's wife had just started University and wanted to make some money in her spare time, they bought Replicars, moved it into their garage, and renamed it Marque Products.

They stocked all of the diecast lines that were available at the time, and also all the white metal kits. However there were a number of models that were not being produced. Gene contacted John Day and had him make up 50 models each of the 1952 Porsche that won its class at Le Mans, the Porsche 904 and the Porsche Carrera Abarth, and sold them through his mail order company. Dale King made him two

Precision Miniatures
1948 Indy Novi USA 1980

more Porsche masters.

Around 1977 Gene was approached by Lloyd Asbury with the idea of making their own white metal kits. Lloyd had been the pattern maker for IMRA which produced the 1973 Indy Eagle in 1:40 scale and then went out of business. Once Lloyd had left IMRA, he showed Gene a master he had improved for him, and Gene was sold on the idea. Precision Miniatures was formed, they agreed to a business plan, and Gene bought the required centrifugal casting equipment and moulding machine. Lloyd contributed his three 1:40 scale Indy masters, which became the first Precision Miniatures kits, and they started production.

In the space of 8 years, Precision Miniatures (PM) had designed, mastered, and cast about 30 models, built an international reputation, and then finally disappeared from the 1:43 scene. An innovative company, they introduced photo-etched wire wheels, and their first in house PM kits were as good as the best European kits, according to Wayne Moyer of Model Cars, who had the enviable task of reviewing them as they were issued.

Precision Minatures
Ferrari 250 Lusso

Wayne described the PM company as a result of a perfectly matched partnership. Gene had left his job in the computer industry to operate Marque Products, and continued to be a model enthusiast who understood the hobby, but with the knowledge, business sense and ambition to promote and manage a thriving business.

He similarly described Lloyd Asbury as a superb master modeller capable of designing and creating a detailed and accurate miniature automobile, and then reducing it to parts that could be cast cleanly and assembled easily. Whilst Lloyd was the principal pattern maker, Dick Armbruster made 2 or 3 masters for the partnership, and Western Models made the 1953 Corvette.

The early PM kits were marketed through Marque Products, which was based next door to Gene's address for PM. Wayne describes the PM Indy kits as very cleanly cast, complete with photo-etched parts, and reminds the reader that when he wrote in 2009, the kits were 30 years old!

The photo-etched wire wheels came with the Ferrari 250 Lusso pictured here, released in 1979.

Wayne notes in his profile in 2009 that in the early 1980s, PM was the only kit maker he knew that issued kits with all the major mould lines removed.

In mid 1981 Gene sold Marque Products to concentrate on PM, and Marque Products continued to sell both PM kits and factory built models. During this year there were casting difficulties with a Hudson model, which had been mastered by Dick Armbruster. By October 1982, Gene had received an offer too good to refuse, and had gone back to work in the computer industry full time. Gene continued to work evenings and weekends at PM, with Lloyd Asbury continuing the casting. Sales and model development was slowing up, caused mostly by the labour of love for Lloyd that was the Hudson Hornet. It was Lloyd's favourite car, but not high on customer's wants lists.

Tendering for a contract to make 1:32 promotional models was unsuccessful, and PM lost valuable funds on that. Wayne Moyer records that many more factory built models were made than was first apparent. A number of builders were making in batches of 12 to 24 models, including Nestor Spinelli, and also Jim Waters, Mike Arensdorf, and Jack Hudson.

By November 1984, Doug Johnson had purchased Gene's share of Precision Miniatures, and Lloyd Asbury had remained as a major shareholder, and continued to run the casting equipment for Precision Miniatures Incorporated (PMI). Within a few weeks, PMI had moved from Irvine to Newport Beach. Under Doug's direction, PMI's emphasis moved towards fully finished models, and in due course no further new kits were produced. All the models were labelled as PMI, and Made in the USA 1984, although some were made as late as 1987. In due course, Lloyd also sold his share of the company to Doug.

Wayne Moyer describes the quality as being variable, and records that PMI disappeared quietly in 1986. There were plans for a signature series of models, but the moulds and names were sold, and Gene was involved for a while with a third owner in some high quality hand built models.

Wayne's conclusion in 2009 was that PM was not the same after Gene went back to full time employment, but that whilst it lasted, 2 very talented people produced some of the best 1:43 kits made in the USA. It is a testament to these models that they still hold their own against similar models produced today.

Arjan De Roos
de Roos Autominiaturen

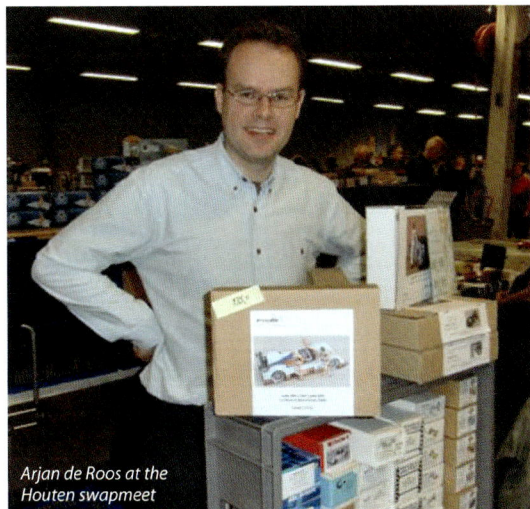

Arjan de Roos at the Houten swapmeet

As a kid Arjan de Roos was fascinated by models of all sorts. Especially plastic model kits got his attention. At an early age he was building several kits his father bought for him. Later on he spent his first earned money on bigger scale models with even more detail. All these of course were to be built precisely according to their instructions.

One day a friend took him to a specialist model car shop in Holland. The shop was crammed with car models, big and large. It was like a candy store! Especially the 1:43 scale models got his attention, some with amazing details, even engine detail.

As building had his main attention he opted to buy a white metal kit, a Ferrari 500 F2. With his experience of plastic model kits, a white metal kit was something different. It was not as sharply cast as a plastic kit, but it had something a plastic model lacked.

It was the mid 1980s, a period when white metal kits had been on the market for some time. On the other hand, French companies especially, had introduced resin as a material for model car kits. It meant that various companies issued some new kits at regular intervals. It was a wonderful time to be a model car enthusiast. Kit makers developed models of all sorts. Some brands developed models within weeks, after a race or a press presentation. Also, through the years kits developed in detail, finesse and realism.

In 1991 Arjan had his first opportunity to visit a model car meeting in the UK, and not a regular swapmeet or car show. No, ModeleX, as it was called, was a specialized meeting for the artisan makers of model cars. It was a meeting for both collectors and traders. But what had attracted him really was the open UK National Kit Building Championship. In between his studies he was still building kits and had wandered in the direction of super detailed kits, where not only outside detail, but especially engine and cockpit details, were to be added as much as possible.

The meeting was a 'warm bath' and those who visited will not easily forget it. Two halls of the National Motorcycle Museum were crammed with small booths for a variety of English and foreign exhibitors; even attracting makers from Japan and the USA. They all showed their latest models and made the show a spectacular event.

This meeting was organized through the 1990s and demonstrated that a specialist meeting for this niche product was appreciated and fruitful. For Arjan in 1991, it had started as a visit for the Kit Building Championship, but convinced him to start a business of his own. It was a first step in getting important contacts in this world. Some people he met in Birmingham he still contacts regularly and became friends with some of them.

One prominent participant and most valuable contact Arjan made was John and Pam Simons of Marsh Models. They managed to bring out a wonderful series of CanAm cars, and Le Mans racers that are strong In Holland. CanAm is not such a popular collector subject and he was elated to see them turn to making more Ferrari models in recent years. In fact, his contact with them started when all Marsh's models were fully white metal kits. Their series then had 13 references. Today it has grown to 180.

One of their models was the first that Arjan could be named as being the instigator. Having made the Ferrari 512M Sunoco, he offered to send John some documentation of the only works Ferrari 512M that competed. And what a wonderful model was developed. Not only crisply cast in white metal, but also with double depth photo-etch material for extra detail and realism. The whole cockpit was made out of this aluminum lookalike material with etched in rivets for splendid detail. It was nice to be involved with such an innovator. In later years Marsh Models moved partly from white metal to resin casting especially for body parts. Still they produce wonderfully realistic kits of great sports cars.

Other important makers from the UK are Scale Model Technical Services and Scale Racing Cars. SMTS is popular in Holland as they make several English brands such as Aston Martin, Jaguar and Lotus while SRC made smart kits (now produced by SMTS) predominantly of Formula 1 racers. They are simple but detailed at the same time. At ModeleX, he also met Make Up Co. Ltd. from Japan, at that time making hyper detailed kits like their spectacular Ferrari 250 GTO, with opening doors and bonnet, full wiring and other incredible details.

Arjan left ModeleX, that year not only winning an honorable third prize in the Kit Building

Championship, but also with important contacts in this fascinating world. Based on this he has developed a business in Holland, supplying collectors and enthusiasts with the kits and accessories they look for. A business that has not only brought a lot of contacts, but also visits to a variety of companies, busy making the most interesting models.

As in Italy, the land of passion for red cars and speed, one also finds several model car makers who got their inspiration to make white metal models in the 1970s.Around Loano in the Italian Riviera, a group of car enthusiasts had assembled to make this area the 'silicon valley' for model kits. The Tron brothers, from whom Paolo had discovered John Day kits and introduced them to Italy, were setting up a sales organization with their own kit series. They were joined by Luca Tameo, a young boy from Milan who had started to make models of Formula 1 cars and with a primary interest in Formula 1 models, had developed a great skill of model making.

Claudio Riva, who started by selling ice creams on the beach specialized in the casting of white metal parts for many named makers as well as other brands. Together with his Meri Kits, he specialized in the whole casting process of white metal and up in the mountains he had a studio for the development and production of kits, for his own brands and those of others. When Arjan visited them he was always astounded by the various moulds from many famous makers such as AMR, BBR, Dallari, Robustelli, and Tron. Together with his wife, and sometimes sons, Claudio Riva involved himself in many projects

From Tron in Italy, Arjan had the opportunity to offer a wide range of Italian brands to the Benelux collectors and builders. Makers that often operated from their garage but delivered car models that incorporated their love for cars as well as their skills. Also, Tron masterminded great white metal kits, of course, mostly of Ferrari cars.

Luca Tameo developed as a real specialist in Formula 1 kits, going from simple to multi part and material kits, remaining loyal to white metal as the base for his models. What he crafted by hand is nowadays heavily developed with the use of computer technology and precision manufacturing, often reflected in price, but

AMR Ferrari 250GTO

at the same time in the quality of his products. His small but professional company also had to withstand the money greed that is an integral part of Formula1 racing nowadays. It hasn't stopped him and Arjan believes he is probably the most well known brand for white metal kits.

Having mentioned the great companies from England and Italy, one other country brought forth a man with a company that became a phenomenon. Andre-Marie Ruf, the maestro from France, who, first from Paris and in later years from the south of France, made kits in his own particular style. AMR was started in the mid 1970s, and was not the first to produce in white metal. That is a feat of English makers. Andre, however, always wanted to make a statement with each model he produced and by doing so earned great respect and admiration from collectors and colleagues. Most of his white metal kits impress when built, some not exactly to scale and somewhat larger, like 1:40 or 1:41, and always quite heavy due to Andre-Marie's typical internal construction. He promoted himself and the artisanal model making scene from a cottage industry to an artistic level. Today, some years after his death in 2004 some of his kits are highly sought after and change hands at prices triple or even ten times the original price. His death left a void, although his son in law Michael Craig continued with his own series called Piranha and Mount Ventoux Montage, but built only.

Now in 2011 the white metal kit still exists. Maybe, no longer as popular as it used to be, but still a group of collectors do have a great interest in them, either to build or collect. A great joy for all of them and, through his business, Arjan is happy to offer that opportunity.

André-Marie Ruf
AMR

Since 1975, André-Marie Ruf has created nearly 600 models in several ranges.
Nowadays, the only places to find these oldies are swapmeets, auctions or internet web sites.

Born on February 16th 1946, André-Marie Ruf was mad about cars before he could speak. His studies took him into a technical job in the French automobile industry. He began his modelling career customizing Norev model cars.

He decided to launch AMR on the 1st of April 1975, and with his wife, Marie-Claude, they decided to sell built models only. He wanted to improve on John Day kits that he considered to be the standard at that time. His first model, a

AMR Tenarif Aston Martin DBV8 Vantage

1200 Porsche Turbo RSR, that raced at Le Mans was built and launched in 1974.

After 4 more built models, he launched his first kit in 1976, the Ferrari BB NART Sebring 1975. He named the range X.

Jean-Pierre Viranet joined his team, and as he was keen on single seaters he created Formula 1, 2, and 3 models. These models were known as X-Tenariv.

Being responsive to the world wide market, and his customers, the next year saw the appearance of the first American car, the Corvette Greenwood Gr4 seen at Le Mans in 1976. A Belgian customer asked for the Minerva AR 30 HP of 1932. By 1978, a partnership had been established with Minichamps, and for the Boutique Auto Moto in Paris, André-Marie made several Porsche 935s.

AMR were one of the first to introduce photo-etching for the first time in the model car world in1979, with the Ferrari 250 GTO. He also created his now legendary wheels.

In 1980 Renault launched the Renault 5 Turbo, and asked André-Marie to produce 3500 kits of this car. AMR was inspired to create the ground breaking white window boxes known all over the world by AMR kit customers. As a minor sponsor of Rondeau, in 1980, AMR won Le Mans!

Capitalising on this in 1983, AMR won the 24 hours of Daytona as a sponsor of the Porsche 935 T-Bird. AMR started the factory built models again in 1984, and were building models for Annecy Miniatures and other suppliers.

In 1987, despite a good level of sales, but facing serious money troubles, André-Marie RUF sold AMR to Paul Gunther Lang, CEO of Minichamps. The AMR team continued to build for other ranges, and for Annecy Miniatures they delivered 350 sets of Ferrari

F40 and 125 C.

From February 1993 to March 1994, André-Marie worked for Le Phoenix. For this company he sculpted Cobras and Ferraris. However, in April, he returned to make models under his own name. By October 1998, André-Marie settled down at Camaret sur Aygues, in the Vaucluse, and in 2003, launched his range of super detailed Titan 1:12 curbside resin kits.

Sadly, in August 2004, André-Marie Ruf passed away, and the company shut its doors one year later, in September 2005.

Dave Sinclair
Miniauto

A number of specialist model car traders operate successfully in the USA, but few have been part of this industry as long as Dave Sinclair.

Dave built car kits as a child as there weren't many built up models. He used to build models from wood and/or cardboard and recalls they had heavy metal spoke wheels which could be treacherous if you were not careful in handling.

He was fascinated by mail order at an early age, primarily as it was a business you could start in those days with very limited capital. His father had built a chain of ten cent movie theatres with virtually no capital. He would go into a town, see an old opera house closed down, find the owner and propose that he open that theatre, and make money for both himself and the owner. They had nothing to lose, so usually agreed, and he soon had theatres in several states providing 3½ hours of entertainment for a dime.

Whilst considering mail order as a business, Dave found a pair of salt and pepper pots in the shape of the Venus de Milo. He advertised, and to his surprise had responses from people who also had collections of salt and pepper pots (known as shakers in the USA). He soon became the 'salt and pepper king' with sets shaped like TV sets, animals, shoes, and famous buildings. After a few years he sold the salt and pepper business. Some years later, while working as Advertising & Sales Promotion Manager for a dental equipment manufacturer he got the desire again to run his own mail order company.

It began as a sideline in 1964. One of the items Dave had was a Matchbox silver plated Rolls Royce mounted on a porcelain ash tray. So many people wrote to ask, 'what other little cars do you have, preferably not attached to an ash tray?,' that this became his inspiration to specialize in miniature cars.

Dave found that in the toy sections of most department stores in the USA only three ready built lines of model cars could be found. Matchbox, Dinky Toys and Corgi Toys, all diecast in England. After some searching, he found diecast models in Italy, France, Denmark, Portugal and other countries that were never exported to the USA. The first line he imported was Rio from Italy, which included a few American cars, such as a 1928 Lincoln, a 1909 Chalmers, and a 1908 Thomas Flyer. Dave began to import them and for a few years was the exclusive dealer in the U.S.A.

The key was that they were designed to appeal to adult collectors. Sales grew slowly but steadily for ten years. Dave diversified, selling hundreds of larger 1:8 scale kits by the late Pocher Company of Italy, including those of Alfa Romeo, Mercedes and Rolls Royce. He even imported ½ scale Ford GT 40s and Ferraris with petrol engines from France, for wealthy kids to drive around the family estate.

Then in the early 1970s some enthusiasts in England and Canada discovered how to build model cars similar to the way lead soldiers are made. Firms such as Western Models in England and Brooklin Models in Canada started offering these models of American cars ready built, and sales began to improve as eager collectors began to order these models despite the fact that they cost several times more than diecasts.

This was a turning point, for up until this time diecasting was practically the only method of making model cars other than crude cast iron toys. Dave's knowledgeable customers soon realised that handbuilt limited editions rapidly appreciated in value, whereas diecast models seldom do.

Dave worked closely with John Hall of Brooklin in their early days, together with Western, and perhaps the most colourful man in the white metal model business, the late Richard Briggs of MiniMarque43. Dave recalls Richard's enthusiastic collecting of full size cars as well, favouring Packards, and recalls Richard making annual trips to the big Auburn Cord Duesenberg auction and meet in Auburn, Indiana.

He would fly into New York, rent the largest Lincoln he could find and load it with suitcases and boxes filled with 1:43 scale cars. The weight of his stock would lower the car's rear end as he pulled into Dave's driveway in Erie, Pennsylvania.

The only model cars, diecast, or handbuilt, that were actually, or presumably, built in the U.S.A. were from Motor City U.S.A. of California. These were excellent models, all of American marques including many hearses and ambulances. At one point, without notice, Alan Novak cut off delivery to all dealers declaring he didn't need them, and would market his models himself. Within a few months he was begging dealers to return, which most did, and finally Motor City built their last 1:43 scale models about two years ago.

Dave has watched as some firms making handbuilts have ceased trading, whilst other new ones have sprung up. He recognizes that the condition of the world economy has taken its toll on this industry as well as everything else. But in the USA, wise collectors who may have lost money in the stock market, have come to realize that hand built limited editions are perhaps a safer investment. He can see the day when models he has sold will appear on Antiques Roadshow programmes.

In the current market, in his 46th year of trading, Dave saw his gross sales up in 2010 slightly over 2009. He has customers all over the world, in Australia, Moscow, Rio, Sao Paulo, and Tokyo, as well as many other places. He occasionally takes buying trips to Trade Fairs in Milan, Nuremberg and Paris for his suppliers of hand built models don't find it economic to travel to the American trade shows due to their small quantity production.

Dave doesn't foresee any major problem for the miniature car business. He has seen some collectors tightening their belts and limiting themselves to a lesser spending figure these days, but only a few have stopped collecting altogether.

Julian, Margaret & Nicholas Stewart
Durham Classics Automotive Miniatures

Julian and Margaret with their son Nicholas

One of the few white metal model ranges to originate from Canada, Durham Classics Automotive Miniatures is run by the husband and wife team of Julian and Margaret Stewart together with their son Nicholas. The company, established in 1980, is based in Oshawa, Ontario, which is east of Toronto.

Julian is a native of England and grew up in Croydon, south of London. Like most young British boys, his collection of toys included Dinky Toys as well as other things mechanical, but Dinky and other miniature vehicles really captivated him. This passion was instrumental in helping him develop the Durham Classics line.

Julian was educated at a technical school which led to an engineering apprenticeship and a career in engineering drafting which proved useful in developing his model cars. Julian emigrated to Canada in 1967 and as a design engineer worked for Phillips Electronics. Here, Julian worked with another expatriate, John Hall who became a major player in model collectables and founder of Brooklin Models.

One day John brought a toy collecting magazine to work 'The Toy and Train Collector' and showed the classified ads to Julian. American dealers were offering high prices for 1st issue Matchbox Yesteryear models. Seeing the opportunity for a quick profit they began scouring shops in Toronto for these models, which were selling locally for 69 cents to $1.49 Canadian.

This hunt was originally a quest for a little cash, but it had an unexpected effect. Julian felt like a child again, and his long forgotten love of toys came back to life. He was a diecast collector once more and especially sought out Dinky, Solido, Rio and Minic. His colleague John Hall was also into collecting diecast models in a big way!

John moved to Brooklin, Ontario and he and Julian would get together and talk about cars and models. Not content with buying other makers models, John started making his own resin models and then, ultimately white metal models. Seeing

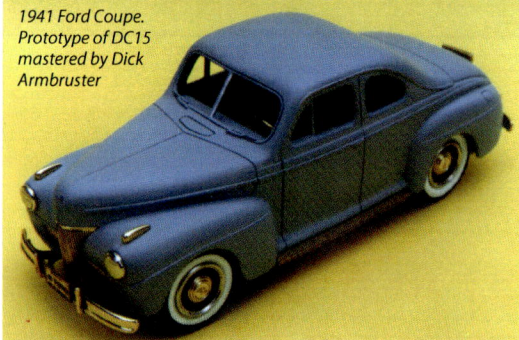
1941 Ford Coupe. Prototype of DC15 mastered by Dick Armbruster

John create his Brooklin Models inspired Julian and he told John he would like to give it a try. So, he bought some tools and carved a very hard block of Canadian maple into the Brooklin 1932 Packard Light 8. Collectors will note the JS77 initials cast into the baseplate although these were removed on later editions. Julian has always stated that the pattern maker gets no recognition for the creation of his work. So, when Julian produced his own models he made a point of placing the creators name on the underside of most of his models.

Following the issue of the 1932 Packard Light 8 Julian produced the master of the 1934 Chrysler 4 door Airflow. The year was 1979 and the Canadian government was not too friendly towards small businesses. So, John decided to pack up his toys and to return to England where the Thatcher government was much more encouraging to entrepreneurs.

Julian had enjoyed seeing his masters produced as handbuilt white metal models so when Brooklin relocated to the U.K. he missed this excitement. Even though Julian had considerable talent to produce the masters he had never been privy to the moulding or casting process. This would have to be learned from trial and error. He felt like a chef who couldn't operate a cooker.

Then Julian heard that one of his co-workers had done some work in a costume jewellery company and had some experience of white metal casting procedures. With the help of this co-worker Julian tracked down the company and sought out a no longer used centrifugal casting machine. However this machine proved unsuitable for casting model car bodies.

Ever the engineer, Julian began tinkering with designs for producing his own casting machine. A lathe, drill press and milling machine were purchased and work on the casting machine began. After much trial and error and endless hours of work with alloys, moulding rubber and melting furnaces a sample body casting was produced. This all took place in the basement of Julian and Margaret's house! However they were both excited by the results of their first

model a 1934 Chrysler Airflow 2 Door Coupe.

Julian and Margaret took 10 Airflows to the Canadian Toy Collectors Society toy show and listed them for $55.00 each. At one show they didn't sell a single piece! However now, many years later it has been reported that some of those Airflows produced without windows, running on Dinky tyres and shipped in homemade boxes, change hands at prices in the thousands of dollars!

Following the Airflow, Durham Classics produced a 1939 Ford Panel van which became their company logo. Julian adopted this vehicle as a logo because he had never seen a van which carried its spare tyre on the outside behind the passenger door.

Over the years Durham has produced many promotional models for organizations, including McDonalds, Ontario Provincial Police, Canadian Aerospace Heritage Foundation and many others. The company has produced over 35 models with specific Canadian logos including Canadian Automotive Museum, CCM Bicycles, Toronto Telegram newspaper etc.

Julian then built a vacuum forming machine to produce the vehicle windows and machined the injection molding die to produce the black and whitewall tyres. As production capacity increased, so did demand. The model production process was taking every moment of Julian and Margaret's time.

So in 1985 following Margaret's encouragement Julian left his well paid job and launched Durham Classics as a full time operation. Julian and Margaret were rapidly outgrowing their basement operation and began looking for commercial premises.

In 1986 Durham Classics focused on premises for rent in Oshawa. At that time there was practically no space available which was a reflection on how good the manufacturing economy was in Oshawa and Canada.

However, after much searching Julian and Margaret were able to rent the front half of a 1700 square foot unit which was all office space with a tiny area that could be used as a workshop. So, in 1986 they moved their equipment and set up shop

DC28 1953 Chevrolet 1/2 ton pick up.
100th Anniversary of 'Bibendum', the Michelin man 1998

at 595 Wentworth Street, Unit 63, Oshawa. This was to be their manufacturing base for the next 20 years. Advertisements were placed in the papers and they found that the skills they were looking for were a rarity among the local applicants. So they employed a cross section of the people applying and decided to train them themselves.

Gradually the workforce grew and in 1994 they had a staff of 12 and were leasing the full unit. They installed a fully enclosed spray booth and expanded the casting area.

Later in the 1990s they attended their first ModeleX show in Solihull and met many other artisan companies, many of which are no longer in business. They returned to ModeleX six times in the 1990s and won the Best Stand trophy three times with the help of one of their UK collectors, Keith Pillinger.

In the late 1990s the business was diversified and produced many castings for other companies, not model related. A second larger industrial unit was leased to handle this work.

Julian and Margaret continued to lease two units until 2006 at which time their son Nicholas experienced a severe illness. This together with the downturn in the economy made it necessary for them to close the original unit.

The range of Ford Ranch Wagons

With contract casting work occupying much of their time, inevitably they were neglecting Durham Classics models. However, with many requests for their older models being made, in 2008 they decided to turn once again to model cars.

With increases in rent and other costs, they have now decided to downsize and move their business closer to home.

With a much reduced workforce, Julian and Margaret continue and are proud to be the sole producer of handbuilt 1:43 scale white metal models in Canada.

Thomas Wolter
Tin Wizard Model Cars

Thomas Wolter at the Houten toy fair

Tin Wizard was founded in 1979 by Gerd Breiter. The first model produced was a VW Golf in street and racing form, and a subsequent theme was a range of Bugatti models. Shortly after Tin Wizard's foundation, Herr Breiter was visited by his childhood next door neighbour and playmate, Thomas Wolter. Thomas and Gerd had not seen one another for many years. Thomas had studied mathematics and physics and had gone on to qualify as an optician. Although Herr Breiter started the business, he did not have the training or expertise for the work of model making. He was more at home in an office doing all the paperwork - accounts, invoices, letters, etc. Indeed, Thomas felt it was difficult to understand why Gerd started this sort of business.

Tin Wizard Jensen Interceptor kit

Tin Wizard Jensen Interceptor Ready built

However, Herr Breiter had been searching for someone to help him with the technical side of the business. Thomas joined the business and started making the patterns, the moulds and looking after the general production. There were a few others running the machines, cleaning the parts and helping with all the other work needed. It was a time for learning as the quality of the models was poor and they knew they could do better

During the early years their production consisted mostly of German cars, BMW, Opel, and in particular, Porsche as they had received some orders from the Porsche factory.

They produced parts for Danhausen and other companies in Europe and the USA who were producing model cars. They also produced complete models in white metal and resin for other companies. Sometimes things did not work or turn out as expected, but all the while there was fun in what was being done and gradually they improved their techniques. They were pioneers, finding new ways to do things, getting better all the time.

In 1984, they exhibited at the Nuremberg Trade Toy Fair for the first time. This was a good decision as business was going well and it encouraged them to keep on with the work.

In 1993, Herr Breiter decided to retire from Tin Wizard, fearing the threat from the Chinese producers. Thomas then found himself 'alone', taking over all the office work as well as making a new start and feeling his way in a changing market.

Whilst all the time doing contract work, Thomas continued to improve his pattern making skills and even started to do his own litho work for decals and photo-etched parts. He bought a 'Repro' camera and, a year later, he bought his first Mac computer. He learnt to work with 'Freehand' and 'Photoshop' and was then able to do decals and photo-etched parts to a standard and quality he could not achieve before. It was a good decision – he threw the big camera away!

Having experienced so many problems with industrial electro-plating suppliers, like poor quality or loss of parts, Thomas decided to build his own in-house plating system, also a good decision. He was able to achieve the quality and reliability he wanted.

In due course, he made contact with Peter Comben of Enco Models at ModeleX and they had stands side by side there on several occasions. They started to work closer and closer, sharing 'know how' and as a result Peter moved his business to Germany for a few years. This resulted in the revival of the Enco Models range, which is now produced to the high standard that Peter desired.

In 2003 Tin Wizard began working with CAD programmes and since then has been able to produce perfect models. Thomas still does masters by hand, in conjunction with CAD. He finds this a perfect way to work and is pleased to have found a keen young assistant to learn the craft and eventually take responsibility when he decides to retire, although he does not see that happening for a few years yet. Thomas enjoys his work and derives great satisfaction from the technical challenge of getting new models into production. Since the beginning, more than thirty years ago, they have constantly looked for new ways to improve their skills. Key to this are his staff: Jörn Herring who has been responsible for white metal casting and building ready-made models since 1995, Stefan Himmel who has done the painting since 1991 and Malte Grünberg who is the CAD technician and has been with Tin Wizard since 2002 doing white metal casting and, more recently, mould making.

The market has changed significantly since they started. Then, 99.99% of their production was sold to the trade. Now, 95% of their models are sold direct to collectors. They do not manufacture the same number of each model as in earlier years when at times, they had 9 employed people. In those days they made more than 1000 pieces of some models. These days, about 300 pieces of a new model are made, spread over a few years. Today as a small team they only produce a small number of some models. Thomas does not concern himself with precise numbers and, indeed, does not count them.

Today, his position is that he can attend to and deal with anything to do with running the business, be it master and mould making, production, artwork, marketing or, his pet hate, office work, in which he feels the Germans hold the world record for complexity!

Tin Wizard BMW

Robert Budig
Modellautos

In 1982, Robert and his wife Ilona, founded an antique store in Leibnizstrasse in former West Berlin. When his daughter Mascha was born in 1987 he started to work with model cars. Even during the first years of the new business, he realised his special interest was in handmade white metal and resin models. The first models of his own production were a Rumpler Tropfenwagen and an Amphicar, chosen because those cars were designed and built in Berlin. Then in 1994, Robert first visited ModeleX in Birmingham. Delighted with the new international contacts made there, he started to produce other handbuilt cars with the help of Brooklin Models, Tin Wizard, Germany, and some Russian manufacturers. During the time of co-operation with Brooklin, the Volvo Duett Hearse and the Ford Ranger F1 Hearse became available.

Robert frequently visits toy fairs in Great Britain, e.g. the NEC toy fair in Birmingham, and Barry Potter's fair at Sandown Park, whilst on the continent you can find him at the fairs in Houten, Netherlands, and Aachen, Germany. During the years, many other models were built to order for Modellautos Budig, including the Mercedes C111/IV , Mercedes G4, Mercedes WaWe 9000 (a water canon car of the Berlin Police), Kleinschnittger, Fuldamobil N2, S6, S7, and the Nobel, all being special German bubble cars.

In December 2011, Robert and Ilona celebrate 30 years trading from their original store.

For the future, Robert sees that it is worth focussing on hand made models, since a renaissance of such models is now occurring.

CHAPTER SEVEN
COMMERCIAL BREAK

Whilst it was racing and sports cars that seemed to be the first choice of the early makers, models of commercial vehicles were soon to follow cars, and these took the form of replica Dinky Toys vans from Dave Gilbert and of course, Transport Replicas by Jim Varney, whose dedication to public transport in those days shone through.

Bryan Garfield Jones and Derek Barratt followed with their advanced kits of larger lorries and delivery vans, not forgetting the handbuilt Dennis tanker by Motor Models. Military trucks featured in Milikits and Bill Barnes' releases. By 1977, Alan Smith had entered the field providing a new level of detail and complexity, and featuring articulated vehicles for the first time.

Bill Barnes
Nene Rubber & Plastics

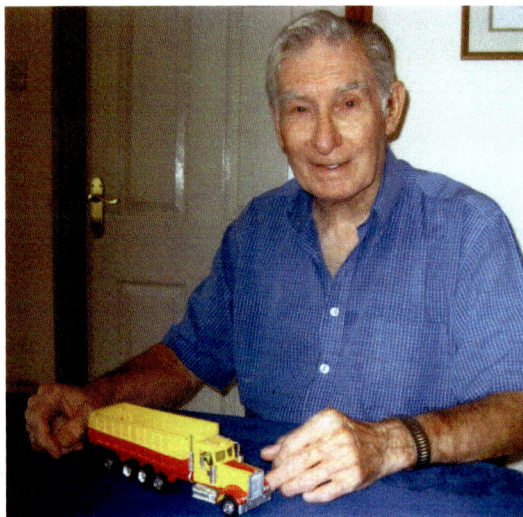

Bill Barnes, another pattern maker and builder of many years experience, has spent most of his working career involved with wheeled transport miniatures, although his childhood sowed the seeds for a life with aeroplanes.

Not the Dinky Toys for Bill, his first model build was a Miles Master aeroplane from a balsa kit by Sky Leader models. This was way back in 1940 when he was just 7 years old! As is often the way, his dad thought he could make a better job of it, and so they took it apart and built it again together.

Through the war years Bill lived with his family in north London, and he concentrated on making models of the military planes he saw. Come 1952 National Service called him, and he joined the RAF as ground crew. He found time to continue making his model planes, not just for himself though, now he could make them for his mates too. Purchasing a kit for 1/9d and selling it for 7/6d to friends helped him develop his early entrepreneurial skills. His work in radar did not lend itself to work in 'civvy' street when he left the RAF, so he joined the USAF as a communications Engineer in 1954, and worked with them until 1959.

He achieved his aim of returning to the RAF, acting as an aircraft engineer serving on Canberras, Valiants and Victors, finally the Blue Steel cruise weapon, until 1972.

A whole new field, the car industry, specifically Fords making small parts, beckoned to Bill. He remained with Ford until 1990, but during this period wanted to experiment with creating his own products in his spare time. He first formed Executive Model Enterprises in 1975, to make and sell 1:76 and 1:60 fairground and military vehicles. Later, Bill formed Nene Rubber & Plastics in 1980 making spare plastic and rubber parts for the car industry. The former company was jointly with a partner to whom he eventually sold his share.

1930s Sunshine binder in 1:16 scale

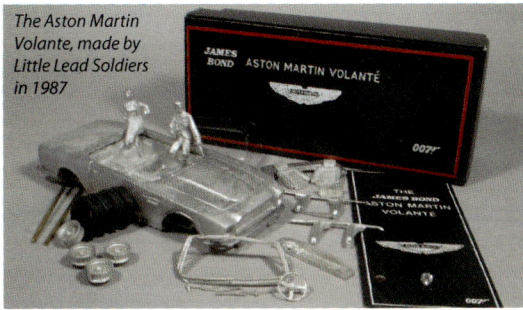

The Aston Martin Volante, made by Little Lead Soldiers in 1987

Bill was keen to develop a way of producing one piece bodies for model vehicles, as until now all model kits were created from sheet metal, resulting in kits with sides, front and back, roof and chassis. He used the techniques employed in the jewellery industry, and having met Peter Comben, who had developed cold cure silicone rubber moulding, he found he was able to use plastic for the masters. Peter had just left Mettoy, and the two developed a sound working relationship, resulting in a well-oiled manufacturing process. This was helped further by Bill letting Peter use a corner of his Nene Rubber and Plastics factory.

Also around 1975, Len Buller had been keen to develop 1:60 military vehicles. Up to that time Len had been modifying existing diecast models, by adding detail and re-painting in military livery, and selling them on. Bill needed tin canopies for a project of his, contacted Len, and the scene was set for B&B Products that has grown and remained until Len retired in 1990, and passed over all his moulds to John Fisher's Kingfisher Models.

Bill's method of working has not changed since his early days, in that he creates a pattern of any commissioned piece from plastic, passes this to Peter Comben who then makes the mould and casts the required number of castings. Bill then takes over for building and painting.

In response to a specific demand for fairground vehicles, Bill created the Tober Models range, which has become very successful, and has been sold both by other retailers and through swapmeets. One consistent retailer for Bill over the last 26 years has been Bob Pitkin, who whilst trading at some toy fairs, has also become a regular at all the major outdoor shows during the summer months. In 1980 he was approached by the Fairground Association, who asked Bill to make a model of the Scammell Showtrac, in 1:48 scale, together with a trailer. Bill estimates that he has produced more than 850 of these.

Bill met Frank Rice-Oxley, founder of Roxley Models, in 1980, and as he was making a Morris 8 van at the time, Frank expressed interest in taking a few for his Post Office Telephones series. The latest in a long line of models commissioned by Frank from Bill has been a 1925 Albion Express Support Vehicle, for which

Bill did the research, Peter Comben undertook the casting as usual, and Bill assembled and painted.

Bill created the master for the Aston Martin Volante, made by Little Lead Soldiers. This 1:43 model was made for the launch of The Living Daylights film in 1987. It was initially marketed through Harrods of London and Odeon Cinemas at the film premiers. We believe that probably no more than 1000 have ever been sold.

Other makers Bill has developed patterns and co-ordinated the moulds and castings for, through Peter Comben, have included Alan Smith's commercial range, Rod Ward's Bond Minicars, and some Reliant 3 wheelers for Bob Pitkin.

Currently, the demand appears to be for farming equipment – not surprising when Bill lives in Norfolk! Bill is finding that retired farmers are seeking an individually commissioned piece of farming machinery in 1:16 scale, often costing up to £1,000 each. In his wooden workshop at home, having downsized from a double garage, Bill assembles, and his wife Sandra undertakes the final detailed inspection and all the paper work.

Bill has had difficulties with his vision, but a recent operation has corrected this well, and his order book is full. Projects in 2010 included a 1:16 Ferguson Centre Baler, two patterns for Bond Minicar Types A and G, 3 wheelers, some patterns for Alan Smith, a model for Roxley, and various earth moving equipment models.

One area not usually covered by Bill is trains. However, he was recently approached by a sculptor to produce a large model of a locomotive entering St Pancras station, suitable for display on a table. Bill obtained all the drawings, but the sculptor customer was not able to use them, preferring to be able to see and feel the 3-D image. Bill therefore created a 4mm master for him, from which the sculptor created a 4 metre long bronze sculpture!

At 77 years young, Bill feels that the secret of his success has been his versatility to rise to a challenge, producing masters in any scale. He has never employed anyone else to work with him and still used his kitchen table, but early in 2011, after much consultation with Sandra, Bill decided to retire. Failing eyesight and ill health has meant he can no longer achieve the standard he expects of himself.

We wish Bill and Sandra well!

1936 Scammell

Derek Barratt
MetalModels

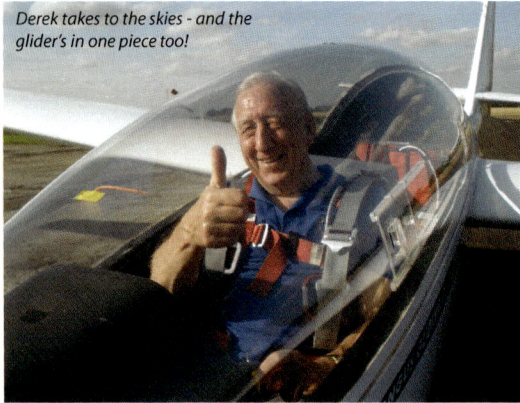
Derek takes to the skies - and the glider's in one piece too!

Here we have a collector enthusiast who has not only contributed to the road vehicles story, but also, later in this volume, to the development of white metal model aircraft.

Derek Barratt was a wartime baby, and grew up in Southgate, North London. Later, in 1963, he became aware of the corner shop known as Beattie's. Stamps were their major stock, but Derek saw a small box of old Dinky Toys in the window, and a 30d Vauxhall caught his eye. He bought that car for 2/6d, and still has it to this day.

At the time Scale Models were running a column on model cars, written by Cecil Gibson, who would feature new white metal releases, including those from Paddy Stanley and John Day, together with information on obsolete diecast. In 1965 Derek attended the first ever swapmeet in Anstey, Leicestershire, at the home of Cecil Gibson. He bought some Dinky Toys and was smitten.

By the late 1960s and early 1970s, Derek was an enthusiastic collector of all things Meccano, from Dinky Toys to Hornby '0' gauge, and he attended various swapmeets as a trader, to further his hobby. He had joined the Maidenhead Static Model Club, where he met many key people in the hobby, such as Mike Richardson and Graham Bridges.

Moving to Norfolk in 1973, Derek met Royston Carss, a Hornby railway enthusiast, and editor of the Hornby Railway Collectors Association magazine.

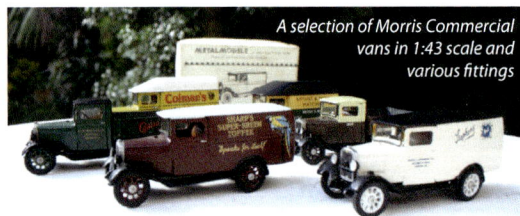
A selection of Morris Commercial vans in 1:43 scale and various fittings

He lived nearby, so Derek helped Royston collate and staple the monthly issues. After two years of friendship, they both wanted to develop fine scale railway vehicles, so Royston proposed they jointly set up a partnership. MetalModels was born!

Derek believes they were the first people to apply etched brass construction to railway vehicles other than locos. Royston did the initial drawings, and together they would spend evenings and weekends developing the business. They selected Bailoy Engineering in London, a small firm of just 2 people, to produce both the masters and the castings for white metal items in the kits.

It was a natural progression from this point to consider road vehicles, and as Derek knew an owner of a Morris Commercial truck nearby, he led on measuring and producing the drawings. Again, Bailoy did both the master and the casting. These were to be kits, including transfers, and Derek admits now that their priority was accuracy, and less focus was given to assembly!

The Colman's Mustard livery on hiline roof van

To achieve authentic liveries, they approached the editor of the Old Motor magazine, Prince Marshall, who put them in touch with Ted Gaffney. Ted was in his 80s, and had been a delivery driver for Harrods. This well respected role had included maintaining his vehicle in impeccable condition. Whilst driving around London and southern England, Ted would carry his own sketch pad and record the liveries and advertising of lorries and buses. These sketches were then transformed into watercolours, which in due course he lent to Derek, who used them as the basis for 12 different liveries.

The Morris was released in 1976, produced in van, open and tilt versions, and approximately 800 kits were sold.

The partnership was dissolved in 1980, in order that each partner could pursue different directions, but it was not until 1989 that Derek saw an article in the Sunday Telegraph on Dennis Knight's range of Helmet aircraft. These were filling gaps in the line up of Dinky Toys aircraft Derek had amassed. After collecting these for a while, Derek concluded that he could add further to this collection by making his own, so in 1995, his Supermarine S6B was launched. The master of Tommy Atkins was used, and Tommy also did the casting for Derek.

His 'Speed in the Air' series followed over the next three years, and for this the name MetalModels was resurrected. More recently, Derek has teamed up with friends Wojtek Benzinski, Paul Howard and Chris Sayer, due to increasing difficulty in achieving satisfactory pattern making. This has led to the quartet making the move towards use of rapid prototyping, using computer modelling software to produce the drawings which instruct the machines that create the master.

Derek, is as enthusiastic as ever for the future of white metal model aircraft, but is aware of the need to embrace new techniques in achieving constantly improving quality.

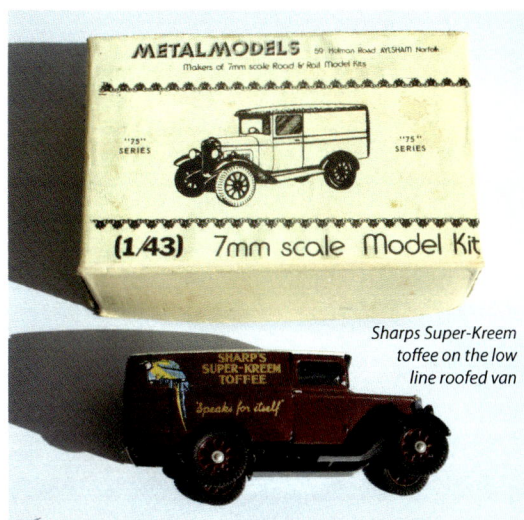

Sharps Super-Kreem toffee on the low line roofed van

John Fisher
Kingfisher Models

The development of the use of white metal for commercial vehicles followed a number of different paths. John Fisher believes that it was the sudden rise in the values of Dinky Toys Foden trucks for restoration or chopping that led to serious collectors like him seeking another way.

He recalls his childhood as having to make do with Yesteryears and Corgi Toys, whilst his older brother had the superior Dinky Toys, Shackleton lorries and other 'forbidden fruit' not to be played with.

On leaving school John joined the Civil Service, and by the 1980s he had begun to re-kindle his interest in trucks and fairground vehicles. With the cost of Dinky Toy Fodens climbing, he realised that it was possible to create a replica cab and chassis. Firstly he experimented with resin replacement cabs, but these shattered too easily. John's first white metal Foden cabs followed soon afterwards.

John had been trading at local toy fairs for some time, buying and selling models for his own collection, but in 1985 John registered Kingfisher Models and he began offering a few of these cabs for sale, after he used some for his own collection. John is also an enthusiast for 1:1 scale vehicles, owning a Scammell Highwayman and a living van.

From this modest start, John went on to stock some of Geoff Moorhouse's developing range of Heavy Goods. Prior to 2000, he acquired the Model Trucks range from Alan Dean. This was followed by John Winnett's commercials range, after he had reached a point when he wished to cease trading. John also extended his range of Dinky style kits and developed the spare parts list.

After giving up work, John and his wife Elaine shared the responsibilities of running the business. John has found he is able to create the simpler patterns, such as those from existing diecast vehicles, but more complicated shapes require the skills of professional pattern makers.

Kingfisher Models' comprehensive catalogue can now be accessed on his website, which also has links to other suppliers such as Geoff Moorhouse's Heavy Goods.

John feels that in 10 years time the white metal market will have diminished considerably.

Mike Forbes
Marquis Models

Mike Forbes, editor of Diecast Collector magazine from its launch in 1997, started the Marquis Models business on a part time basis in 1991, although the idea dated back a year or so before then. Basically, the concept was to provide replacement cabs for the 1:76 scale lorries from Exclusive First Editions, which were then widely available at discounted prices at toy fairs. Mike thought that, as he wanted to change the AEC cabs for something else, others would too.

The first two masters were the 1950s Leyland, so

Mike Forbes

called 'mouth organ' and 1960s Foden S24, re-worked from the original Budgie Toys and Lone Star Impy models, long-obsolete. Mike similarly made the other masters from re-worked Matchbox, Budgie and other obsolete models, while the chassis were based on the EFE parts.

The first 100 castings were produced by Hart Models, more or less as a favour, as Tony and Bob were amused by Mike's idea. He took these to a Maidenhead Static Model Club night, where they virtually sold out to other 'dealer' members. Hart Models did not want to continue production, but Mike met Chris Andrews of Jus-Ryte Modelcraft, based near him in Northamptonshire. Chris then took on the production of the castings, as well as the vac-form glazing units.

The range was added to, until there were ten different cabs available, one of which has two variants, plus a number of chassis, bodies and other parts, designed to convert EFEs into different types of vehicle, or they could be used to build a complete EFE style lorry.

The Marquis Models range, named after Mike's house, The Old Marquis, was available for ten years or so, demand falling off as the original EFE lorries became less common at toy fairs. Ironically, the 1:76 scale market has since taken off again, with a number of new ranges of lorries, with which the Marquis parts could also be used. In fact, the late Don Craggs, the man behind Base Toys, had a set of Marquis cabs from Mike years ago, and some of the Base Toys bear a striking resemblance to the Marquis items. Similarly, EFE has more recently produced several of the vehicles in the Marquis range.

The cabs were basically one piece castings, designed to be easy to use, although a few had a separate base to aid in fixing to the chassis and were supplied with vac-form glazing (also available separately) and a fixing screw, with an instruction sheet In a plastic bag, as were the various parts available. Something approaching 500 of each casting were produced and sold over

the years. In theory, production could be restarted with new moulds, but the price would hardly be competitive with the low prices of some of the current diecast ranges.

As his main business was in press and public relations, Mike was well placed to send press releases to the model magazines and others, along with a few adverts, to market the Marquis products. They were mainly sold by Mike directly by mail order and at toy fairs, as well as by a number of other traders, notably Gary Hames of the Toy Exchange in Southampton and other toy fair traders like Bob Pitkin.

Mike produced a photocopied leaflet and order form which was sent or given out and which brought in sufficient orders to keep the range going for some time, with a number of regular customers. Finished models, both conversions and complete Marquis Models were also offered, including a few incorporating other Jus-Ryte parts, like the Scammell based on the old Budgie/Trucks of the World castings. At the same time, Marquis Models marketed a number of other conversions, mainly based on various Corgi models. These were produced in conjunction with Len Jefferies and the late Pete Molen, and included re-finished Corgi Volkswagen vans in 'Toblerone' and other liveries, police cars based on the Corgi Ford Zephyr and open top Guy Arab buses.

Although not marketed as Marquis Models, Mike is still producing 1:50 scale lorries, based mainly on Corgi, often using white metal cabs from Kingfisher Models, in liveries like British Road Services and Pickfords plus, more recently, customers' own colours.

Mike has recently retired as editor of Diecast Collector, and we wish him well in pursuing his interests in both journalism and the model car world.

Geoff Moorhouse
Heavy Goods

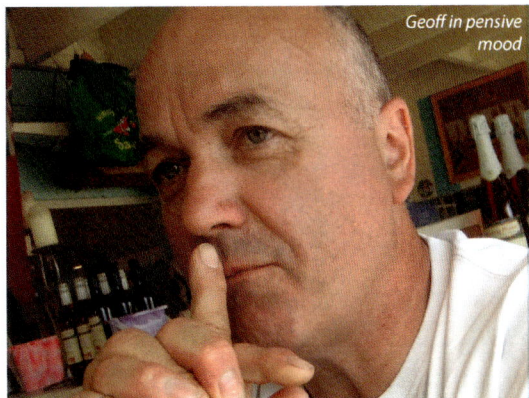

Geoff in pensive mood

Model making was always an ambition for Geoff Moorhouse, and he started making military vehicles from scratch in his teens. However, he soon found the drawback was that once finished, however pleasing the result, he only had one model to show for all his efforts. So even at that time Geoff started looking at ways of casting components.

When it came to employment, in the early 1970s, Geoff achieved his ambition to work for Meccano in Liverpool as a Product Designer. Sadly Meccano were behind the times and struggling, based on a number of issues including an outdated Victorian factory. Corgi had been producing ever more working features, and Dinky Toys were forever trying to catch up. Geoff recalls that at one stage they produced a model with a large number of plastic parts to reduce costs, and despatched these to their suppliers as usual. Not surprisingly, to us now, many stocks were returned, as customers still wanted the feel of quality that solid metal models would provide. It was

AGM no.1 De Soto Suburban Sedan

of course the use of metal in the models that was reducing their viability.

Geoff's role as Product Designer was mostly in developing mechanisms and designing prototypes. Some of the models was involved with included the Foden Tipper, Bren Gun Carrier, German Half-track, and Triumph TR7.

Geoff was made redundant from Meccano in the mid 1970s, and began working for himself making resin mouldings for continental model makers. This included the 1949 De Soto sedan, including the popular New York taxi version. This model he also marketed as his own range, AGM, and later produced for the Sun Motor Company in metal.

Heavy Goods Scania 112

After a few months Geoff was offered a job by Mettoy, and went to work for them at their drawing office in the Northampton. By 1979, Mettoy too were struggling and found it necessary to make redundancies. He took this opportunity to leave and make a go of working for himself again, based on contacts made with Dutch collectors. Another ex Mettoy employee Peter Comben made many of the patterns for him, and Tyler Casting undertook the casting. Geoff's role was to do the initial research and design, followed in due course by the building if required, and the packing and despatch. The 'Heavy Goods' range was born! The first model had been the Seddon Atkinson 400 produced in resin fully built, but this was not that viable and metal kits proved a better option for the market at that time.

Both Peter Comben and Tyler Castings moved on and Geoff eventually ended up doing the pattern making and casting himself. This included working for other makers; one was Rod Ward and his Sun Motor Co. range including the Ford Mustang, Humber and transkits.

An early and significant link was with Dirk Miedema, in the Netherlands, the proprietor of Miho Truck Kits. Geoff visited Dirk and persuaded him to transfer from resin mouldings to white metal, and from then Geoff was responsible for all Miho production. Sadly, Dirk has since passed away, but his wife continues with the business. Geoff enjoyed the creative element of his association with Dirk and sees some of the Miho kits as his best work. It also provided a significant part of his business.

His own kit range is still popular and well known; even the very early kits are still in demand. Although much of the white metal business has been overtaken by the Chinese diecasting industry, his ability to work for others, and to remain small and flexible, has enabled him to survive.

In addition to the casting he has now become a retailer, in order to supplement his earnings, and buys in stock to sell via the Internet. Geoff has noticed that he is getting more people of mature years coming to him for kits, building for nostalgic reasons, but recognises that this may be a temporary

Heavy Goods Foden FG6 Tipper

reprieve, and that inevitably young people may not be seeking white metal as a kit building medium.

Hopefully Geoff's Heavy Goods business will continue to satisfy that collecting need for some time yet.

Frank Rice-Oxley
Roxley Models

An excellent example of enthusiastic collectors taking their vision into business is Frank Rice Oxley and his son Simon.

Frank was born in 1928, and fondly recalls being given no less than three Dinky Toys 29 series Double Decker buses for one Christmas from his sisters, forming a complete fleet! He would have been about 10 years old, and also remembers them being given away later.

Later, whilst in the Army undergoing National Service, Frank developed an interest in historic Post Office vehicles, but it wasn't until 1955, whilst attending hospital in Epsom for X-rays, that he saw a veritable mirage of post office vehicles and he was hooked. He read books on the subject, and found he had a flair for retaining detail. He had entered the publishing world, and progressed to Chairman of the family business, Metal Bulletin, founded in 1913.

With a resurgence of interest in Post Office vehicles

after spotting two Albion vans in Oxford, Frank founded the Post Office Vehicle Club. This club is now flourishing and has a membership of over 200.

In 1986, two years before retiring from the family business, then having become a non-executive director, Frank formed Roxley Models with his son Simon, now 34. They had regularly been scouring the toy fairs and swapmeets in the south of England, looking for appropriate models to strip and repaint as Post Office models, initially for their own amusement.

However, with the arrival of Mabex on the scene, the pace quickened, and they began trading at the toy fairs, and issued their first mail order catalogue in 1988. The models may not have been completely authentic, but there was a steady demand for them.

The white metal involvement came from Alan Smith, of A.Smith Automodels, who approached Frank offering to make post office models for him. Initially they fell foul of the Post Office regarding Royal Mail licencing arrangements, but after the application for a licence was successful, Frank got official work from the Post Office, which also attracted the inevitable royalties to pay to them as well!

Early orders included 60 High Top Post Bus models, which Alan did the patterns for and cast, and supplied in batches of 25 or more. Specialist vehicles

A Vauxhall Astravan, BT livery

Morris van

included Royal Mail Nightrider vans in black livery, together with four in concept green livery to indicate an environmentally friendly build. Unfortunately, these were so gadget laden, that the trial had to end prematurely as the real thing was supposed to be fuel efficient and was anything but!

A Hong Kong Leyland DAF riot van followed, together with Sherpas to a number of postal regions.

Much of this side of the business has contracted due to the Hart Smith Models going into receivership. However, Bill Barnes, now living in East Anglia approached Frank with a proposal. He had seen

a 1930s Morris Linesman's van in a scrapyard, had measured it up in detail, and offered to make the model if Frank took a regular stock. This he did and Bill continued to cast and produce models for Roxley.

Frank had opened his first shop in 1988, at Smithbrook Kilns near Cranleigh, Surrey and subsequently, in 2000, he moved to Great Bookham. Simon's interest in railway accessories has meant the stock has diversified, but interestingly they have found that with the televising of James May's series on BBC2, a sudden upsurge in demand for Scalextric and Airfix kits has occurred. This meant that their shop recently experienced the best Christmas sales in years.

It is an interesting comment on the development of the white metal hobby, that a Roxley Models Hong Kong Police riot van, originally retailing for £55, recently achieved £220 at an auction.

Frank and Simon now have a website that is helping to widen their field of influence, and they have reflected on building a hobby into a business that is now beginning to turn a profit. It has always been a family affair, with his daughter also part of the sales staff until a short while ago.

Brian Salter
Model Historian

Brian Salter in his workshop

Brian was born in 1941, and recalls that since the age of 2 when he threw one of his sister's diecast toys out of his pram into a ploughed field, he has been destined to be connected with toys and models!

Brought up in Harrogate, his family moved to South London in 1946. Brian fondly remembers his grammar school promoting handicrafts, woodwork and metalwork, for those not so keen on sports. Handily, nearby was BEC Models, for some at least almost an after school club, all encouraged by the

hands on proprietor Frank Vescoe. Pre Christmas Saturdays were spent helping out at Philip Duckers, just 200 yards away, a traditional toy shop, just entering the toy soldier market on their own account. Even his first full time job involved models – grass trimming with a model village, suitably instructed by two former land army girls. Somehow the die seems to have been cast!

More normal employment followed, and although somewhat exotic at times, and with quite severe changes of direction, the earlier enthusiasm remained. This was all the while complemented by a growing interest in the social and industrial history behind the miniature products.

A period of coach driving, mainly a summer occupation, gave Brian more time for such interests. Come December 1990, Brian noticed some illustrations, in Model Auto Review, of Hart Models military products, and was intrigued.

Then, shortly afterwards, whilst engaged as a

The Recovery Position - Transport of Delight
Bedford TJ AA Rescue, and Danish Falck Rescue truck

Arguably the world's two most dreaded Land Rovers - Transport of Delight's Judge Dredd and SAS Land Rovers

supernumary tea boy in Roxley Models shop, two men appeared. In conversation with Frank Rice-Oxley, as luck would have it, the pair was Tony Molay and Bob Herridge, proprietors of Hart Models. The opportunity was grasped, and Brian enquired of the possibilities of trading Hart's range at collectors' fairs. Without further ado, terms were arranged, and a factory visit and sample order agreed. A table at Sandown Park toy fair was duly booked. The potential of the product was proved to a whole new audience.

Hence, Transport of Delight was born. Alan Smith Auto Models came on board in due course, plus a number of similar smaller more specialised ranges. Initially Brian knew little about white metal, just being the main retailer quite literally 'on the road'. Eventually the Transport of Delight name started to appear on some of the boxes of some very specialised Land Rover models.

Brian's close contact with the Solihull factory and many users of the marque over the years, encouraged Harts to look favourably on such diversification. The first result was access to the Queen's Royal review vehicles, and subsequent models meant that Harts had no difficulty negotiating an official Land Rover licence when such things became a necessity.

The foregoing then resulted in another unique opportunity; permission, indeed a request to model the then current operational SAS desert patrol vehicles. The resultant quality was confirmed by an American reviewer, pointing out the high price, but saying it was 'the best he'd ever seen of its type'. Another exclusive came from the Judge Dredd movie. Solihull supplied some 30 or so very special vehicles to populate the 22nd century streets. A few hardened enthusiasts said they should never have been built, let alone modelled, but it was a superb model of a horrible vehicle, and sold well.

The fabulous patterns for these were made by Glenn Thomas, with castings by White Metal Assemblies. Other well known, in Land Rover circles at least, but unusual types also resulted from the services of Paul Dimmock, Arthur Trendall and CMA Moldform. As well as in house work, a series of approved Automobile Association vehicle models was a further speciality.

Partly due to the shift in the market place, but initially at least to changed personal circumstances, Transport of Delight came off the road at the end of 2004, to slowly wind down.

As an aside, Brian's name continues as the owner of the Bayko trademark. Using the skills and contacts built up since 1990 completely new style parts are made to supplement this famous 1934-64 building toy. A much more sedentary existence is now devoted to what Brian calls creative research, all very much shared by his wife Ann with her different but compatible and sometimes overlapping interests. Sadly, this was not to continue, as Ann died in 2010 after a prolonged illness.

Tony Molay & Alan Smith
Hartsmith Models

Tony Maloy

The commercial vehicle origins displayed so clearly in Hartsmith Models lay with two men, Alan Smith and Anthony Molay, both of whom have made a very comprehensive contribution to this industry.

Tony Molay, like so many of us, built Airfix and Tamiya kits as a child, preferring the military vehicles. Having served his apprenticeship with Denzil Skinner, when the company closed down in 1987, due to Denzil Skinner's death, his widow had no interest in keeping it on so it was sold.

Tony, having been made redundant, teamed up with friend and fellow employee Bob Herridge, and bought the business. Together they formed Hart Models and took on new premises in Hartley Wintney. The name was derived from their local Hart District Council. They did, however, still work with the new owners of the old Phoenix works, suitably transformed back into its former function as a painting works, for spraying their models.

Hart Models continued the range of 1:96 scale tanks of all nations, and also developed the 1:48 scale range. Their main customers were the Ministry of Defence (MOD) and British Aerospace. Rapier defence systems tended to be the main source of income.

Whilst Hart Models obtained commissions for model military vehicles from collectors, parts, as well as tyres, were being sourced from established companies such as Alan Smith Auto Models. Hart continued to have a select group of regular customers including the MOD, and large companies seeking models of buildings etc, but the commercial outlet to traders who sold to the general public began to grow. These still were mostly Second World War military vehicles, fairground, and haulage. Also, some Fords were made for sale through A&H Models, LSR Models for Mike Stanton, and others for customers in France and the Netherlands.

*Bedford RS
Bomb disposal*

Tony found that the principal customer, the MOD or a company, would agree to fund the major proportion of the setting up/pattern expenses, and then Hart models were able to increase the overall return by continuing to make for the wider public. Patterns were mostly made in house, although two other pattern makers, Glenn Thomas and Arthur Trendall also produced them. The workforce was usually about 7 or 8 in total, and similarly Tony put some casting out to White Metal Assemblies.

By January 2000, sadly Tony's partner Bob Herridge had retired and subsequently died of cancer, and Tony was on his own. In a similar position was Alan Smith, whose partner Tony Morel wanted to retire. There was a synergy in the range and quality of their products, and so Tony and Alan decided to merge businesses, and HartSmith was born.

Tony Morel continued to make patterns for the new company, which then built up to more than 1000 models and moulds in its range, with both military and commercial vehicles being represented. Both tyres and windscreens are made on the premises, and at that time most casting was done in house. The combined work force numbered 14 and were located in North Camp Farnborough.

Corporate customers still feature largely in their order books, which is important, as it enables then to make large and very specialist trucks and vehicles, in which the mould for the tyres, being a unique design, can often cost £1500 - £2000.

Turning now to the other partner in this duo, Alan Smith also collected model aircraft as a teenager. He served in the Merchant Navy for 5 years, before joining Gresham Lion Electronics, developing electronic systems for submarines, in conjunction with Ferranti and Marconi. Whilst working on electronics by day, at weekends Alan began visiting toy fairs, and was impressed by some of the truck models. He wrote to DAF proposing some alternative liveries, and they suggested that he might paint some models for them!

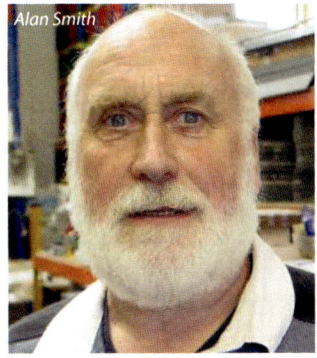

In due course Alan became disenchanted with the internal politics of the MOD, so he decided to follow his hobby into a full time business, and with two friends who were ex-employees of Matchbox, founded A. Smith Automodels in 1977.

For the first 6 months, they worked in a shed in Alan's garden, and their first customer was Portakabin, who wanted some promotional models of their basic product! Alan approached Tony Morel, who was then a Royal Academy of Engineering qualified engineer working as a pattern maker, to make the pattern for him, and they were on their way! This partnership lasted for 23 years and Tony still remains active as a pattern maker.

After the first 6 months, they moved to premises in 459, London Road Camberley to start their first totally original model of the 275 Ton Girder Trailer with Scammell Contractors front and rear. Ten sets of the 275 Ton Girder Trailer were commissioned. This model opened the door for A Smith Auto Models and they began getting promotional work from

Alan Smith

*Ford CMP 1974
Commer Q41*

Pacific Ultra Rotran Girder 4

large engineering companies, such as Leyland, GKN, Scania, Volvo, Ford and Scammell. They made Warrior & Saxon models for GKN, Scammell S24 & S26 Drops models for Scammell and Roadtrain models for Leyland followed from other truck operators and hauliers. With this ever expanding range of models A Smith Automodels began attending toy fairs and sales of built and kit models followed.

In the early 1990s the company had 100 models of the Leyland T45 Roadtrain coupled to a TEXACO petrol tanker completed ready for delivery to Texaco. Unfortunately an electrical fault occurred in the paint shed and a fire soon engulfed much of the shed. The Fire Service was on the scene very quickly. Alan was returning to the workshop, to see all of the flashing blue lights and sure enough the workshop had been damaged. The paint shed was gutted but the casting and assembly rooms were intact but badly marked by water and smoke.

The next day Alan called Texaco to tell them delivery would not be possible at the end of the week as planned. They then made a remarkable and life saving gesture. Submit the invoice in that day and they would pay immediately provided Alan could assure them that they could strip, repaint and deliver the models in 4 weeks. They did just that and stayed in business. It was almost the termination of A Smith Auto Models.

The company then moved to a larger workshop, still in Camberley and remained there for 8 years before moving to Badshot Lee, near to Farnham. Here they established themselves for another 8 years before finally settling in North Camp, Farnborough.

The year 2000 brought about the merger of A Smith Automodels and Hart Models, to form HartSmith Models, but whilst the sales were very successful, a major US customer failed to pay his debts, and so at 65 years of age, Alan took the decision to go into voluntary liquidation. The practicalities of this meant that no purchases could be made for a 6-8 week period, but sales were permitted to clear debts. Just two staff stayed with Alan and Tony, and many models were sold at toy fairs. In the end, the US customer paid up, the liquidator valued the company, and Alan and Tony were able to buy up the remaining assets. Thus ASAM models were born from these ashes. As luck would have it they were able to retain the same telephone number and web site so existing customers had no difficulty in finding the new company. Just by chance the ASAM name which previously stood for A Smith Auto Models was changed to Alan Smith & Anthony Molay and they were again able to continue with an established identity

Now they have made a conscious decision to reduce the volume of the business, despite there being an increased demand. That part of the range which is US vehicles has been sold to a US customer, including the patterns and moulds. At the time of writing, with Alan now in his 70s and Tony 66 years young, they plan to concentrate on kits only, and work approximately 2 days per week.

Alan believes that his business has survived due to the specialist nature of the vehicles they have concentrated on. Whilst the mainstream market for haulage vehicles made from white metal collapsed when Corgi entered it, heavy haulage and special purpose vehicles will always have a place. The future still looks rosy, with toy fairs takings up, and many customers fed up with diecast offerings. It seems that people either want to build the kits for themselves, or will take on a number of commissions and thus purchase a quantity.

Albeit at a reduced level, the future is indeed looking good for ASAM! Alan feels strongly that it has been unfortunate that no one in the UK had the confidence to take on a skilled work force with an established range of models and an enthusiastic world wide customer base.

Adrian Towner
World of Miniatures

It all started around 1968, at the age of 12 with Adrian's interest in model making. He was avidly building Airfix kits and small models. Then moving on to model railways, he joined a local model railway club. Visiting model railway exhibitions Adrian noticed the lack of lineside models, so he decided to travel the exhibition circuit with his own range of small dioramas. However after a

Adrian at work in his new workshop

number of years there came a decline in the railway hobby as videos and computer games became the latest boys' toys.

Adrian felt it was time to try something new. He hit upon the idea of authentic circus and fairground models?

He remembered, fondly, Billy Smart's Circus when it visited Guildford with its music, smells of sawdust and candy floss as you walked towards the big top on a Sunday afternoon. Then, after the performance he would stay behind to watch the pull down and movement of transport, Macks, Royal Windsor and of course Lord Morrison.

During the early 1970s Adrian was working for Messenger, May and Baverstock in Godalming, preparing for sales, and cataloguing antiques. He then realized a long held ambition to join the Fire Service, becoming a retained firefighter in 1978. This gave Adrian the opportunity to pursue his interest in building a model range.

Adrian's first model was an Austin K6, but based on the Dinky K3, with additional brass detailing. Only

ERF 'King Louis' Carters Steam Fair

four models were made as it became clear that there were insufficient models available to convert.

A significant breakthrough occurred in 1989 when Adrian met Alan Smith at the Farnham Maltings toy fair, and with advice from Brian Salter as well, he set about commissioning a pattern for the Austin K6 lorry in 1:48 scale. Bill Fellows provided this, and by 1990 the pattern was finished, and resin casts were taken by CMA Moldcast. Alan Smith cast the parts and built and painted the models. At this stage Adrian was using a spare bedroom as a workshop, where he would receive the models from Alan and add transfers and further detail.

So with permission from Gary Smart, the Billy Smart collection was started, and Adrian began selling his circus models at toy fairs, but this was time consuming.

In 1991, a further 5 models were added to the range, and by 1996 a full colour catalogue showed the extent of the Billy Smart range, and now there are other Circus vehicles as well. Adrian now uses Bill Fellows for all pattern making, and CMA Moldcast for casting. He is occasionally asked to make a special model, and these have included, in 1995, a Dennis Rapier Fire Engine, by special request from Dennis Motors of Guildford. Adrian had often been encouraged by his fire service colleagues to introduce a range of fire engines but by then other makers were in the market, so he didn't proceed with this idea.

So-Coe with generators, Billy Smarts Circus

Adrian has now built a comprehensive website, and has mail order customers from Australia, France, Germany and the Netherlands and the USA.

There are a further 35 models of Billy Smart's Circus to be built by Adrian, and that is in addition to others for Bertram Mills and Carters Steam Fair. The future certainly looks solid and as long as the smell of the candy floss and the interest from the crowd is still strong, there will be a demand for Adrian's unique and extensive range.

Barry Wright
BW Models

The 1:76 scale field is in many ways a specialist area, and Barry Wright has dedicated all his modelling career to it. As is often the case, his dad bought him Airfix kits to build in the 1960s. In 1965 Barry joined the army, and became interested in the vehicles he encountered there, as a construction engineer. In later life he regretted not taking pictures of these.

Barry married in 1974 and left the army in 1976. Once in civvy street, Barry joined the Civil Service, and resumed building Airfix kits, but just the military vehicles. Come 1987, Barry moved from Birmingham to Northumberland, where he encountered a local branch of the Miniature Fighting Vehicles Association. This branch was in Newcastle, and it was the first club that Barry had joined. They took part in annual competitions around the country, and Barry was persuaded to enter his models in the competition which took place in Glasgow. There, he was amazed at the standard of other competitors, but pleased to have won a trophy for best resin model.

The person presenting the prizes was Gordon Brown, of Cromwell Models, makers of resin kits in 1:76 scale. They chatted, and Barry was asked if he was interested in making some masters for the resin range. He gave it a go, and in the following five years to 1991, made between 30 and 40 masters for them.

By 1991, Barry was keen to make a particular

1:76 Land Rover 90Gs

vehicle in the range, but Gordon was reluctant as the cab of the truck concerned, had window pillars that would be very fragile in 1:76 scale. The answer was to use white metal.

Barry asked around, but no one else was actively interested, so he sought advice, and acquired his own casting machine and associated equipment, for £300, and decided to do it himself.

The result was that BW Models started in June 1991. By 1992 Barry had got some kits ready for sale, and placed advertisements in the military model press. Over the next 18 months he attended many toy fairs and model shows within reasonable travelling distance, whilst still continuing to work as a civil servant. He has always been a one man concern, but gradually expanded, and in 1994 asked a friend to assist with some masters, to increase the range of kits available in his range. Barry has seen steady growth since, and in 2009 had the best year for some time. He feels that people are now more shrewd about how they spend their leisure time and money, and thus try to do so profitably to them.

Thor Missile System with tractor and trailer

Finally in 2004 Barry retired at 55 with a reasonable pension, and has been able to concentrate more on his white metal business.

The work has continued to go from strength to strength, which Barry attributes to being clear about what customers want. He will listen to ideas, but takes care to assess the likely demand for a new model. Land Rover variants have always been popular, and recently a long term customer opened a model shop in Belfast and asked if he could stock his range of Northern Ireland military vehicles.

Both the flow of ideas and subsequent suggestions have generated a large increase in the number of Northern Ireland related vehicles in the range. Barry finds that each model will break even financially at about 40 models being made and sold, and some will achieve this in 12 months, whilst others are yet to make it.

He never drops a model from his range, as there is still an occasional demand for every one of them. This is a good example of a specialist producer who has found his market, and serves it well. It is reassuring that such models will continue for some time yet.

CHAPTER EIGHT

ON THE BUSES

The aura that surrounds everything related to buses is quite staggering. We are all aware of the popularity of collecting bus numbers as a child, and thus all the major tinplate, then diecast makers have made sure that our memories of buses familiar from childhood are available for us to enjoy. Correspondingly, there have been many model bus enthusiasts who have sought to fill gaps in their model bus collections by making their own models.

Whilst the interests of both Ray and David have been predominantly cars, it has still not been easy to locate and record the stories of some of those early model bus makers. Many companies, such as Westward, no longer appear to be in existence, and others were small and transitory in their influence, and are not mentioned here. However, here are some of the fascinating stories we have uncovered from those which persisted, and became icons of a very dedicated field of modelling –

Anbrico
Model Railways and Buses

Anbrico is one of the earliest producers of model buses we have found, and the following history is based on the Anbrico Scale Models: Hand Built History website, with acknowledgements.

The name Anbrico first appeared in 1932 when it was used in connection with hand built scale models, in particular model railway items in 0 gauge for the home market. As the years went by the firm became known as Anbrico Scale Models and all types of models were made for sale in countries all over the world. The firm was also producing for other firms in the model trade. Some larger models were built from 1952 in 1:12 scale for bus and coach operators for use in booking offices around the UK, and some models appeared on the manufacturers stand at the Commercial Motor Show at Earls Court in the early 1950s.

Anbrico Scale Models produced the first 00 models of the new British Railways Diesel Multiple Units

00 Bedford Short Tipper

(DMUs) about to be supplied to the Leeds/Bradford area in the early 1950s. A model shop in Leeds bought the first batch of 6 twin units just weeks before the real prototypes appeared in service. As a result of this order and adverts at that time more orders came during the following weeks from model shops in Manchester and London. Over the next few years the range increased until all types of DMUs and rail buses were produced in 00 scale.

In the early 1960s the introduction of a 00 range of coaches from the big four operators (LMS, GWR, LNER and SR) required part time staff to be employed to assemble parts. From the start the range was inclusive of finer detailed items such as screw couplings, sprung buffers and braided vacuum pipes and of course the lining found on these earlier carriages. Around this time a well known model firm dealing in the larger scales asked if Anbrico could supply them with a range of 0 gauge pullman coaches. This work was undertaken and a range of pullmans was produced for them over several years. In later years they were produced only to special

AC 00 Railcar

00 Bradford Balcony Standard Tram

order as required for individual customers.

Over the years the ranges became very popular and production methods were changed and improvements made to give a more detailed appearance from experience gained from the range of '00' coaches being produced. Some twin car units were mounted on a scale length of track on a wooden plinth, intended to be given to potential customers throughout the world as Christmas presents that year from British United Traction. In later years after being 'handed on' these turned up from various places to be motorised by Anbrico for use by the new owners on their model railways.

As a result of numerous requests from model railway enthusiasts, a range of 00 diesel locomotives was being built up, and in due course these included the option of the inclusion of extra detail as required by individual customers.

In the early 1960s a small range of ready to run trams was produced in 00 which came as a result of a trade order. This became popular with both customers in U.K. and abroad as they were available on either the '00' or 'TT' gauge chassis, and absorbed a considerable amount of their small skilled staff's time.

In early 1965 an order was received from British Railways Scottish Region for a 00 model of the three car Glasgow suburban electric Blue Train to be mounted on a length of scale track on a wooden plinth with posts and overhead wires. The completed model was presented to the Queen and Duke of Edinburgh on a visit to see the line in Scotland in July

LMS Brake Van

1965. As a result of this initial work the Glasgow Blue Train was later added to the lists.

By 1968 the first in a range of 00 cast metal bus kits was introduced which included popular British double and single deck buses and coaches. It was decided some time later to transfer the range of brass trams over to cast white metal kits. This range covered the lack of types available for use with model railways, but added interest was found from enthusiasts who just enjoyed making models of buses and trams. One enthusiast group that was just starting saw the advert and made contact to ascertain if the types they were interested in could be produced for them.

Kit production continued until July 1987, during which time some 80 cast metal kits were available including one N gauge diesel locomotive with the '00' kits covering buses, trolleybuses, trams, lorries and one diesel locomotive.

00 Burrell road Locomotive

The hand built model section was closed some time later after the completion of some outstanding orders for models and patterns for firms in the model trade. The Pudsey premises containing the model side of the business and showroom were sold and converted into a 4 bedroomed house. All items connected with the scale model business were sold off to other firms and private collectors when the old premises were emptied for the conversion. All the models from the showcases in the Pudsey showroom became part of the private collection of one of the business partners, to be retained to illustrate the history of the firm since the original models were made in 1932. Most of the range of bus kits pioneered by Anbrico have since been introduced in complete form, in various liveries, by several diecast firms, and can be seen in model shops throughout the UK and in various other countries.

Since production ceased there has been a sharp rise in the second hand sale prices of all the hand built models. eBay prices in particular show this when unopened kits appear for sale, with the fully built models as a rule fetching a lower resale amount.

00 Fowler SE

However the range of ready to run 00 railway coaches and DMUs very rarely come up for sale. These are often sought through collector's adverts in most of the popular model magazines.

Anbrico Video Services was established in the late 1970s, in independent premises, to cater for the customer looking for prototype information on some of the lesser known private railways in Europe and, in particular, Switzerland. Over the years a range of over 130 hour long video films was produced from the information collected in Austria, Czech Republic, Germany, Holland, Ireland, Italy, Portugal, Switzerland and the U.K. covering railways, light rail, trams and trolleybuses.

00 Isle of Man railcar

These films were used by transport bodies when considering the use of light rail schemes, but the main users were of course enthusiasts from all over the world, with many tapes going out to America and Canada. Over the years Anbrico has done work for several of the major construction and demolition firms in the UK either 'in house' or filming out on location with one of these firms still using the services after more than 18 years.

As well as orders received, direct work has been undertaken with several groups of photographic shops throughout the UK, offering transfer from ciné, slides and prints to video. No job was considered too small, as often copies of a subject were received that had a running time of only 2 minutes, received from solicitors, police or law courts in the Leeds area seeking a same day turn round.

00 Nettle Railcar

Other subjects have included weddings either in the UK or abroad. Several video productions were undertaken either to advertise a product on television such as bathrooms or showers. Copies illustrating holiday resorts and apartments were also undertaken for holiday companies.

A comprehensive website provides ample information for the customer, and so the long established Anbrico name lives on.

John Gay
Model Buses

Almost all model bus collectors around the world will know the name John Gay. John's lists of buses for sale are legendary, and his knowledge of the bus scene is limitless.

It's not surprising therefore, that the first toy he remembers being given by his parents for Christmas in 1944 was the Dinky Toy 29c pre-war double decker. He was 6 years old at the time and living in Pembury. The shop where it was bought in Tunbridge Wells was apparently rationing the toys they sold, so he was lucky to get it! John remembers that he carved the rear stairs out as he felt they were unsightly, and did the same with the next 29c.

As with many other children in those days, John travelled to school by bus, and it was this daily exposure to omnibus pleasure on AEC Regents that fuelled his growing enjoyment for collecting, along with the fact that his father worked for Maidstone & District Motor Services. In 1949, on moving to Tunbridge Wells, five Brimtoy buses were disposed of by his parents, probably because they were never played with but most of the Dinky Toys survived. John would often buy another toy cheaply, in order to swap it for yet another model bus at school. He has kept a record of these early exchanges through his personal notebooks. By the early 1950s, while still at school, John had around 80 diecast model buses and 30 cars and trucks in his collection, mostly Dinky Toys.

He began his working career with a shipping company in London, moving on after a year into

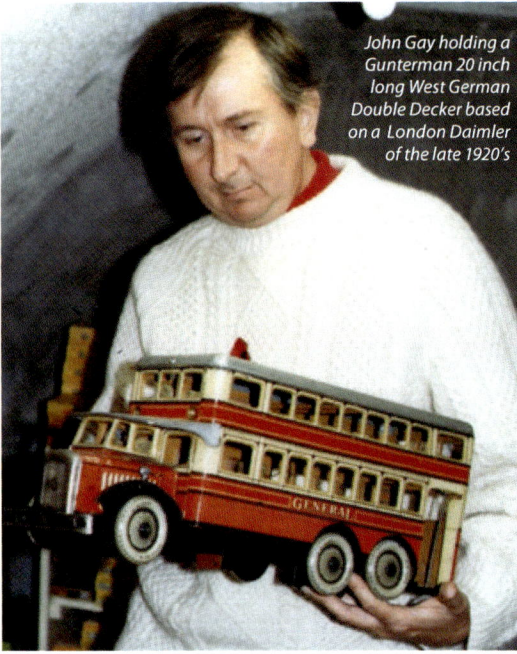

John Gay holding a Gunterman 20 inch long West German Double Decker based on a London Daimler of the late 1920's

when they found it increasingly impossible to buy ink for it that they decided to bin it in 2004, join the 21st century and computerise their lists!

Around 1976, with magazines promoting the hobby worldwide, John found that his export business really took off. It was not long before well over 50% of his models were exported every year, including a large proportion of buses. Domestically, bus kits featured strongly in sales right through to the late 1990s. During the 1980s, as many customers were from the USA, annual business trips were made to ensure good relationships were maintained.

John recalls that when EFE were launched in 1989 this was a bad day for kit makers of buses. The market became very competitive, evidenced by Corgi Toys using many of John's models as a guide for their new products, this work being carried out by Bassett Lowke. John was all set to buy the Bassett Lowke company for £25,000, the seller's price, when it suddenly fell through without explanation and the next thing, there was an announcement that Corgi had purchased the company.

commodities, and then into the Royal Air Force for National Service, where he trained as a typist. He returned to the city to the same company and at the age of 21 became the youngest member of the London Commodity Exchange, trading in coffee. In the early 1970s the city was changing and after 3 different jobs he left in1974. By this time John's collection had reached well over four figures for buses plus even more cars and commercial vehicles. His experience of trading models for his own collection determined this as a possible career path, creating a business out of his hobby. He became self employed in 1975, with his wife Valerie joining him in the business in 1976, taking over production of price lists and all the back office work essential to making everything run smoothly. One of his first purchases was not toys but a large secondhand commercial size Roneo duplicator, which ended up lasting nearly 30 years! It was only

Pirate Models Bristol K5G Maidstone & District

John began stocking white metal kits right from the outset, including early ranges such as Anbrico, Brackenborough, Pirate and Westward. In 1992 John bought Pirate, soon followed in 1994 by buying Lowland from Barry Lester. John immediately commissioned new models and these started to come into production in 1993. By 1996 this had doubled turnover for Pirate. Most new models were OO except for five HO French models for Paris. The Wistow Company came into John's ownership in 1997, with its 7mm lines of buses and trams. After acquiring the white metal bus companies, John continued to work with Ron Charlton, who had always made the majority of bus castings and also used Barry Lester as his pattern maker.

Partly inspired by a visit there in 1982, John decided to expand his kit range to include Hong Kong buses, the first being 2 Seddon Pennines based on existing UK kits. They only needed new fronts/

Pirate Models AEC Regent LPTB

Pirate Models Dennis Lowliner Aldershot & District

rears and proved very successful. This immediately prompted John to commission new kits and these started to come into production in 1996. These were the first accurate scale kits by any maker for Hong Kong and developed rapidly into a range of over 60 variations. Sales fell away quickly as most were immediately copied by volume manufacturers, with ABC using the Pirate Guy 'Long Dragon' in their advertisements. At this stage John feels that it was a tribute to the expertise of Barry Lester, in his view a brilliant pattern maker, who only had measurements and photos to work from to produce the patterns for Hong Kong buses.

The Pirate OO range has been added to every year, accounting for some 80 new kits plus many more variations. Barry Lester produced high quality patterns for Pirate which john feels are among the best in the range. Working closely with John, kits were greatly improved with detail and weight. The original RT bus for instance was reduced in weight by 25% when the pre-war and coach versions were introduced. Manufacturing of Pirate kits from 1968

was in the hands of Ron Charlton whose dedication and expertise over the years has assured the success of Pirate, and he continued casting until his retirement in 2002. Since then Dave Ellis of South Eastern Finecast has been providing an excellent service.

In 2007 several new HO kits were issued for the USA, bringing the total to 33 variants.

White metal bus kit production is probably now at an all time low and looks set to stay that way. Most of John's customers are 60 plus, technical skills are no longer taught, therefore John finds that virtually no youngsters are coming into the hobby. He feels that there will be a niche market for kits not produced by the bigger manufacturers, but even these may be short lived as most manufacturers are also 50 years and more. If demand for the specialist metal alloy drops too low, the raw material may also no longer be available, but John hopes that is a long way off. Fortunately there are still modellers who prefer the feel of a white metal kit to that of a resin kit. He feels confident that with a wide range of buses not copied, he is in a good position to supply that niche kit for the specialist.

Pirate Models Leyland P2 Sheffield

The Model Bus Federation

Co-founders Bob Heathcote and Martin Popplewell

Two enthusiastic bus modellers, Bob Heathcote and Martin Popplewell founded the MBF in 1968 as a way of extending their hobby by communicating with other modellers and swapping ideas and tips to help improve their modelling. Both founder members

were pupils of Bradford Grammar School, and discovered they had a common interest in buses, and also model buses.

Bob Heathcote is a native of Huddersfield, but had moved to Bradford and his interests in the late 1960s were directed more towards trolleybuses. Bob remains a central figure within the MBF and is currently a committee member as well as membership secretary. He currently resides in Sheffield, where he has taken up the position as Reverend of the United Reform Church in the city.

Both Bob and Martin were instrumental in persuading early white metal kit manufacturers, such as Anbrico, into producing 1:76 scale bus kits, initially for the benefit of MBF members.

In later years, the MBF has been responsible for a small range of white metal bus kits in its own right,

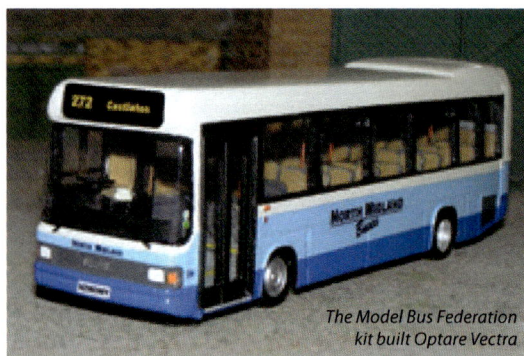

*The Model Bus Federation
kit built Optare Vectra*

these being the all Leyland, Royal Tiger 1950s coach, produced by Mark Hughes models, and the MAN Optare Vectra kit, produced by RTC models.

Since these white metal kits have been produced, the emphasis has been on the production of resin bus kits, and a number have been made available to MBF members.

The Federation has grown over these 43 years to become an organisation of over 1000 members worldwide. It has an elected committee, and aims to share and promote new ideas, relating to model buses, trolleybuses and trams.

Within the UK it has a regional structure, with each geographical area organising its own shows, trips and meetings through local groups led by an area secretary. An impressive colour journal is produced and distributed every month, and its own in house sales department provides a stock of kits and spare parts to keep members enthusiasm high!

National meetings involving all members provide an opportunity to meet other modellers from around the country, and some of these involve shows and competitions.

The Federation has a publicity officer, Karl Kingston, who looks after the promotion of the club, and other officers, who run each part of what is a vibrant organisation.

CHAPTER NINE

TRAINS, PLANES AND BOATS

In the early days of developing casting processes, model railways were the subject that seemed to attract considerable interest from potential producers. Firstly, lineside accessories would appear, and then rolling stock, followed by the first locomotive kit.

A dedicated band of enthusiasts have found that model planes in white metal have been a viable proposition. For obvious reasons, white metal was not thought to be an appropriate material for model boats, but history recorded here tells us otherwise.

Trains in White Metal

Whilst white metal is a medium best known for model cars, there has been a small but significant sector of the model railway market that has benefited greatly from the development of white metal as a model material.

1899 saw the very first Bassett Lowke catalogue, and the fortunes of the big producers such as Hornby and Trix have been well documented, yet the model railway industry and hobby has been reliant since the 1950s on a cottage industry of producers making white metal kits.

It has been recorded that Frank Vescoe of Bec Kits saw and utilised the use of centrifuges first. Certainly Bec's rolling stock took a few more years to appear but Vescoe, the Keysers and Bob Wills all knew one another. Is it reasonable to think they shared technology, which leaves us very unclear who came first!

Nevertheless, all model railway enthusiasts will wish, at some stage, to personalise their locomotives, rolling stock or lineside accessories, in order to create a fictitious place, to create a more super detailed train, or just to enjoy the construction of a unique or scarce piece of railway history. The early producers of white metal castings met the demand for such enthusiasts to create their own rolling stock, and special locomotives. We are indebted to Robert Forsythe for his assistance, from an extensive library of both information and photographs, in compiling the following summaries.

Cotswold

Cotswold Scale Models were supplying kit built locos in 1968, from Wotton under Edge, and a year later, announced their own kit of a mechanical horse, with a locomotive coming later that year. Buses followed, and it is known that they had first moved to Kingswood, then in 1971 to Bristol. Westward Scale Models also used the same address in Bristol at that time. Locomotive kits followed, and were well known for their brass milled chassis. Cotswold had taken over the range of R&J supplies, and Ron Charlton was the proprietor by 1975.

By 1981 Cotswold and their associated ranges were all transferred to Nu-Cast and Bill Stott.

K's

The manufacturer known as K's is often credited with the issue of the first white metal kit. In 1957, it released a kit of the GWR 0-4-2T, and earned itself a place in this history. Its full commercial name was N.& K. C. Keyser Ltd, and the N was father or Pop Keyser, as he was mostly known. He was of German origin, and opened a tobacconist shop which

K's SR Brake

became a model shop in the 1940s at Hanover Court in Uxbridge road, London. The whole family were involved, including Mrs Keyser and their son Ken. Ken was making scratch built locos from 1946, which were displayed in the shop.

K's GWR Railcar

Ken saw a jeweller's centrifugal casting machine and realised it could enable the production of small items in white metal. He began with small components, then complete wagon kits. By 1957, despite the fact that Bob Wills was already at the same point, K's launched their first locomotive kit at the Model Railway Club show. This was a complete package, including wheels motor and gears.

K's K62 Coronation Loco

As the range grew, the family moved the business to a purpose built factory near Willesden Junction station, where they remained for the next 12 years. Pop Keyser died in 1966, and it was down to Ken and his two sons Melvyn and Graham to orchestrate the next stage of the company's development, involving relocation to a factory in Banbury.

Ken's sons had seen the rise in plastic rolling stock kits, and oversaw the investment in injection moulding machines, and plastic used for rolling stock, and from 1970, resin wheel centres. In 1978 the whole of the TT range of products was sold to Adrian Swain, trading as ABS.

Locomotives continued to be manufactured until at least 1983, but after that K's history is less clear, with other players involved in the wholesaling and marketing, including Nu-Cast, which led to adverts for bodies appearing as Nu-Kays. Ken Keyser died in 1989, and a year later the HMC Group bought much of the K's ranges. The name and ranges were then subsequently acquired by Autocom, but with a statement that the marketing would still be under the Nu-Cast banner.

Nu-Cast

The Nu-Cast company history begins in a retail shop started by Bill Stott, a model railway enthusiast who had moved in the mid 1960s to Shotton, County Durham.

From local exhibitions he progressed to part time trading, then gave up his job with the Salvation Army to launch Nu-Sto Scale models in 1969. Six prototype handbuilt cast locomotive were on offer, and with the advertising of the shop, a Q6 model was also to be available as a kit.

It appears that the development of the shop then took precedence, and by the end of 1974, just three more locos had become available. Whilst Nu-Sto Scale models continued for some years as a shop, Nu-Cast Model engineering became the kit and

handbuilt production facility in separate premises. Apparently, a range of car kits known as Auto Replicas were part of Nu-Cast in 1979.

Investment continued, resulting in claims of the best loco kit range available, and a move in 1987 to a factory unit north of Hartlepool. It seems that rumours were rife of Bill Stott purchasing the K's range, and of moves to Lincolnshire, but what is known is that Adrian Swain, who had been involved for some time in the design work for Nu-Cast, bought the range of wagons and the Wickham trolley in 1992. By 1993, Nu-Cast had moved again to Andover, and the two names of K's and Nu-Cast had been integrated into one business by Autocom.

Wills

Bob Wills' story and his success in the white metal business has been documented elsewhere in this book, but as far as trains are concerned, Bob's first loco kit was launched at the October 1955 Model Railway Show. He had started with 0 gauge white metal castings, but 00 gauge components were added at the show. White metal wagons came along and by 1962 there were eight in the range. These still feature in the South Eastern Finecast catalogues.

Wills LSWR G6

Bob's first wagon kit pre-dated the K's release, but it wasn't until 1959 that his first two locomotives appeared. By 1964 22 locos were in the range, with a preference for southern and Great Western prototypes.

During the period up to 1980 new releases dropped, but the fine definition of Bob's kits was now well known and popular. Through this time Bob chose to develop the manufacturing operations as a separate company, known as Industrial Display Company Limited, with him as Managing Director. Whilst this remained the structure for the Wills Scenic Series until 1997, the Wills Finecast range of rolling stock was transferred to South Eastern Finecast in

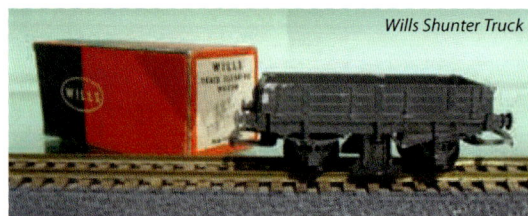
Wills Shunter Truck

South Eastern Finecast SEC/SR/BR Kirtley R1 044T

June 1988. By acquiring the Stephen Poole range of wheels, and developing a nickel silver chassis kit for his loco kits, Bob ensured that Wills were still at the forefront of innovation in this field.

The need to upgrade the loco range with etched metal components, and to develop the Scenic Series in a totally different media, led Bob to pass over the business to Dave Ellis, and South Eastern Finecast then carried on the same traditions. The company was sold in April 1997, but Bob Wills remained a frequent visitor to Dave Ellis in Forest Row.

By March 1999, all Wills Scenic Series production was moved to the Ratio factory at Buckfastleigh, which meant that Wills had become a part of Peco.

With the acquisition by Dave Ellis of Wills, the development work associated with incorporating etched nickel silver chassis, re-engineering the twenty year old kit components, and entirely new kits began. Dave used a network of people to assist with design, which included Alistair Rolfe of Modeltec and Paul Vine of Precision Miniature Arts. Paul was originally one of Dave's Saturday lads working in the shop. Ray Rogers became involved in the mid 1990s, and by 1999 Alistair Rolfe had launched his own range called No Nonsense Kits.

South Eastern Finecast SR/BR Class 'W' 264T

Ron Goult of Little Engines established a working relationship with Dave which entailed Goult redesigning kits for Dave, whilst Dave cast the Little Engines range.

More on Dave Ellis's role in developing and sustaining the model car ranges of Wills can be found elsewhere in this book.

GEM

George E Mellor entered the model railway trade in 1929, and remained involved until he died on January 3rd 1994. Born in 1911, he grew up in Colwyn Bay and never moved away. Amongst Mellor's products, GEM's 4mm cast white metal loco

kits were well known, appearing in 1964.

Before that GEM's main stock in trade had been 16.5mm gauge trackwork and a wide assortment of handbuilt rolling stock. The company had no casting ability, but George was an innovator and the success of Wills and K's was not lost on him nor was Tri-ang's early success with TT gauge.

GEM LMS 460 Prince of Wales

One of the lines in the GEM 1956 catalogue was the small range of products under the S&B name. The S in S&B stood for Rex Stedman of Leeds Model Company fame. After Stedman died in 1959, GEM obtained the S&B business and with it the ability to cast in white metal. The result was that from 1963 GEM joined the league then composed of K's, Wills and Bec to become one of the four big names in 1960s white metal railway kits. By the end of the decade GEM's contribution had been established in TT and OO, with a leaning for the LNWR engines so familiar to anyone living on the North Wales Coast in George's lifetime.

The TT range although extensive in its day withered after the 1970s, until ultimately in 1993 it was sold to 3mm Scale Model Railways with which it remained. By then GEM was actually in the hands of the gentleman who owned the company until 1997. This was Roy Dock, one time editor of the Model Railway News, who left that magazine for life with GEM. A Railway Modeller announcement stated that from the 1st of

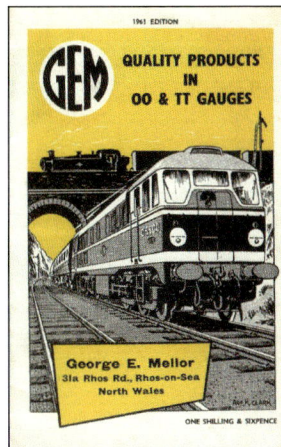
1961 GEM Catalogue

1963 GEM Catalogue

May 1977 GEM was a partnership between Dock and Mellor. Dock became financially responsible for the company, Mellor retaining a 'fatherly' role. Twenty years after his involvement commenced Dock was a sick man. He had been with the GEM stand, as so often, at the York Easter Show in 1996. Later that year a stroke laid him low.

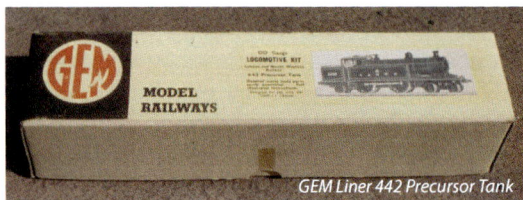

GEM Liner 442 Precursor Tank

The upshot of this was the September 1997 announcement that the whole GEM range as then constituted had been sold to Terry Henson's Thameshead Models of Bedford. Since 2000 kits have been upgraded and re-released. In that year the N gauge GWR 28xx appeared and by early 2007 twelve in OO were available again. The modern releases all have an etched nickel silver chassis kit which Terry's team has produced.

MTK

Did Colin Massingham and his Modern Tractions Kits become legends in his lifetime? Undoubtedly Colin did a tremendous amount of good for railway enthusiasm, whether in the world of full scale preservation, or in the realm of modelling. In both he was a pioneer of interest in modern traction.

Colin was 57 when he died on the 30th January 1996. Since the early 1970s, he had been a significant figure in the world of Modern Traction. He was a practical person, happy in the company of railwaymen, preferably in a cab. He drove lorries, preserved buses, and in 1970 decided to make model railway kits. He was running the Slough Model Centre then and from there, Modern Traction Kits was launched with its first release for a cast white metal Class 24. In the early 1970s as his range expanded, his interest took on full size locos. In 1973 he was instrumental in the purchase of the first main line diesel to be privately preserved, the D821 Greyhound.

Initially his medium was cast white metal but later punched aluminium and etched brass were enthusiastically adopted. He realised punched aluminium enabled effective production of multiple units and coaching stock. His was a cottage industry and he expected the modeller to help himself. The standard he set was workmanlike not exhibition.

Colin's choice of prototype was staggering, and he only needed a prototype to be suggested and he would have a go at producing a model. Many of his choices were offered in different scales and they evolved in specification frequently. After his death, the 4mm scale models went to Alistair Rolfe's No-Nonsense Kits, much of the 7mm range is with Nationalised Railways, whilst the 2mm scale models have seen a variety of owners.

Colin remained up to the minute to the last and even in the late 1980s and 1990s quite a galaxy of new units appeared of prototypes, and Colin was usually the first to sell a new model.

Aeroplanes in White Metal

In scanning the entire white metal model industry, it is clear that model aeroplanes were a small but significant part of the story. The following information has largely been put together with the assistance of Derek Barratt, whose range called MetalModels covered both commercial vehicles and also aeroplanes. Derek had been assembling a list of the smaller, low-volume producers from around 1985 onwards and the following therefore excludes most of the more recent ranges of 1:200 scale jet airliners. The majority of these models – and there is a bewildering host of them - originate in the Far East.

1:200 has been given the name 'The Collector's Scale' first in MetalModels advertising, to illustrate the advantages of the scale for displaying a collection of aeroplane models, reflecting the fact

Wojtek Benzinski's Rapide

that quite a number can be arranged in a relatively small space.

This scale had already been used in the U.K and France by Dinky Toys, who together with Solido, Tekno, Mercury and Tootsietoy dominated the

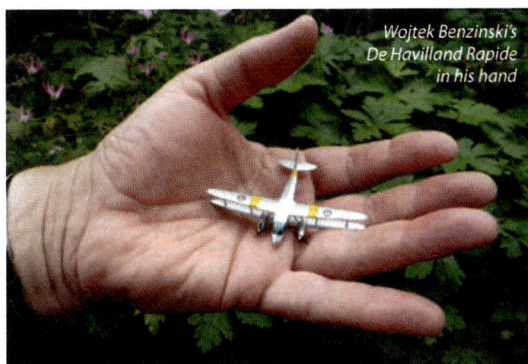
Wojtek Benzinski's De Havilland Rapide in his hand

market with their diecast offerings. Plastic aeroplane models were also prevalent in the 1940s and 50s, with Wiking of Germany monopolising the 1:200 plastic scene for many years. All of these brands, had ceased making small-scale aircraft models by the mid-1960s, and it was at this time that these older toys became recognised as obsolete, collectable items. Within a couple of decades many examples, especially those in good condition, were getting scarce and the rarest models were becoming much too expensive for most collectors. In fact, these toys, for that is what they are, actually covered only a limited number of originals. The complete small scale Dinky Toys range from 1934 to 1965, for example, covered less than fifty basic castings.

Chris Sayer's Fairey Autodyne A

A void became apparent, with collectors frustrated at being unable to add to their collections when they discovered that their favourite planes were not modelled. At about this time, the war gaming hobby was expanding to include aerial conflicts as well as land and sea battles, and an increasing number of enthusiasts were in the market for miniature aeroplanes. In response, a number of castings appeared, mainly from small cottage manufacturers in England, to meet war-gamers' requirements. These standardised on the very small 1:300 scale which, although ideal for the intended purpose, usually offered little in the way of detail. A few of these manufacturers then began to offer slightly larger 1:200 models and in so doing, laid the foundations for a whole new chapter of model aeroplane collecting.

As a result, since the 1970s a number of 1:200

producers have appeared on the scene. Some delivered models that are high volume, high pressure die-casting, or from injection-moulded plastic, requiring expensive machinery capable of producing large quantities. By contrast the English low-volume makers adopted a far more affordable technique of casting low melting point, lead-based alloys (white-metal) in rubber moulds using simple centrifugal casting machines.

Chris Sayer's Beech 7

Foremost in England amongst the pioneers of the early 1980s was Dennis Knight, creator of the Helmet Miniature Aircraft range. Dennis himself made some of the masters for his 1930s type biplane models, whilst commissioning originals for the bulk of his range from others. Notable amongst these were Brian Lawrence and C.A. 'Tommy' Atkins, the latter being responsible for the majority of Helmet originals.' Indeed, it is fair to say that many of the subsequent English producers owe a huge debt to Tommy as the master pattern maker responsible for creating the originals of many of their models. Without his efforts there would be far less of the English 1:200 production.

Other early birds in the field, responsible for their own masters and models, included John Alcott, Leighton Fletcher (Aerocrafts), and Rod Langton (Langton Miniatures). Skytrex Ltd was also an early pioneer.

Chris Sayer's SR177

The 1990s saw a raft of new entrants to the 1:200 field, including Armitage Models, M. Johnson's Miniature Aircraft Models, The Norfolk Group, Metal Models, Aircast, The Aerodrome, Hempsall Models and Vapour Trails, all commissioning their masters from Tommy Atkins. Amongst other makers arriving on the scene three names are well known to collectors; Martin Beacom (Small World Models), Western Models – a major producer in the field - and Eclipse Models, these three being unusual in not relying upon Tommy Atkins for their masters.

Chris Sayer's TSR2

Below are a few details about some of these producers, which may shed some light on any examples of their models that new and future collectors may acquire.

Leighton Fletcher's range known as Aerocrafts featured fighter and trainer types, frequently those flown by the man himself. Interestingly, both Tommy Atkins and Leighton were R.A.F. fighter pilots in the 1950s. Not only did Leighton create his own patterns but he also produced the castings, by adapting the traditional jeweller's method of pouring hot metal into a handheld mould. He developed this technique to an advanced level, achieving some intricate results including a one-piece Gladiator. His models were always sold as plain castings. Sadly, Leighton Fletcher passed away in 2010.

Paul Howard (left) with Dennis Knight (right). Paul has just agreed to buy Dennis' Helmet business and they're shaking on the deal

The Aerodrome was the title adopted by David Austin for a series of 1:200 models, predominantly of civilian types, as an offshoot of his well known Dinky Toys trading business. The masters for this series were again the handiwork of Tommy Atkins. It is thought that only a small number of finished models appeared on the market, built by various people for David. A small, engraved windsock under the wing identifies his models. MetalModels later purchased most of the masters. David would often be seen at Christie's and Phillips in London

purchasing rare Dinky aircraft at what were felt to be high prices. Later, at The Aerodrome in Oxford, they would appear on his list and seemed to sell, even at those high prices. His most successful venture was his white metal reproductions of the proposed but unreleased Dinky Toys D.H Flamingo to which he assigned the appropriate number 62f.

Simon de Montfalcon created a limited series of attractive models in the mid 1990s under the Aircast name. These models, including the Supermarine 224 and SARO A1 flying boat jet fighter, were all derived from Atkins masters. It is believed that they were sold either as plain castings or in finished and painted form. Aircast disappeared from the scene after a few years and the fate of the original models is unknown.

In the 1980s John Alcott produced a limited number of beautifully made 1:200 models of large aircraft, initially modifying Dinky Toys Comet castings with white metal components to create Nimrod, MR2 and AEW3 surveillance 'planes. In association with Victor Bailey, John then produced a Lockheed Constellation and a Bristol Britannia wholly in white metal sold in Veteran & Vintage packaging, the trade name of Victor Bailey's Portslade-based collectable toy business. Finding the material not up to the quality he wished, he turned to aluminium, and created a Liberator and B36 Peacemaker. However, this medium proved too expensive and the project under the Veteran & Vintage banner was shelved. They were expensive models for their time, in line with their superb quality, and survivors still stand comparison with later competitors today.

Michael Armitage produced a B-58 Hustler model in the early 1990s and this model was later acquired by Derek Barratt who reissued it in more detailed form in his MetalModels range. An F-111 was also proposed but the master was sold on to Brian Keates before any were sold. Michael was one of the original makers that pooled resources in forming the Norfolk Group.

Over the last fifteen years or so Wojtek Benzinski

John Alcott, who made aeroplanes for Veteran & Vintage, and for himself

has applied his skills to a variety of other maker's castings, especially Aerocrafts, and the superb results grace many a collection. As a former British Airways engineer, his painstaking approach is self evident and nowhere more so than in his new array of Cloud Break models, introduced in 2007. They encompass a diverse range of subjects, focussing on previously neglected types such as the DHC Beaver and Otter, Noorduyn Norseman and a choice of Austers. A further development is a link with Metal Models to produce models of the principal USAF jet fighters of the 1950-1965 era and the first fruits of this collaboration should appear in 2012.

Derek Barratt's Lockheed C 141A
Starfighter Airpower Series for MetalModels

Richard Bizley worked as a talented sub-contractor for Western Models, finishing their products before establishing his own range of modern jet fighter models. Not surprisingly, Western provided the castings for this range, known as Eclipse, and the models are particularly noteworthy for Richard's excellent, highly detailed finishes. More recently Richard has devoted an increasing amount of time to his successful Bizleyart company, as he is also an extremely talented painter, and Helmet Miniatures have taken over the marketing of Eclipse models.

Dennis Knight, based in Betchworth, Surrey, was behind Helmet models, offering either fully finished items (with or without wheels & propellers, according to customer choice) or as plain castings for the buyer to assemble. Factory finished models may be identified by the DK monogram with date, painted on the undersides. Later Helmet releases included larger resin models, sourced from Ron Crawford's HBM range, with Helmet additions of metal propellers and undercarriages. Paul Howard and Ann Lister, who continue production of both kits and finished models under the Helmet Historical Aircraft label, purchased the entire Helmet range and business in 2007.

Fred Hempsall employs his model making skills across a variety of fields and his professional abilities

are very evident in his 1:200 aeroplane models. His production includes models from his own catalogue as well as finishing other maker's castings to customer order. Fred has long collaborated with Tommy Atkins in the joint production of models of unusual subjects, usually types close to Tommy's heart. These shared projects, and items such as the inter-war period R.A.F. flying boats, may be found on Fred's list. It may also be mentioned that at various times in the 1990s, prior to the overall disposal of most of his moulds and masters, Tommy sold off considerable quantities of uncollected and other forfeit castings, of various origins, along with some speculatively produced castings, to recover his outlay. Fred, amongst others, purchased these in some quantity and a dwindling stock of these items still remains, allowing occasional manufacture of otherwise long-gone models. Another speciality from the Hempsall works includes the full refinishing of Western Models products, to a professional standard, with the client supplying the model.

Melvyn Johnson released a series of R.A.F. jet fighter and trainer models around 1992-1995 under the Miniature Aircraft Models label. These included some unique types in this scale such as a Gloster Javelin and Folland Gnat. All were sold built, painted and boxed. The masters were subsequently sold on to Brian Keates.

Derek Barratt's Rockwell B
1-A Airwell Lancer Airpower Series

Langton Miniatures, still in operation at the time of writing, produce an eclectic mix of 1:200 seaplanes and flying-boats, covering types that saw action around the coasts of Britain in WW1. These are sold as kits with whitemetal and etched brass parts, which are so well presented they appeal as collectable items in themselves and it is almost a shame to make them! Transfers (decals) are included. Langton Miniatures also produces an extensive range of ship models, including six different North Sea craft in

Derek Barratt's Speed in the Air Series

1:200 scale to complement the aeroplanes, along with three WW1 RNAS vehicles to the same scale.

As indicated above, Derek Barratt started the MetalModels range of aircraft in 1991, the name being resurrected from an earlier range of model railway items. The first years were spent building and painting other maker's items for resale, notably Aerocrafts and a number of the early HBM models (the first HBM models were metal castings, prior to the appearance of the universally known resin range). The first actual MetalModels product, and the first of the Speed in the Air series, was the S6B. A second series of 1950s/1960s USAF types was launched later, most production being sold through Collectors Aircraft Models under the Airpower label, whilst a more recent introduction is the Golden Age range featuring various types from the 1930s. The majority of output 1500+ to date has been of fully finished, boxed models, though a few kits were sold. All finished models carry either the MetalModels or Airpower decal below, or in the case of other makers' castings, a DB monogram may appear. These decals were never included with any kits.

Mick Armitage, Melvyn Johnson, Derek Barratt and Chris Sayer were all aviation enthusiasts living in Norfolk, England, in the early 1990s. The first three had already commenced kitchen-table production of 1:200 models of small types under their own labels. However, all four had a common desire to produce models of rather larger types and, to share the heavier costs that would involve, the Norfolk Group was formed between them for this purpose. The first joint effort was the Short Sunderland (the master being provided by Tommy Atkins, as was the case with most of their models), which was generally sold in kit form, though a handful of built-up models were also produced. This was followed by a short series of USAAF types, namely the L4 Piper Cub, C-47, B-26 and finally various marks of the B-17. The latter started life as a multi-part Atkins master which was passed to Leighton Fletcher for extra detailing

and which emerged, cast by Leighton, with larger, one-piece, components. All, like the Sunderland, were usually sold as kits with just a few fully finished examples being offered. Various transfers were available for the C-47, allowing it to be finished as a USAAF Skytrain or an R.A.F. Dakota, or even in China National Airways DC-21/2 form! One footnote, to answer future historians who may stumble upon it, is that a few models were advertised, and may even have been labelled, as Macadam kits, from the acronym MickAndChrisAndDerekAndMelvyn.

During this period both Mick and Melvyn left the group to follow other interests, whilst Wojtek Benzinski joined to add his expertise to the effort, particularly in the shape of the later B-25 model.

Chris Sayer has blessed his new array of 1:200 kits with the appropriate name of Shed Models, reflecting the inner sanctum from whence the new arrivals emerge! The choice of types in this new, 2008, line up also reflects considerable discernment, as it comprises models of aircraft never seen before in the scale, including many gone but by no means forgotten machines. There is a definite link to local history with two impressive Boulton Paul creations, in the shape of the Overstrand and Sidestrand 1930s bombers, as well as a diverse array of minor and experimental types. Shed models will mainly be available in kit form though it may be possible to undertake fully finished articles to order.

Martin Beacom, proprietor of the Small World brand, has long been associated with quality modelmaking as the constructor behind many of the models sold through Aviation Retail Direct (formerly Mach 3 Models) under various in house labels. His skills are nowadays crystallised within the Small World portfolio of classic airliners and transports. It is also likely that the choice of models will be expanded as Martin reintroduces items from the now departed Western range, finished to his own impeccable standard.

The Norfolk Group, Standing Left - Wojtek Benzinski (Cloud Break Models), Standing right - Paul Howard (Helmet Historical Aircraft), seated left - Chris Sayer (Shed Models), seated right - Derek Barratt (MetalModels). Summit meeting, Duxford, Sept 2010

Vapour Trails was the name chosen by Brian Keates for his models and as such, is not to be confused with the earlier output of plastic 1:200 aeroplanes from Corgi Toys under the same brand name. Brian's list of models grew rapidly in the mid 1990s and their fine quality made them sought-after items. Later, Brian acquired Tommy Atkins' inventory of masters and moulds, comprising those models that Tommy had created speculatively and for his own satisfaction, which added yet more types to his already extensive product list. In a further move Brian elected to supply Collectors Aircraft Models, on their customary exclusive basis, and direct sales of Vapour Trails models correspondingly ceased. CAM re-branded the range as Skyfame models. Today, in 2008, CAM lists Brian's F-4 Phantom and this model is something of a tour de forces, in that Brian offers the model in the markings of every single RAF squadron that operated the type. Further details are currently awaited regarding the availability of the rest of the Skyfame range.

One of the big guns in the English 1:200 story, Mike Stephen's Western Models, was already a long established and respected producer of fine quality model cars, before attention was turned to diversifying into model aircraft. The impetus for this move no doubt arose from Mike's aviation interest as a keen private pilot. The first Western aeroplane

Wojtek Benzinski

to appear, and a marker of the quality to follow, was the Bristol Freighter. This was swiftly followed by numerous classic airliner releases, together with USAF transports and the mighty B-36 and B-52 bombers. Few collections today are without some Western issues and they remain a significant element in the English 1:200 story. The business was sold in 2007, on Mike's retirement, and though the masters have reportedly gone abroad, some future Western model derivations may appear here from Small World Models.

Boats in White Metal

Alan Dixon
D & M Casting Company

White metal model boats are few and far between, but The D&M Casting Company made a range of lifeboats for the RNLI, and Alan Dixon, was the man to 'launch' them.

Alan joined the family business, Walkers Town Model Centre, in the early 1970s. This was a model shop selling railway, Scalextric, plastic kits, flying models etc. It was during this time that Alan and his partners recognised that there was a gap in the market for accessories in N gauge railways. With this in mind the firm began to make these items, such as street lamps, station furniture, people etc. This then developed into working N gauge model engines such as the Princess class, Black 5 etc. They also produced a range of vehicles for another supplier. The name D&M, of which Alan was the D was created to keep the casting of metal kits separate from the shop business.

This business continued for several years, but then came the decline in model making, or more accurately the start of computer games, and the bottom fell out of the market. One of the partners left the business, the other continued but in a very smaller way, whilst Alan tried to develop the metal casting side. Being an active supporter of the RNLI, and knowing the buyer for them, the beginning of the range of Lifeboat models was nigh!

Alan's first contact with their pattern maker was a fortuitous meeting, when he came into the shop one day and one thing lead to another. He was a very

D&M Castings Oakley Lifeboat

D&M Castings
Oakley Lifeboat Box

skilled man who was already an industrial pattern maker. Alan recalls that he had fingers like bananas but could create the smallest and finest brass patterns he has ever seen. Sadly he died some years ago.

D&M Castings' first premises were in a room upstairs above the shop. This was fine to begin with, but when the RNLI commissioned them to make the range of boats it was clear that they needed larger premises and a floor in a mill complex was rented that had been taken over by a metal fabrication business. All the equipment used was home made such as the casting machines, melting pots, mould press etc.

The D&M range continued right up to the end of the business. D&M only sold in the UK, although Alan had arranged to go to a trade fair in Belgium, and had created display units etc. Then the Falklands war broke out and the ferry he was due to sail on was commandeered for the war. He never got there. The production runs for the RNLI were for a new model every 6 months, with a view to creating the entire fleet past and present.

The company did operate a mail order side, but only with the D & M range, as well as through a wholesaler.

D&M Castings advertised in railway magazines, and their wholesaler also attended toy and model fairs with their products. Packaging was in cardboard outer boxes with smaller components packed in plastic bags inside the box.

Alan's role was a jack of all trades. He cast the items, along with one full timer and a couple of part timers, and made up the sample items for the customer. He also did some pattern making, usually the easier bits. No one else manufactured for them.

The end for D&M came thanks to the tax man. Alan was at a stage when he had to give serious thought to expanding the business or staying as they were. During this time he received a tax demand for several thousands of pounds that both he and his accountant knew they did not owe. On appeal they were told that they must pay the amount or face prosecution, and if the tax office was wrong then they would get the money back. Several thousand pounds for what had really become a one man business was for too much to absorb.

After having many sleepless nights, Alan got up one morning, picked up the phone and told the accountant to wind up the business because he was so annoyed by the attitude of the tax office. He did get the money back exactly 2 years later, but it was too late. Alan then became employed full time by the RNLI, and had no desire to return to casting. Therefore, there will be no more white metal lifeboat models from D&M, but haven't they made a significant contribution in every way to our appreciation of the work of the RNLI, and to the use of white metal for model boats.

CHAPTER TEN

BREAKING THE RECORDS

Many books have been written on the subject of the fastest car on earth, better known as the World Land Speed Record. The UK has featured large in taking, holding and retaining this record for substantial periods of time, indeed Thrust SSC currently holds the record at 763 mph, set in 1997, and Bloodhound SSC is on course to increase this to 1000 mph or more in 2012, with American and Australian cars also in contention. It's not surprising, therefore, that those model enthusiasts who are dedicated

followers of these attempts have gone to great lengths to reproduce their favourite cars in miniature. In the UK, a few record cars appeared in the Dinky Toys pre-war 23 series of racing cars and are now very collectable.

The post war years brought a flurry of record contenders from Australia, the UK and the USA and consequently provided a significant selection of cars for the specialist producers to model. Such specialists are fairly few in number, extremely dedicated to their chosen path and generally work in reasonable collaboration with each other. We have been fortunate to record the stories of some of them in this chapter.

Jason Ferns
HB Models

It was good to hear from a relatively new entrant into the white metal hobby, and Jason Ferns is one such enthusiast. At 40 years of age, Jason, too, remembers his Dinky Toys, but just as important were his Action Men! It was the evolving project that was the Thrust SSC bid to achieve a supersonic World Land Speed Record that caught Jason's imagination, and in 1996 when it was reaching its final stages, he obtained all the versions of this incredible car made by Lledo.

A few years later, by coincidence browsing at the Havant toy fair, Mike Stanton overheard him seeking LSR models from a trader, and offered to give him a complete listing of all model LSR producers. Jason joined the club, but he found that many of the prices were beyond his reach.

However, he found the RAE Piccolino range much more affordable, and began with these. At this time, Keith Edney was focusing more on his 1:43 range of cars, and subsequently began to reduce his time in the white metal model field. However, Jason was able to buy some kits from Keith, and then went on to the 1:43 range.

He loved his Piccolinos, and when he found that they were no longer being produced, he approached Keith to explore the possibility of buying some of the master patterns. A deal was struck, and Jason came away with the initial 12, together with all the moulds, decals, etched parts and remaining castings.

Initially Jason hoped that Ian Jones would be able to re-cast them for him, but due to Ian launching his new resin series, there was no time. Ian recommended a local caster and model maker, who arranged for the masters to be repaired. With this work completed, new moulds were made as the old ones were no longer serviceable.

Jason's model of Parry Thomas's car, Babs

H.B.MODELS
1927 Babs

Jason's plan has been to produce the new Piccolinos in small batches of 5 at a time, to satisfy both his own collection and those of his immediate friends. He began with all the Bluebirds, the Golden Arrow, and a Sunbeam. Jason has also had the master for Babs, Parry Thomas's car, made for him, together with the castings. Should this trial prove a success, he may consider making a more serious business from it.

It is so heartening to find a relatively new arrival on the white metal scene who is motivated by the same ideals as the more experienced producers, and has the energy to enable this medium to be used to continue satisfying a small but key section of the collecting fraternity.

Ralph Foster
Pandora Models

Ralph Foster at work

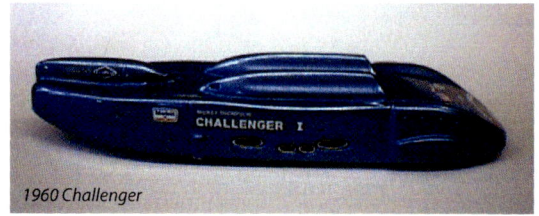
1960 Challenger

On leaving school in 1962, his first job was as an engineer with the NCR, and they provided their own training school. Later, NCR trained their engineers for the electronics age, and it was this that caused Ralph to hanker after the traditional processes, so he turned to kits once again. He discovered that white metal was the medium of choice for collectors, and found high quality kits by Wills Finecast, Auto Replicas and later Western Models.

Triumph Gyronaut

To begin with Ralph built kits for his own collection, but like many in this field, he found some of his favourite cars were not available in sufficient quality and detail, and felt sure he could build his own. He gained much encouragement from Colin Baxter of Scale Racing Cars, and others within

Airfix kits have been an inspiration to so many collectors, and another devotee is Ralph Foster, who created Pandora Models. Ralph always preferred the vehicles Airfix made to planes, and made these kits all the way through his school career. He was always a fan of the metalwork classes at school, and sure enough he chose to train for a career in engineering when he finished his education.

BMW

Triumph Thunderbird

the industry he had got to know, and in 1985, he took the plunge to manufacture. His first subject was the Sunbeam Silver Bullet, and he turned to Richard Stokes, who he regards as the best, for his first pattern, and was very impressed with the way the pattern parts fitted together like a jigsaw. He chose Keith Williams and John Allen of Scale Model Technical Services to undertake his casting for him, and the result was a best seller. Altogether, 750 examples of the Sunbeam were sold, on a world wide basis, without any advertising, through friends and via specialist trade outlets.

1928 Bluebird

In consultation with friends, he concluded that as his models were to be fresh out of the box, what better name than Pandora! There have been a total of 20 in the series so far, mostly sold as kits, but some handbuilt by Ralph. He recalls with particular fondness the first of the Bluebird series, the 1927 car, which was the first purpose built example, and paved the way for the complete range of Bluebird cars, later versions of which displayed full engine detail under removable engine covers.

Ralph is fortunate to have a small well house in his garden. This originally served his village with water, but has proved an excellent workshop. Here he prepared and fettled castings for the kits, painted and assembled the handbuilt versions, and packaged the finished product in his own boxes for despatch. In due course Ralph bought his own casting machine and cast the bodies of the smaller white metal cars himself. He also experimented with resin bodies for some cars, using Dave Buttress at CMA Moldcast.

1926 Babs

Come 2002, Howard Statham had decided to take a rest from the LSR Productions line, as it had been a part time hobby interest, and Ralph purchased the patterns, remaining stock and the right to sell LSR. He has since held these in abeyance, as in 2003 he realised that with the onslaught of the Chinese manufacturing industry, either his range should be manufactured there, or be closed down permanently.

The Well House has therefore slumbered, but in the meantime, Ralph has been keeping a close eye on the white metal market, and believes he has identified a small upturn in demand for Land Speed Record cars, in limited numbers. As we were putting this profile together, Ralph was dusting down and stripping out his workshop in the hope that he might again launch his Pandora range onto the collectors market. Watch this space!

Stutz Blackhawk

Ian Jones
Mach One Models

Ian Michael Jones was born on Christmas Day 1958 in Carlisle, Cumbria, but moved to Derby at the age of two, when his father was transferred with Rolls Royce following the abandonment by the British Government of the Blue Streak rocket programme on which he worked.

An unspectacular academic career was followed by an engineering apprenticeship at Fletcher and Stewart's, a local company specialising in sugar mill machinery, however it soon became apparent to Ian that this was not really what he wanted to do and so he took a position in the parts department of a local Ford dealer. This lasted for a couple of years before an opportunity arose to join another local engineering company in the sales department. The British Organ Blowing Company, as the name suggests, produced

Ian Jones

rotary blowers for church organs, diversifying into other industrial fan applications but more importantly giving Ian the resources to nurture his very basic scratch building skills. Having access to the workshop during lunch breaks and at the end of the day, he had a variety of machines, tools, material and expertise in all things engineering to draw on to enable him to satisfy his interest and improve his skills.

It was about this time that he met Ralph Foster of Pandora Models who specialised in Land Speed Record Models and it was suggested to Ian that perhaps he might like to produce a pattern for the Budweiser Rocket Car and ultimately put it into production. Thus in 1992 Mach One Models was born, the name being derived from the fact that the Budweiser rocket car claimed to have broken the sound barrier, Mach One, on land.

The production of this initial model was trusted to CMA Moldform who produced the resin and metal parts, the transfers (decals) being produced by a local company Kaylee Transfers. Ian then either built them up or packed them as kits. The annual model show, ModeleX proved to be very beneficial at this time in gaining potential customers and making contacts for the business and so it became apparent that the 'day job' was getting in the way of the model making Following a promotion for his wife Julie, he felt financially able to resign from the British Organ Blowing Company and set up Mach One Models on a full time basis which he did in February 1994. However, later that month his wife announced she was pregnant and so on November 3rd (Dan, their first son was actually due on October 28th, ModeleX weekend) of that year, following Dan's arrival, Mach One Models was once again a part time enterprise, as Julie would be returning to full time work following her maternity leave, and Ian would become a househusband. A second son, Ben, followed on Boxing Day the following year.

Ian continued to expand the model range during this time, in the main buying patterns from other Land Speed Record Producers such as Fred Harris of Replicast, Geoff Brown of GB Models and the Green Monster pattern from Mike Mcnally of M.A.E

in Canada, via Howard Statham of LSR Productions. He was also commissioning original patterns, for example the 3-engined 1928 White Triplex, from established pattern makers such as Richard Stokes. At this time, some of his metal casting was being done by Peter Comben of Enco Models, with the resin castings still being produced by CMA.

It was at ModeleX that a contact was made and the opportunity to buy a centrifugal casting machine presented itself. The machine was very primitive by today's standards but would enable Ian to reduce his costs by casting the metal parts himself, leaving CMA to do the resin work. Obviously, a melting pot was required and during a conversation with Doug McHard of Somerville Models, he told Ian that he had a melting pot that was no longer required and provided Ian collected it, he could have it for free. The catch was, it was attached to a vast automated casting machine that Doug no longer required. However, after much grunting and heaving, the machine was loaded onto a trailer and deposited in Ian's garage, where the melting pot was removed, and the remainder of the machine sent for scrap. The melting pot gave many years of service, finally expiring about five years ago, when a new one had to be purchased. The casting machine continues to give good service although Ian still cannot fully understand the 'black art' that is white metal casting. He can stand at the machine for hours trying to get a particular part to form!

The current range of models amounts to more than 30, all available either as kits or fully built models. Mach One Models have diversified into Water Speed Record boats, a range acquired once again from Fred Harris of Replicast.

As to the future, Ian continues to produce patterns and models, though as with most low volume model producers, he is affected by the huge resources the Chinese manufacturers have at their disposal and has latterly turned his efforts to larger scale models, and although many have been started, none have been completed. A familiar story amongst the 'artisans'. It is hoped that Ian's two sons will become involved in the business but at the time of writing have shown little inclination to do so, telling him that the contents of his work room will be consigned to the skip when he dies! He's sure they're joking! Aren't they!!!!!

Art Arfons' Green Monster

Howard Statham
LSR Productions

LSR productions was formed in 1983, by three Land Speed Record enthusiasts, to produce accurate Land Speed Record models to 1:43 scale. Billed as 'Models by Enthusiasts for Enthusiasts' the watch words were accuracy, detail and correctness. It was a hobby activity for the partners who all had full time jobs - Mike Stanton in Aerospace, Howard Statham in IT, and Fred Kaesmann in Military Liaison, and also an acclaimed and successful author. The models in the range were numbered SKS01 onwards, SKS being the initials of the 3 founders.

In the 1980s, information on LSR cars was quite difficult to find, many contemporary photos were wrongly captioned, the vehicles changed almost every time they came out to run and precise dating was vital. To design and build an accurate scale model of an obscure record car required much researching. Brian Lawrence of Lawrence Designs and Models (LDM) was the original pattern maker, had an existing business, and was not a partner in LSR.

Mike had produced his 1:43 scale Goldenrod model and was in contact with fellow LSR enthusiast and speed record historian and author Ferdinand (Fred) Kaesmann.

Brian had already made the brass pattern for Mike's Goldenrod. Brian was a master pattern maker and under the name of LDM had also produced a small range of 3 land speed record models. (See the Brian Lawrence profile). One of these was the original LDM Thrust 2. The LDM pattern was based on drawings of the proposed Thrust car at a late

stage in the vehicle's design but before the design of the actual car was finalised. Consequently, it had a number of changes when compared to the car that ran at Bonneville in 1981 and 1982, including fin strakes, the cockpit canopy glazed on top, and the intake profile and wheels.

Howard Statham had always been interested in the Land & Water Speed Records since seeing information on the various vehicles in the Eagle comic in the 1950s. Apart from the excellent centre spread cutaway drawings, Eagle also did a series of half page colour collections, Land Speed Record cars one week, Water Speed another week etc.

After seeing Western Model's 1933 Bluebird at the Model Engineering Exhibition, he bought a kit of it from them and so started his collection of 1:43 scale models. This led him to buying a kit of Goldenrod from Mike and so started the journey that led to LSR Productions.

Having been a modeller since childhood days, like many others he started with the first Airfix Spitfire kit, had been in the International Plastic Modellers Society (IPMS) for many years, and started the IPMS Kent Branch with meetings in Sevenoaks. Having started to collect 1:43 scale Land Speed Record cars, he decided to produce a model of his own and began work on a pattern for the 1965 Spirit of America. He used plastic modelling skills to do this and made the pattern in car repair paste, the two part soft putty used to fill car bodywork holes. Howard still has this pattern and says that even now when he looks at this old master, which never went into production, it holds up well with modern incarnations of the 1965 Breedlove car.

Howard knew Mike from seeing and buying his Goldenrod at one of the Eastbourne Historic Vehicle Club fairs at held at the Winter Garden in Eastbourne in 1982. On a later visit to that fair he sought advice from Mike about the sonic model and how to make it in limited quantities. He made a simple cold cast mould in soft rubber and produced a few test shots, but was using ordinary liquid resin which, when it set in such a large lump, generated considerable heat and cracked.

An interesting aspect of Brian Lawrence's patterns was that he had an uncanny ability to capture the correct look of the real car in miniature. Making a model pattern is not just about getting the measurements correct, it's about the model looking like a small version of the real thing. He would work from basic dimensions such as the length or the wheelbase and a few photographs. Few pattern makers had that skill.

Howard recalls an interesting aside concerning Brian. Some years ago, Brian was involved with the real TSR2 project and was at Boscombe Down when

Thrust 2

the
prototype
TSR2 fell off the transport
trailer bringing it from Weybridge, and
how horrified they were when it lay on its side on
the tarmac. This story was told at a time when such
information was far from the public domain. It has of
course since been published by others.

During the late 1980s, a series of 1:144 aircraft was
planned and patterns were made for the a range of jet
aircraft. Mike had produced patterns for the Hunter 3,
DH 108 Swallow, Supermarine S6B and Hughes racer
and Howard bought these. He also bought the 1:144
patterns for the LDM TSR2 and DH Comet racer from
Brian. The TSR 2 was sold on via SMTS but Howard still
has all of the other patterns, although no aircraft were
ever produced by LSR Productions

The Thrust 2 pattern was acquired from LDM,
modified by Brian and Howard to represent the 1983
Thrust 2 and an agreement made with Richard Noble
of Thrust Cars Ltd. to produce the model under licence.

During this time, Howard lived in south east
London and Mike lived in Hampshire and they used
to meet up in a Little Chef restaurant about halfway
between the two for planning meetings.

Howard drew up the complex artwork for the
decals, Mike using his experience to source boxes
and decals, and the vital casting experience, which
came initially from Western Models and latterly from
Scale Model Technical Services.

Brian made the main body as a single piece but
in the late 1970s, when this was cast by Western
Models, the body was too big for current casting
methods. It was therefore cut down the centre line so
as to be accommodated by the casting machine. By
1981, it had been re-soldered together and all later
LDM castings and all LSR Productions main body
castings were cast in one piece.

The boxing up of kits was quite easy, Howard
did all these on his kitchen table, developing
a production line method that enabled kits to
be boxed and ready for despatch in a home
environment with little trouble or inconvenience to
the household. However orders for built models from
Thrust 2 sponsors quickly materialised and volume
production of such a complex model became a
major problem. Fettling and spraying batches
of about ten models in a home environment was

severely challenging and much credit goes to his
long suffering wife for accommodating this. Who else
would tolerate spraying in the kitchen!

Soon the building of LSR Productions models
was farmed out, a little to SMTS but the
majority to Paul Willit who traded
as Precision Miniatures based
in Taunton, Somerset. The
approach was to have the
models about 90% built by
the outsourced builder and for
Howard to complete the fine
detail parts and the decals etc.

The logistics of farmed out building became
the achilles heel of the operation because it
became impossible to maintain the high standards
demanded by Howard with such long geographic
distances involved.

Mike's Goldenrod was subsequently added to
the LSR catalogue. Howard modified the pattern
to include separate exhausts for improved detail
accuracy and ease of building. Work also started
on the design and development of the pattern for
the 1922/23/24/25 350 H.P. Sunbeam which in 1923
became the first land speed record Bluebird driven
by Malcolm Campbell. The pattern was cleverly
designed so that a common chassis and some parts
were used for all versions while some body parts
were special to one version.

The Sunbeam pattern was made by Alistair Duncan.
Alistair was a silversmith who later also made the
1926 & 1927 Babs patterns for LSR. He used his initials,
AD, from his accredited silversmith hallmark punch
set as identification on the castings. The actual 350
HP Sunbeam was measured and photographed at
Beaulieu Museum. When measured, the car was
representing the 1922 car, but subsequently the
pattern was used to represent the later cars.

Mike and Howard developed the very fine wire
wheels that even today are among the finest in the
business. Each model wheel was constructed of 5
brass turned parts and 3 precision photo etched
parts, all soldered together in a jig. This allowed for
very fine spokes of 0.5mm diameter and yet a very
strong assembly. Later, a larger
version of these wheels
was produced for
Pandora

1922-1925 350 H.P. Sunbeam

to use on their 1927 Bluebird model. Mike designed the turned aluminium wheels to represent the aluminium covers of the real wheels on the 1924/25 cars. The late Rod Kilby, one of Mike's neighbours who ran a small precision engineering company in Hampshire, made the turned parts for all the wheels. Rod also supplied SMTS with turned parts, the initial contact being facilitated by Mike.

Sometime after the 1983 Thrust 2 record, Richard Noble embarked on a new venture. This was to produce an inexpensive enthusiasts' private light aircraft called the ARV Super 2 (Air Recreational Vehicle). This was very innovative for the 1980s and for a variety of reasons the venture failed but not before Richard had persuaded Howard to produce a promotional scale model of it. LDM made the brass pattern to 1:48 scale, a common aircraft scale. The model was produced in limited numbers but the model venture was no more successful then the real thing. Howard tells us he still has a pile of castings in his garage. The story of the ARV Super 2 is an interesting story in its own right. It was powered by a three cylinder 2-stroke engine designed and built by Hewland of racing car gearbox fame. Richard Noble still owns and flies one today.

LSR Productions was always a hobby to the trio but at one point, Howard seriously considered going full time on the venture. He produced all of the artwork for decals except for Goldenrod, and was able to modify brass pattern work as required so he made preparations to go full time. He amicably bought out the other two partners and invested in some new models.

He had patterns made for some new models, which included the K4 Bluebird boat in the three main versions (3 pointer, jet and prop rider), Babs in its 1926 & 1927 incarnations and City of Salt Lake. He also bought some patterns from other companies who were either running down or had patterns that didn't fit their range. These included the 1966 Green Monster and the part completed pattern of the 1965 Wingfoot Express 2 from Mike McNally, and the Mercedes T80 from Western Models. He also bought the old LDM patterns for the other two record cars in the LDM catalogue, the 1978 Malcolm Olley Jet car and the Barry Bowls rocket car. The engine used for the jet Bluebird K4 was actually the Malcolm Olley Jet car engine slightly modified to fit the boat.

Sales outlets were mainly retail shops such as St Martins Accessories, Grand Prix Models, and Wheels Model Cars, as well as other manufacturers who had loyal customers, and of course to collectors in general. Sales were to all parts of the world, but all in small quantities and mostly to the UK. Figures for total production runs are not available but are thought to vary from less than 200 for the 1922 Sunbeam to about 800 for Thrust 2.

In the late 1990s Howard decided that LSR as a full time job was not financially viable and the burden of producing a large range of models as a hobby was too much. Also, he observed the burgeoning threat from the Chinese who could produce cheap high quality models. He sold off the patterns but allowed LSR Productions to remain dormant.

Most of the cars went to either Pandora Models or Mach One Models. The Wingfoot 2 was only partly made and it went first to Mike who did some work on it and he then sold it to Pandora who had the pattern completed and issued.

Regrettably, the models that went to Pandora did not see ongoing production, and along with their range of Bluebirds and Silver Bullet are out of production and very difficult to find.

At the time of writing, Howard had just retired from his regular day job and was planning a new model. It is quite possible that LSR Productions will again produce accurate scale models from new patterns.

Mike Stanton
Mayes Models/MS Models

Mike with examples of the range of models he produced

To Mike, all the good modellers he ever met started out as young modellers that just got older....There does not seems to be a middle way unless you are talking about collector/modellers, a totally different breed. He considers himself an old modeller with leanings towards collecting; that is his excuse for the story that follows.

Balsa wood, tissue and dope, Jetex power and diesel are all to blame in some way. As an unruly youth he well remembered destroying his Jetex

Rolls Royce Armoured car

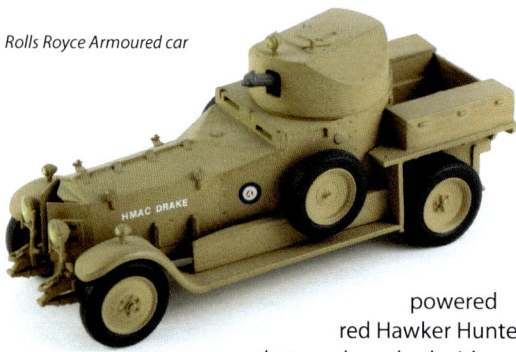

powered red Hawker Hunter that was launched with a powerful Brocks banger in the fuselage one fine day. The mid-air destruction was memorable and seemed a fitting ending at the time. The motor was recovered and did the same for his DH 110 and Attacker. These were unforgettable endings that marked this passing era.

In later years the advent of plastic kits and the new white metal car ranges from John Day, Mikansue, Auto Replicas, Grand Prix Models and others re-shaped his interest in building and collecting. Most of the models were worthy of note whilst others were totally frustrating in scale and quality. Before them, Merit plastic kits figured largely along with the gems from AMT, MPC, and Pyro from the USA. A few still survive in Mike's collection including one of his first Merits, the hand painted 500 Cooper Norton; what a little gem.

Mickey Thompson's Challenger 1

With his RAF career closing in the late 1970s he decided to produce and market a model of his own to continue the hobby interest. The 1920 Rolls Royce armoured car was chosen as it was a particular favourite and not been done before in 1:43 scale. The Mayes Models name was chosen to keep alive in a small way the double barrelled family surname that had not been used for generations. The 'Milestone Series' range name suited the type of vehicle he wanted to produce, i.e. all milestones in their particular field. These names were only used on the Rolls Royce and the first Goldenrods, the wheel driven record car of the Summers Brothers in the USA, another huge personal favourite. Talking to Bill and Bob Summers was an exciting experience whilst sorting out an agreement for Goldenrod production. Sadly, Bob died early in life but is survived and well represented by his brother Bill.

Starting out from scratch was a struggle, the white metal model industry was relatively new and producers were very secretive about suppliers and methods. He was fortunate to meet Brian Lawrence of LDM Models who was a superb pattern maker, and Mike Stephens of Western Models who did his initial casting and helped out with advice and ancillaries for the models. Mayes Models became incorporated into LSR Productions around 1983, (see the entry for LSR from Howard Statham in this chapter for that part of the story.) The Rolls Royce pattern was eventually sold to the late Richard Briggs who incorporated it in his Minimarque43 range selling fully finished versions with little extras added. Where it went after Richard sadly passed away, Mike is not sure. There are armoured car models out there that still look very familiar to him. Goldenrod went to LSR Productions.

Some years after this, Mayes Models reared its head again when it produced the 1959 and 1960 Mickey Thompson Challenger LSR cars in conjunction with a local collector friend John Cockayne. They also introduced Monty's Humber and General Alexander's desert finish Ford staff car. The excellent patterns for the two army vehicles and the 1960 Challenger were made by Arthur Trendall from Berkshire. Castings were done by Hart Models in Hartley Wintney, the surviving partners from the Denzil Skinner organisation that had closed down in the village. The pattern for the 1959 Challenger was produced by Mike from the 1960 version, so not entirely all his own work. Mayes Models ceased trading around the 1990s, the names and military patterns being retained by the family of the late John Cockayne. Sadly, John died in 2009.

Putting a timeline to all these happenings proved hard, likewise keeping away from models was proving harder. MS Models, became another of Mike's re-incarnations and still survives to this day in minor ways. Once again he was back in business! The Mercedes C1-11-IV, and the ARVW research vehicle patterns were purchased from Andy Martin of Aardvark Models in the USA. Andy was a fellow ModeleX exhibitor, the show being a mecca for the white metal industry at the time. The rocket powered

Monty's Humber

Wingfoot Express 2, ex MAE Models, was purchased from Howard Statham. The Wingfoot Express and the ARVW were eventually sold on to Pandora Models. He upgraded them to the excellent items that they are today. The Mercedes was sold to Robert Budig of Modellautos in Berlin, and was marketed by him after a considerable amount of re-working had been done on the pattern. There were a few 1:144 aircraft patterns made by Tommy Atkins as mentioned in the LSR entry, although cast, they never went into production and now reside with Howard Statham. Mayes Repro, another venture, had a little flourish with signed prints of the record breaking Meteor and Hunter aeroplanes, and are still for sale at the Tangmere Military Aviation Museum, where the actual aircraft reside.

The years passed and life takes over and the hobby/business interests wax and wane with demand and energy. Mike's next peak seemed to be from 1996 with the production of the Kawasaki Lightning Bolt LSR motorcycle of Don Vesco. What a really great guy and a tragic loss to record breaking when he succumbed to cancer. The large scale model of the Gillette Mach 3 Challenger produced for the team, was a labour of love as Mike was part of the team that saw it break the UK record driven by Richard 'Rocketman' Brown and only just failed to beat the outright world record at Bonneville in the USA in 1999. Being a biker fan these really fast two wheeled streamliners always fascinated him and made for a great collection as far as he was concerned. There are not that many, which is also easier on the budget. Prices are changing, costs are increasing and the large discounts the trade expects make model production on a small scale very difficult. Bike models were never big sellers for Mike and it will be interesting to see how the new 1955/56 Triumph record breaker bikes from Spark/Bizarre fare in the market place. His model of the Bonneville streamlined Vincent as ridden by Russell Wright was another 'must do one day' model, the pattern being beautifully produced by Phil Edwards. Work is still in progress on that one, ditto the 1961 Joe Dudek Triumph record breaker. Mike promises to dig out that pattern again one day!!

A few nostalgic moments for him include the first UK swapmeet he attended at the Monkey Island restaurant near Maidenhead on the river Thames. You had a suitcase or a box full of models and that was it.

You traded in the queue or joined the rush to set up and sell as soon as you were let into

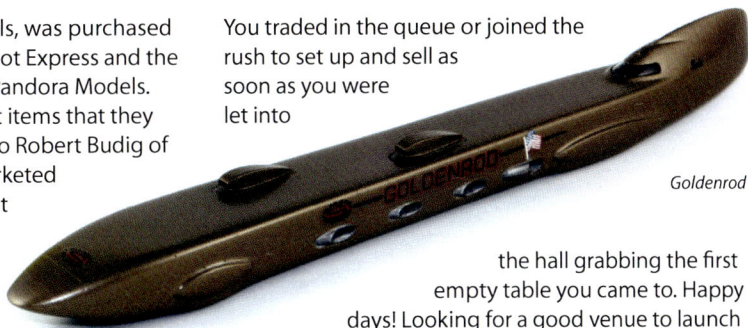

Goldenrod

the hall grabbing the first empty table you came to. Happy days! Looking for a good venue to launch his new Rolls Royce model that was supposedly going to set the collecting world on fire, he booked a table at the Windsor swapmeet and set up eagerly. No sales or much interest apart from the organiser, Mike Richardson of Mikansue fame, congratulating him on a nice model. Great expectations, but no sales. Mike asks if anyone remembers the champagne launch that Western Models held at a very early Windsor school swapmeet of their new Jaguar XK 120 model? They had a great time and if you were lucky you got a drink and some peanuts. That was how to do it in style...

Finally, Mike remembers he received a phone call from Rolls Royce requesting 50 of his brand new armoured car models to commemorate a recent tie up with Vickers. The armoured car had a Vickers machine gun in the turret. At the time only one built example existed that had just been taken to the Rolls Royce showroom in Conduit Street, London for approval together with 49 sets of raw castings! This was the entire model stock and Mike was still serving in the RAF at Thorney Island at the time. Queen and Country had to come first, and there was no way he could honour this order, so reluctantly had to turn it down. We can all be wise in retrospect and all foolish at some point in our lives. Mike had no excuses either and rests his case as just another old modeller.

Vincent Black Lightning LSR

CHAPTER ELEVEN
THE CHEQUERED FLAG

The field of motor racing was, indeed, the birthplace for many of the very early white metal model car makers, as has already been talked about in chapter four. However, at that time, in the early post war period, the pattern makers and producers had relatively few real life examples to copy and reproduce in model form.

In the 1950s, a new era of racing cars began to appear under the banner of F1 and a World Championship for drivers was established, based on eight races, compared to the twenty that are to be run in 2011.

Diecast manufacturers Dinky and Solido, in France, lost no time in producing models of these new racing cars and they were very popular ranges with collectors of that time. They were surely the catalyst for the handbuilt fraternity to get increasingly involved with similar ranges and produce sophisticated examples which would appeal to adult collectors seeking more refinement.

As the years passed, more and more races were added to the F1 calendar, bringing an increasing number of racing cars which could be modelled. At the same time, other forms of racing took hold, notably sports cars, of which those raced at Le Mans became a sure fire collectable range.

Some manufacturers committed themselves totally to racing and/or sports cars whilst others established various ranges and included these as part of their production.

As can be seen in this book, motor sport has provided the specialist manufacturers with exceptional scope and the collectors with boundless choice.

Colin Baxter
Scale Racing Cars

Scale Racing Cars was started in the late 70s by Colin Baxter and John Phillips, born out of the dissatisfaction with the quality of the Formula One models available at the time i.e. badly cast standard suspension or simply too easy to assemble thus making it an expensive hobby. Their aim was to produce 1:43 white metal kits.

They used to call at Grand Prix Models and later Lamberts of Ley Street, Ilford, on their way down from the North to Brands Hatch. After a few trips they mentioned to Brian Sloman at Lamberts that they would like to manufacture their own range, and asked if he knew a pattern maker? The following Monday, he rang them to say pattern maker Richard Stokes was seeking new work. A meeting was arranged with Richard to discuss a pattern for an 'Embassy Lola', but he wasn't sure he could do what they wanted. However, a price was agreed with the proviso that if they didn't like the master they didn't have to pay for it. Being Yorkshire men this appealed to them! In due course they met Richard at Donington Park to collect the master and were overwhelmed by its quality and workmanship.

Their problems were now about to begin, as neither of them had any experience of white metal model production and they spent hours on the phone wading through the Kelly Directory, finding a tyre manufacturer in Northampton, a jewellery caster in Oxford and a screen printer in Dewsbury. After the production of their second master they came to the conclusion that they had to cast and produce tyres in house. They bought a Saunders 9" bob weight casting machine and then had to learn how to use it. After months of trial and error they managed to produce their third model in the garage where everything happened, only outsourcing the transfers. They had some assistance and instructions

Formula 1 Lola Ford

from Doug and Roly McHard at their home in Lincoln. They realised they had made a mistake with the 9" machine which was great for the small parts but not so good for the larger parts. Through Richard they sourced, from John Hall at Brooklin Models, a second hand 11" air operated casting machine, which gave much more control on the mould pressure, making the larger parts easier to cast. John also showed us how to make vac forms for windscreens.

Now with two casting machines, a vac forming machine and a compressor they had outgrown the garage. They moved into Salisbury Hall, an old house in Hull converted into office and workshop units, taking one small workshop unit in which they carried on casting and building most evenings after work, and weekends.

In the early 1980s Colin was made redundant and started working full time for Scale Racing Cars, and Richard came in as a partner, with the responsibility for making the master patterns. The range increased and the market for handbuilts became more prominent so Paul Blenkirom was employed as an assistant. He learnt fast how to batch build models to a very high standard and the handbuilt models as well as the kits were much sought after all over the world.

The kits had a break even point of 250 and all except the three later models achieved this quantity. They also made a Ferrari 312PB in several versions, in limited editions of 500 kits, all of which were fully subscribed. They manufactured three limited editions of 150 handbuilts - a Maserati 250F, Fangio, a Mercedes W196 short wheel base, Moss, and a Ferrari Dino 246, Hawthorn, all fully subscribed. The building was done by Colin and Paul and all the spraying was carried out by Ralph Foster of Pandora Models, who was second to none with a spray gun. Distribution was via retailers at home and abroad and at toy fairs, auto jumbles, classic and racing car shows. One show where they always made an

impact was ModeleX. They were present on most occasions during its eleven year run and won the trophy for 'Best Stand' in 1993 and 2000. Promotion was by photocopied sheets, colour photos and by editorial in magazines. The kits were initially packed in small corrugated cardboard boxes and later in black and yellow printed boxes with the built models in better quality two part boxes with a lift off lid.

Richard Stokes made all the masters except one, Colin did all the casting after they bought the casting machines, made tyres on an injection moulding machine and all the vac-forms. Paul did all the spraying and building except where mentioned elsewhere and the artwork and printing of transfers were subcontracted. John did the office/paperwork for several years until Colin took over and also did all the packing and dispatch. All the research for the models was done by Richard and Colin. The end of Scale Racing Cars as manufacturers came in 2003 because of the lack of sales due to cheap imported 1:43 scale toys. However most of their standard kits and built models are still available, now produced by Scale Model Technical Services.

They liked to think they were innovative in introducing scale models with lift off body parts, full engine details and accurate decaling. Their models were certainly at the forefront of F1 modelling for almost 20 years.

Where are they now? John is now a director of the company where he has worked for most of his life, Richard is helping to raise the next generation of master makers, Paul is a van driver for a paint distributor and Colin is a full time carer for his wife and a part time angler.

On behalf of John, Richard and Paul, Colin would like to thank everyone who supported them and who gave him twenty or so years of happy times doing something that he loved.

David Buckle
Formula 1 Models & Prints

The well known shop premises in Swanage, Dorset were originally founded in 1985 by David Buckle as Formula 1 Models & Prints. Initially it sold old diecast toys, but David soon became known for holding a large stock of performance white metal models, complemented by a fine selection of prints of performance and sporting vehicles.

He was a F1 enthusiast and the models he traded reflected this primary interest. In 1989 he relocated the business to his home, changed his trading name

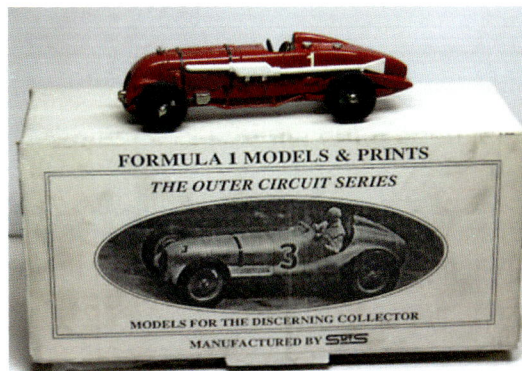

4.5 litre Birkin Bentley

to Formula 1 and spent more time at toy fairs. He was a regular at ModeleX and was awarded the 'Best Stand' trophy at the 2003 show at Warwick Hall, Stoneleigh Park, Coventry

He launched the Outer Circuit Series of racing car models of cars that were seen on that pre-war Brooklands circuit. Made for him by SMTS, the series was short lived and only John Cobb's 24 litre Napier-Railton and the Birkin Bentley were modelled but fewer than the anticipated 400 of each were made. David died in 2004.

Colin Fraser
Formula Models

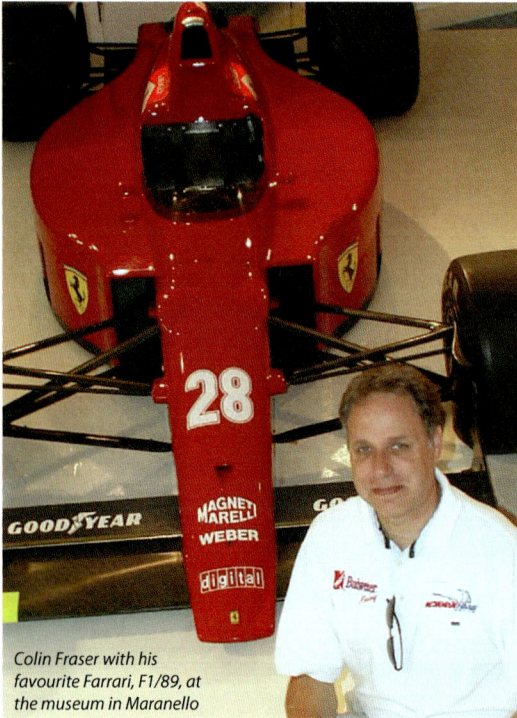

Colin Fraser with his favourite Farrari, F1/89, at the museum in Maranello

Proprietor Colin Fraser has been in the hand built models industry since 1988, albeit part time for the first couple of years. His father used to make control line and free flight model aircraft as well as cars from Merit kits, and was instrumental in Colin's interest in modelling.

His love of cars, particularly the racing variety led him to make his own, as there were not many models available then. At that time, living very close to Brands Hatch his interest in motor racing allowed him to see many races with the iconic cars he came to love. It was at the model and book shops there that he first saw both Solido diecast models and later the iconic John Day range of white metal kits. These fired his enthusiasm and having seen both the JPS Lotus 79 and Ferrari T3 of 1978 race, he wanted to make models of these cars. Fortunately he saw an advert in Motor Sport magazine that led him to

purchase kits of the Lotus and Ferrari by mail order from Grand Prix Models in St Albans and also to visit Lamberts of Ley Street in Ilford, Essex, as that shop was closer.

Colin says he owes a lot to Brian Sloman of Lamberts – indeed, he goes so far as to say that he would never have got involved without him. He did the job - always having a good selection of kits in stock. It was there too, that he met John Simons who at the time was building customer models for Lamberts.

Colin always had an interest in Indy cars, following the 500 mile race from the mid 1960s, indeed, he was irreversibly drawn to these cars. There not being a recognised manufacturer of model Indy cars, he decided to produce his own model of the Chaparral 2K, subsequently becoming the recognised UK producer of Indy car models, building them full time at home from 1988. It was from his friendship with Brian Sloman, for whom he made customer models, the support of George Maxwell at Mini Grid, a popular source for quality models in Unionville, Toronto, Canada and Steve Matero of Motor Sport Miniatures in New York that he was able to secure orders to take the Chaparral project forward.

Knowing that Scale Model Technical Services, who were based near him, were producing models and offering a service to potential new manufacturers Colin contacted Keith Williams and his partner John Allen. They agreed to produce kits of the Chaparral model for him, from the creation of the master pattern to preparing decals, photo etch, sourcing tyres and casting the metal components. Some 150-200 models and kits were originally produced, and it pleases him to know that this model is still in production and available today. Peter Kenna made the original master of the Chaparral and other pattern makers that have done work for Colin include Bob Hine, Ian Pickering, Christian Sargant and Dick Ward.

Throughout his career, Colin's work has frequently been inspired by the motor racing stars and the cars they drove – Graham Hill, Chris Amon and Nigel Mansell, to name but a few. Ferraris have been a theme for him and through this he met Nathan Beehl who ran the Ferrari Model Club and also worked at Grand Prix Models.

Nigel Mansell's move to Ferrari gave Colin no

alternative but to make a model of the first Ferrari, 640(F189), he drove and this decision led him to a meeting and help from the car's designer, John Barnard, who also designed the Chaparral 2K. This project was never released by Formula Models, being purchased by the Japanese model shop Raccoon. Further commissions came from First Formula, Pro Line, Aone Planning and Crescent Models.

Over the years Colin found that Indy car models could not sustain him full time as a model manufacturer and he has had a long and fruitful relationship building as a sub contractor for Marsh Models and others, including Charter models and Ghost Models as the need arose. He builds proprietary kits in small series under the name Automodel Art, two of which were signed by designers John Barnard, a Ferrari 412 T2, and Rory Byrne, the 1995 Michael Schumacher World Championship winning Benetton B195. Additionally, he has added a range of US F5000 models under the Yank name.

His interest in Indy cars led him to follow NASCAR racing and although he has never ventured into making models of these cars, he has a fine collection of diecast models of the cars that were racing in the early 1990s.

From time to time, Colin has worked for himself in both Illustra's and SMTS's premises with some cross working as the need arose. Since March 1997 he has had a workshop in Court Lodge Farm, Wartling, Nr. Hailsham, Sussex, next to Marsh Models and Model Assemblies.

John Haynes
Historic Replicars

John Haynes was born and bred in Brackley and from an early age formed an interest in motor racing, regularly cycling to Silverstone to watch races. From school he joined The London Brick co and completed an engineering apprenticeship. After that, engineering was his way of life until redundancy in 1980, when he returned to his first love and commenced making model racing cars.

From success at this, he formed his own business, Historic Replicars, making 1:43 scale model racing and sports cars. The models were keenly sought after and examples can be found in most handbuilt model collections.

In the early 1990s, virtually all handbuilt models were 1:43 scale. John decided to experiment with 1:24 scale models and successfully developed a line of Jaguar models, for which he will be remembered. He continued with both lines until 1994, when he retired due to ill health. Most of his models are still current, now being produced by K&R Replicas.

John maintained his interest in motor racing and the model scene until he passed away in April 2002.

Roger Taylor
Autographic

Autographic was the name given to a small range of model racing and sports cars produced for Roger Taylor, after a long time involvement with motor sport illustration and automobile art.

Over a 35 year span, starting in 1965, he produced hundreds of 4 view scale drawings, many of which were published in the magazines of the time, including Model Cars, Miniature Auto World and Scale Models. His wife Margaret ably supported him by re-arranging the detail and the race history of each car and typing up the information into a readable description. Many of Roger's own photographs were used to illustrate these profiles.

The Autographic model cars, manufactured by Western Models from patterns made by Robin Housego, first appeared at the end of 1989. The first model was a Mercedes Benz 300SLR in both

1953 Cunningham C4R

Mille Miglia and Le Mans air brake versions. Tourist Trophy and Targa Florio examples completed the set. These were followed by three versions of the

1957/58 Vanwall, 1956 Maserati 250F, 1953/54 Cunningham C4-R and the Maserati 450S Costin Zagato Coupe.

For Roger, his drawing work and the models were only a hobby. Promotion at work demanded too much time for the models range to develop and production came to an end after just two years.

Much later, after retiring, Roger and Margaret moved to Hastings and subsequently made contact with SMTS. There, he found employment in a welcoming environment, reviving his drawing work on the computer and saw three of his models, Mercedes Benz, Vanwall and Maserati 250F, relaunched as Blueprint (BP) Models.

Carrie & Dave Wade
Little Smashers

Dave Wade

This is a story of enthusiastic artisans, and includes the Isle of Man to add glamour! It begins when Dave Wade recalls always being fascinated by the Le Mans racing cars; not for him the glamour of Formula 1.

Dave married Carrie, and together they lived in Barton Le Clay in Bedfordshire. Dave had noticed that whilst winners of Le Mans were modelled, the tail enders rarely got a mention, let alone models produced of them. So, in 1981, following the Le Mans 24 hour race, he decided to make a model of the IBEC 308 LM. The car was based on Hesketh F1 suspension and mechanicals and a detuned small valve Ford DFV engine. The model was entirely home made, apart from the wheels which were from Scale Racing Cars, and the decals from a specialist in Hitchin.

Before it raced at Le Mans for the third time in 1981, the real car was garaged in Milton Keynes, where Dave was able to visit and take measurements.

The car was driven by Tiff Needell and Tony Trimmer before being retired after 5hrs and 45 mins having suffered gearbox and electrical problems. However, after the race, when it returned to its garage, Dave was faced with the news that it was to be cut up and put in a skip! Dave had an AlfaSud at the time, and he persuaded the owners to help him put the sections of the racer on the roof of his car, and then drove it back to his house in Bedfordshire, for it to lodge safely in his back garden!

Dave had a day job too, as a metallurgist, and so was familiar with the properties of different metals. He set about sculpting a pattern out of Milliput, and created a resin body, which was mixed at home and cast using bath sealant! To create the chassis and engine detail, Dave made up a centrifugal casting machine from a bedside cabinet, a dimmer switch, a strimmer motor and aluminium tread plates used as the platform to support the mould rotating at 175 rpm, intended to confine the molten white metal solidifying from 200 degrees C. Luckily it never went wrong...

And thus Little Smashers came into the model world! The name was taken from the northern England expression for something small but beautiful.

The model was by Dave's own admission a bit rough in places, but they set out to sell 100 of them, and this was achieved. He sold approximately 30 in built form, and the remaining 70 were packaged as kits in cardboard tubes (from photocopier paper reels) with plastic bungs in the ends, and sold via Lamberts of Ley Street. The fire extinguisher on the model was represented by an electrical resistor, and the towing eye by a bra hook! The roll over bar was fabricated from garden wire...

Aston Martin Nimrod 1983

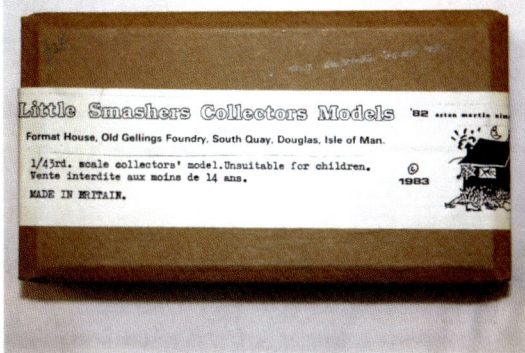

In 1981, Carrie's parents lived on Jersey, and on their visits, Dave would join a fellow Le Mans enthusiast for a drink. After knowing him for three years he discovered that a friend, Pat Evans, coincidentally, was also a pattern maker. Pat had been producing patterns for Tony Bellm and his Bellini range. Tony had a pharmaceutical factory on Guernsey, and had engaged the workforce there to build the Bellini range of models.

Dave asked Pat to produce the pattern for his next subject, the Aston Martin Nimrod in two versions, one the Pepsi sponsored car that raced at Daytona, and the other at Brands Hatch, sponsored by Bovis. He was very pleased with over 1000 models sold of a non Le Mans car. Dave obtained a vac-form machine to make the sign on the roof of the model and the windows Casting was undertaken by Brooklin Models and the packaging by Carrie and Dave. By this time in 1981, they had moved to Douglas in the Isle of Man, and the address appearing on the instructions for the Nimrod was Format House, Old Gellings Foundry, South Quay, Douglas. This was a friend's building company base, useful as a mail address.

Dave had always wanted a model of a Maserati 300S, and for this he created the pattern and cast all the white metal components for the Nurburgring 1956 Moss / Behra car. About 30 items were sold, and later in 1982 Dave made a 1:24 scale version, again finding a friend, Dr Pete Moran, to master the model for him. At the time Pete was a medic on the RFA Sir Galahad stationed in the Falklands, presumably sculpting away on the master while waiting the arrival of casualties. The model is a beautiful representation of one of the most attractive sports racers ever made.

Next it was the turn of the URD which raced at Le Mans in 1986, and for this Dave made the pattern, and passed the job of the resin body and the vac form for windows to Provence Moulage in France. The wheels were locally made on the Island. Again, this sold well, with 250 pieces going to collectors

via Dave's regular outlets of Grand Prix Models, Lambert Ley Street, Wheels of Totnes, Classic Models of Carlisle, Elite Models of Stratford and several continental outlets.

1987 saw a pair of Tigas, both Le Mans versions, made under the new name of Libra Miniatures – Dave's birth sign. These were followed by three different Chevron B16s, which sported a resin body and white metal components, with white metal ancilliaries. The first was cast by Tim Perry, and the others by Chris Arnott of CMA Moldcast.

Carrie and Dave began to see the quantity and quality of diecast and resin products coming from China at competitive prices challenging the market for handbuilt and kit models, and decided to cease production in 1990 as they became distracted by their other love, blues music. They established the Manx Blues Club and the Big Wheel Blues Festival, a successful event still running with Dave as its lifetime president.

Whilst in the Isle of Man, Dave was working as a Health & Safety consultant, but in 2006, after 25 years of regular travel to and from Cheltenham to visit their daughters, involving flights and ferries, they decided to move to Cheltenham themselves.

Dave now plans to continue enjoying his extensive collection of Le Mans and other sports racing car models, but is also very involved in painting seascapes and organizing musical events. Will there ever be any more Little Smashers? Dave says his adage is "Never say Never"! "Making models is no longer a hobby", says Dave, "it's a serious business. I remember being inspired by various people in the hobby, such as pro builders like Pete Campbell, photographers such as John Cope and others in what was a model producing community who would do what they could to help. Even the car manufacturers and sponsors were generous in their requirements for royalties. Although I didn't always agree with Brian Harvey's views, I would most certainly support the view that without his journalistic and commercial efforts, the white metal model industry would never have existed, never mind helped create the successful international businesses of today".

Nimrod 1982

Steve Ward
Penelope Pit Lane

Steve about to pour molten metal

Another Airfix kit enthusiast, Steve Ward, found that his parents thought that static kits were a waste of money, so at 13 years of age he began an interest in war gaming and slot racing. The latter gave him a life long interest in motor racing.

Steve pursued a career in the Police Force and upon leaving after 15 years in 1989 he decided to work for himself, creating dioramas of street scenes and some nudes. He named his business 'Something Different Dioramas'.

Still war gaming, now with Skytrex products, and finding that there were important omissions in their range, Steve made a range of ship masters from balsa and plasticard. Never having done anything like this before he bought a Tiranti casting machine and made coldcure moulds to produce the ship kits in white metal. In 4 years the business grew to a range of 450 kits including tanks, aircraft and 54mm 'Dads Army' figures. He was now using a hydraulic casting machine and a vulcanising press, using jewellery type disc moulds.

Steve had a very good friend from school days, John Shinton, known to many in this field, who had served his pattern making apprenticeship. John

was able to help in such fields as creating masters, moulds and casting, together with artwork drawing for photo etching and water slide transfers.

Steve used a Tiranti casting machine to make the first mould, but he soon wanted to improve the results of his model making skills, and to enter 1:43 scale. Steve's real love has always been racing cars, and so he set out to develop a range of 6 white metal racing cars, under the Penelope Pitlane name, and the two ranges ran for some time together. For these patterns Steve began to use Cebatool resin synthetic wood, an expensive medium, but capable in various degrees of hardness to be sanded, cut and shaped without any grain to affect the finish.

The white metal racing range launched in 1995 comprised BRM V16, HWM, Connaught B-type, Cooper Bobtail as well as the official Arrows Formula 1 car. This was only a short lived development, as Steve rapidly realised that the diecast companies, hitherto concentrating on current F1 cars, were now challenging his market by producing historic racing cars too.

To achieve the level of quality Steve wanted, he turned to CMA started by Chris Arnott and Dave Buttress in 1990, whose castings Steve found were so fine that they could go straight into the kits.

Steve's love of motor racing extends to visits to the Festival of Speed, where on one occasion he recalls sharing a marquee with John Shinton. Steve observed that another stallholder selling 1:8 scale racing car models had samples on show which he felt he could produce to a better standard. Steve then set about creating a 1:8 scale Lotus 18 in resin for display and sale at ModeleX 97.

Arrows F1

Unfortunately, for Steve the only buyer was John Surtees, and as a result, and with associated personal reasons, Steve ceased trading for 8 years. In 2006 the name of Penelope Pitlane was re-launched, specialising in slot cars with resin bodies, white metal detail parts, and photo-etch chassis, which Steve realised was the ideal medium for easy assembly adjustable slot car chassis. These chassis, which accept a range of electric motors, are selling well. He is now commissioning his own 48-spoke wire wheels, with tyres and motors coming from China.

In summary, Steve has re-established his love of motor racing, both current and historic, using 21st century materials and production sources. His business is developing well, and the future is promising.

CHAPTER TWELVE

THE SHOP FRONT

Bob Wills found suitable premises to open his shop known as R. Wills Scientific Hobbies in Coulsdon in 1946, and Frank Vescoe opened his BEC Models in Tooting Bec in 1953, making these two of the earliest pioneers we know to have launched shops dedicated to the sale of models, both railway and cars. As the hobby developed, and diecast models for the collector began to emerge, there was clearly a demand for specialist model shops that stocked static metal models of most forms of transport. These shops often spread the risk by stocking model railway locomotives, rolling stock and accessories, as the two hobbies often coincided.

These specialist retailers then found that swapmeets were opening up the market place to part time traders operating as a hobby in addition to their full time employment. A certain amount of animosity developed, with these sellers sometimes being referred to as 'weekend warriors'.

More recently, eBay has offered yet more scope to both these groups of retailers, and some have grasped this opportunity aggressively. Casual, part time traders have been able to sell models that are surplus to their collections, whilst serious full time retailers have been able to extend their 'shop front' to include on line shops with lengthy listings of white metal models for sale. The following is a medley of these retailers, many of whom have given their views on the state of the market.

David Angel
The Angel Collection

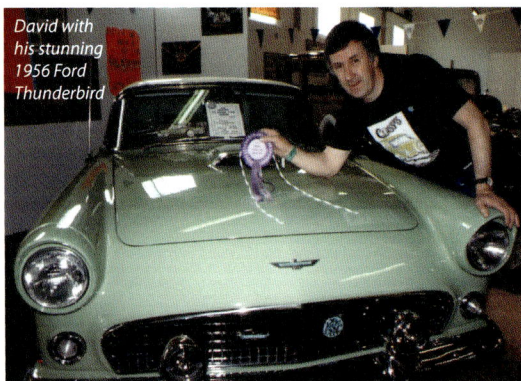

David with his stunning 1956 Ford Thunderbird

David Angel was a war baby and after the war his father bought, repaired and sold second hand cars, particularly American ones, for a living. David remembers being taken to school, along with his brother, in a succession of 1930s Ford V8s, Pontiac Coupes and similar cars. At one time, his father had an SS100 and later a Cord Sedan finished in purple. It had a faulty gearbox and eventually sold for £500, paid for in proper fold out white £5 notes!

When David was 17 he learnt to drive in a Railton Fairmile convertible and after passing his test in a 1949 Morris Oxford, not surprisingly, drove many American cars. He was, by then an apprentice panel beater and in his spare time helped his dad repair written off Nashs, Studebakers and a Jaguar XK 120, which he drove to work on completion, much to the surprise of his senior workmates!

In his younger days, David collected Dinky Toys, mostly American, and he modified quite a few with a hacksaw into convertibles and pick up trucks. Later, he built a model scrap yard for his younger brother with, of course, damaged Dinkys in it. He also built him, from scratch, a yellow and black pedal car in American style with four headlamps and big fins.

After marrying Carole in 1962, he repaired written off cars and sold them for a living, before expanding into selling repairable cars and dismantling late models for spares. He also found time to build and race his own lilac coloured 'Angel Autos' Minis and a Mk 1 Escort in Autocross and televised Rallycross with much success in the UK and Europe, accompanied by Carole and their children Stephen and Maxine.

Being in the car salvage business David acquired many older classic cars, many of which were American. These he stored away until the early 80s, when having designed and built a new house with a purpose built six car garage, he was able to display them along with other American cars purchased later. One of these, a '56 Thunderbird, he stripped to its bare chassis and restored it to what was described by Classic American magazine as 'Britain's Finest Thunderbird'. Now resplendent in authentic Sage Green, it was a stunner and won many 'Best of Show' awards.

On buying the first of four 1955/56 Thunderbirds in 1983, David joined the Classic Thunderbird Club International (CTCI) and attended all the bi-annual international conventions in the USA from 1984 to 2006, some twelve events all in different locations!

About this time, at the Bristol Classic Car Show, David bought his first Brooklin model, a 1952 Studebaker Starlight Coupe in black, which was a coincidence as his Dad had owned one in the 60s that David had done bodywork on, and that was black too!

Through friends, David became aware of model car swapmeets. Attending an evening meet in Salisbury in 1987, he was taken by a new release from Brooklin Models being offered by specialist retailer John Martin. He bought the model, a Chevrolet Nomad, together with a model magazine. Reading the magazine later, he found an article about a Brooklin special produced for Webers, an American nostalgia/toy store 69th anniversary – only 69 made! Wow that's a challenge, he thought. 'I must have one' was his reaction and thus began many years seeking out rare limited edition Brooklin Models.

In 1988, Brooklin Models produced 100 models for John Hammick of Merley House Model Museum. David went to the museum and bought one and thus started a long friendship. John was building a large collection of Brooklin models for the museum and they helped each other add models to their collections, spending many evenings on the phone comparing notes, etc.. This association resulted in their co-production of the Brooklin Collection Guides and later the three Brooklin videos, each complete with a limited edition Brooklin model.

More friendships developed when David met John Roberts, an American car enthusiast at a Wessex Model and Toy Collectors club meeting. David joined the Wessex club and purchased their 1987 club model - another limited edition. Through talking to John about the real American cars he owned, he was introduced to Brooklin's founder, John Hall, another American car enthusiast, resulting in him measuring and photographing David's Kaiser Manhatten and adding it as a new model to the Brooklin range.

David's meeting with John Hall was very significant as several more cars from his collection were later modelled by Brooklin. These included a Ford Fairlane Skyliner, a Chevrolet El Camino and a 1960 Edsel Ranger convertible. From the Lansdowne range, a Ford Consul convertible and a Capri were also used. It also resulted in David driving John's daughters to their weddings in his Ford Skyliner and Edsel convertible.

David's Thunderbird and Brooklin model enthusiasm gelled, with John agreeing to produce 200 Sage Green 1956 Thunderbirds for him to take to the CTCI Convention in Dallas in 1988. These were well received and David commissioned Brooklin to produce limited edition models for all the International Conventions over the next decade. These included alterations to the master to produce a 1955 model, followed by the complete reworking of the original master to produce a 1957 standard model which was then included in the Brooklin range as well as producing a boxed triple Thunderbird set in an edition of 300 for the 1994 Convention.

Two years later it was modified in an edition of 500 'Birdnest' models for the Bend, in Oregon, Convention. At Bend, David saw the full size racing Battlebird and thought it would make a fantastic model and Carole took many photographs of the car and the signwriting. Upon returning to England, David showed the pictures to John Hall and suggested the idea of reworking the 1957 master to form the Battlebird for the next convention in Dallas in 1998. John said the master would need 'major surgery', but agreed to produce 500 models. It was later used by Brooklin in the factory special 'Speeds Week Thunderbird Set'.

With John's retirement at this time and Brooklin introducing a 'no more specials' policy, the 1998 Battlebird was the last CTCI special produced by them.

However, still wanting to continue the Thunderbird theme, David commissioned Durham Classics in Oshawa, Canada, to produce three Convention models, culminating in 2004 with three different models for the 50th anniversary of the Thunderbird launch and decided that would be the end of the ongoing series of CTCI models – a grand total of sixteen! Durham also produced models in Angel Autos and Inca Trail livery for David.

Since 2000, David has commissioned several detailed and refinished models in his 'Angel Collection' series of models. These were produced by Richard Hutchins and later by Mike Stephens, founder of Western Models Ltd. All have been issued in low numbers and the series are Code 2 models produced with the kind approval of Brooklin Models.

In the late 1980s, David bought a large collection of models including over 250 Brooklin models, with the rare Mobiloil Ford van and an S M Baily Dodge van, from a collector in Florida. Together with his wife Carole, they took a winter break in the sun to pack them up and bring them home safely, not forgetting to pay the duties at Heathrow!

On another occasion he bought a collection of rare Brooklins and Corgi Toys from Paris, obtaining many rare issues for his collection as well as a large stock of items for re-sale. He once sold an 'instant' collection of more than a hundred Brooklins to a new collector in the USA, and later, on the phone to a man on his hospital bed, David quoted on quite a few examples and then asked him which ones he was interested in buying and the reply was 'I'll take them all!', so a deal was agreed.

David was an early member of the Brooklin Collectors Club, the San Francisco Bay Brooklin Club and the Brooklin Club Deutschland (the last two now both defunct) and attended many of their meetings, making many friends. Along the way, he met many manufacturers, model makers and other dealers.

For David, his model collecting and dealing has been a 'Great Experience.'

Ralph & Kathleen Avis
St. Martin's Accessories Ltd

Ralph and Kathleen in the shop

Ralph Avis commenced work at Beatties in High Holborn, London in 1967. After a couple of years there and visiting Motor Books and Accessories in St Martin's Court from time to time, he joined that company and moved with them in 1970 to larger premises at 95 St. Martin's Lane.

Motor Books was sold in the mid 1970s and the car accessories and models then assumed the current name. Later the car accessories, which were in the basement were sold off and the upstairs was given over solely to model cars.

In 1985, Ralph and his wife Kathleen bought the business which quickly became a necessary port of call for overseas visitors and London based model collectors, being just a stone's throw from Trafalgar Square, right in the heart of London.

In the late 1980s they launched Classic Supercars, an exclusive range of white metal models manufactured in total by Scale Model Technical Services (SMTS) It was a small range, spread over 2-3 years and comprised a Cobra 427, a Cobra Daytona Coupe, a Porsche 930 Turbo, a 1963 split window Corvette and Roadster, which were all sold as kits and built models in the shop and by mail order.

Otherwise, they stocked all the important white metal ranges including Abingdon Classics, AMR, Brooklin, Classic 43, Danhausen (Metal43), K & R Replicas, Lansdowne, Minimarque43, Marque One, Omen Miniatures, Precision Miniatures, Somerville, etc., as well as several resin ranges.

Handsome was the name given to a range started by Peter Accini, a member of staff who later emigrated to Australia. In the event only one model was produced, a Police Ford Zephyr, also made by SMTS.

A very collectable 1980s model is the limited edition (under 100) Brooklin 1935 Dodge van finished in cream and dark green, with St Martin's logo to each side.

As well as running the shop, Ralph raced a 1965 Shelby GT 350 in national and occasional overseas races during the 1990s/early 2000s.

In the late 1990s, the long standing husband and wife team increased by one when Danny 'the manager' Offord came to join them and all three are still working together.

Their London shop has recently closed after 40 years trading, but they are now selling by mail order, and will continue to stock new releases and show what they have on their website.

Ralph and Kathleen's very well established model shop in St. Martin's Lane

Charles Barnett
Midas Models

Charles at Sandown Park toy fair

Charles Barnett's stepped display of white metal handbuilt models will be a familiar sight to those who frequent Sandown Park, N.E.C., Windsor and other major toy fairs, but he hasn't always majored on white metal.

Throughout his life, Charles has always been fascinated by cars, and had his share of Dinky and Corgi Toys as a child. However, unlike many of us, he managed to hang on to his own toys as he grew older, and by the mid 1960s he had amassed a significant collection of these, together with some Spot-On models, and a few examples of the then foreign makes such as Solido, Mercury and Politoys. He had his eyes opened to the concept of collecting model cars as a serious hobby by Brian Jewell's book, and the then encyclopaedic work, 'Catalogue of Model Cars of the World' by Jacques Greilsamer and Bertrand Azema.

Whilst at college studying marketing and advertising, Charles began looking for examples of cars not modelled by the major diecast manufacturers. This was the time of the early kits of John Day and Motorkits, and models by Brooklin and Western Models, and Charles acquired a number of these.

His collection has grown over the years, and was the driving force behind his entry into trading in models. He attended what were the first swapmeets where true exchanging took place, in the north of England. These were in Huddersfield, in a room above the Co-op Dairy, and in Bradford, in a basement under a city centre chapel!

Charles took a job in marketing support with a member company within the Tootal Group, based in Congleton, Cheshire, which specialised in fabrics made from man made fibres. From there he went to the mail order company Empire Stores in Bradford, working on the selection of merchandise for the catalogues.

A spell with a furniture company in Leeds, managing sales support, followed, but redundancy there led Charles to take a post with an entertainments company, also in Leeds. A further spell of redundancy, when that firm too went on the slide, persuaded him to join the Civil Service in 1981.

The two spells out of work had however, led him to develop his model interests, and to travel further afield around the growing number of swapmeets and collectors fairs. One event in London, for example, brought him into contact with Max Kernick and John Roff, where Charles was impressed with the quality of their Abingdon Classics models of MGs.

By this time, Brooklin Models were developing a higher profile, and on one occasion when Charles called into the factory in Bath to collect a few spare parts, he was introduced to, and treated to a long chat with, its founder John Hall. Charles was impressed and a long association with Brooklin began. A meeting a short time afterwards with fellow enthusiasts Brian Harrison and Mike Marlow, who had founded the Brooklin Collectors' Club, saw Charles become the newsletter editor for that club. Thanks to Mike's canny budgeting and positive approach, he was able to produce a high quality publication worthy of the Brooklin product, which he continued to develop for several years.

During the 1980s, other makes began to arrive on the scene, and many of these were happy to market their models through specialist dealers, so Charles' trading sideline slowly changed emphasis, away from diecast and towards the handbuilt white metal replicas.

His involvement with the Brooklin club led to his attending the annual show of the Canadian Toy Collectors' Society, and he made some good contacts during this trip, notably with Julian and Margaret Stewart of Durham Classics, which ultimately led to Charles becoming their main European distributor.

The trip also sparked Charles' love affair with North America, which he now visits 3 or 4 times a year, and where he has developed a growing

Midas Models Rover P2 in various colours

Midas Models Rover P2 in Dove Grey

Charles' view of the market for handbuilt models now is that it is more affected by the retirement or closure of some of the key producers in the industry. After all, most of these businesses are run by one man or one family, in contrast to the development of the much cheaper mass produced diecast products from China. He recognises that the customer base has shrunk, but finds that for every customer who moves away from handbuilts to the mass produced items, there is another who, growing tired with just amassing diecasts, moves toward the solid feel and limited nature of the more collectable white metal pieces. He finds that collectors of handbuilt models rarely sell their whole collections, but rather, will trade away duplicates, or models that have been upgraded, and will usually prefer to exchange these against new models, than sell them for mere cash!

Charles retired from his Civil Service career in February 2011 to be able to devote more time to his hobby. It is always a pleasure to deal with him, and he deserves every success in the future.

number of customers and suppliers. Meanwhile, he has developed his regular pattern of attending major collectors fairs in the UK. Over the years, he has commissioned several special models under his 'Midas Models' brand, with both Durham Classics and Somerville Models. These have all been well received and are now sought after.

Mike Coupe
Spa Croft

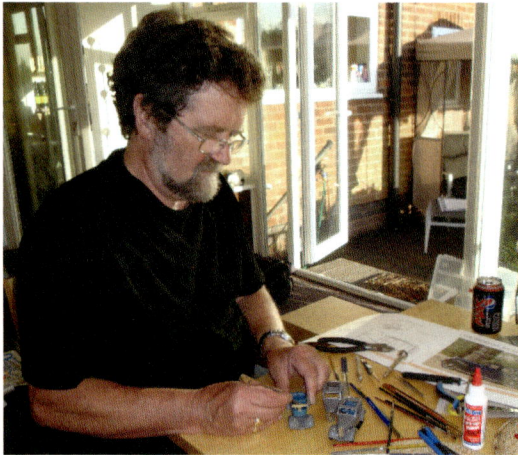

Mike Coupe has been an enthusiastic collector of model cars for longer than he cares to remember. It all started in the late 1940s when Mike had his first Dinky Toys Buick Viceroy, and, together with a Ladybird book on cars of the time, he began collecting the Dinky Toys pictured in that book. These included Standard Vanguard, Riley, Rover 75, in fact, all the 40 series, but that Viceroy wouldn't go away. It was chopped and turned into a town car and later was repaired with Plastic Padding! His collecting was then overtaken by the draw of the girls in his teens.

The interest came back in his 20s, when Mike

recalls picking up later Spot-On models, such as the Hillman Minx, cheaply and also Models of Yesteryear. Another hobby of his was collecting records of the era, and this led to him becoming a local mobile DJ. He spent a lot of time at the Shoulder of Mutton Inn in the small hamlet of Hardstoft about seven miles south of Chesterfield in Derbyshire. When the landlord asked him for ideas to generate some income, he suggested a swapmeet, but not too often as there were others in the area. And so Mike took the initiative, and in 1983 he launched the fondly remembered Hardstoft swapmeet at the Shoulder of Mutton. Alternating with the nearby Nottingham International swapmeet, it was held once every two months on a Tuesday evening. A feature of the swapmeet was a draw where the customer whose entry ticket was drawn at the end of the swapmeet, would receive a £5.00 voucher to be spent on the night at any of the stalls present. Needless to say, all dealers present waited with eager anticipation to see if their takings would be boosted by another fiver. As a comparison with today's toy fairs, the number of tables was between 30 and 50 at a cost of £5.00 per table. The swapmeet had a five year run, only curtailed by the pub closing!

After 12 months, Mike had accumulated a profit of £300, so he thought he'd start a model car business, and approached John Hall of Brooklin Models to supply him. Known as Brock Miniatures, trading began in 1984, and was gradually built up over the next ten years or so, based solely on mail order and toy fair appearances.

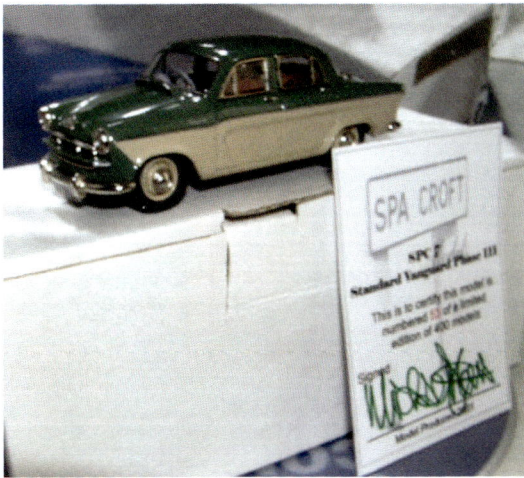

In 1995, an idea which had its beginnings a few years earlier came to fruition, and Mike launched his first model, the Series II Morris Isis, at the ModeleX of that year. The pattern for this model was made by Pete Kenna. Mike shared the ownership and launch of the model jointly with Roger Tennyson, then of Jemini Models. With a new business comes the need for a name. John Hall's choice of name, being the place where the first Brooklin model was made, was the inspiration for Mike, and so he selected the street where he was born, Spa Croft. Mike's intention was to model the cars that were around that area during the period from 1930 to 1960, whilst he was living in Spa Croft.

In recent years, as the name Spa Croft Models took precedence over Brock Miniatures in the minds of the collectors, Mike now trades under the new name for both manufacture and retail of white metal models, and has been supplying high quality models, from a range of quality manufacturers, of British and American cars to model collectors for the past twenty five years.

Until 2003, Mike had been supplying the specialist trade with Spa Croft releases, but in that year he changed his pattern maker to Ian Pickering. He also opted to assemble the models himself, and only supply direct, as it would have been too pressurizing to be assembling bulk orders for trade suppliers. In response to demand from his customers, Mike also ensured that there was added detail in the subject chosen. The first model under this new regime was the Morris 14. Previously, Mike had used Moldcast to cast his models, and subsequently GTA Models for both assembly and some casting. Pat Land now paints the bodies and interiors, whilst castings are produced by Maurice Bozward of White Metal Assemblies.

However, overall, Mike's business approach is one of relaxed trust. Like many of his colleagues, he regards the white metal business as a 'fraternity of gentlemen of leisure not bound by the formalities of life'; in other words, contracts are sealed by a shake of the hand, not the written word.

Mike's wife Pauline was the sleeping partner in the business, accompanying him to swapmeets and ModeleX exhibitions, but since she passed away in 2004, he has chosen to restrict his sales outlets to eBay and his very comprehensive website.

Each Spa Croft model is meticulously finished, with much research carried out to ensure accuracy. Every model is produced in two colour schemes and total runs consist of 400, but in addition, an extra 100 are reserved to produce limited runs of other colour schemes, including a sub range, Le Car Noir. As the name implies, this is a range of all black cars, limited to 50 pieces, produced in response to collectors' demands for cars in the colour which they remember, invariably black.

The majority of the Spa Croft range has been mastered by Peter Kenna, one of the UK's most sought after pattern makers, and more recently again, Ian Pickering. There are now 11 models in the range, the most recent being the Humber Pullman. New models either due or planned include a Morris 25 Coupé.

Mike considers his customers to be very loyal to his theme, and the demand for Spa Croft has not been adversely affected by the recession. Indeed, with the value of the pound dropping, interest has increased from Europe and the USA. Mike finds amongst his handbuilts, there is consistently high demand for the popular Lansdowne range. He hopes to continue with approximately 2 new models each year for at least another 3-4 years, by which time the big 70 will have arrived!

We wish him continued success with the classic motors of post war Britain.

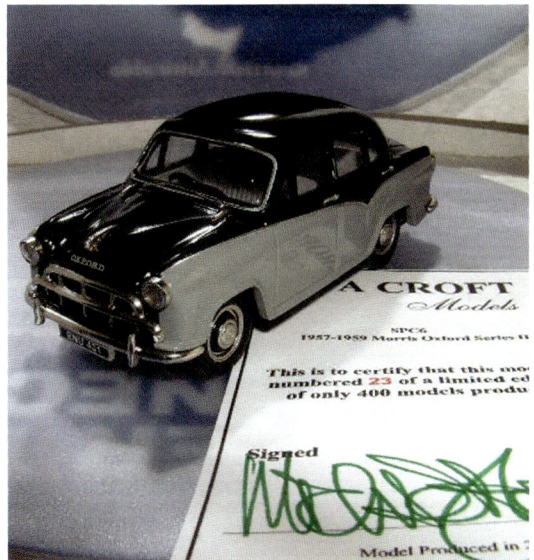

Rae & Ann Dobbins
Merrymeet Model Cars

Rae with his Lotus Elan Sprint

Rae's interest in model cars and cars in general originates from childhood building Airfix kits.

Rae was never a fanatical kit builder but he reckons to have built many models over the years, including remote control planes and boats, the last being a slope soarer glider of the Red Arrows Gnat.

Rae's employment took him into production management, and after 25 years working for an employer 25 miles from home, his beloved Lotus Elan Sprint was no longer suitable for everyday transport and he was forced to buy a 'sensible' car. He had planned to use his Elan for competitions and to tow it with his new purchase of a Landrover Freelander.

Rae's model collection had by this time featured mainly classic sports cars with a few Le Mans cars and 60s F1 cars

Rae thought a kit of the Freelander towing a 1:43 Elan would be a good subject for a model and started looking, which was when he found Merrymeet Model Cars, and added his name to the mailing list. In 2002 Merrymeet was being run and owned by Peter Radcliffe, and when the first mail arrived from Peter in that year it announced that he was about to close the business through ill health.

At the same time, the company Rae worked for announced its closure, and so, after much discussion with his wife Ann, a major career change brightened the horizon and he bought Merrymeet Model Cars.

His first task was to see exactly what he had bought, a lot of stock was old and out of date and

whilst Peter's objective had been to have a stock room full of models for him to build, Rae's was to have the company more financially secure. Most models are available from suppliers at short notice so stock is kept low, to about 300 models, and new orders placed regularly with the major suppliers to meet demand. Help and advice is always available including a build tip CD as well as spare parts should any be missing or damaged.

Although back in full time employment with soulless electronics, Rae now has part time work with something that he really enjoys. His leisure time more recently has been spent competing in motor sport events with his son Marc in a Mini Cooper S and rebuilding his Lotus Seven and Elan.

Attending the Le Mans 24 hour race has become an annual family event. Although specialising in Le Mans kits Rae has varied the range by adding more classic sports cars and 60s and 70s F1 cars. He has recognised that model making is a hobby that is mainly done outside work time, and with the business being run from Rae and Ann's home, if they are in they will answer the phone at any reasonable time seven days a week. E-mail or Fax are regular means of customers ordering too.

Rae sees the future as bright, and being a worldwide supplier means one country's recession is normally balanced by another's upturn; demand from Far Eastern countries being particularly high now.

Retirement is nearing now for Rae and he sees this as a positive opportunity, being able to spend more time on Merrymeet Model Cars with perhaps a more comprehensive news letter and quicker turn round of models He currently works as an IT co-ordinator for a special needs school, a job that he finds to be extremely rewarding and challenging at the same time.

Handbuilt Transit van and space frame on the roof from an MEA Kit43 kit and a Lotus Seven by SMTS

Les & Peter Duplock
Model Road & Rail

There are some characters in the model car world that are almost universally known, and Les and Peter Duplock are two of this breed!

The two boys were brought up in North London. Their dad, who was originally a Ford mechanic with Hollingsworths in Hastings, joined the RAF at the outbreak of WWII as an aero mechanic where he met his wife Irene. A move to London saw him enrolled as a bus driver and their mother a 'clippie' or conductor working out of the Holloway bus garage.

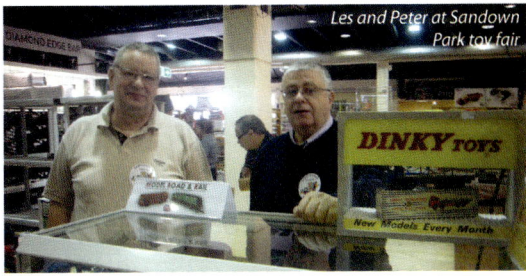
Les and Peter at Sandown Park toy fair

Interestingly, Terry Parsons, also a driver there, later became more widely known as Matt Munro the singer! Les recalls how every week, after collecting his modest wage, his father would return home with 2 Dinky Toys clasped in his hands. He would offer both hands to both boys, and they would choose. Les' memory tells him that he got the Vauxhall Cresta in green and grey, whilst Peter got the maroon and cream version!

Both boys accumulated a large collection of Dinky Toys, but Les recalls that whilst he would use a blowtorch to strip and then paint them, Peter kept his pristine in their boxes. His parents had obtained a hardware shop in Islington, north London, and the boys began selling their model cars in the shop. By 1968, the family moved to premises with a newsagents shop in Penge, south east London, and their interest in cars was re-kindled.

However, the fire really began when Peter bought a 36 series Dinky taxi at a traction engine rally, and Les placed a small advert in the shop seeking his favourite locomotive, the Battle of Britain class. The response brought a collection in, which was duly purchased, some parts kept, others sold, and thus a larger advert was placed. More collections came and were sold, and the business was born.

By the time Les and Peter took the plunge and moved to a run down model shop in Worcester Park, Surrey, which they found in Dalton's Weekly, Peter was working for Legal & General Insurance, and was helping Les with marketing behind the scenes. They brought with them a vast collection of stock, and so Model Road & Rail was born in 1981.

Les's favourite vehicle of all time has always been the Austin FX3 London taxi, and when he got

Model Road Replicas Austin Taxi for Christmas

to know Brian West, of the London Vintage Taxi Association, they realised that there was no accurate model of the FX3. Having decided to fill the gap with his own range, he researched a few potential white metal manufacturers, and settled on Scale Model Technical Services. He sought and obtained approval from Carbodies, the makers of the 1:1 scale version. On reflection, it is ironic that the real cab at the time cost £1000, and the brass master for the model cost £1100! Les and Peter decided to call the range Model Road Replicas, to link it with the shop, and liked the Dinky Supertoy box art, so used that pattern, but with green stripes to also link with the shop colours.

Model Road Replicas Vauxhall Victor F type

The taxi was well received, and to continue the range, Les and Peter decided to use Brian West's F-type Vauxhall Victor as the next subject, as there was not a good model of this car either. Mk II Ford Consul, Ford E83W van, and 300E van, together with the Routemasters, all followed. MRR had assistance from Tim Bubb, a regular trader at Maidstone toy fair, who worked at the South Eastern Gas Board, for the livery of the E83W van, and Paul Harrison at Ford for original drawings of the vans and the Consul.

Model Road Replicas 1:76 MRR6a AEC Routemaster RMF

Each model was made in the lower hundreds, and some still appear on eBay today. Les reflects that the white metal market has declined since the quality of diecasting from China has risen, but also notes with satisfaction that when Ertl published their catalogue featuring their new Austin FX3 taxi, the illustration was based on the MRR model!

More generally, Les feels that whilst white metal model subjects were chosen from gaps in their diecast line up, the manufacturers follow the lead of cars already made by white metal ranges.

As a retailer, Les reflects on the halcyon days of Matchbox Models of Yesteryear collecting and selling, when the market was buoyant, and notes that the fun of chasing and finding elusive rarities is now almost lost thanks to eBay.

These days, Les has joined the ranks of eBay sellers, and is also promoting his associate company TOY444 Auctions (TOY 444 taken from the company van's registration) as a way of both reducing his remaining stock since the shop closed, but also serving the needs of collectors.

Model Road Replicas 1:43 MRR4a Ford 300e van 7cwt

Brian Harrison
B & L Models

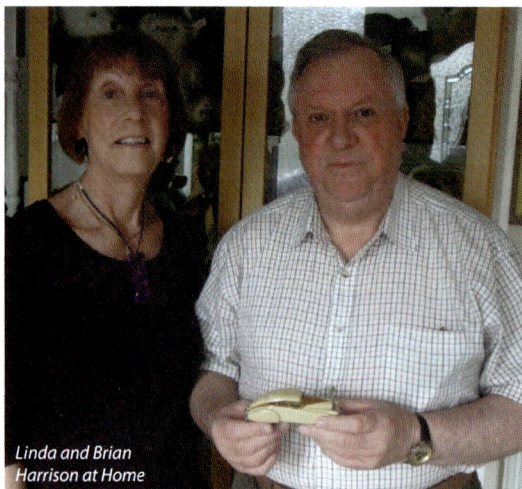

Linda and Brian Harrison at Home

Brian Harrison, who formed B&L Models in 1989, is based at his home in Bradford, West Yorkshire. Like most people into toys and models, he started with Dinky, Corgi, Lledo, etc., then he bought his first Brooklin model from a shop in Halifax and since that day he has been hooked on what he considers the best value for money handbuilt models on the market.

He placed an advert in Collectors Gazette wanting Brooklin Specials and received a phone call from a Canadian gentleman visiting Harrogate offering him six 1986 Canadian Toy Show models which he bought, keeping one and swapping the others for additional Brooklin models he wanted.

In his search for the rarer models, he talked with John Hall, then owner of Brooklin Models who pointed him in the direction of the Canadian Toy Collectors Society show in Toronto. Thus guided,

he went there in 1990, 1991 and 1997 and also attended the Bay Brooklin Club AGM, which club is now defunct, but in the late 1980s/1990s always held their meeting during the weekend of the CTCS show. These weekends were always a great social occasion and opportunity for sharing experiences with fellow collectors from all over the world. Who in that fraternity could ever forget gathering at Tony Romas for supper the night before the show?

He also went to Germany as part of the German Brooklin Club weekend there and was a regular stallholder at ModeleX, the show for handbuilt models run by Ray Strutt, which was held at The National Motorcycle Museum in Birmingham during the 1990s. For Brian, ModeleX has to be the best show he ever attended as a dealer.

In his early days as a collector/dealer he helped Bill O'Donnell, a true gentleman who 'showed him the ropes' They went to many shows together and Brian would help Bill set up his stall and learn the 'tricks of the trade'. Yes, this was to be the life for him. He quickly realised it was what he wanted to do and in 1989, set up B & L Models.

At the time, he was still working for a large telecommunications company, but this was due to change as he became more and more involved with his hobby, come second job. In 1994, he quit his full time job to concentrate on the models and has never looked back. It was the best thing he ever did, apart from marrying his wife Linda, the L part of B & L. Without her support he would still be working for the same company

He still attends a few shows, but nothing like as many as he did in the 1980s/ 90s. Whilst he specialises in Brooklin models, he also stocks other manufacturers' handbuilt models, selling by mail order from home. He can be contacted by phone, fax, mail or email.

Nigel Judge

Nigel - specialist retailer

Nigel recalls his 30 years of model collecting and dealing beginning when he collected toys as a boy, with birthdays and christmases always a time to welcome the latest Corgi to the toy box. The first major development was the arrival locally of a full shop window display of Hot Wheels. These models, the track, and the paint finish made obsolete anything that came before!

At University in London in the mid 1980s Nigel stumbled across a shop selling second hand toys at Charing Cross underneath the arches, (run by John Teychenne) and it was only then he realized that old toys had a value. He started hunting for them and began selling them at venues such as Farnham Maltings, Gloucester swapmeet and Sandown Park.

His passion for white metal models was ignited at the time he first saw those made by Western Models, and although some look dated now, they were superb at the time and were distinctly different from anything else. It was only the high price which was a deterrent, as they were about half a weeks' wages for Nigel at the time! The 'new on the scene' Brooklin Models, and some smaller companies like Marque Models, John Day and Mikansue were all competing for attention, and were modelling rare cars forgotten by diecast manufacturers.

The discovery of David Buckles' model shop, Formula One Models & Prints in Swanage was a third catalyst, as that range of models and their continued improvement was a focal point for him. It persuaded Nigel to try to concentrate on these models and leave the diecast ranges to the others. Of course he was still on the look out for obsolete Tekno, Solido and Marklin diecast models to supplement his paltry selection of handbuilts and even dealt in Franklin Mint if the price was right to turn over a profit.

After being made redundant Nigel spent a year as a full time trader before working as a teacher, and the weekends, long holidays and any spare time were reserved for his hobby, girlfriend permitting. The joys of teaching meant that the long holiday breaks were

when his focus became the auction sites which are the main supply of models. Nigel is now well known as a white metal dealer and has a regular clientele who are often surprised at the variety and selection of models he has available.

Nigel recalls one customer who was looking to buy models of all the real cars he had acquired, but had never seen a model of a post war Hillman he once owned. Fortunately, Western Models had just released the model and Nigel had it on his table. The customer had an envelope with 'new fridge money' written on it, which was swiftly ripped open and the model purchased; the fridge had to wait!

Nigel has some very keen customers who have massive collections, and one of them uses 4 A4 sized books listing the models he has as reference. Most of these are white metal. Nigel suspects they must weigh a fair bit and are worth a fortune!

Nigel's highlights in white metal collecting begin with the Pathfinder range, convinced that their subject choice and quality made them very desirable. The potential for investment was a bonus, and they still hold their own in the current market where the values of modern diecast models are dropping. He regards Somerville Models as slightly better than Pathfinder Models in quality, their last issues such as the Ford Prefect and the Vauxhalls still being state of the art. Pete Kenna together with Spa Croft and Crossway Models are now producing British cars that Nigel enjoys and which remind him of British cars long forgotten. He believes that Brooklin's Lansdowne range has come on leaps and bounds over the last decade. For Nigel, the top of the range for white metal models are Top Marques, still the epitome of excellence and quality, with J & M Classics nearly as good although the scale looks sometimes inconsistent to him.

Nigel's golden era of white metal was the 1980s, with Daimler House, SMTS, Motor City USA, and Minimarque43 all actively promoting the hobby, He senses that the standard of modern diecast and resin models in the 21st century are now good enough to give the collector pleasure, but the feel, the subject, the weight and the exclusivity of white metal models will, Nigel believes, ensure a following and hopefully new collectors will come on board.

Nigel speculates that in the future it will be interesting to see if new customers emerge in the next generation, and if they will know the difference between a Riley and an Alvis. Unlike the older tin plate and diecast toys, white metal models can, in his opinion remain relevant as the producers can change with the fashions. He predicts Ford Capris will be the Squires and Frazer Nashs of the future so he believes it is all rosy in the handbuilt garden.

Nigel plans to continue his passion to collect and deal

in handbuilt models, and awaits with thumping heart for the next Spa Croft model, together with the one off Jowett Jupiter fastback promised by J & M Classics.

The best model of all time? Well, Nigel's choice is a mundane car in reality. He would choose Pete Kenna's Standard Vanguard Phase 2 closely followed by the Top Marques Alvis Grey Lady which is perfect right down to its badge bar.

Tony Mclellan
Langley Miniature Models

The staff team, Tony with his son Ian, and his mother Noreen

So often we have found that white metal model makers have been family based, and this one spans 3 generations!

Originally running a grocery shop in Maidenhead, it all really started with humble beginnings in a hardware shop in Langley Green, near Crawley, Sussex. Tony and his wife Pam had been considering other lines to stock, and had tried handicrafts, but the interest was not great. Pam's father was an enthusiastic railway modeller, and Tony began to be fascinated by this hobby too.

It didn't take long before Tony had established Langley Models in the back room of the hardware store, and was stocking a full range of plastic kits, Tri-ang, Hornby and Fleischman model railway equipment, and radio control models.

As the demand for model railway models and accessories increased, particularly in N gauge, customers began asking for signals. Tony made a set of signals out of brass, and soon realised that this was a long winded way of producing a quantity of signals. Another helpful customer told him of a friend Tony, who had worked for Corocraft, the founders of

The mould store

Schwaroski crystal, casting jewellery. This company was also based in Crawley, and Tony Mclellan believes it had been the first to use a bob weight centrifugal casting machine in the UK. He made the mould from the brass signal, the customer took the mould to his friend and production began.

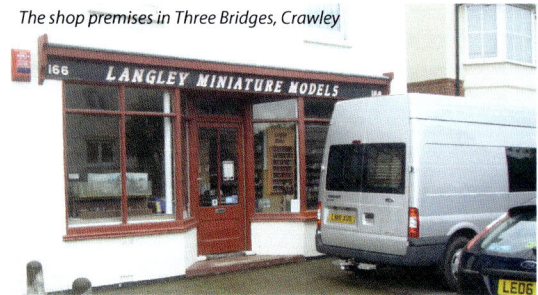

The shop premises in Three Bridges, Crawley

Meanwhile Pam had been watching BBC Nationwide covering a local business feature, which she felt was boring, and so she wrote inviting them to visit their premises at Langley Green. A film crew arrived and were with them all day. As a result word got around, and customers came from far and wide both for kits, and with ideas. As the castings were returned from the caster, Tony and Pam were packing them and despatching from the rear of the hardware shop. As an engineer by trade, Tony found it was not difficult to experiment with brass patterns, and began to develop their range with lorry kits. He contemplated making rolling stock, and locos, but concluded that with experts such as Bob Wills in the market, the gap was for scenic and lineside accessories.

He first continued with N gauge, but then branched into 00' As the business grew, it became necessary to employ the services of some freelance pattern makers, and these included Ian Harrah, in Brixton, who had previously made 15mm figures, but was able to make horses, vehicles, and fairground rides, all areas Langley Miniature Models was moving into. Tony was keen to produce simple one piece cabs for his lorry kits, as other makers were still working with slab sided construction.

With Langley Miniature Models outgrowing the hardware shop, and their enthusiasm for the business leaning in that direction, the shop in Langley Green was sold in 1977, and Tony and family moved to a house with a garage, where the model construction could continue. The family were seeking a level of self sufficiency through their white metal business, and

Tony stated he would give it 2 years!

Three years later, such was the success of Langley Miniature Models that they began to think of bigger premises. When walking along Three Bridges Road one day in Crawley, Pam spotted a grocery shop for sale. Without further ado, they bought it, and offered their son Ian a minor partnership in the business. They soon set about removing the Victorian kitchen at the rear, and extending the premises to create a workshop, storeroom and packing area. Acquisition of both a casting machine and vulcanising press enabled then to carry out the whole casting process for many of their kits entirely in house. Contract work for similar other businesses such as Scalelink is also part of their everyday work.

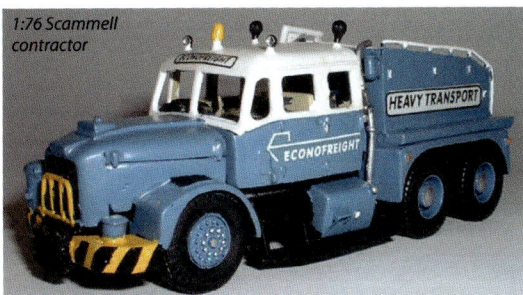
1:76 Scammell contractor

The same premises remain Langley's base to this day, and are also home to their dog Tess and a sprightly green hen parrot named Oswald which enjoys temporary refuge in the many boxes around the storage area, in addition to its cage.

Soon after this move, Tony's mother Noreen joined the team, as the range of models was up to 130 different lorry kits, and around 12 different boats, featuring river, inland waterway and harbour craft. Ian had begun making the patterns for new models, according to new ideas from customers, or just something different that they wished to make. Fairground models, buildings, cranes and dockside accessories, figures, and many more in both N, 00 and 0 gauges all feature in their comprehensive catalogues. Tony finds that different models vary in their popularity, with most lorry kits being made at 100 a time, whilst an autocoach in brass sold 4,500 examples.

1:43 Fisherman in a boat

1:76 Scammell Highwayman

Around 1990, Tony's son Ian had been studying for an engineering degree, and was working in the shop on Saturday mornings. Since the separation of Tony and Pam, Ian has joined the business as a full partner with Tony, thus ensuring the continuation of the business. Tony also feels that whilst the Chinese diecast makers such as Oxford Diecast, Classix and Base Toys appeal to the enthusiast who prefers to simply place a model on the layout, his ranges meet the needs of the dedicated modeller who wishes to sculpt and create a model unique to his or her model railway scene. Tony and Ian both visit around 20 – 25 model railway shows each year, all over England, using an 18' x 6' display stand featuring their models in built form.

Apart from their pattern makers, and two part time workers, this remains very much a family business, and the enthusiasm for the continued growth of the business appears to pump through both Tony and Ian's veins. Indeed, to produce increasingly difficult projects particularly for '0' gauge, Ian is experimenting with new and innovative ideas using resin as the medium. Some 40 years on from starting, the business still goes on with the range constantly continuing to grow, and a solid future appears to be ahead for Langley Miniature Models.

1:76 Hunt scene (above) & 1:76 Market scene

John Martin
JM Toys Ltd

John and his car at JM Toys HQ

Many collectors will know the well known sight of a wall of 1:18 scale model cars covering many tables at the major toy fairs, and adjacent to this formidable array is an equally substantial display of the very best in quality white metal handbuilt models.

Those who have obtained their models from JM Toys for some years will know that it was founded by John Martin, and John's story deserves recounting here. John hails from an engineering background, having commenced a five year apprenticeship with GEC Marconi in Portsmouth at the tender age of 16. There he developed his model and tool making skills, including working on prototypes of satellites and torpedoes. He left Marconi at 21 to improve his skills at Plessey, and then at 25 had an opportunity to work for himself. He founded three companies, J Martin, Toolmakers, MDM Engineering, and a third making agricultural spraying equipment. It was his tool making company, though, which cleared the path towards toys, as this company made tools for the production of Airfix kits, Palitoy model railways, and similar work for other toy companies.

John recalls how he found old toys when he was

Russell Martin at Sandown Park toy fair

holidaying in Devon at Shaldon, where he had a flat for the family just by the little zoo. He found himself at the nearby Bairnscroft hotel listening to a chap from Birmingham, who owned a model shop. He was then intrigued by the model shop in Teignmouth which displayed a wide range of model railway items. He became hooked, wanted to both collect, and to become further involved, so he bought a company making the controllers, and then acquired the Fleetline Model Company, owned by Brian Parks, which made white metal model miniatures for model railways, and railway accessories in N gauge, such as farm animals, fencing etc.

Morris J Van promotional
for British Diabetic Association in red

He transferred his skills from managing engineering work to counting toy sheep on the kitchen table, as he and his wife found themselves responsible for packing the sets of animals and other accessories.

On November 9th 1979, John opened Cowplain Models, near Waterlooville, Hampshire, stocking mostly model railways, kits and some obsolete diecast models. During the following 5 years, he consolidated his position in the toy field by purchasing first the stock and then the freehold of Tony Collett's model shop In Portsmouth which also specialised in model railways. He finally sold the shop to Chris Hitchin in 1984, and whilst he had an agreement with Chris not to trade in competition locally, John began trading at a few toy fairs elsewhere around the country. At the Salisbury swapmeet he met David Angel, who traded as Angel's Autos, owning both a collection of about 20 American cars, and also a scrap yard in Dorset. Meanwhile, John became attracted to the new Brooklin Models range, impressed by their weight and strength, and remembers with frustration how he was still gathering his knowledge on Brooklin, as he let 2 Brooklin models without windows go very cheaply at a swapmeet, not realising that these were 2 very early models finished in this way at the Canadian factory. On his travels John began collecting Pathfinder models, and met Pete Kenna of Kenna Models. As his knowledge grew, he was approached by Richard West, the first editor of Model

Viscount models Triumph Dolomite in yellow and white

Collector, to write a column on white metal models. He declined, but his collection was photographed at home for the magazine.

He also travelled to the Brussels swapmeet at Woluwe, where on one occasion he found some odd coloured Brooklins, and wrote about his find in the Model Collector magazine.

Imagine his surprise when he got a call from John Hall, supremo at Brooklin, quizzing him on where he obtained them. It became clear that these models had been removed from a workbench at Brooklin Models. John Hall was happy for John to keep the models, and as a result a strong friendship was formed.

The pattern is becoming clear, as John expands his knowledge, trading in white metal and his personal collection, so friendships are made. He travelled to Canada and the USA, visiting the Canadian Toy Collectors Society annual show, and buying collections of Brooklin models along the way. He believes at this stage he had amassed one of the biggest collections of Brooklins in the world. Indeed, John's collection, and those of John Hammick and David Angel, were the source of all the listings in the first Brooklin Model Guide. Roly and Doug McHard, of

Viscount Models Ford Cortina Mk III 2000E

Somerville Models, were also amongst the friends he made along the white metal trading route, as he was stocking large quantities of models from all the key British and foreign manufacturers.

Throughout this period of expansion in the model world, John continued to own his engineering company, only closing it finally in 1992.

As a result of his long term diagnosis of diabetes, John became involved with the British Diabetic Association, and realised he could make a difference through his involvement with model cars. John organised with Brooklin Models to produce a special BRK 31x Pontiac sedan delivery as an ambulance, had 500 made, and donated all the profits to Portsmouth hospital and the BDA. He has been

Brass master for Morris J Van

amazed at the generosity of collectors that made this possible. Further projects included a special Lledo model which raised £30,000 for the Portsmouth hospital, and funded groups of diabetic children in need to enjoy holidays on the Isle of Wight. Other manufacturers also supported the fund raising, including Pathfinder Models with special colour variants on its Morris 'J' van, and Pete Kenna with a special Standard Vanguard pick up.

By this time, JM Toys had become one of the biggest distributors of white metal models world wide. Certainly, John was regularly ordering a substantial number of each colour of the Pathfinder Models as they were released. This increasingly close link to the specialist makers led to special models, such as those in the Viscount Range in the 1970s. These white metal models came about through a joint partnership with Pathfinder owners Jeff and Sue Sharrock. Sadly, the range had to stop at 2 models as Jeff's ill health meant curtailing all but the mainstream Pathfinder range.

JM Toys would handle all the major white metal ranges, importing Durham Classics, and were main retailers for Brooklin Models, Scale Racing Cars, Kenna Models, Western Models, RAE Models and

Somerville Models, together with Minimarque43, Pathfinder Models, Illustra Models, Scale Model Technical Services and many others.

Nowadays, John feels that the market continues to be reasonably buoyant, but sales are more web based than at toy fairs. He feels this is a backward step, as traditionally, it has been a pleasure to share with customers face to face the weight, definition and detail that white metal handbuilt models offer. His flagship range has always been Brooklin, which includes Lansdowne, but surprisingly, may not have done. John explained to us that prior to the Lansdowne range's launch, John Hall of Brooklin had been proposing that John might commission Brooklin to make a range of British cars. John Hall's main interest was always American cars, and the European connection was satisfied by the joint venture with Eddie Anderson which created the Robeddie range. John discussed the idea with John Hammick, and together they felt they could enter into a business arrangement with Brooklin, on the basis of approximately 150 pieces of the each model.

They got as far as researching the possible subjects, concluding that the range should be called Westminster, and would be launched with an Austin Westminster. However, when John Hall suggested that 1,000 items would be the batch supplied, they realised that this was too big a risk. A year later, Lansdowne was born and launched 'in house'.

John's health has suffered as a result of his illness, and he has been steadily handing over aspects of the JM Toys business to his son Russell, who will acquire a thriving and comprehensively stocked model car business, with a few thousand models on the internet based JM Toys eBay shop alone. At the time of writing, this hand over is expected to be completed by the end of 2011.

John is now able to reflect on the extent of the loyalty and friendship he has gained from his many loyal customers from as far afield as Australia, Canada, New Zealand, South Africa, South America, and the United States.

Whilst he would now like to put up a sign over his door 'Gone Fishin!' he nevertheless is still tempted by his first love, and recently bought another substantial collection of Brooklin models – they say it's in your blood don't they!

Bob Pitkin
Tober Models

Bob has sold Tober models for some years, both at toy fairs and outdoor shows in the summer months. Tober is 'gypsy' for fairground vehicles and equipment, and these models were originally created by Bill Barnes, from Norfolk, whose story appears in Chapter 7. Bill's production included a large range of fairground vehicles.

Bob soon became a major retail outlet for Bill, as the range was very attractive to both casual and regular visitors to steam rallies. More recently Bob has been selling Bill's 3 wheelers, simple models that are easily mastered.

Peter Stoyle
Peregrine Model Cars

Peter behind his stand at Windsor toy fair

Peregrine Model Cars is the culmination of a successful journey by Peter Stoyle, who is one of the small band of traders who have established a niche in the relatively exclusive market of handbuilt model cars.

Peter was first introduced to model cars when, in 1969, he and his wife Kathy had the idea of a vintage car sitting atop their wedding cake. The selected vehicle was none other than the Y4 Matchbox Models of Yesteryear Opel, in white, of course.

Before marrying Kathy, Peter had owned an Austin Healey Sprite MkI known as a Frogeye, but once married, Peter's interest in classic cars began to bear fruit, and his first sortie, in 1972, was to bring home a Ford Y-type on a trailer behind his Ford Cortina 1600E, bought for £50 from a farm on Dartmoor. This car never got fully restored, and was eventually sold on to make way, in 1975, for a Daimler SP250 Dart joining the family. This car was in ivory, and Peter fully restored it. It has been in the family for many years, and now is his daughter's pride and joy.

During these early years of married life, Peter was working as an electrical fitter in the dockyard at Plymouth, in a team of six setting up navigation systems. By the early 1980s he had begun collecting, firstly Matchbox Models of Yesteryear. This brought Peter in contact with Ray Bush, who ran the UK Matchbox Club, and Ray became a firm friend.

When Ray retired in June 1986, Peter bought his entire collection including rare prototypes. With Ray's advice and encouragement, Peter planned to begin trading in secondhand model cars, beginning with the Bush collection, together with his own Yesteryear collection which he decided to pass on. He began in a small way part time whilst still working in the dockyard, but a few months later, in September 1986, Peter had the opportunity to take redundancy from the Ministry of Defence, and the model car business became his full time occupation.

Amongst the clients Peter met was John Hammick, who purchased a number of the rarer prototype Yesteryear models. When in 1988, John planned to open the Merley House Museum, he had intended to use the newly launched and popular Days Gone range to promote the attraction. However, with Peter's growing interest in handbuilt models, he persuaded John to consider a Brooklin model instead as the special for the Museum. 150 models were commissioned of the Dodge van, with Merley House logo, and John and Peter had 75 each. These now command a premium.

This venture helped establish the name and specialist nature of Peregrine Model Cars. Peregrine as a name was simply easy to remember, and as a result, the nickname of Peregrine Pete for its owner was almost inevitable! With the arrival on the scene of the much loved Pathfinder Models range, it was not so surprising that Peter should suggest to Jeff Sharrock that they produce a Daimler Dart model. Amazingly, Jeff had a Daimler Dart too, in maroon, and so the two Pathfinder issues were painted in their two colours, complete with correct registration numbers. Subsequently, Peter also commissioned Pathfinder to make a Metropolitan Police Daimler Dart, complete with chrome Winkworth bell, which again is now very sought after.

The early years Peter recalls with much fondness, enjoying his developing reputation as a specialist in Yesteryears and spares for that range. He was reassured that he would be able to make a reasonable living, as prior to this, he had never even attended a toy fair!

By 1990, he was travelling across Europe to Belgium, France, Germany, Italy and Luxembourg on a monthly basis, selling obsolete diecast models at toy fairs, and

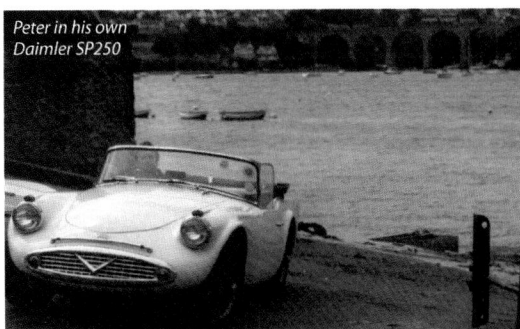
Peter in his own Daimler SP250

also beginning to pick up handbuilt models that had hitherto not been seen in England. Peter had always intended to obtain retail premises in Plymouth, but somehow he found trading from home, with the flexibility to travel in Europe in search of interesting new models, more appealing and rewarding.

Today, Peter's table display is a glittering array of the best of the handbuilt makers, both resin and white metal, with a particular leaning towards Rolls Royce. He is a reliably full stockist of J&M Classics, Top Marques, Brooklin and Lansdowne models. He recalls with amusement an old lady who examined a Top Marques Rolls Royce closely, observing the price tag of £250, and then commented "It does seem a lot of money to pay for a child to then play with it!"

Peter has continued the occasional promotional theme, working jointly with Pete Kenna of Kenna Models on a Standard Vanguard Phase II liveried as the Monte Carlo Rally entry, and also an MGTD Police car in black. This followed the successful Metropolitan Police Daimler Dart.

He has retained a small collection of models of cars that are significant to him, such as the Daimler Dart, as well as a small selection of Ford Anglia 105Es, a range of BMW estates, as this is what he drives now, and also the Z3M roadster. Perhaps surprisingly, the more vintage era is represented by a line up of Shackleton lorries.

Business is surprisingly picking up after the recession, leaving Peter optimistic enough to have been employing his daughter part time for the last 15 months on selling via eBay. He acknowledges that the quality of Chinese and Far Eastern manufacturers has improved immensely, but strongly feels that there are customers who will choose a handbuilt model costing considerably more than a diecast as it represents exclusivity, and the models are often of subjects never covered by mainstream manufacturers.

There are, for instance, many Rolls Royce and Bentley enthusiasts who will purchase every new model of these marques that are released. Peter can claim both Royal and celebrity clients amongst those who have regularly purchased from him.

Steve Traffic
BMC Garage

A man with a BMC mission is surely Steve Traffic. Steve recalls buying a Spot-On Mini van at a collectors shop in late 1991 or early 1992, which reminded him of school holidays when his father took him round the country collecting documents for his work in the only available works vehicle - a green mini van. There was no works car available at the time, nor couriers! As a result he approached Brooklin Models to make a Mini van and pick up in white metal for him. This was around the same time that Gems and Cobwebs had released their Jaguar Mk VII. Brooklin agreed to produce the Mini van and pick up, and thus Steve launched British Motoring Classics, now bmc43.

The first 5 liveries of the Mini van Mk III were released in December 1992 with 3 different vehicles all produced by Brooklin in various liveries and plain colours.

Brooklin found a master maker for the first 3 models, and Steve obtained permission to develop a range of models from MG-Rover at their Head Quarters in Warwick, and the original Heritage centre at Syon Park in West London, some time before the Heritage centre at Gaydon was built.

Gift set 'Pedal Car company'

The third Mini van, a MkI, was produced in Lansdowne Models livery, following a request from John Hall, the then Brooklin owner. Brooklin made British Motoring Classics models were supplied in a blue coloured version of its Lansdowne box with gold coloured labels, but the glue holding these boxes failed and they tended to spring open, so Steve changed to plain white boxes with printed labels.

There were to be further models in the range, the fourth and fifth being a Riley Elf and a Wolseley Hornet but Brooklin wanted to concentrate on its Lansdowne range. Consequently, Steve decided to seek another source for complete models. He arranged for these and others including a Mini Clubman saloon and estate, Mini Cabrio, and a Mini

Hot Dog minivan

Traveller to be produced on a sub contractor basis by Western Models. The range was named Miniclassics, now merged into bmc43, and ran for some years until production was taken over in house.

Operating from a toy collectors shop, and later an antiques centre, meant that all his models and kits have been produced on this basis.

Steve believes he was fortunate to get Brooklin's agreement to make the first 3 models, and also in finding MG-Rover so helpful and even commissioning some models for the company. At the 1993 Earls Court Motor Show, the 1994 Monte Carlo Rally Rover Mini Cooper, to be driven by 1964 winner Paddy Hopkirk, was unveiled on the next but one stand. Rover received special dispensation to use rally number 37, the same start number as the 1964 winner. A model was quickly produced in the Miniclassics series of the 'press-presentation' livery, with decals produced speedily from photographs taken at the show, and Rover used some of the models for publicity purposes.

Steve has mainly worked for himself, not employing any staff. He did not set out to expand and has been content to maintain a steady production rate, with new models and ranges, at his own pace. One of the best items produced in the

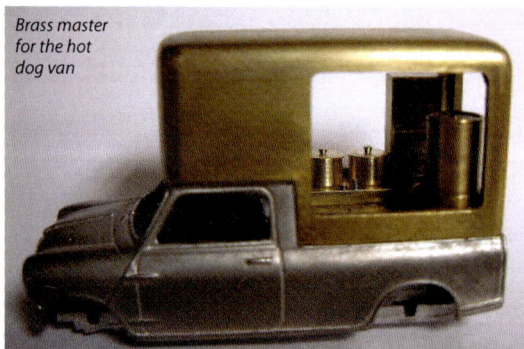

Brass master for the hot dog van

range is a Cooper Car Company set, with mini van, trailer and racing mini. The set was completed with an Omen Miniatures figure of John Cooper, which the late great John and his son Michael gave permission for Steve to produce.

As techniques have developed over the years there have been a number of changes to make building and painting simpler, and as a result, Steve has found that many collectors now document the variations that have arisen.

Production numbers are generally 1 - 200, and none has, to date, exceeded 500 units. Most are still available, some only currently as kits, and these are usually released after fully built stock has sold out, but no limits are set on any of the range.

The company has relied in the past on toy fairs, and classic car shows, but increasingly mail order and the website have become more important, as the entire range, and the more recent resin slot car ranges can be fully promoted in colour.

There are no plans to stop at the moment, and production has become mostly models partly made in

Mini pick up - film unit

resin, mainly due to the high cost of shipping complete white metal models. Steve has also begun producing models in other scales such as 1:32,1:50,1:76, and some of the latter two are in white metal

Given the overall state of the market at present, Steve is likely to make smaller runs of unusual derivatives in the future, such as a Mini pick up with a Riley Elf bonnet, Mini Clubman van, in other words vehicles that exist in the real world as conversions, and are legitimate subjects!

Graham Ward
Promod Ltd

Graham with a selection of current Promod Models

Graham Ward is one of our more prolific entrepreneurs, but has perhaps remained more behind the scenes than others.

He recalls always having been interested in real cars and trucks and started collecting Matchbox

at a young age with his pocket money. He always preferred them to Corgi and Dinky Toys as he felt that he got more cars for his money. As he grew older he started to make model kits of cars from Airfix and AMT, and the constructing bug started.

When Graham was about 14 he joined the Matchbox UK and USA clubs and started trading and corresponding with other collectors worldwide. He found himself enthusiastically seeking models with different labels and colours, and exchanging for examples not found in the UK. Graham now feels that this is something that is missing from modern collecting, the hunt for rare variations and odd colours.

In 1982 Graham launched Promod with a shop. He decided to start working on his own, as he had previously found that he soon got bored in his earlier jobs, and decided that working for himself was the way forward. He had a friend called Bill Deane, who was a leading Britains dealer, and Bill gave him encouragement to go it alone. Bill's adage was that if you start with nothing you have nothing to loose.

Graham's first shop was in Longton in the Potteries selling diecast, trains and kits. Soon after he commissioned a number of special models from Lledo, Matchbox and Corgi at a time when they were prepared to manufacture specials. The ranges were limited and apart from Lledo quantities quite large. As a result, he saw a gap in the market to produce what are now called Code 3 models, based on other models, the first one being a Van Hool coach by Efsi. These were all hand painted in coach paint from the real vehicles.

Promod Bedford S type

The first models to be issued under the Promod name were a joint venture with a company from Balsall Common called Gearbox which had grown out of the Boston-Nicholls pewter company from Birmingham.

However, there were difficulties with this venture. Gearbox produced very fine complex models in limited numbers, and the companies that were seeking Graham's Code 3 service were seeking large quantities of exclusive models. Gearbox wanted only to produce models with many fine parts and Promod needed models that were simple and easy to build in quantity. He considered investing in his own manufacturing but decided that it was more cost effective to sub contract the manufacturing and only do the painting and building himself. Graham recalls, on one occasion, a car company wanting 2000 hand built models, stating a price, and delivery time in 3 months. This was a challenge but his suppliers agreed they could achieve the deadline. He asked the customer for pictures and plans but they refused, saying it was top secret and they could reveal nothing until the launch. The only problem was they wanted the models for the launch!! Unfortunately therefore, Promod did not proceed with that order, but Graham was not surprised to discover that the real car was a complete flop as well, no wonder with marketing people like that behind it.

Promod has made exclusive models with runs of only 50, and also up to 3000 hand built models for some customers. Today Graham limits the collectors models to 150-250 of each, although as well as cars and trucks, Promod produces kits which are not

limited. Promod's range of pillar boxes and telephone kiosks are also unlimited and continue to sell year, in year out. Models which are not limited are brought back sometimes modified in new versions/liveries.

For some time Graham's market has been worldwide, and he sells direct as well as supplying shops. Many of his sales are direct to companies, and for collectors he advertises through collectors' magazines and real vehicle magazines.

The Promod production involves contracting out the pattern making, and all the casting. Graham then builds the models in house so he can keep an eye on quality. With ever increasing prices from China, with some Chinese diecasts, even in 1:43 scale retailing at nearly £100, it is now possible for the British handbuilt industry to compete again.

Promod Karrier with milk churns

Graham is planning to expand with new ranges including more kits, and new areas such as soft skinned post war military vehicles. He is also planning the gradual re-launch of the Somerville range of models which Promod purchased on the death of Doug McHard. Rod Ward, acting on behalf of Doug's widow Roly, approached Graham, and the subsequent sale included all Doug's machines and moulds. Graham's plan is to keep Promod's models fairly simple in detail but affordable for those who find the mass produced models becoming to expensive. To this end, he has already simplified the castings of the three Vauxhalls in the range, and re-cast these, partly at the request of Vauxhalls. These can now be found on eBay.

Graham takes an optimistic view of the future, and foresees the market going full circle with there being growth amongst the specialist companies again.

Rod & Val Ward
Modelauto Ltd and
Sun Motor Company

Within this business there are few that have succeeded in becoming a retailer, producer, publisher and household name. Rod Ward and Modelauto are two such names.

Rod had originally qualified as an architect, and

Rod at ModeleX

Sun Motor Co. Humber ambulance

Val as a technical librarian, and prior to getting involved in the model car business, they had owned a collector's shop called Sun Antiques, named after its location in Sun Street, Haworth, Yorkshire. They brought their combined organisational skills to the then usually more amateur activity of toy dealing, and established Modelauto Limited, in Leeds, as a leading distributor of handbuilt models and kits.

As proprietors of the shop, Rod and Val also saw a need for an enthusiast based regular magazine devoted entirely to model cars, and so became the publishers of Model Auto Review magazine.

The Sun Motor Co range was set up in 1983 by Rod and Val, using the 'Sun' name from their previous business, as they had found that from time to time, some ranges or models would disappear from the market, but stiil have some sales potential. They considered ways to keep them going, whilst ensuring that there was no intention of competing with any of those ranges, whose proprietors were all friends of the Wards. This became the driving force behind Rod's production for the next 20 years.

As a result, Modelauto was among the first firms to have promotional models made by handbuilt artisans such as Michel Dubray, Doug McHard at Somerville and John Hall at Brooklin Models.

There were four Sun sub ranges at the start. Series 1 consisted of 1:43 scale fully finished cars, Series 2 1:43 transkits and conversions for existing diecast models, although this series only lasted for a year or two. Series 3 were reproductions of old toys and Series 4 were 1:76 scale white metal kits.

Beginning with Series 1, Geoff Moorhouse had worked at both Meccano and Corgi on the design of diecast model cars, and he produced his own range of 1:43 polyester resin handbuilt model cars for a short time under the AGM name (his initials), but was personally more interested in trucks. He was developing a 1:50 white metal truck range, called Heavy Haulage. Rod asked Geoff if the two AGM cars could be slightly modified and cast in white metal for Series 1 of the new Sun range. The first of these two

models was a De Soto Suburban 1948, modelled in a number of guises including a taxi, police car, fire and ambulance cars, and finally a hearse.

The second AGM was a 1954 Bristol 450 Le Mans. Geoff had always liked the Bristol, but he thought the Dinky Toys version looked rather bland, so he created a proper scale model. It was so good, in fact, that Provence Moulage later copied the Sun casting, without permission, for their 1:43 resin kit of the 450. To extend the scope of Series 3, Rod proposed making a copy of the old Chad Valley Humber Super Snipe, and asked Geoff to prepare it for casting. Geoff didn't like the toy, and suggested making a more accurate master for Series 1. This appeared as a private car in 1984, and later also as a police car and Bristol Fire Brigade car.

When Vic Bailey, proprietor of Veteran and Vintage Models in Sussex, discontinued his range of Dinky and other copies, they were 'adopted' to launch Series 3 of the Sun Motor Co. There were seven white metal replicas of pre war diecast Dinky Toys, plus an MG racing car. However, once the original castings ran out, Series 3 was discontinued.

Series 4 consisted of copies of Dublo Dinky Toys and Matchbox models, previously cast under the RADDS name by toy spare parts specialist Steve Flowers. This Series, also did not last long.

All the white metal models were cast for Rod by Maurice Bozward, of White Metal Assemblies, whose excellent work, especially for large castings, was known to all in the trade. Geoff Moorhouse continued to provide masters for Rod, of a number of new models, for the white metal ranges. These included a Humber Super Snipe Tickford drophead, specifically requested by an owner who approached Rod to make a model of it. Existing diecasts also provided a base for additional models in the range, such as a fire appliance based on the Corgi Classics Thornycroft lorry, a VW Beutler estate and Beetle cabriolet, based on Tomica Dandy 1:43 models, and a Bedford ambulance based

Model Auto Review shop in the 1970's

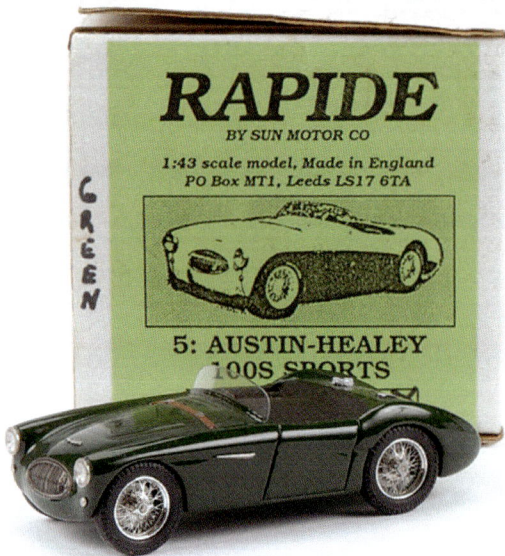

Sun Motor Co. Rapide Austin Healey 100S

on an Ertl 1930 Chevrolet truck.

When polyurethane resin kits and handbuilt models began to flood in from continental Europe, Rod was determined to find out about the new resin technology, asdid Chris Arnott. Chris had been a barrister in the RAF, but retired young to set up manufacturing model locomotive kits as Vulcan Model Engineering.

Through this activity Rod met Peter Kenna, who had trained to make brass locomotive patterns at Keyser's. Chris set up CMA Mouldcast to go into resin moulding, and asked Pete to make the master for a 1:43 Rover P6 3500S, so that the process could be tested. CMA later made other 1:43 resin models, a Riley RMA Bonallack coupe and RMA saloon.

As a result, Rod began to develop his own Sun polyurethane resin models, the first being a 1:43 Bugatti T251 Grand Prix car developed from an old Circuit Series kit, achieved with the permission of the range owner, Bryan Garfield Jones. 'Garf' gave permission for the remainder of his racing car kits to be copied, but Rod did not pursue the project.

Geoff continued to produce further model masters for Rod, but he eventually became busy with his Heavy Goods truck range, so Rod advertised for more pattern makers or skilled scratchbuilders. Most of those who responded were useless, but a few recruits contributed to the Sun Motor Co and other future ranges, as well as becoming good friends to Rod and Val.

Max Tomlinson, a Bugatti specialist, produced an excellent Bugatti T40, equipped with beautiful photo-etched wire wheels, which were supplied by Bob Wills, of Wills Finecast and Auto-Kits. A Cadillac 75 long wheelbase limousine from 1952 followed, based on the Ertl sedan, and mastered by David

Farrance. In 1988, although there were lots of cars which could have been added to the Sun range, Modelauto was also selling many other model car ranges. At that time, there were fewer truck models on the market, so it was decided to develop that field, initially with heavy haulage trucks; Diamond T M20, Rotinoff Super Atlantic and Scammell.

Up to that time Rod had avoided using one source for pattern making, casting and building, as he preferred to place the work in different parts of the market according to demand. These models were an exception, being entirely made by A Smith Auto Models, as a way to get quality models to the market fairly quickly. This was a decision regretted later, and it was never repeated.

Later truck releases were produced by other pattern makers, mostly Bill Barnes, who also made his own Tober Models range, and cast by various companies, mostly CMA, but also Maurice Bozward and Pete Comben at Enco. Assembly of models was undertaken by various specialist builders. Over the next few years the Sun Motor Co truck range grew quickly, eventually including almost 200 different kits and handbuilt models.

In 1991 the Sun range was split into three different ranges. Sun Motor Co then continued to include trucks, buses and emergency vehicles. In response to demand, a new Bugattiana range was devoted to Bugatti models, incorporating the T40 and Loiseau car mastered by Max Tomlinson, and then augmented by a series of French made Bugatti masters from the DB range. These were much admired models made by Denis Baudet, who had been diagnosed with a serious illness and was retiring from model making. Eventually the Bugattiana range included over a dozen different models, some white metal, others in resin. The range was finally sold some 15 years later to Georges Pont of CCC models, so the DB models returned to France, along with much of the Rapide range.

Rapide became the third new range, focussing on classic cars in 1:43 scale. The Ford Mustang Boss and Humber Super Snipes were the only models carried over from the Sun range, and an ex. DB Austin Healey 100S joined them. More important were two more 'orphans', this time adopted from Pat Shrimpton's Marque One Models (MOM) range.

Sun Motor Co. 105
Humber Super Snipe drophead

After
protracted
licence negotiations with
Bentley Motors, a revamped version of the MOM
Bentley Mark VI 1949 was released, joined by the ex.
MOM Jaguar Mark VII, also fully licenced at a time
when many small model firms slipped their models
out quietly, hoping that brand owners didn't notice.
The Jaguar had such a large single piece white metal
body casting that only Maurice Bozward could
produce it. These four Rapide models were well
received in the early 1990s, but it was hard to get
suitable pattern makers for the next subjects which
Rod and Val wanted to make.

Pat Shrimpton decided that, with an ongoing
court case between Chrysler and a model company,
he didn't want to risk allowing his Chrysler models
to transfer to the Rapide range, licenced or not.
By now Modelauto was distributing dozens of
specialist handbuilt ranges on a wholesale basis,
including Goldvarg Collection, Kim's Classics, Tin
Wizard, Autocraft and Micro. For the Rapide range
Bill Barnes mastered the BSA Scout sports car and
Scout aerodynamic coupe, once again with Bob Wills'
superb photo-etched wire wheels. At the same time
the American Austin Bantam sports, originally in
the old Mikansue kit range made by Mike and Sue
Richardson, was also adopted.

As many of the Mikansue masters eventually
ended up with Keith Edney's RAE models, Keith cast
and built the little Bantam for the Rapide range.
Bill Barnes then developed other Bantam pickup
and tanker variants, followed in 1996 by Gérard
Dahinden's much admired Belle Epoque and Epokit
range of 1:43 masters, which were acquired by Rod
and Val when Gérard retired. These too were added
to the Rapide range. They were models of classic
French cars, produced by CMA for Modelauto, and
mostly sold in kit form, as it was becoming more
difficult to get builders capable of the high standards
required, charging sensible prices.

In 1998 the stable of these three model ranges,

Sun, Bugattiana and Rapide, was joined by a fourth,
Bijou. This range encompassed various unusual kits
and handbuilts such as the Bugatti T50 'Baby' made
by Auto Replicas and the Austin Pathfinder. It also
became the home for a whole new range of mostly
resin transkits, to make 1:43 models of cars not
previously available, based on mass produced diecast
models, mostly mastered by Bill Barnes.

In the mid 1990s Modelauto was one of the
first model companies to have a presence on the
internet, and launched its website. Originally a broad
based e-commerce shopping website, it gradually
concentrated on model cars, model aircraft, books
and Model Auto Review. With the success of the Auto
Review books in the 21st century, Rod and Val Ward's
book and magazine publishing activities came under
the umbrella of Zeteo Publishing.

In the late 1990s another of the handbuilt ranges
being distributed by Modelauto was Scottoy, white
metal reproductions of old Mercury models, made
in Italy. Jonathan Scott was sceptical when Rod
suggested re issuing the Mercury Lambretta and
Piaggio Vespa scooters, accompanied by a large
order. In spite of Jonathan's doubts, the scooters
became the biggest selling Scottoy Models. When he
then re issued the Piaggio Ape open three wheeler, a
van body was made for it in England and it was sold
in the Bijou range.

By the early years of the 21st century it was
becoming more difficult to produce ranges of
handbuilt models and kits. Much of the Sun Motor
Co range, and other 1:50 commercial vehicle ranges,
were undermined by the same subjects appearing
more cheaply as Corgi Toys diecast models, so there
was little point in expanding the range. Prices for
resin and metal casting in Britain had also risen to
the point where production was costing more than
the retail price of a kit. As components ran out,
therefore, subjects would be gradually phased out
from the Sun, Bugattiana, Rapide and Bijou ranges,
and nothing new was added. All of the French car
subjects in the Bugattiana and Rapide ranges were
sold to Georges Pont in France, and various other
masters were sold to other interested parties.

Remaining stocks of many models were still
available from Modelauto, during 2010 at 1990s
prices, and most of the masters were retained
in Yorkshire, but there is little prospect of any
future production.

Modelauto continues to produce the magazine
and publish books on motoring related subjects.

CHAPTER THIRTEEN

THE VOLUME PRODUCERS

By the mid 1980s some white metal producers had begun to stand out as particularly successful, profitable and expanding. They had taken on staff teams, sometimes had in house casters and builders, and were able to co-ordinate a manufacturing process akin to mass production. We have drawn together a few of these producers that we believe were particularly successful in achieving this forward step.

Bernie & Graham du Cros
Gems and Cobwebs

Bernie and Graham Du Cros at ModeleX

Originally in the antiques business with a shop in Maidenhead, known as Gems and Cobwebs, Bernie and Graham found they were acquiring old toys, including Dinky Toys and other makes, and in 1982 turned the business over to old models and toys.

After a period in Hungerford, they moved to

Gems & Cobwebs BMW

Cornwall in 1988 and took over a garage for a while, selling light commercials and petrol, but also continuing the model business. Model Garage was a play on the word model meaning scale model or excellent service. Having been in the trade since the late 1970s they had been asked for many model vehicles which at that time had not been made.

Meanwhile, Ken White, a keen collector of diecast military models, had been working in Cyprus between 1986 and 1989, and on his return to London, working in the Egham area, he visited toy fairs and met Bernie and Graham. He bought most of Bernie and Graham's stock of military aircraft, and then became interested in the business potential of white metal models. He had funds to invest, and jointly with Bernie and Graham, successfully applied for a grant to develop a factory in Redruth.

Graham had become friendly with John Hall, who agreed to produce the first three models in the new Gems & Cobwebs range, the first being the Jaguar MkVII.

Milestone Miniatures Jaguar Mk VIII

Ken visited the Gems & Cobwebs factory regularly, and together with a friend from Cyprus, also entered into discussions with John Hall when he was

Milestone Miniatures Vauxhall Wensum

considering selling Brooklin Models in 1992/93. Gems & Cobwebs needed its future to be assured once the grant ended, and so a plan emerged to bring together Gems & Cobwebs and Brooklin Models. Despite initial enthusiasm, the new partnership never materialised, and each went their separate ways.

After a while they developed the brand name of Milestone Miniatures, and created not only a wide range of model cars, but also two further ranges, one for Brooklands Museum, and the other a range of American cars known as 43rd Avenue.

They tended to use a variety of pattern markers, but in due course also chose to do their own casting and total assembly, and at the peak of their success the company employed 12 staff.

Model Garage, already a well established business, was subsequently sold to its present owner Rod Hunt in 1992. The home of that business has moved over the years, but is currently based in Colyton, East Devon at the premises of Rod's other business, Colyton Antiques Centre, which he acquired in 2000.

Just prior to ceasing production in 2008, Milestone Miniatures produced a model of the R.N.L.I. Tamar Class Lifeboat. This is now a very rare model, developed as a prototype and made for approval by the R.N.L.I. This was granted and a run of less than 50 units of these then new Tamar lifeboats was produced as presentation items to crew members on special occasions. With the exception of the aerials and some of the railings the model is produced from white metal and hand assembled. This example pictured bears the name of "Spirit of Padstow" and is number 16-04. It is the only one produced with this livery. The model is 5.5" long and is displayed on a wooden display plinth with a glass cover.

Spirit of Padstow - Tamar Class Lifeboat model

John & Jenny Hall
Brooklin Models Ltd

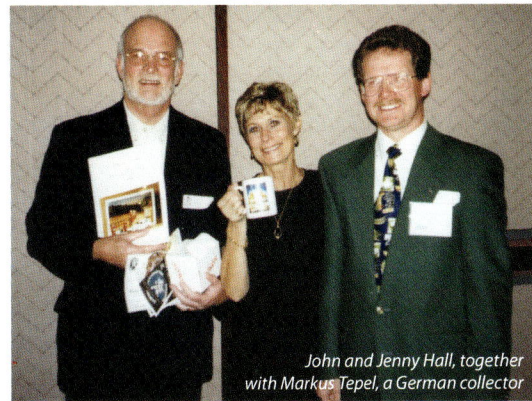

John and Jenny Hall, together with Markus Tepel, a German collector

When John Hall emigrated to Canada in 1965, little did he know that he was destined to become the owner of, probably, the most successful model making business in the history of white metal modelling.

Born and bred in south London, John graduated with a degree in design engineering after studying part time at a local college at the same as following a design apprenticeship.

Growing up in England in the 1950s was an education in itself, with so much development in all activities and spheres of life. A teenager in those years was a very lucky individual and so it was with John. For him, particularly, it was music and cars that grabbed him, however, both from America. Rock and Roll performers such as Elvis Presley were instrumental in him joining a local rock band, and the American cars of that era – the big, fast, gas guzzling monsters that were seldom seen in England but were

BRK25 - 1958 Pontiac Boneville (limited edition 500)

part of the American influence that was to set him on a course that, in time, was going to change his life completely.

His early employment was with electro-mechanical engineering firms and this held his interest until 1965, when, with his wife Jenny, they emigrated to Canada, seeking a better life style. They chose to live in Ontario, near the United States border so they could travel in that country as well. During this time John worked for Phillips in Toronto and Chrysler in Detroit, and on the Gemini and Apollo space programmes with De Havilland. In these positions, he gained experience in casting techniques from plastics and diecasting associated with the aerospace industry.

In 1969, John moved from industry to teaching, taking up an appointment at Durham College in Oshawa, Toronto, teaching in his chosen line of work. When he wasn't doing that he was pursuing his interest in automobilia and collecting, which he had started in 1960. In this pursuit he met up with Julian Stewart (later of Durham Classics) who had similar interests and together, at times, they searched the Toronto toy shops for Matchbox Toys, Dinky Toys and old tin toys. In this they were successful, finding many pre and early post war Dinkys and Matchbox toys, mostly in their original boxes and display cases, selling at their original prices!

For John, these acquisitions later enabled him to found Canada's first antique toy shop, called Toys of Yesteryear, which he ran for a number of years. It was then that he thought a lot about making his own scale model cars and spent time exploring all the avenues which might allow this to happen.

In 1973, after several years moving around Toronto, John and Jenny settled in a small rural town called Brooklin, some 35 miles north east of Toronto. The basement of the house would prove to be ideal as a workshop to make, paint and build model cars.

Eventually, in 1974, John made a pivotal decision to resign from his teaching work at Durham College and commenced working from home, designing the equipment necessary to be able to build finished scale model cars that would appeal to collectors who, at the time, largely had to build what they wanted

One half of the casting room

from kits. At this point, Jenny took employment, so that John could concentrate producing models, as well as looking after their two children.

One of his first models was that of a 'plow', to sell as a souvenir at the annual 'plowing' match held in Toronto. However, his enthusiasm far outweighed their appeal to the spectators, who only bought 200 of the 2000 he had cast and his memory is more about the hundreds he melted down, than the cast model itself. If only he could have foreseen how the collecting world was going to develop! Today, the 'plow' is a very rare piece and would be a wonderful item for a Brooklin collector to come across.

Gluing the models

Notwithstanding this set-back, John was continuing to dabble in model making and scratch building for himself and other collectors.

He was one of the founder members of the Canadian Toy Collectors Society, together with Ron Faithful and Tony Topley and through the CTCS met many more collectors. John went to his first toy show in Buffalo, New York and it was there that he was encouraged to make his first model – a Pierce Arrow. Being a car that he loved, it was not long before he had made two master models in resin and begun the casting. They were very crude by later standards, and the casting rate was just ten models per week, to achieve a total of 86 models! But for John, it was a great success and bode well for the future. Hand painted, with a resin base and no windows, it became car No.1, and is now very sought after.

The Tucker Torpedo was to follow and was the first model produced by Brooklin Models and a Ford Model A became No.3. By the end of 1974, with equipment installed, the basement of the Halls house became a small factory. With two employees, plus John, Brooklin Models was underway!

Initially, John did everything, carved the master, made the moulds, cast the pieces and together with the two employees who painted, they all assembled the models. As time passed and more models were being produced, so more staff were employed. During the next few years, the quality improved, thousands of models were produced and the name of Brooklin was firmly established in the collectors market, but predominantly in North America.

In October 1979, the Halls took the decision to return to England and all 'Made in Canada' production ceased. The company re-established itself in Bath and has remained there ever since. Initially they occupied space in Huggett Electrical's premises, but subsequently took a new unit in Pines Way Industrial Estate, close to the old railway station, where it is to this day. In this new situation, Jenny took an active part in the business, looking after the administration and all the other paperwork.

It did not take long for the Brooklin name to be recognised and the company expanded rapidly to cater for the explosion of demand from its new found collectors market in England and Europe generally. The company's strong beginnings in Canada assured that its collector base there has been maintained. The formation of clubs in England, Germany and the USA also created greater establishment for the Brooklin name. In the spring of 1988, Brooklins models were re-launched as the Brooklin Collection and this continues to the present time.

In 1993, a new name appeared within the Brooklin portfolio, joining The Brooklin Collection, RobEddie (now discontinued) and US Model Mint. For some time there had been talk of introducing a range of British models to complement the American vehicles. The idea, originally mooted by John Martin and John Hammick, was for development themselves, with models made by Brooklin. However, John Hall decided to develop the range himself, choosing the Lansdowne brand name after the Lansdown area of Bath. He added the 'e' at the end but was never sure why!

The choice of subjects followed the Brooklin philosophy of modelling previously rarely available models in this scale. The Austin Healey Sprite was a miniature of John and Jenny's first car, and it joined the Vauxhall Cresta, MG Magnette and Minivan to get the new range off the ground. Other models swiftly followed, again bringing new subjects to collectors together with new castings that echoed classic choices from the Dinky Toys' heyday of the 1950s.

On one occasion, when the new range was being established, John travelled to a remote rural location

An assembly line

to measure a Vauxhall Cresta. He was ushered into the living room of a small cottage where smoke from the log fire filled the room. Settling down to talk to the car's owners over a cup of coffee, he asked if he could smoke. "We'd rather you didn't", came the reply through the gloom!

In the course of time, some great names from Britain's motoring heritage of the 1930s have appeared under the Lansdowne banner. The AC 16-80, Jensen Dual Cowl Phaeton and Saloon, Triumph Gloria Flowfree, Railton Fairmile and Morris Ten Series 111 are just a few examples. Family cars have not been forgotten with Austin A90, Humber Hawk Estate, Hillman Minx and Triumph 13-60 Estate being just a random selection among the large range available. More recently links have been established with Bentley Motors and Bristol cars, and officially authorised models from these two great marques have begun to appear in the range.

Lansdowne Jensen H Type Dual Cowl Pheaton

In 1994, Brooklin celebrated its 20th anniversary, with a gathering in Bath of members from all the clubs. A cruise on the River Avon, together with a tour of the factory and a dinner, made for a very memorable occasion. A bonus for twenty members came when a draw for that number of an exclusive special model was announced.

Besides the standard models, in both ranges, limited edition 'specials' have been made for various clubs and organisations – The Brooklin Collectors Club, the San Francisco Bay Brooklin Club, Canadian Toy Collectors Society, Classic Thunderbird Club International, Maidenhead Static Model Club, ModeleX, Wessex Model & Toy Collectors and many others besides. The longest running of these 'specials' were those for the CTCS, issuing its 33rd consecutive annual model in 2011. These are all very collectable and some have achieved large sums of money at auction, or on eBay.

In 1997 The Buick Collection arrived. Unique in concept, this new range represents the development of Buick between 1934 and 1939, the classic Harlow Curtice era. Curtice had been brought into the company in 1933 and is generally credited with saving Buick from oblivion by introducing the 40 series, a Buick designed for the popular market.

Showing Harley Earl's early influence the 1936 models marked a new direction for the company even though this was to be a stand-alone design year.In 1937 the range was redesigned yet again, the new models causing a sensation. The idea of a one make model collection was enthusiastically received by collectors and 20 models have already been issued, with the rollout of further models set to accelerate.

Other ranges that have appeared since include International Police Vehicles (IPV), Rod 43rd and Community Service Vehicles (CSV).

Nigel Parker & Tim Fulford

In August 1998, a management buyout was arranged between the Halls and Nigel Parker and Tim Fulford, who became the new directors, with the other staff becoming shareholders. John and Jenny subsequently retired to Vancouver Island, Canada, but later moved to Sydney, Australia to be near their family.

When asked how he got started in the business, Nigel replied that his interest in cars goes back to his childhood, and although he was not originally interested in models, he later became fascinated with the engineering and production of handbuilt models. After finishing college in 1982, he started in the paint room at the Brooklin factory at the suggestion of his friend, Tim Fulford, who had joined some 10 months earlier. Moving on to the casting room, and later to mould making, by 1990 Nigel was Production Manager for John Hall.

In the years since, Nigel and Tim have pushed

Lansdowne Austin Atlantic

the quality of their models to new heights, building on the traditions and values set by the company's founder. Models in the current range now feature improved detailing, with the fine touches of plated hood ornaments, windshield wipers, door handles and fine chromed wire trim.

The Brooklin factory, nestling in the corner of Pines Way Industrial Estate, covers 5,000 square feet on two levels, with tight passageways and stairwells connecting the various production areas. Currently there are around twenty five staff.

Nigel Parker, Managing Director

Brooklin Models Limited is currently the world's leading manufacturer of 1:43 scale handbuilt white metal models. Their manufacturing process includes the creation of brass masters, which generally come from independent pattern makers, but are further engineered by Darren Mould and Ian(Mr P) Pinker to suit Brooklin's casting and assembly processes. Rubber moulds are created by carefully sculpting strips of virgin rubber around the masters, all of which is subsequently encased in a steel frame, and vulcanizied at over 300°F. These vulcanised moulds are principally made by Neil Parker. Centrifugal casting machines are used for creating baseplates, headlights, wheels, dashboards, seats and all the other small parts. This work is carried out by David Heath, Production Manager, together with Ian Carpenter amongst others. Bodies are specifically cast by Andrew Bodely, and once fettled and prepared, together with sub-assemblies, are then hand spray painted with automotive quality paints, one of their team being Bob White. Final assembly and packaging is also accomplished by hand, one model at a time, by a team of technicians, the longest serving of which are Sue Hotham and Steve Bodely. Most of these specialists are multi-disciplined and can move to different departments as the need arises.

The manufacture of the models involves six production areas, each operation requiring three weeks to produce the models in a total eight week cycle. Overall, approximately 20,000 models

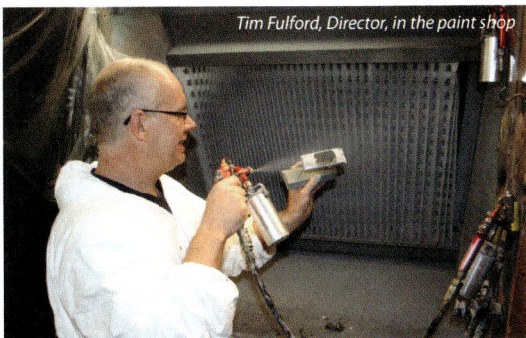
Tim Fulford, Director, in the paint shop

are produced in a given year, with the average production run for an individual model over a five year period rarely exceeding 1000 models.

From the late 1990s through the 2000s, Nigel and his factory staff have introduced an amazing number of classics to The Brooklin Collection. Likewise, Landsdowne models have grown in number as befits the years that have passed. Their other ranges have not been overlooked and show a healthy growth as well. .

Now, at the start of the fourth decade at the same location, all of the staff named, as well as Amanda Hookings, the Office Manager, have been with the company for at least 14 years or more, some as long as 28 years. "Brooklin Models are the sum of the company's staff, not the premises and machines"– so says MD, Nigel Parker.

(Back row from left to right): Mark Cable, Andrew Moseling, David Heath, Richard Brinkworth, Martyn Bowell, Andrew Bodely, Ian Carpenter & Steven Bodely. (Front row left to right): Susan Hotham, Neil Parker, Angela Bonfield, Darren Mould, Sarah Noble, Robert White, Sandra Egginton & Nick Lay.

Amanda Hookings, Office Manager

Doug & Roly McHard
Somerville Models

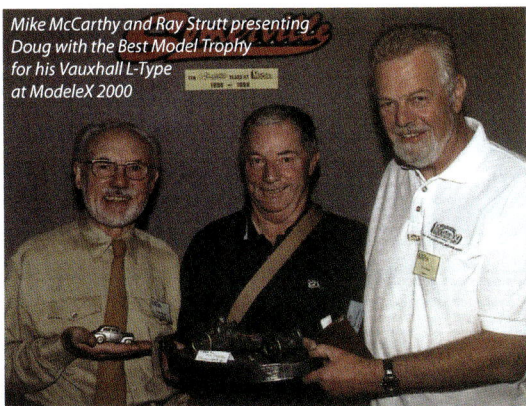
Mike McCarthy and Ray Strutt presenting Doug with the Best Model Trophy for his Vauxhall L-Type at ModeleX 2000

For many collectors of hand built white metal model cars, those produced by Somerville Models are considered to be the finest available, certainly considering models of British cars. They were renowned for their high quality, fine definition and distinguishing characteristics.

Sadly, whilst examples can still be found in the market place, no 'factory' models have been available since the death of their founder, Doug McHard, 8 years ago, when the business was closed and subsequently sold by his wife Roly. However, whilst no finished models have appeared under the new ownership, some have been released in kit form, albeit now with a reduced number of plated parts.

Doug was well involved with the toy hobby from an early age, making models for himself. Following service in the RAF, he turned to photography and journalism, becoming assistant editor of Model

Popular Somerville casting - the Vauxhall L-Type

Somerville Austin taxi kit

Aircraft magazine and subsequently editor of Meccano Magazine. He later became marketing director for Meccano Ltd, with responsibility for Dinky Toys and Meccano ranges.

Following redundancy in the late seventies, he set up his own model making business, concentrating on British cars of the 1930s, 40's and 50's. It was very much a family business, with the help of Roly, and a small team who lived near to his home in Billinghay, Lincolnshire, where it all happened. Everything was done under the one roof from pattern making, by Doug himself, to the finished model, except perhaps any decals that were required.

Hillman Minx Series 5

Such was the appeal of the models Somerville made that advertising was not really necessary, but did appear from time to time to announce the arrival of a new model or range. Allied to this they used a production method

whereby a batch of a few hundred models would be made and only repeated again when the cycle of different models had been completed. This could take many months and consequently encouraged collectors to purchase soon after a release to avoid waiting a long time for another opportunity.

Mock up projects in primer

At ModeleX 99 his Vauxhall Velox L type was chosen as Best Model, an award he was very proud of and, indeed, a just reward for exhibiting at every show since its inception in 1990. A diversion was the work they carried out for both Saab and Volvo, although large scale production for these companies was turned down in order to maintain the cottage industry style that Somerville epitomised.

At heart, Doug had a passion for aircraft modelling and flying, and was a legend in those circles. Such was his standing that he took to judging rather than competing and flew his own models after the competitions were over. He was doing just that when he collapsed and died at RAF Honington in Suffolk on 28th August 2002.

Ford Van produced as a memorial to Doug

Somerville Ford van made for Val and Rod Ward's Silver Wedding anniversary

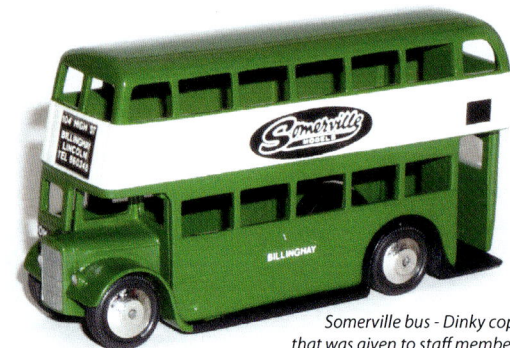

Somerville bus - Dinky copy that was given to staff members

Jeff & Sue Sharrock
Pathfinder Models

Jeff & Sue Sharrock at home

Jeff was always interested in transport, visiting his local bus garage as a child, collecting Dinky and Corgi Toys as well as being a regular train spotter. In the early 1980s Jeff, in his early 30s with a young family, was a successful deputy head, then acting head of a comprehensive secondary school, but needed a fresh challenge.

He was visiting toy fairs to add to his model collection; his entrepreneurial spirit kicked in and he started to have stalls dealing in models. He and his young son Jonathan became regular faces on the swapmeet circuit. Jeff liked the feel and quality of white metal models, particularly Brooklin Models, and decided he would like to produce a range of slightly unusual cars of the 1950s and 60s, typified by the PFM 1 Jensen 541R, their first model. He went into partnership with Bill O'Donnell of LSJ Models, a friend and fellow dealer at swapmeets. It soon became clear that a small niche business would be better suited to single ownership so Bill opted out. This was a perfectly amicable decision and Bill remained very supportive. John and Jenny Hall of Brooklin Models were also very helpful both with advice and more particularly with castings. Other professionals also produced castings for Pathfinder Models.

Daimler Dart SP250

From the start Jeff used some of the best pattern makers: Alistair Duncan, Pete Kenna, Ian Pickering and Richard Stokes. Assembly, spraying and finishing were initially done by local art and craft teachers. Jeff showed the models at swapmeets and built up a solid customer base, selling direct to personal customers and also to retailers. Models were sent for review purposes to Collectors Gazette and Model Auto Review. Things were gathering momentum and a business adviser was engaged who proposed expansion into a work unit. However, Jeff decided to 'do his own thing' preferring to keep things small and manageable, running the business from home. He came up with the brainwave of producing one model at a time, in limited runs in 2 colours, 300 of each, with numbered certificates. This commenced with PFM7 Wolseley 6/80, still one of Jeff's favourite models in the range.

Morris 6 Special for G&W Engineering

This decision proved hugely successful and PFM went from strength to strength.

Initially, Jeff explored arrangements with a number of potential casters to supply to this increased quantity, including Illustra, who made one model for them. The range was now getting known outside Britain through continental dealers. In 1991 Jeff was approached by the main Rover dealership in Amsterdam to do a special commission of a Rover P5. This was so successful that other commissions followed, among them were Ford models for Geir Andreassen of Minicar 43 in Norway and various models for the late Denis Wheatley of G&W Engineering who was a personal friend and model collector.

Graham Price of GTA Models had done the casting, assembly and spraying of the Rover P5 and Sue and Jeff were so pleased with the results, and with their working relationship with Graham, that he went on to do all further models for PFM. They fondly recall meeting Graham half way between Bangor and Devon to take delivery of completed models. Jeff's wife Sue, together with Linda, a friend in the same village, did all the hand detailing. Sue also did the checking, packing and the paperwork involved in

Vauxhall Friary estate special for G&W Engineering

1962 VAUXHALL CRESTA FRIARY ESTATE

This is to certify that this is No. 75 of a limited edition of only 350 models produced exclusively for G & W Engineering Ltd. by Pathfinder Models.

running a business. It was Jeff's interpersonal skills and understanding of people that was the key to the unique hand written newsletters that were mailed to every regularly subscribing customer. These were individually addressed, gave full details of planned models throughout the forthcoming year, and expressed many personal comments on the significance of each car to Jeff or Sue. A genuine relationship was thus built with each and every customer, which all customers appreciated, and was a brilliant marketing approach.

Jeff's own Daimler SP250, used for Fiona's wedding in September 2010

Customers liked what PFM were doing and wanted more. Jeff started a range of continental classics, a range of vans for special commissions, and Viscount Models with John Martin of J.M.Toys, to cater for interest in 1970s cars. However, in 1994 Jeff was diagnosed with a brain tumour and underwent major surgery. PFM continued but other ranges were restricted. Jeff and Sue realised at this time how many friends they had made through the business, both in the manufacturing and selling. Everyone was very supportive. PFM had always had a very good relationship with customers, many of whom became friends over the years, phoning for chats and visiting the home. Christmas cards are still exchanged with many. One customer regularly visits from quite a distance, sometimes in his wonderful two tone pink

Vauxhall Cresta Friary Estate. Such friendships have meant a great deal.

Jeff has been the decision maker in the business and chose which cars to model. He took the opportunity to indulge his own taste in cars. The Wolseley 4/44, Reliant Scimitar GTE, Morris 8 Series E, Jensen C-V8 and Daimler SP250 were all based on cars owned by the family. The Daimler has now been passed on to son Jonathan who shares Jeff's passion for cars, and the Daimler in particular. It was used for their daughter Fiona's wedding in September 2010, along with Jeff's Saab 900 classic convertible.

Jeff always intended that PFM would have a finite life and kept customers informed of future plans to finish after a certain number. It was decided that PFM 36, the AC 2 litre saloon would be the final model in 2002. Jeff and Sue have very fond memories of their PFM years. Sue's personal favourite models are the PFM 3 Bristol 401 in metallic blue, and a special Daimler SP250 which Graham sprayed to match Jeff's own car whose colour was not original and couldn't be used in the range.

Many collectors have wondered what happened to the brass patterns of the Pathfinder range. One of the early patterns, PFM3, the Bristol, was purchased by a company known as Cheshire Scale Models, the owner of which we understand emigrated to Australia. The remainder of the patterns was then kept by Jeff and Sue. However, as there were funds tied up in the pattern costs but there was no further use for them, They decided that they would retain some as keepsakes, and the rest would be sold. A very acceptable solution came in the form of Greg Clay, a serious white metal collector who was keen to become their custodian. All the patterns were passed to Graham Price who then polished them, and mounted each one on a piece of perspex before a final price was agreed by Jeff and Sue with Greg. There was an agreement between them that the patterns were not to be used for manufacture for some considerable time. Eventually some were sold, the majority went into a private collection, whilst Crossway Models had some and Mike Rogers of J &

An Example of a 2-color prototype for determining colour schemes

Brass master for Daimler

M Classics had the Daimler and Jowett Jupiter. The Austin Herefords and Devons were an arrangement with Pete Kenna, and the Fords similarly a joint venture with Geir Andreason of Minicar 43 of Norway. Interestingly the pattern for PFM10, the Jensen C-V8, is owned by the Oxford Diecast Company, together with a number of others, but they have no plans to make a C-V8 at present. We believe that SAMS Models obtained the Mk3 Cortina which then went on to Crossway. We also understand that a mystery briefly surrounded the master of the Ford Corsair. This was sent through the post to Dave Turner for a review, which Dave did and sent it back in due course. When Dave received a call from Sue Sharrock asking when it would be coming back, he realized it may be lost. He reported this to the Royal

Mail, and strangely, a few weeks later, a white van drew up at Pathfinder headquarters, and handed over the master!

Looking back, PFM owed its success mainly to Jeff, the ideas person, to Graham's craftsmanship, to Sue's attention to detail but perhaps most of all to the very personal service. Jeff and Sue were, and still are, complete technophobes, and ran the business with no computer/FAX machine etc. Customers seemed to like their hand written letters! Jonathan and Fiona are still trying to drag them into the 21st century but Jeff and Sue are still holding out against it, preferring to enjoy the quiet life of retirement as much as possible, (despite Jeff's second brain tumour in 2007) by escaping to the warm sunshine of Lanzarote in the winter months.

Brass pattern for Vauxhall Cresta Friary estate

Roger Tennyson, John Billinger, Carl & Amanda Merz
Jemini and Crossway Models

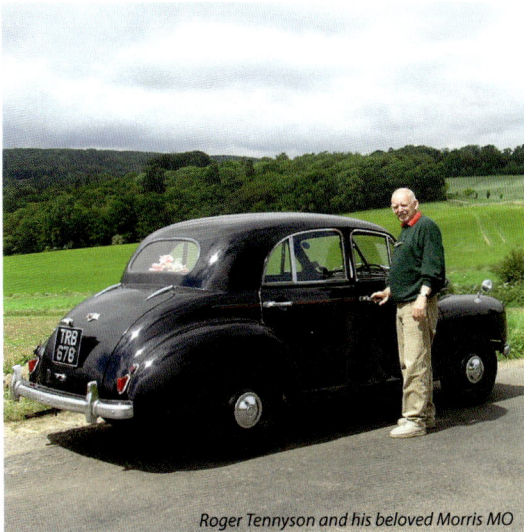
Roger Tennyson and his beloved Morris MO

Some significant producers have now retired from the scene, but take an active interest in both miniature and full size classics. Roger Tennyson is one such enthusiast, who has been surrounded by classic cars from an early age.

Roger recalls growing up within a classic car loving family. His father served in the RAF during the war, and when demobbed became an Aero Engineer with Rolls Royce. His love of old cars meant Roger and his brothers grew up with such wheels as Railtons, Talbot, Alvis, Daimler, Triumph, Auburn, Jaguar, Riley, Rovers, and at one point a Rolls Royce Doctor's Coupe in black & yellow. It had tiny seats in the back that faced each other and they had a great time there.

As children they always had Dinky Toys and he recalls his first restoration attempt at about 10 years old. He tied a piece of string around the axle of a 38 Series Dinky Lagonda and dipped it into the tin of paint with which his father was painting the window frames. Needless to say the mess made is more the reason for the memory than the finished result. Like most children of that era Roger progressed to Airfix and Revell plastic kits and was always modifying them, but his first love was always cars; the odd boat or plane purchased for him were always built but not with the same enthusiasm.

Roger Tennyson's conversion on the Morris Minor

During the 1980s Roger found some of his old Dinky Toys in a box in the loft and feeling sorry for them he found the correct colours and restored them. He also began to collect from autojumbles those that he could recall owning as a child, and restored these too. A friend saw these and asked Roger if he would restore his models. This started Roger on the toy fair circuit, purchasing battered Dinky Toys, restoring and selling them. It was whilst at a Buxton toy fair that he was asked by a fellow police officer from Cheshire to produce a model of the Cheshire Police Rover 90 in green. At first, Roger had no idea how to go about this, as white metal models were beyond his reach and awareness. However, at the same time, as a committee member of the 6/80 & MO Club, Roger, in company with the club treasurer, John Billinger, visited Jeff and Sue Sharrock at Pathfinder models. It was there they saw the Rover 90 model, which was the correct model on which to base the Cheshire Police car.

John was also a model enthusiast, and for a while the two had been restoring Dinky and Corgi Toys for their own enjoyment. John and Roger then took the step of creating Jemini Model Reproductions and an agreement was made with Jeff and Sue for Jemini to produce the Rover as a limited edition under licence from Pathfinder. The name was derived from the initials of the two partners, and 'mini', being an iconic British car. The models were supplied to Roger and John in

Abbey Classics kit of the Triumph 200 Pi estate

kit form, sprayed and built by Roger in his converted shed, and boxed by his wife Joan in the kitchen. Roger continued restoring the Dinky Toys whilst John was busy producing Dinky reproduction boxes.

It was at this time that they discovered ModeleX, and took a shelf in one of organiser Ray Strutt's glass cabinets to display the Rover. From then on they became regular exhibitors until the last ModeleX at Stoneleigh Park. However, the white metal bug had bitten and further investigation into master makers and casters in order to produce their own models was made. They followed the Rover with the Wolseley 6 in both civilian and police livery, using a master from Martin Field and cast by Peter Comben of Enco Models in Lincolnshire. Roger's visit to Enco regenerated his police interest again, as Enco had produced the Mk1 Sunbeam Tiger as a kit and he knew the Metropolitan Police had used the Tiger as a traffic patrol car. Pete Comben agreed to produce a police model on the understanding that it was cast by him, thus another police car joined the range. Some were built by Roger and some by a builder in the Northampton area.

Fine detailing by Carl Merz

By now Jemini was becoming recognised. They received much support and advice from Pete Kenna, and asked him if he would produce a master for them. Through him Roger became aware of GTA Models in Exeter, who were at that time building for Pete, and who built their Wolseley 1300 Mk2 saloon mastered by Pete. Roger even tried experimenting with some old diecast models, creating a Mini Clubman estate from an old Corgi Mini van and a Dinky Clubman. The result was cast by Enco and sold as a kit. A few were sold built up, but the finished

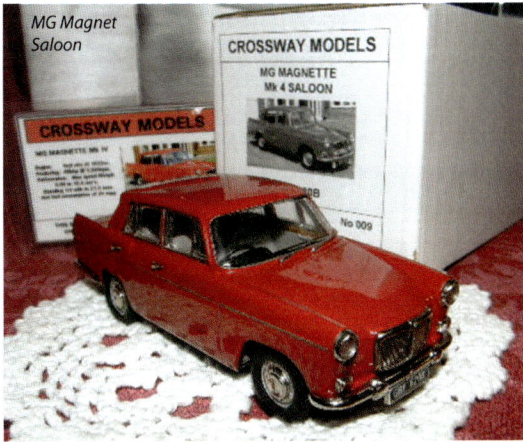

MG Magnet Saloon

article left a lot to be desired. Roger still has the master, but is not proud of it!

However, Pete Kenna converted the Wolseley 1300 into a 2 door 1100/1300 saloon and an MG 1300 for Jemini along with more police items that Roger produced using Lansdowne models as a base, with the consent of Nigel Parker at Brooklin Models, who has also been very helpful to him. They produced a Staffordshire Ford Zephyr in conjunction with JM Toys, and a Lancashire MGB using the K&R Replicas kit. Pete also introduced Roger and John to Maurice Bozward at White Metal Assemblies who cast a large number of their models.

The Jemini partnership however became strained when Roger and Joan moved to a 200 year old cottage in Lincolnshire, called 'Crossways', in need of restoration. They were deeply committed to the renovation, John had family problems and the partnership eventually floundered. They had been warned at the start that a business partnership was a little like a marriage, sometimes doomed to failure; a hard lesson indeed, but they agreed to go their separate ways on an amicable basis.

With the demise of Jemini Model Reproductions, Roger and Joan decided that they would continue with white metal models. Whilst staying with friends, the conversation turned to a name for the new business, and it was suggested that they use the house name and call it 'Crossway Models'. John retained the Jemini name, and when his difficulties were overcome, Jemini continued making reproduction boxes and dealing at toy fairs.

At ModeleX, Roger had met Glenn Thomas, who had introduced himself as a master maker and asked about future work. Roger suggested producing the Rover 75 Cyclops master, which Glenn agreed to do. Cast by CMA Mouldcast and painted by GTA, the final building was down to Roger, and it became the first Crossway model. Roger had been working on a project to create the Wolseley 16/60 as a 1:43 scale

model, and had a master, part completed. This was sent to Glenn Thomas and he created the second model, again painted at GTA, although the two tone paintwork presented a challenge.

A Triumph Dolomite Sprint followed, but then Roger took a different route. At a previous ModeleX Roger had discussed with David Buttress of CMA the possibility of using their Riley RMA resin kit as a base for creating a white metal model. They proceeded with this, creating a new master to produce the model in white metal. Roger used GTA again for painting and built the models himself.

Another agreement with Pathfinder saw the conversion of their Morris J Van into the Post Office Telephones Planners van based on an existing vehicle in Birmingham, again cast by CMA and painted by GTA, with help from family to complete the detailed interior. Crossway later purchased the brass master of the J Van for future model ideas.

Around 1996 Roger realised that he could not continue building the models fast enough on his own to satisfy both trade and customer demand, working from a small room at the back of the cottage. Joan had mentioned this to one of their neighbours and they were introduced to Carl Merz. When Carl visited Roger and Joan, he formed a real enthusiasm for the models and was soon a regular at 'Crossways' when he had some spare time.

Carl and his wife, Amanda were expecting their first child. Amanda was leaving her job to look after Billy when he was born and she was looking for part time work, so she took over the office at Crossway. Roger never enjoyed the paperwork and accounts, whilst Amanda excelled at them. By 1999, when Amanda's maternity leave ended, she became a permanent part time employee of Crossway.

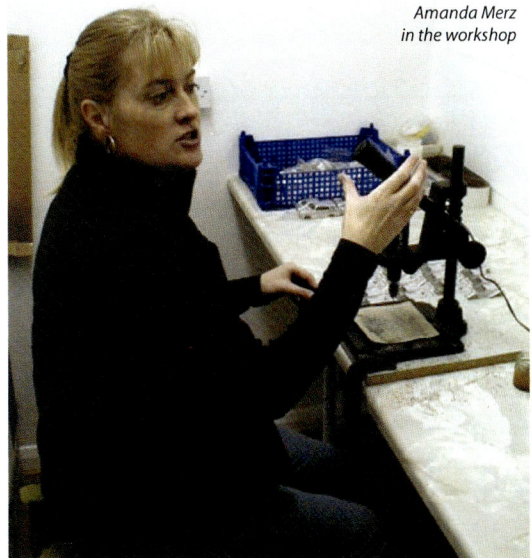

Amanda Merz in the workshop

Master for the Morris MO

Her ability to understand the different models from each producer was impressive, enabling her to talk to customers with experienced fluency.

With Carl & Amanda in the team, Crossway Models grew, and at 'Crossways' production was moved to a new workshop with its own drilling and painting rooms. There was a large area at the front for building the models, leaving the old workshop area as office space for Amanda. Carl had dexterity at building, and also an exceptional eye for detail whenever a new master arrived. He would look at photographs of the car and then the master, picking details out within minutes when Roger had taken days!

Carl also has an excellent sense of humour, and Roger recalls that when he first joined Crossway, and was asked by family members what he had been doing, he replied "pumping up tyres" and the classic, "tuning in the radios".

Roger, Carl & Amanda decided that instead of just retailing their own models they would also become retailers of other manufacturers' items, and Amanda took control of this side of the business. By agreement they became partners, but at the same time Joan and Roger were considering selling 'Crossways', the house where all the work was done. Carl designed and built a new workshop at his own home, around an existing shed in their back garden, complete with a new office for Amanda. By this time, the model range had increased rapidly and a new kit range, Abbey Classics was introduced. The first two Abbey Classics models were the Ford Cortina Mk3 1600L and the Mini Clubman and 1275 Saloons, both designed to have full engine detail incorporated in the kit. The Cortina created a lot of interest when it was launched at ModeleX where Roger was presented with a picture which still hangs in his office. Both models were variations from existing masters and were converted to full engine detail by Glenn Thomas. Glenn continued to work with them and was responsible for most of the masters and their conversions at that time.

The Crossway range was on a limited edition basis, all certificated, with main runs being 600, in several different colour schemes to give the customer a choice. Smaller runs were used for the police and rally ranges, of usually 100 but sometimes as low as 25.

A Crossway Newsletter was developed and sent out to existing customers, proving very popular. It is still produced. They also sent model samples for review to the main model press, Collectors Gazette, Diecast Collector, Model Auto Review and Model Collector. With some help they also created a website for Crossway Models, together with a review site White Metal Model Reviews where Dave Turner would review new models. They also attended as many of the larger toy fairs as possible, keeping customers informed.

A personal ambition for Roger has been the commissioning of the master for the Morris Oxford MO, a replica of his own car, which has been in the family since the 1980s. Again, it was Glenn Thomas who made an excellent job of the master. However, with abundant separate plated parts, it was a pain to build, but the finished item was well worth the effort. During this time Crossway had also started to use another master maker, Lawrence Gibson, who did some excellent work and is still working with them.

Roger was also responsible for the development of a range known as Emmy Models, jointly with a friend based in Switzerland, but produced in the UK. This was fraught with logistical difficulties, and was a short lived project ending in difficult circumstances.

Unfortunately, Roger began to have health problems and standing in the spray booth or sitting at the bench all day became very difficult, so in 2005 Carl and Amanda agreed to purchase Roger and Joan's half of the business. Roger retired to manage renovation of their new home with builders doing the main work. His health has improved considerably

Carl Merz in the workshop

since then and he still enjoys tackling model projects, including sorting his huge collection of authentic British police car models converted from many manufacturers' examples. Roger and Joan's main interest now is disappearing into Europe in their motor home, seeing parts of the world they had never envisaged visiting, and thoroughly enjoying it.

Crossway Models has gone from strength to strength under Amanda and Carl's ownership, continuing to specialise in mail order distribution with a worldwide customer database, sending out both a paper copy and e-mail to its customers detailing all the new releases that it is able to supply. eBay has also helped them and they sell significant numbers through their eBay shop.

As they produce all the Crossway range as limited edition runs, they only have a couple of traders that they supply on a regular basis, they sometimes struggle to supply even their own customers.

However, they do attend the NEC Classic Car Show each year to promote their products to a

Armstrong Siddeley pattern for Crossway

wider audience.

Amanda and Carl continue to be primarily manufacturers of both the Crossway and Abbey Classics kits range of models. However, they are also retailers of other manufacturers' models that they are able to lay their hands on. They do not make their own castings 'in house' but use two companies to cast for them, White Metal Assemblies and CMA Moldform.

CHAPTER FOURTEEN

THE PARTS BIN

Peter Cox and Guy Harrison's story in Chapter 1 of how they discovered the new potential market whilst on the floor of a Spittlefields warehouse is the stuff of legends! Renovating old playworn Dinky Toys soon became fully achievable, first with radiators and tyres, and then progressively more spare parts. It seems there was room in the market place for a number of retailers of spares, but slowly Steve Flowers began to mark out his supremacy! At most toy fairs, however, there are still one or two traders who can be relied upon to supply a range of tyres and wheels. Of course many parts are also made in resin, and Barry Smith's BTS Mouldings business, based in Hastings, has become the major supplier of all things resin.

Steve Flowers
Steve Flowers Model Supplies

Steve in his workshop

Most collectors know the name Steve Flowers as a comprehensive supplier of spare parts, but how did he get into this business? Well, it's not surprising to learn that, like so many others, he too had a substantial collection of Matchbox, Dinky and Corgi Toys as a child, along with his brother.

As a teenager, girls, of course, pushed toys into the background, but his models had not been given away, they remained in his bedroom cupboards at his parents' house. When at age 23 Steve happened to be walking past some old antique shops in Leicester,

his eye was drawn to some Dinky Toys in the window of one. He negotiated a price of £5.00 for twenty, but to this day Steve is not sure why he bought them. Was it for his young son, or was it nostalgia?

Some were similar to those he had owned, so he went back to his mother's home, and found his old collection just waiting for him! He was working in the transport field at the time, and he begun investigating how to make spare parts out of frustration when his own models needed repair. He had a basic knowledge of tool making, and so set about making his own spares. At first, he was using car body filler and Milliputty to create the patterns, and then, casting a few spares.

Having repaired quite a few old toys, he then visited antiques fairs, armed with his bag full of swaps, in the days before toy fairs. Amongst the traders who were prepared to take some of his repaired models as trades, was Rod Ward, of Model Auto in Leeds. Rod was keen to take a regular supply, and so in 1976 the spares business was established, initially during evenings and weekends, whilst Steve continued with his transport day job.

Initially the main material used was white metal, being easy to cast and mould. As the business grew, Steve found he was able to go full time, achieving a better income than his permanent job. Trading was intensive, visiting many toy fairs, in order to market his range of spares. With this step forward, he was able to invest in tooling to make more complicated parts. In 1980 he began making and stocking windows, transfers and tyres, and by 1985, he was moulding plastic spare parts. Whilst years ago, replacement Dinky wheels were always white metal, the spun aluminium replacements are now spun steel, producing an accurate result.

Steve visits toy fairs less frequently now, as he is engaged full time in manufacture, but occasionally uses the opportunity to survey which models are requiring spares, in order to judge the viability of making a new part. Examples of the level of sophistication include the toolbox of the Corgi VW breakdown pick up.

His customers were very local in the early days, but now he is proud to provide a service to many European collectors, along with those in America, Australia and Canada. Not only has the internet increased the volume of sales dramatically, but the world wide market has meant Steve is constantly creating new parts for ranges made by French Dinky Toys, Solido, Tekno and others. As his ability to make spares in the original material has grown, so the percentage of spares made in white metal has become much less. Indeed, most of his new parts coming onto the market are plastic or tin.

Steve is reflective about the recession, demand for his stock requires that he works 7 days per week, with

Steve and his hard working team

business being almost solely mail order, and it is just seasonal fluctuations that he sees each year.

He remains a faithful collector, filling in gaps in his Dinky Toys line up, but also includes some of the Oxford Diecast models that he feels are strong contenders now.

Long may the collectors market receive a comprehensive service from people such as Steve.

Martin Jewell

Martin at Windsor toy fair

Martin grew up helping in a toy shop, which was the family business, situated on the Hangar Lane gyratory system in west London. He remembers joining a slot racing club at school, and when he went back to his old school fete, he found Dinky Toys being sold there.

At the time, his father was looking after his uncle's newsagents shop in Pinner, and Maidenhead Static

Model Club member Ian Cooke dropped in with an advertisement, and his uncle put the two in touch. As a result, Martin attended one of the first Windsor toy fairs in 1974.

Martin was working for AEC in an engineering shop, but subsequently took over his uncle's shop, and began attending the MSMC meetings, trading, and buying in collections.

In order to improve his Dinky Toys for sale, he first bought tyres from Platform One. He then went to an engineering exhibition and saw silicone moulds available for casting, and began producing spare parts himself.

With the arrival of Steve Flowers most of Martin's spares business has now reduced, but he still sells spares direct on eBay. Martin continues to trade at the major toy fairs in the south of England, often sharing a table with Graham Thompson, where he specialises in Spot-On models in all conditions.

Colin Penn
Motorail

Our research seems to suggest that Colin Penn was the third person to manufacture white metal spare parts, the first two on the scene being Mikansue and Pirate Models.

Another spare parts manufacturer was DG Models,

run by Dave Gilbert, featured in Chapter 4.

The late Dave Jones used to make spares for early Dinky Toys, Britain's and Charbens as well as his Dinky style cars. Colin originally obtained the spares he needed for himself from all 3 of these, but then started making them himself because he needed parts that no one else made.

It all started for Colin at his local model railway club. One of the members was an Enfield Council

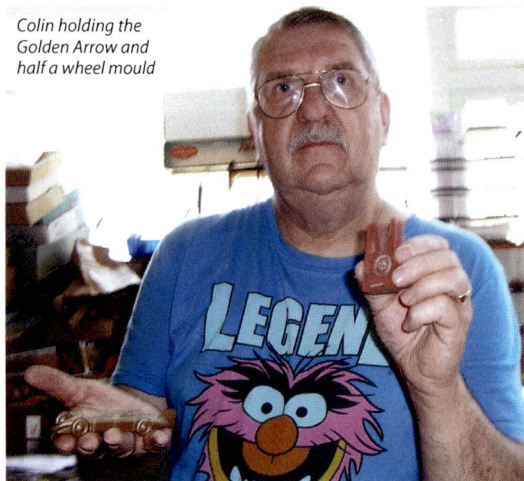

dustcart driver. He brought to the British Railways Staff Association club a pre war Johillco Golden Arrow record car which had only 1 wheel and presented it to me. At the time there were very few swapmeets and Colin had never seen one for sale before. He decided to try to restore the model and at first used 4 spare Dinky wheels with rubber tyres. However he wanted it to be more authentic and he recalled reading an article in an old Railway Modeller magazine about reproducing wagon sides by making up the sides and ends in plastic and then making rubber moulds and casting them in white metal. He had one original wheel and thought this could be used, as a master, to create a mould and through this process make another 3 wheels. Colin found a supplier for the rubber and made himself a two part mould which worked well. The Golden Arrow is still in his collection.

Following this experiment, he had a quantity of left over rubber and decided to see what he could create with it.

Johillco 'Golden Arrow' complete with Colin's first casting of a wheel

Returning again to his model railway interests, through his local model railway club, another member offered Colin a carrier bag of Scalextric cars and bits for £5.00. He recalled his younger days playing with his brothers, and as a result, he started collecting the cars. Many of the early cars such as the Mercedes, Austin Healey and Aston Martin had separate bumpers which were often missing or broken, so Colin started making white metal ones which eventually became chrome plated. This was before Barry Smith came on the scene with his lighter

resin ones, produced under the name BTS Mouldings.

In fact it was Colin that introduced Barry to the spare parts circuit, as he was working for a company making resin car body shells, and Colin asked him if he could produce windscreens in clear resin. His business was built up from there. Colin was also making Scalextric drivers' heads, and concentrated on the more obscure parts, rather than the Dinky spares as produced by Mikansue, Pirate and DG Models.

Martin Jewell and Steve Flowers came on the scene much later. Another dealer, from Bognor Regis, who used to have a stall at the Woolwich toy fair in the foyer, was Bob Walker, and he specialised in selling spare parts.

Steve Flowers began by acquiring Colin's parts, and supplying them more cheaply. Colin had created a replacement plastic card carrier for the Dinky searchlight wagon, complete with a bolt cast into the base so that it could be fixed to the base with a nut. He used to supply them to Martin Jewell until he learnt that Martin was getting them cheaper from Steve Flowers.

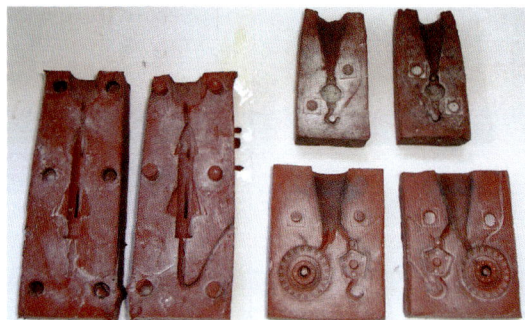

Hand poured rubber moulds for Dinky and Meccano crane hooks, a tractor front wheel and a rocket for the Lone Star Rocket Launcher

When Colin checked what Martin was selling, it was his own casting, but recast in all white metal including a cast bolt. It was slightly smaller due to wastage and as a result had less detail definition. Colin is proud of the comments from the public that his castings were better quality, but acknowledges that Steve's are much better now.

Colin continued to make and supply spares until the 1990s including the resin parts by Barry and the tin parts by Steve. However, the number of parts was growing so high that he decided to leave the business to Steve and Martin in order to could concentrate on the Copycat Models and the retail business. Colin still dusts off his moulds on occasions and makes bits for his own use. He has also devised a technique for producing one offs without the need for a rubber mould. He closely guards this industrial secret as he does not want to take large amounts of work, but if given a small part, he can run off 2 or 3 copies within an hour!

John & Chris Stockton
Photo Etch Consultants (PEC)

The vast majority of white metal models will have photo-etched parts, and the vast majority of these will have been made and supplied by PEC, launched in 1988 by John Stockton.

John recalls enjoying the likes of the Dinky Toys Thunderbolt as a child, but building kits or collecting did not feature in his childhood. Indeed, his first employment was in the process engraving industry, but he soon found that this was highly trade union controlled, and his boss at the time decided to seek an alternative industry to enable greater and more flexible development.

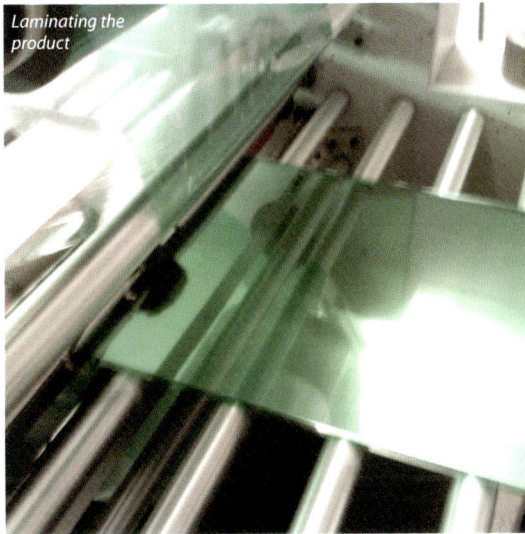
Laminating the product

During the war years, photo engraving and etching was in its infancy in the USA, finding a purpose in lightening the airframes of aircraft, by removing unwanted metal. In 1963 John and a colleague were despatched to the USA to investigate this new process, and duly returned with a licence and all the necessary equipment to put in into operation here in the UK.

John explains that the etching process involves a number of stages. A sheet of the required thickness of metal is coated with a light sensitive material, and then a suitable camera takes images of the eventual product, the resultant film of which is placed on each side of the metal sheet, describing the shape that is to be retained. Ultra violet light is used to expose that image, then acid is applied to the bare areas of metal, leaving behind the coated areas. After removal of the coating, the product left is the piece needed.

Whilst John's company was the first in the UK with this invention, Kodak were heavily involved in the

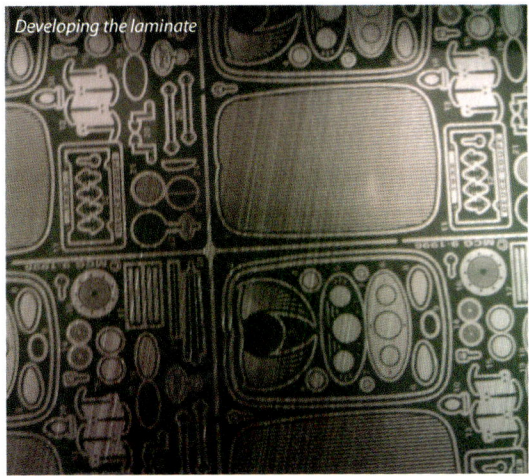
Developing the laminate

USA and soon were promoting it in the UK too. The process was immediately applied in the developing electronics industry, but it took 3-4 years before the potential was really understood.

By 1968, with the arrival of printed circuit boards, electronics development was really taking off, but alongside were applications in modelling such as stanchions on model boats, and miniature windows and doors for architectural models to promote housing developments.

John recalls John Simons of Marsh Models being one of the first white metal producers to recognise the potential for model cars. After a brief period when John worked for a company that did not have the highest standards or integrity, in 1983 he took a major career change and worked for a while for a competitor. In 1988, John had launched PEC, and immediately began exhibiting at ModeleX to promote the etching process to model car producers.

It has been steady expansion since then, with modellers increasingly seeking improvements in

Etching the shapes

Cleaning the sheet

John and Chris are confident that whilst collectors and modellers continue to demand higher quality and detail, their product will continue to be in demand, and the recession has not affected them at all.

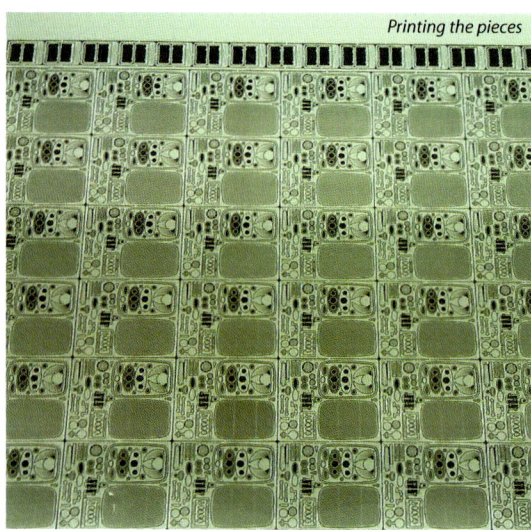

Printing the pieces

definition and quality, resulting in windscreen wipers, door handles and bonnet motifs being photo-etched. John has enjoyed the loyalty of 17 employees for many years, and when in 2005 he chose to retire, and move across to make way for his son Chris, these experienced people remained with the company.

THE ADAPTERS & FLATTERERS

The supply of white metal kits and handbuilt models provides a rich source for enthusiastic modellers, keen to create something unique to them. So many have done this with Dinky Toys, but the malleability of white metal has meant that so much more is possible. However, to create a model at least as beautiful as the original handbuilt, whilst removing a roof is a skill held by relatively few master model makers. Here we follow the story of some of them, and also focus on the alternative way.

Why not create something new, either a straight copy from white metal of a classic Dinky toy or Spot-On model, or alternatively a model in the style of a Dinky Toy that was never made. Those craftsmen who have created a living for themselves from this art deserve to be recognised too and their stories are recounted here.

Victor Bailey
Veteran & Vintage

Victor Bailey and John Alcott

One of the key figures in the early days of the use of white metal for replicas was Victor Bailey. Victor has been a collector since he was 5 years old, but it wasn't until 1969 that he decided that he had too many model cars, and wanted to part with some of them.

His mother had shop premises in Portslade, used mainly for storage, and so Victor agreed with her that he could use the window to sell some of his collection of 3000+ Dinky Toys and other diecast models.

Without any advertising until 1972, Veteran & Vintage was borne, but the response was not as Victor had planned. The shop was popular, but many customers brought more models in to sell, and soon Victor had more stock than he had started with!

By 1972, customers were finding that good condition Dinky Toys were expensive, and there were no good restorations or copies available. Victor then embarked on a small range of replicas of models that both he and his customers wanted. This began with the Taylor & Barrett fire engine and AFS Tender, which were followed by Dinky toys 34a Royal Air Mail Service car, 60y Thompson Refueller, 33 series mechanical horse range in various liveries, 31 Holland Coachcraft van, the 22h streamlined saloon, and 22g tourer. These replicas were limited to 100 items each, and were sold through the shop and at the Windsor and Sandown Park swapmeets. Victor also had a list of enthusiastic collectors who would be informed of the next release.

Victor's friend John Alcott assisted with the assembly and finishing of these models, and their joint interest in model aeroplanes led to Victor proposing a Veteran & Vintage range of white metal Dinky style aeroplanes. John had previously made modifications to Dinky Comets with added white metal components to create the Nimrod, MR2 and AEW3 early warning versions. Together they launched a short Constellation and a Britannia, but the inherent weakness of white metal made it unsuitable for this type of models and very few

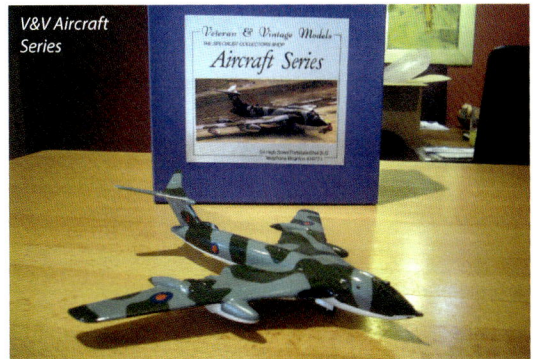

V&V Aircraft Series

were made. They turned to aluminium, made further models of a B36 Peacemaker and very few of the Liberator, until this medium was found to be too expensive. They had satisfied their own interest, but it was no longer a viable proposition to make more.

As the market for white metal replicas waned, Victor turned to restoration of Dinky Toys Guy vans, mostly Weetabix and Lyons Swiss Rolls liveries. He was most insistent that every one of his restorations should have 'V&V r' engraved on the base, but he recalls one French trader acquiring one and filling this in!

By 1985 Victor had become more interested in collecting and restoring tinplate, so majored on these areas at the shop, and also had a regular table at Sandown Park toy fair.

He closed the shop in 2003 and has now retired. He enjoys travelling, theatre, and visiting grandchildren.

Taylor & Barrett fire engine copy

Dennis Goodman
Debo Toys

Whilst the MICA replicas of early Lesney Toys are quite well known, the DEBO white metal replicas are less so, and were made in the late 1980s and early

Rag & Bone cart replica by Debo

1990s by Dennis Goodman and Rob Miles. They are also copies of the early MoKo/Lesney Models, originally distributed by Moses Konstam. Both Dennis and Rob were interested in all that Lesney and Matchbox produced.

We believe the first in the range was the Rag and Bone Cart and Colin Penn supplied the original model which was used as a basis to create the mould. Colin still has the very first casting from Debo in his collection. It is understood that Dennis and Rob also made the Soap Box racer, the Horse Drawn Milk Float, an ice cream vendor, which may be the same as the Copycat one, and possibly three others.

This range was made quite separately to the replicas made by the Matchbox International Collectors Association, and it is not known who made the moulds or cast these replicas.

Sadly, Dennis passed away in the 1990s and Rob Miles died around 2006.

John Hodges
'Odgi' Toys of Yesterday

As a youngster, John Hodges had been a keen model maker, so it was no surprise that later, after doing an apprenticeship in mechanical engineering, he began making items and exhibiting them at the National Model Engineering Exhibition in London.

When trying to find out more about the cars that Dinky Toys had produced, he came across several references to the 38 Series Triumph Dolomite that he initially understood may have been produced as a prototype, but never made it into production. That being the case, he thought that if he could produce the model it would appeal to true Dinky Toys collectors.

In pursuance of this idea, in the late 1970s, he became aware of the two materials that would make the production of this and, perhaps, other models possible. One was Milliput, an epoxy resin that enabled him to fabricate the Dolomite 'master' and the other was the cold cure silicone rubber into which the molten white metal could be poured to form the casting.

Everything worked according to plan except that he found the whole process very laborious. The gravity castings were fairly poor and required a lot of time finishing, so he tried three or four commercial casting companies, none of which gave him satisfactory results, until he crossed paths with a specialist caster, Peter Comben of Enco Models who, from that moment on, made all the castings he subsequently required.

Such was the success of the Dolomite, finding space in many Dinky Toys collections, that John decided to make more 'toys that Dinky might have made', calling them Toys of Yesterday. He went on to make 12 or so others during a 30 year period, all being made at home in limited surroundings.

After minor finishing to the castings he applied one primer/undercoat followed by three coats of acrylic automotive paint, all from aerosols. The bodies were then hand polished and smaller parts such as seats, radiators and wheel hubs were hand painted.

Box making was quite a laborious process too. They were originally made with white cardboard printed with label and covered with yellow film. They were then hand cut round a 1/4" perspex former and formed up around a wooden block. Later on, when yellow film became unavailable, the labels were computer printed on yellow card and covered with clear film.

Samples were sent to magazines in England and many overseas countries. The vast majority of his production was sold by mail order through editorial and occasional advertising publicity. Word of mouth brought in many other orders and a few traders were selling them at swapmeets and toyfairs. A lot went overseas, to America, Australia and Canada, mainland Europe and South Africa.

On one occasion, an American customer who had purchased quite a few of John's models arrived at his flat straight from Heathrow, complete with luggage, hoping to get a visit to the 'factory'! John never knew if the visitor was disappointed to only find a flat, as he was out and his brother answered the door, but he did get a cup of coffee!

After 20 years or so with no new models appearing, demand dwindled and eventually ceased. This suited John as he had begun to look for other outlets other than the demands of his one man business. He still plays around with ideas connected with the model making business, and has produced some new masters, but is not involved in the sale of cars produced from them. In his spare time he now enjoys clay pigeon shooting and cycling.

Ian Law
PP Copy Models

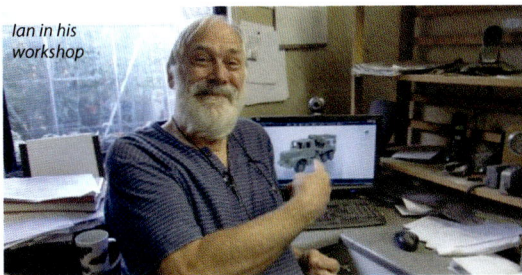

Ian in his workshop

If there's one man who more than any other typifies the creative and imaginative energy that many collectors have then it's Ian Law. Many collectors will experiment with a careful chop for their own amusement, but Ian has taken his abilities in this field to another plane altogether, developing a significant market in adapted models in the Dinky Toys style, almost all of which are true representations of real vehicles.

But Ian's roots go back to the golden era of Airfix kits, when they were 11½d each. He built most of them and then progressed to balsa wood aeroplane kits, all whilst he was around 9 – 12 years of age. Ian was living in Finchley Road, West Hampstead at the time, and in his lunch hour at school, he would jump on the train and head for Holloway Road, Highbury, to the Toys, Toys, Toys shop to constantly add to his building repertoire.

His other love was cycling, and he proudly talks of the first love of his life, his Soleil d'Or bike, used throughout his teenage years. However, Ian's world was about to change! A friend who was a collector of Minic Toys suggested they visit the Dorking Halls toy fair in 1980, and this was Ian's first glimpse of the vast range of old toys still available. Shortly after this, he gave

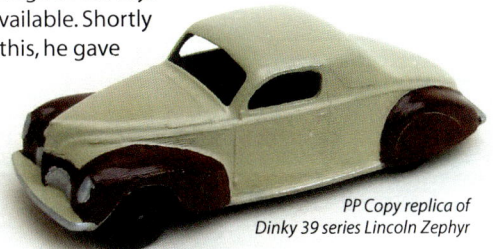

PP Copy replica of Dinky 39 series Lincoln Zephyr

Bugatti for Club Dinky France

up working in the greengrocery business, and moved to Worthing. He happened across Dave Bull, who ran a collectors shop in Lancing, and bought his first Dinky there, the Bedford Refuse Truck, for £5.

Whilst Ian immediately found repairing and restoring very rewarding, at no time did he get into seriously collecting Dinky Toys.

By 1985 his repairing and restoring had built up to a business sufficient for him to open his business unit in Brighton, which he initially shared with Chris Stonor, called Collectamania.

When collectors told him that the sources of 28 series Dinky van replicas were a little sporadic, mostly coming from DG Autocraft, he decided to start making copies himself. No sooner had Ian started, than a toy fair trader said he would take 50 from him, and thus he was into higher quantities!

Ian managed to get a friend who was in the casting trade to let him practice on his centrifugal casting machine. He gave up Collectamania, and launched his own business under the name of Presents Past. Ray Strutt guided him with his advertising, placing pieces in Collectors Gazette, with a front page article in the September 1989 issue. It was a small step to name his range of copy models, PP Copy.

This prompted some enquiries, including a call from Leslie Hurle Bath, who a decade earlier had worked with Barry Lester. Leslie owned Replicars BV in the Netherlands, and ordered a massive 2000 examples of a promotional 28 series van model, for sale in the store 'De Bijenkorf', followed by others. The first 2 payments from Leslie, Ian recalls, enabled him to place a deposit on his first house! A subsequent order from Leslie was a quantity of the Triumph Dolomite roadster, to be marketed under the Replicars name. Ian had previously arranged with John Hodges of Odgi Toys to create the pattern in resin using the original drawings from Dinky Toys. Sadly, Leslie died in the early 1990s and his son Randolph, who took over the business, did not wish to continue the arrangements with Ian.

At this stage the materials being used by Ian included 'Printers Lead' purchased from the dimly lit backstreets of London in $1/2$ ton quantities, and casting took place in Ian's garage. Ian's copies of the Spot-On range of sports cars have sold well over the years, and still the Daimler Dart SP250 is regularly

ordered by the car's owners' club.

The Dinky Toys Club of America ordered a promotional issue of the Dinky Toys Trojan van in red, white or blue. Whilst resolving how to deliver these models, Ian and his wife Christine, together with his son Steve, decided to deliver them personally. To combine business with pleasure, they flew to Detroit to complete the delivery, and went on to Baltimore to the toy fair organised by the Dinky Club. Ian was amazed at the acute shortage of Dinky Toys in the USA, and the demand for the few items he took with him meant that he was sold out!

This was too good an opportunity to miss, and Ian and Christine then opened a unit in a collectors mall in Adamstown, Pennsylvania, which lead to a further 5 units being taken in the next 3 years.

Whilst on one of his visits to the mall, he was asked by a stallholder to obtain an example of the Britannia Beanie Baby bear. Prices in the USA meant a minimum value of $300, and thus began a regular ordering of quantities of the Ty produced cuddly toys in the UK, followed by despatch of the Britannia on a regular basis! He was selling large quantities here in the UK, and also exporting considerable numbers to the USA, but was only stopped and searched once by the US Customs! During this period in which Ian had been diverted by Beanies from his preferred pursuits, he was still occasionally contacted by people to undertake commissions, including a run of 25 Dinky aeroplane copies.

Many white metal makers have found that the arrival of eBay has improved their business, and in Ian's case, eBay opened up the enthusiasm for Dinky Toys to collectors worldwide, but meant that his sales in America could no longer support keeping the units in the mall.

A major breakthrough came in 1998, when Ian got the call to produce 300 pieces of a promotional model for Club Dinky France (CDF). For a short while, Len Buller, trading as B&B Military Models, had been providing these specials, and it was Alain Gransard who asked Ian if he would make CDF3 the Citroen 2CV in grey. At the time, Alain was trading in old toys at his shop in Paris called Le Grenier de Grandmere.

A year later, Guy Girod, President of Club Dinky France, decided to take over the ordering direct, and Ian found himself producing

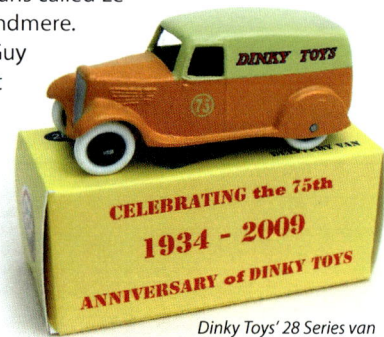
Dinky Toys' 28 Series van copy for 75th Anniversary of Dinky Toys

the next model which was a Studebaker Fire Chief car.

The club then alternated the issue of a B&B Models vehicle, with an Ian Law product. However, after Len Buller died, Ian was asked to take over the entire issues, and from 2002, the requirement has been for 2-3 models per year. In 2010 it increased to 6 models per year! These special issues are usually in quantities of 100 – 200, but repeat orders continue. Plans are already in place for the 2012 issues.

The process is quite fascinating, in that Guy Girod will send Ian an A4 sheet depicting the car he wishes to be modelled, always based on a pre-existing French Dinky Toy. However, it will have significant changes, such as from saloon to convertible or estate. Perhaps it will be a delivery van using a different cab unit. The sheet sent will also show the parts of other vehicles required to create the finished product, and finally the real car, as all are based on a real vehicle.

For the last seven years Ian's output has been mostly for CDF, and a book is to be published shortly featuring all the club models. This will be a fascinating read, and can be obtained from CDF.

Special promotionals for both the Maidenhead Static Model Club (MSMC) and for the Dinky Toy Collectors Association (DTCA) have also emanated from Ian's workshop, but Ian's 'bread and butter' lines and his promotionals for France represent the combination of clever design, unique creation of a master, followed by truly International quality control!

Ian's master pattern for such a conversion is created by first identifying which original toy vehicles will be contributing parts of their construction to the finished product. He then orders a small number of white metal castings to be taken from these original toys, produced for him by a Birmingham based casting company with a flair for detail.

This then provides Ian with a soft metal base with which to cut, file, alter and then solder together this new design. Thus a rough pattern is produced, which is then sent back to the casters. The staff there will clean up the inside of the casting, add on detailed casting ridges, and machine cut the shut lines of doors, bonnet etc, before taking a mould and casting the finished product.

Once this has passed the eagle eye of Ian, a production run with that mould is assured. An example of this process is in the Bugatti type 101 featured as the CDF model for 2010. The pictures here highlight the ingenuity involved. The Bugatti's side panels and doors are taken from a Corgi Riley Pathfinder, the bonnet and front wings are heavily modified Dinky Jaguar XK120, and the windscreen and rear end from the French Dinky Simca Sport 8.

Ian estimates that it takes him a total of 1 full day, over a 3 week period to produce the master, then a further 10 days for the castings to return, ready for assembly. Whilst Ian originally undertook his own casting, the ever present need to improve quality meant that he sought out and found his casters, already well known for their quality war gaming figures, and also badges and pins for football clubs.

Ian finds it difficult to envisage ever retiring, as his work fuels his addiction to his one consuming hobby, collecting lead figures. For Ian now, eBay has enabled him to seek and find many obscure figures, as well as his models reaching a wider audience, thanks to other CDF members.

Fred Lewis

Amongst the builders and adapters names that feature alongside Brooklin Models on the Internet is Fred Lewis.

Fred started collecting model cars in the late 1950s. The first ones were Matchbox 1:66 scale to place around his father's HO railway layout. Some time later Fred got interested in 1:43 models such as Corgi Toys and Dinky Toys.

Later in the 1960s Fred started to buy John Day kits and build them. He still has some John Day, Mikansue and other early kits that he purchased then.

As his collection grew he decided to concentrate on Ferrari sports racing cars. Fred reckons he has probably built around 400 kits of Ferraris. Some of the makes purchased included AMR, Annecy Miniatures, Bosica, CAR, CL Modelli, C-Scale, Gamma, Grand Prix Models, GT Turner, Illustra, Leader, Meri, MOG, Precision Miniatures, Provence Moulage, Record, Scale Racing Cars, Starter, Tameo, Tron, and Western Models.

In 1980 Fred purchased a kit of the 1962 Ferrari GTO for $650.00 and built it. This was produced by the Make-Up Co Ltd of Japan and consisted of 500 pieces to which Fred added probably another 50 pieces. It was the most detailed 1:43 model Fred had built or has ever seen. A similar kit was sold on eBay about 10 years ago for $2400.00. Fred has never seen another one that has been built.

Eventually models of American cars of the 1950s started to be made in 1:43 scale. These are the cars that Fred had grown up with and so it was inevitable that he should start to collect them. Even though there are not many kits of these cars, Fred buys them and will then either rebuild them to create better models, or in some cases he will change them completely into another model.

The base models that Fred adapts are often

1954 Ford Skyliner

from Brooklin but from time to time also Conquest, Durham Classics, MiniMarque43, Motor City USA, and Western Models. He tries to avoid diecast models as these are not worth putting so much time into. He usually undertakes customer requests but he finds that some want very extensive changes such as making a convertible from a station wagon. Even though he is able to do this, he would rather not do these conversions any more as the time involved makes them very expensive and it is more time than Fred wants to put in on just one model.

The 1954 Ford Skyliner pictured was created from Durham's 1954 Ford Panel van. At the present time Fred is scaling back somewhat, but his website features these re-creations in abundance.

Barry Lloyd
B-Line Models

Barry Lloyd is a Vanwall racing car enthusiast and in that capacity knew that there was a Vanwall that had not been modelled. He decided to put the matter right and produce a small run to satisfy himself and a few other enthusiasts besides

Mikansue made their Vanwall Special kit with the surface radiator in 1979/1980. Barry bought one, (still unmade...!) and thought it would make a reasonable basis for the second version with the scoop over the radiator tubes. He thought about it for so long that Mikansue had stopped making the kits, but luckily RAE took them on. So, he decided to have a go, and bought 6 RAE kits.

He thought it would be a bit of fun to make half a dozen, and try and sell the surplus so he would end up with a 'free' one for his own collection. He thought he would make as good a job as he could out of the fairly basic kit, so got some South Eastern Finecast wire wheels, and decent filler caps from Grand Prix Models. The rather weedy kit exhaust pipe was replaced with one from an old C Scale Vanwall kit, and Wessex Model and Toy Collectors club member Arthur Clapp cast some copies for him.

Arthur also cast the radiator scoops from the 'master' Barry had made from some spare white metal, and turned the brake discs from some nice shiny metal! He says the rear axle De Dion tubes were little lengths of aluminium tubing with the ends flattened, but can't remember whose steering wheels he used – they may have been Lansdowne ones.

After that it was just a question of cleaning up the original castings and putting them together on a mini production line! The 'Vanwall Special' decals came from the original kits, the race numbers from

The surviving 5!

his bits box - some sheets of numbers he had picked up from somewhere.

He had intended to make 6, but unfortunately after spraying the bodies he put them aside to harden off, and one body ended up touching the edge of the box they had been put in. He tried to 'T cut' the resulting mark out, but ended up going through to the primer... After a certain amount of bad language he couldn't face stripping it and starting again, so the 'run' was reduced to 5 rather than 6!

He still has that spoilt one, and a couple of old Mikansue kits he picked up on good old eBay, and maybe, just maybe, one day he will make B-Line Models No.2 - the 3rd version of the 1954 Vanwall Special, which had a conventional radiator... But don't hold your breath!

He says that he can only consider them as 'chops', the B-Line Models thing was very much tongue in cheek, which is why he left the RAE labels on the boxes as well as his own. At best, he says, they do demonstrate that quite a nice model can be made from fairly basic beginnings, but it just took him the best part of 25 years to do them!

Barry is also a member of the Wessex club, was newsletter editor for 11 years, currently vice chair and, would you believe, has a taxi business called B-Line!

Kevin McGimpsey & Stewart Orr

MICA and Perfect Toys

Kevin McGimpsey

Kevin McGimpsey and Stewart Orr are names synonymous with Matchbox Toys and MICA (Matchbox International Collectors Association). They have been lifelong friends and enthusiasts of the Lesney and Matchbox names, and in 1968, aged 16, Kevin was buying Bentley variations in Boyles sports shop in Belfast, believing that he and Stewart were the only Models of Yesteryear collectors in the world!

Stewart's mother owned the Pandora Sweetie shop in Bangor and fortunately for Stewart she stocked Yesteryears. More surprisingly, his GP, Doctor Brown had a complete set of 1st series Yesteryears and was prepared to accept recent releases in exchange for these early ones!

During the period of 1970 to1980, Kevin's collection was 'moth balled' and placed in his parents' attic, while he went to University to read law, and then into the army. He met up with Stewart again in 1977 and although Stewart still collected Yesteryears, Kevin had no interest in them.

Kevin was married in March 1981 and his mother boxed up his belongings, including his collection, in Ireland and sent them to him in Farnham, Surrey. The enthusiasm returned, and Kevin soon found Kevin Baker's Tangley Model Workshop in nearby Guildford, which stocked Yesteryears. He then met a friend

Motorbikes and three wheelers

of Stewart's, Keith Mortimer who was a dedicated collector and trader.

Kevin joined the UK Matchbox Club on 31 June 1981, and later attended the Windsor swapmeet in Slough, with Stewart. They were amazed by the dozens of tables of model cars, many of them Matchbox.

The Falklands war broke out in April 1982, and Kevin recalls entering Port Stanley in mid June. In the general store, he came across six 1st series Yesteryears that included a Y4 Shand Mason fire engine with the crew still on the plastic sprue. The price was around 25p each. They were dusty but otherwise fine. Kevin packed them in a souvenir brass 105 Howitzer shell, and brought them home.

At a dinner party in March 1983, one week after leaving the army, Kevin established Major Models, his business venture with Stewart. They each put in £200 in cash and £500 of their collections, valued at their retail price, and published a monthly 4 page listing of what was for sale.

Later that year, Stewart suggested that they published a Matchbox calendar, featuring the 12 rarest Yesteryears pictured in complementary settings. Not only was permission obtained from Gerry Tekerian, the Matchbox Toys product manager at the time, but he was so impressed that he placed an order for 10,000 when he saw them! The calendars continued to be published for 10 years between 1984 and 1993.

In 1985, Gerry Tekerian told Kevin and Stewart that Matchbox was seeking a new club to take over from UK Matchbox, and asked them to submit a proposal to establish a new one. Dave Smith of Heritage Toys in Lancashire was also invited to make a proposal, but Kevin and Stewart's was accepted and MICA was born.

As a result of this turn of events, Kevin decided not to pursue a legal career, realising he could make his livelihood from Matchbox, through Major Models, calendars, and MICA.

In 1986, the Chester Toy Museum was up for sale, as a going concern. Stewart and Kevin decided to buy it, and rapidly became experts on a wide range of toys. The creation of a dedicated Matchbox room was of course a must, and it was duly opened in April 1987.

In September 1985, as one of their products through MICA, Kevin and Stewart soon produced their first publication called The Collection. This was followed in 1987 by a request from Gerry Tekerian to record the history of Matchbox in one deluxe book. Collecting Matchbox Diecast Toys ...the First 40 Years was published in June 1989, written by a team of expert collectors, with an initial print run of 7,500. An order from Matchbox for 500 further copies came in 1992.

The fee from the project enabled Kevin and Stewart to move the Chester Toy Museum in 1990 to a new home in Lower Bridge Street, where it stayed until 2001.

The connection with white metal for these two friends began in December 1989, when, Kevin and Stewart recall, they were standing in the Falcon pub across the road from the Chester Toy Museum, discussing the next MICA UK Convention. This was scheduled for the following March and they were seeking something unusual to reward those members attending. One of them came up with the idea of producing a limited edition white metal figurine of Leslie Smith OBE, co-founder of Lesney Products.

Road rollers and bulldozers

They needed a white metal manufacturer, and at the time the museum shop had been stocking white metal sets of soldiers and character toys made by Little Lead Soldiers. Their owner was contacted and they were told that a figurine could be made from a photograph of Les Smith. Little Lead Soldiers did a fine job. The Les Smith figure, holding the book, Collecting Matchbox Diecast Toys- the First 40 Years, originally sold for £14.95 and 500 were made to commemorate his presence at the 5th MICA UK Convention in 1990. Now, they can reach in excess of £60.

Following the response to the Les Smith figure it was decided to follow with a copy of an original Lesney Perfect Toy. Perfect Toys, also known as Scale Models or the Early Lesney Toys, were the first toys made by Lesney Products in the period 1948 to 1955. Although a specialist area for collectors, they enjoyed a sentimental place in most Matchbox toy collectors' hearts. The obvious one to start with was the rare soap box racer. This comprised a boy figure, a cart, two axles, four wheels and an elastic band. Lesney Products had made the original in 1949, and co-founder Jack Odell, in an interview in 1988 said, "I remember making the mould myself. It was an absolute failure that never made the grade." It was certainly an unsophisticated looking model, and Kevin and Stewart felt that their example wasn't very good at all. As they did not want the original they had used as a master, they agreed with Little Lead Soldiers that they would make a copy of the boy but would have to start with a blank sheet when it came to making the cart. The model was made, but Kevin and Stewart weren't happy, as some of the models were easily broken. With deadlines to meet for the 1991 MICA UK Convention, they had to take delivery of all those produced. For some unexplained reason some versions retained the Lesney Products legend on the base.

The soap box racer replica was limited to a maximum production of 500. Of the 500 made, the majority of the boy drivers had blue coloured scarves, whilst 25 had red scarves and another 25 had green. The original soap box racer never had a box so they created a replica, using the basic design and colours from the milk float box.

The printers made the box appear old and authentic by printing the design on the rough side of the cardboard sheets! A couple of years later Kevin and Stewart were annoyed to learn that Little Lead Soldiers were selling their own version of the soap box racer. The MICA soap box racer now sells in excess of £100.

A new manufacturer had to be found, and Kevin and Stewart were recommended to try Illustra, based in St Leonards on Sea, East Sussex. Steve Overy, the owner, already had considerable experience in this field, and Illustra were engaged to make the rest of the MICA Perfect Toys range between 1992 and 2005.

Illustra's first Perfect Toy was the covered wagon. A far from mint example was sent to Illustra to enable them to make an accurate rubber mould, and the replicas were centrifugally cast. The full assembly and painting process took place at Illustra's premises. It was a simple matter to reproduce the coloured box.

This Perfect Toy was released in April 1992, and despite being a horse drawn vehicle, was extremely popular, with all 650 sold within a month.

The second model by Illustra was the Rag & Bone Cart with its full complement of junk. At one time the first choice had been the horse drawn milk float but MICA member Dennis Goodman, and friend Rob Miles, trading under the Debo name, had already made a quantity in 1991. The Lesney rag and bone cart is rated as being the second rarest of the early Lesney toys.

At this time, in 1991, the Museum's rag and bone model was missing a couple of pieces of junk, so Kevin and Stewart spent a few weekends at swapmeets looking for the toilet cistern and mangle wheel. Finally, at a Farnham Maltings show they bought a badly damaged cart missing its horse and driver but with four pieces of junk, two of which were the missing pieces. Illustra did a superb job and the

Coronation coaches and horse drawn vehicles

models couldn't be faulted. Originally, in 1949, Lesney made two colour versions of the original rag and bone cart. The rare colour scheme was in pale green with red wheels and a less rare version was in yellow with red wheels. MICA had their first six models painted dark green with red wheels and these were packaged in boxes numbered 1 to 6. The white metal junk pieces are perfect copies and it is virtually impossible to tell old from new, apart from being slightly heavier.

Stewart and Kevin initially rejected a number of Lesney Toys for inclusion in the MICA range, such as the cement mixer as it was relatively common, the crawler tractor/ bulldozer because they thought they couldn't source the rubber tracks, and Jumbo the Elephant as it was made from tin. The large state coach was too expensive to reproduce, and the small coronation coach was deemed to be of little interest, although things were to change. Lastly the Lesney Bread Press wasn't really a toy and was rather boring.

The two rag and bone carts

However, they made a decision to expand the series to include toys not necessarily made by Lesney Products, the first being the Father Xmas and sleigh, complete with sack of toys, which was originally made by Benbros in the 1950s. This replica was released in November 1992 just in time for Christmas. One of the ladies working at the Chester Toy Museum, Juna Cowling, volunteered to make the tiny cloth sacks. She painstakingly cut out each piece of cloth and sewed them into shape before placing the unpainted metal toy of a jester inside. Eventually 475 models were made.

The Aveling Barford diesel road roller followed, and was on sale in 1992 priced at £30. It had red rollers/wheels but no flywheel, and eventually 430 were made. Kevin and Stewart next turned to Morestone, another north London business. They made an extensive range of diecast products including bicycles and horse drawn vehicles. Their ice cream salesman, released in the early 1950s, was

selected, and Kevin and Stewart bought an example at the Farnham swapmeet for £25, which was duly dispatched to Illustra in April 1993. The Perfect Toys Ice Cream Vendor model was on sale in September 1993, decorated with waterslide transfers stating in capitals, 'Ice Cream Stop Me and Buy One'. Just 375 models were made, selling at £31 each.

The penultimate model in the Perfect Toy series was the 1940s motorcycle and sidecar in the fictitious livery of Acme Couriers based in City Road, London. An unidentified manufacturer had made the original model around 1950 and the donor model was again bought at Farnham. It was in fact an army dispatch rider and passenger, and just 375 models were made. The rider and bike were painted grey whilst the sidecar and courier were painted in yellow. The first ten models were painted in a reversed colour scheme. Waterslide transfers were used to decorate each model. It was released in March 1994 at the 9th MICA UK Convention held at the Moat House Hotel in Telford. Price was £32.

This was followed a year later by what turned out to be the last Perfect Toy, made in the 1990s. Kevin and Stewart, whilst researching the series and talking with Les Smith and Jack Odell, discovered that a Muir Hill dump truck was to have been made. Due to a shortage of zinc, it was not produced, but the tooling, was used by another company, Condon. Here was an opportunity to make a Perfect Toy that never was but should have been! Limited to a maximum production run of 400, eventually 375 were made in green and red; with the first ten made in yellow and red. Released in June 1995 it was priced at £35.

One of Jack's early Lesney toys was the miniature Coronation coach, which offered an opportunity for a perfect souvenir for the occasion. The original price of the Coronation coach was 2/l1d (l5p) and there were two colours of plating - silver and gold. Similarly, Kevin and Stewart were able to launch their Perfect Toy Coronation coach to coincide with Queen Elizabeth II's Golden Jubilee in June 2002. Les Smith agreed to autograph each box on all orders received before the cut off date.

The Cement Mixer, finally appeared in 2003, and was very popular. The castings were very accurate as was the paint match. There were two authentic colour schemes but unlike the original, this cement mixer came with its own box. Leslie Smith OBE agreed to autograph a small quantity of the boxes and these were issued to early subscribers. 360 cement mixers were produced.

By November 2004 rubber tracks were available, and the crawler tractor was released in three colour schemes, followed by the last in the Perfect Toys Series, the bulldozer with driver. This magnificent Perfect Toy came in a choice of two Lesney colours –

minty green or orange-red. Each box was numbered and individually autographed by the recently deceased Leslie Smith OBE.

Stewart decided to get out of the toy world, at least temporarily in 2001 and left MICA. Kevin continued to run the club, and he was instrumental in bringing out the small Coronation coach, Cement Mixer, Tractor, Bulldozer and the Road Roller.

Kevin told us, "I ran out of good subjects to 'perfect' and so that was the conclusion of a great series." In 2011 he continues to run MICA as well as working for Bonhams as their golf specialist and Stewart is the toy specialist with Hall's of Shrewsbury, cataloguing and organising 4 toy auctions a year.

Colin Penn
Copycat Models

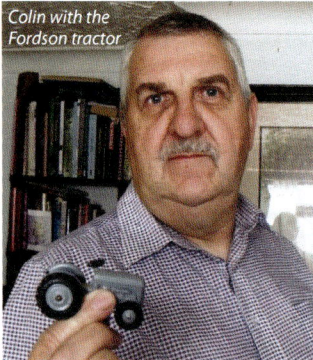
Colin with the Fordson tractor

The name Copycat Models was the brainchild of Jim Varney. During the 1970s Jim was best known for his range of public transport bus kits, covering all periods from horse drawn to diesel, from London to Paris. Known as Transport Replicas, they were accurate and well researched models. Jim was a natural entrepreneur and deserved to do well in business, but fate was not often in his favour.

Jim had an interest in all forms of transport and when Colin Penn first met him in the early 1970s he had an excellent stock of good quality used Dinky Toys. One of the harder models to find was the pre war Fordson Tractor. Although this was mainly made in lead, the front wheels were mazak and were subject to decay as the two metals do not mix well. Jim decided to make a copy of the model to fill gaps in customers' collections. Jim's model was not just a straightforward copy, but an improved model; with the addition of a very accurate Fordson radiator grill that was sadly lacking in the original Dinky model.

Copycat Gully Sucker

And so the first Copycat model was born, and remained alone for many years. However, Jim's model bus kit business went into decline when ready to run, accurate and detailed models were more easily obtained from the likes of Corgi, EFE and other manufacturers. Eventually he sold the model bus kit business, as did Pirate Models, which were in a similar situation. The model bus kit business was shelved and the kits disappeared.

Colin Penn then came on the scene. He, along with another trader, Martin Jewell attended many steam rallies throughout the summer months from the first Enfield Pageant in the spring of 1979 through to the Beaulieu Auto jumbles in the autumn. Tractors always sold well at these rallies with demand far outstripping supply and Martin felt that it was unfortunate that Jim was no longer making the Fordson Tractor. Colin approached Jim, enquiring if he had retained the tractor or if it had been sold with the bus kits. As luck would have it, Jim had retained both the tractor mould and masters. Colin asked if he would be prepared to let him and Martin sell them on his behalf. A deal was struck and they soon received their first batch of Fordson Tractors. It did not take long for Colin and Martin to sell them and request a second, larger, batch.

Several batches later Jim could not believe the change in his fortune and suggested that he might add further models to the range, with Colin being his sole retailer. And so were added the model Ice Cream Vendor, and Tandem & Sidecar. These two models have always been attributed to Morestone, but were in fact made by Agasee and Brooks. Both replicas sold very well.

Jim next selected Crescent racing cars to produce copies of, beginning with the Ferrari and Connaught. Again sales were quite brisk.

Colin is uncertain why Jim chose the Dinky Triumph Herald next, as both Dinky and Corgi had made a version, and neither was difficult to obtain in reasonable original condition. He surmises that it was one of Jim's favourites.

It was inevitable, with the market identified, that soon there would be a copy of the Dinky Toys Field Marshall tractor and this proved to be one of the most difficult models to produce, with the first two

Copycat model boxes, original by Varney below, Colin's version above

masters being failures. The model had to be cut in half horizontally and then rejoined during the building process. A small number of models were produced from the first mould, but these were both very weak at the front axle and had a bad moulding line near the bottom of each side, which was difficult to remove without spoiling the detail. However, this copy has been produced in thousands, finished in the usual orange, wartime green and grey, mainly with rubber tyres.

The Crescent range also delivered the Jaguar D-type, hard to find in good condition. This was paired with the Jaguar XK140 which was an improved Micro Models including racing driver with dashboard, steering wheel and seating. Both models proved very popular both as racing cars and tourers.

Further copies of the Crescent range followed, being the Gordini, Maserati, B.R.M. and Cooper Bristol, and a much improved Charbens Ferguson TE20 Tractor, of which a quantity was supplied for the 2007 Spalding Tractor Show.

During the mid 1980s Jim was supplying Colin with

Copycat model of Micromodels MGA

raw castings, leaving him to decide on the chosen livery. For a copy of the Dinky Morris J van, Colin made three basic versions, Capstan and Royal Mail as done by Dinky, and a GPO Telephones version to pair up with a later model. In addition, by special request, customers could have the model in the livery of their choice.

Interest from classic owners' clubs resulted in No 17, based on the Sunbeam Talbot by Chad Valley, slightly improved by the addition of a crude interior in place of the clockwork motor. Colin produced many of these models in various metallic colours for the Sunbeam Talbot Owners Club.

Still providing many of the ideas, Jim proposed a gully gulper, which utilises the cab from the Dinky 'fish fryer' more commonly known as the dustcart, and the body from the River Series, with a skilfully made joining platform. These proved difficult to produce involving a lot of work, and Colin was never able to recover the true cost within the pricing range. Anyone who has one of these in their collection is lucky as he produced less than 50. Colin made one special variation of this model as a tar sprayer, leaving off the gully boom, and with four spray pipes on the rear. Finished in all over black, it was sold at the Stockwell toy fair, and he never got around to making another.

An unusual choice was the Lion Car DAF Variomatic, and Colin was unable to glean why Jim chose to copy this model. It was not very popular and as a result Colin made only one batch, most of which went to Holland.

Copycat Austin A35

An Austin Healey was a Dinky copy and the MGA tourer a copy from Micro Models, and these were Jim's last input to the range. By 1988 he was growing tired of the business, needing cash input, he offered to sell it to Colin, who therefore acquired all moulds, masters, and unmade, unsold models, as well as the business name and rights to produce the models.

Colin continued to use a variety of sources for his patterns, including items by Crescent, Morestone, Dinky Toys and Tootsietoys. The latter heralded the use of a different caster, who could not produce the quality of the usual supplier, so few were made.

A popular choice was the Austin A30/35 saloon, produced in significant numbers until it was

Copycat Daf Variomatic

introduced by Vanguard, despite an assurance from them that they would not run this model. It was made with cast hubs and rubber tyres and an improvement on the Dinky original.

Colin acquired a Royal Mail licence to produce Royal Mail models in 1989, which all had to be approved by their Intellectual Integrity Department. As a result, copies of the Dinky pre war Airmail Car and the Dinky Z van were produced, the latter as G.P.O. Telephones with a ladder, or as Royal Mail without. The Dinky pre and post war Morris Royal Mail two ton van followed with smoothed sides so that other liveries could be added. A small range of accessories such as mail boxes and telephone boxes, policemen, standing saluting AA and RAC men, and figures directing traffic. The company that maintained all the BT telephone boxes, Unicorn, commissioned a large supply of phone boxes as a give away, and Colin was asked to produce a special

Copycat window cleaner kit

run in black with a figure of a Beefeater for supply to the Tower of London.

Such was, and still is the camaraderie between traders in this field, that as ideas came along for new copies, other producers filled in or took over subjects. The original master of Colin's pre war Dinky RAF refueller exploded in the moulding process, and he managed to get just a few castings made. They were so poor and required so much work that Colin made just one example and scrapped the rest. PP Copy Models had produced this too, so Colin left it to Ian Law and decided not do any

Copycat Mercedes W196

more.

Fellow trader Martin Jewell selected a Lanz Bulldog tractor, originally made by Marklin. It was a heavy bulky casting produced at Martin's request and sold with his permission. It had a limited run, but Martin also produced it himself in some numbers.

Soon, Colin found he had to employ a full time painter, though he still did most of the assembly himself. He was also offering the models as kits in plain boxes, resulting in varying standards of finished models.

Some unusual subjects at this point included two originals produced by Agasee, the Butcher's Boy on his bike, and a Penny Farthing tricycle, with clown figure. In the course of searching for variety, Colin acquired the masters for three more Dinky style racers, but these have not been produced, along with many masters for the Buccaneer Models range which he acquired. Again, he has never produced them, but still has them stored away. They included the Dinky 39 series for the British and USA issue models that have now been produced by PP Copy Models.

During the early 1990s Colin produced a range of over 100 Minic Style 1:1200 ships accessories, many of which were used on a scale model of New York harbour that was built at the Child Beale Wildlife Park near Reading. We believe it is still in their museum.

Copycat Scammell with trailer

By the mid 1990s the popularity of the copies had waned, due to the superior quality of models coming from China marketed by Corgi and Vanguard at a fraction of the price. Colin felt he could not compete, as the charm of a crude hand built model could not match that of mass produced scale models of better detail and definition.

He therefore decided to shelve the business, and concentrate on the retail side of ready to run models, although there was always a demand for the three tractors in the range, as until recently there were few in 1:43 scale.

The last additions to the range were to have been a Fordson Super Major Tractor and Massey Ferguson Tractor, which were derived from the two Matchbox King Size models. Whilst a few have been recently produced they were never given a number. Similarly, a small number of four wheel log trailers to go behind these tractors were also made.

In 2002 Colin decided to start a slow unwind towards retirement and passed Copycat Models onto Bob Pitkin, another trader, who now only retails the 5 tractors that were within the range, although he recently sourced a four wheel timber trailer in 1:43 scale, which has also been produced in small numbers to accompany the tractors.

Colin can still be found as an active stallholder at many of the toy fairs in Southern England, and has many a tale to tell, to those who might care to listen.

Keith Pillinger
My Way models

Keith Pillinger, who founded Bristol Paramedic Ambulance back in 1976, was an avid collector of white metal models years before that date. Not only as a collector but also as a business promotion, he thought it would be a good idea to have a model ambulance produced as a special limited edition. He already had a large number of Brooklin models in his collection and decided to approach that company with a view to them producing the models. Not only were Brooklin Models a well known company, they were based in Bath, Somerset some 10 miles from Keith's Ambulance Station which, of course. was very convenient .

So, Keith went to Brooklin to put his proposal forward to the management who said they would be delighted to fulfil Keith's wish of producing a model ambulance based on their Chevy Nomad van, but it would be a year before they could undertake this production. Naturally, Keith was disappointed but understood and just waited for the months to slip by. Finally one year to the day later Keith returned to the factory with great expectations, only to be told that they had changed their minds and were not able to produce the models! Keith, being very disappointed said "in that case I will produce them myself."

Having given this some thought he went to a local model shop in Bristol and purchased one hundred Brooklin models of the Chevy van. When these finally arrived he dismantled them completely, keeping the plated parts i.e. bumpers, radiator, etc to one side and submerged the original painted bodies into a tub of paint thinners which eventually removed all the paint. This allowed Keith to clean and re-paint them in ambulance white. To achieve a first class 'factory' finish, he even built a water running spray booth, using two pack paint, and achieved the high quality finish he wanted. He then re-assembled the models with appropriate decals.

Although these models were classed as Code 3 Keith felt that it would be incorrect to sell them in their original boxes, giving the impression of factory originals. So he had boxes of his own design printed, depicting the model within, and signed and numbered them all. Great interest was shown in these models by collectors world wide, so Keith decided to produce a series of models, which were all sold and eagerly collected. After the Ambulance, they were liveried as, County Coroners, Blood Transfusion, Funeral Hearse, complete with coffin, and 'I did it my way', all based on the Chevy Nomad. He then produced Pillinger's Rescue in red with gold fittings, based on a Pontiac van, and finally a lime green Pontiac van, also decalled 'I did it my way'. After 100 ambulances, the following four comprised 50 of each and the final two, just 25 of each.

This final model underlined the feeling Keith had about those who said that, being an amateur, he would not be able to undertake such a task. However, the reality is that he successfully completed it, and that the models he produced are now much sought after. As for Keith himself, he has returned now to being a white metal model collector and continues to run his business, Bristol Ambulance E.M.S.

'My Way' & 'Rescue' Pontiac vans

John Roberts
Master Model Maker

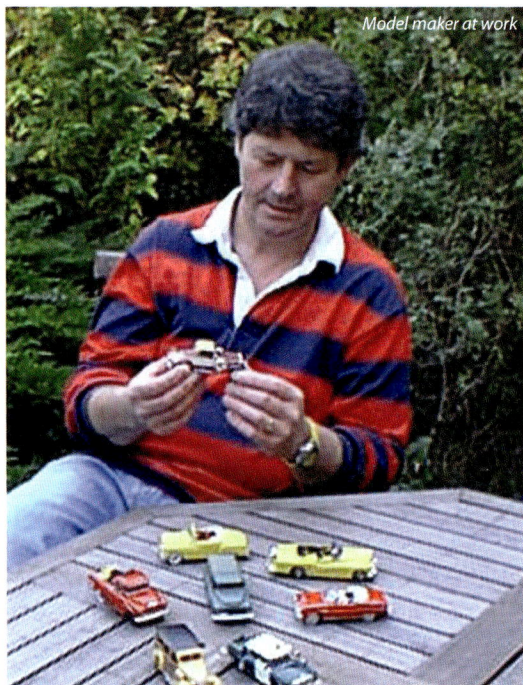
Model maker at work

The term model maker can mean many things. John Roberts' specialism is to create something special from anything, from a block of wood to a standard handbuilt model.

John's interest in model cars goes back to his very early childhood. Like many children brought up in the 1950s, John was an avid Dinky Toys collector and playtimes at school would be spent comparing the various Dinkys he and friends had brought in that day. Many of them were chipped, scuffed and without tyres, a condition quaintly known nowadays as 'playworn'.

John was brought up in Somerset and attended Highbridge VC Junior School. In the breaks he recalls there were usually two ways of playing with Dinkys. One was to race them over the playground at the far end under the trees, although pushing was almost akin to throwing in an attempt to win. The other was to run them along the wall that divided the playground from the local church. The grooves in the sandstone coping can be seen to this day over fifty years later.

The racing section naturally favoured cars of the track – the Dinky Toys 23 series of Cooper Bristols, HWMs, Maseratis and the like. The best two were considered to be the HWM and Talbot Lago as they were larger and therefore slightly heavier. Axles were oiled, and keen types took the bases off and filled the

bodies with lead. These were the Formula 1 boys of the playground. John arrived with his peculiar vehicle of choice, a Commer Breakdown Truck minus its rear bodywork. It was painted red, looked terrible and beat all comers. He is sure this was the one and only time a Commer truck has ever beaten a full single seater racing car grid!

John's father was responsible for starting his obsession with repainting model cars. He had seen some of his son's 'playworn' models and suggested they walked into town to buy some paint. John chose three colours, red, black and beige. The paint came in tins and was made by Japlac. As they walked home his father said, "I wonder how long this paint takes to dry?" John looked up at his father to find he was reading the details on a fourth can which he'd added to the other three when he wasn't looking. This was a can of pale green paint.

Grammar School reared its ugly head in 1959, and John was one of the lucky ones who passed the 11 plus exam. Many who were brighter than him failed this milestone and he lost touch with many friends. He reflects that thousands of childrens' future lives and attitudes were shaped on those single fateful days in summers long gone.

The 1960s brought a new love to John's life in the shape of a plastic bag full of plastic bits, all for the princely sum of two shillings. The Airfix kit had arrived. At first he built a few aircraft and along with everyone else hung them on the ceiling. He then discovered the car kits, which were far closer to home. At first all the offerings were veteran and vintage subjects and his interest did not lie then, nor now, in the early automobiles. However, hope was at hand with the Bullnose Morris and the supercharged Bentley 4$\frac{1}{2}$ litre. John believes he ruined many Bentleys in the name of model making, learning

MGTC with added detail

Morris Minor tourers with added detail

much about the real cars in the process through research based on library books.

One day a visit to his local Woolworths store brought great excitement in the shape of a modern car! This was the Sunbeam Rapier which was Airfix's first attempt at a modern subject. Being a confirmed Rootes Group fan, John could not believe his luck and many a Rapier was wrecked in the name of model making. As the range expanded so did his collection, to encompass Austin Healey Sprite, Ford Lotus Cortina, Mini, VW Beetle, Renault Dauphine, Vauxhall Viva, Triumph Herald to name but a few.

During the Airfix years John still collected Corgi and Dinky Toys, as well as Spot-On. Needless to say, many were repainted and altered and his influences for good or ill were people like Cecil Gibson and F. Brian Jewell who both wrote books on model cars. John still has Plastic Model Cars by Cecil Gibson, which concentrates on the Merit range of racing and sports cars. Mention is made of a product called Barbola Paste. He found some and used it without much success.

Like so many boys his age, he sold most of his Corgis and Dinkys for a pittance and after a few years regained the interest he had as a child and started to buy again. Tatty examples were fine and he would repaint and modify them.

In the early 1970s when John was married and living in North Wales, he learned about Barry Lester and the models he was selling. On a visit to his wife's relations in Salisbury, John went off to see Barry, who also lived in Salisbury at that time. He was just starting up his own company, Auto Replicas. Having made masters for John Day and Acorn Models of Swansea, together with his extensive experience in scratch building, Barry was ideally equipped to start his own range of white metal kits. The ERA

and Maserati were first, followed by the AC Cobra. John went for a Cobra along with some Continental diecasts and a Winross truck. He remembers spending far more than he could really afford!

When John and his wife arrived home he set to work on the Cobra. He'd never worked with white metal before and quickly learned how soft the material was. Luckily he stopped sanding before the chunky Cobra turned into a dainty Austin Healey Sprite! The Cobra was the first of many white metal kits that appeared on John's bench, mainly through scanning advertisements in Model Maker and Model Cars magazines. Western Models, Motorkits, Danhausen, Paddy Stanley, John Day, Varney as well as Auto Replicas soon filled his small workspace.

In 1979 John moved to Wiltshire and a few years later he decided to make a few models in wood for his own amusement. He made a 1955 Buick Century and a 1953 Cadillac 75 Fleetwood. He needed wheels for these and found out about a company called Brooklin Models in nearby Bath. He telephoned Brooklin and spoke to John Hall who invited him to the factory. He made John most welcome, was very complimentary about John's models and readily supplied him with some wheels and tyres. This first meeting would have been 1985 because BRK 20, the Buick Skylark, had just been announced. John returned home with one of these as well as the sets of wheels.

John was in teaching for 10 years as a classroom teacher, and a further 20 years as a primary school headteacher, and so model cars were a hobby and a relaxation, although he was also involved in a small way making models for others. The first was a Sebring Sprite for a local amateur racing driver in the mid 1960s. For the first years of ModeleX John was still teaching but the model cars side was growing, with a steady demand for his work. When he left teaching in

1999, model making became his full time occupation. Thankfully, when he reached 60 years of age a couple of years ago the government remembered he'd contributed to the education system and awarded him a teacher's pension. This has enabled him to work less hours each week, but he still needs to spend some time building models although it's not every day now.

As well as Brooklin, John wreaked havoc with Western Models and Somerville Models and was honoured that both companies awarded him Code 2 status for his conversions on their models. Doug and Roly McHard used to come and see him at ModeleX to discover the machinations he'd inflicted on their beautiful models. The two most extensively modified Somervilles he made were a Riley Kestrel and an Austin 10 Conway, the cabriolet version of the Cambridge. Both had all doors, boot and bonnet open with full engine detail, and the Austin had the roof in the open position. A family friend owned a Conway and so John was able to research the car in fine detail. The Kestrel ended up in Australia and the Austin went to Blackpool. Both were featured in Classic and Sportscar magazine thanks to Mike McCarthy who always used to chat with John at ModeleX. Mike also featured John's work in the 'Collector' series of feature articles. The Austin won one of the awards at ModeleX. Durham Classics also conferred Code 2 status on his modifications of their models, Julian Stewart being most helpful and generous in his praise.

After John Hall retired in 1998, Nigel Parker, the new managing director asked John to become more involved with Brooklin. Whereas before he had been a casual visitor to the factory, occasionally

'Barnato' Bentley
with added detail

helping with suggestions for model subjects, he was now to take a fairly full part as research consultant, helping with subject matter, finding prototypes for measuring, assisting with photo shoots, and so on. Although not an employee John has been made to feel very much a part of the Brooklin 'family' and greatly enjoys the time he spends there.

He also spent a number of years painting cars in oils, and had a few one man exhibitions and some well known customers. He still has a couple of paintings hanging on the wall in his workshop, painted the year his son was born. One day he'd like to pick up the brushes again, and would also like to write more childrens' novels – he wrote five when he was teaching but only had one published.

These days most of John's model making projects involve Brooklin products as, unfortunately, many other white metal manufacturers have either scaled down, changed hands or ceased operations. He still builds model cars but makes less models than he used to. Despite this he continues to have a very full order book and struggles to keep up with collectors' demands. Most people are, thankfully, very patient!

CHAPTER SIXTEEN
THE INFLUENCE OF CHINA & THE 21st CENTURY SCENE

Through the experiences of more than 150 pattern makers, casters, builders and retailers we have built up a picture of how the industry developed, with a burgeoning of new ranges being launched through the 1970s and 1980s, and collecting interest seeming to reach a peak in the mid 1990s. Some people have said that they chose to downsize due to other interests or change of career, others due to health considerations. More recently, sadly some have suffered serious ill health or passed away. A small number became disillusioned with either the market or the bureaucracy with which they had to negotiate.

The original motives of almost all the producers who started in this industry were as motoring enthusiasts keen to fill gaps in the market with more specialist or obscure marques of motor cars not covered by the diecast toy makers. We have seen how Brooklin Models, in particular, has bridged the gap between small artisan and mass production, and also how Danhausen in the 1980s made the major leap to China for mass production, switching to the diecast process.

Slowly but surely, as the cheap labour of Hong Kong and subsequently China, was tapped so successfully by the modern companies producing in large quantities, there have been changes in the market for the specialist white metal handbuilt model car.

However, such is the versatility of the white metal makers and the industry as a whole that it has been able to respond and change direction. Whilst some ranges have been dropped, and/or production runs reduced, in some instances other makers have taken them over in smaller numbers, re-mastering them for better quality, thus retaining that valuable customer base.

Paradoxically, some white metal model producers have told us that the prices of detailed resin models

from China in particular are creeping upwards, allowing the white metal manufacturer scope to re-enter the market with limited runs of new models. Perhaps the wind of change has arrived, and there will be a resurgence, following the current success of white metal kit sales?

At the other end of the spectrum, the late 1990s and early 2000s were the watershed for a number of diecast companies, old and new, to establish their production bases in various parts of China. It has to be recognised that the products of Ixo, Minichamps, Oxford Diecast, Spark, and more recently Neo are now consistently of high quality, with details that have previously only been seen on white metal handbuilt models. From the era when models were created to fill gaps in the diecast line up, the volume manufacturers are now allegedly using original existing handbuilt resin models of obscure vehicles as patterns to create their own resin or diecast versions in high volumes!

The trend from China has been to see reduced production runs, and a number of variations on each basic model – all techniques used by the white metal field years ago. No longer are there production runs of 200,000 – 300,000 as was the case in Dinky Toys and Corgi Toys days.

So are the two methods of production converging together into the same market? Are white metal collectors also buying Oxford Diecast, for example? Certainly, makers such as Marsh Models are in a very similar market to the Spark and Bizarre models, as are Minichamps and J&M Classics, making models of owner classics.

So what does the current market look like?

Brooklin are producing plenty of new models each year, and Durham Classics, in Canada, have re-commenced production to satisfy collectors' demands. However, it is the view of at least one of our larger producers that the tide may be turning. Unreliable factories and increasing costs are causing the Chinese products to reach prices close to existing handbuilts, and in some cases exceed them, one well known manufacturer is a case in point, releasing some 1:43 scale diecast models at over £100 each. Indeed, we hear of rising wage costs, higher shipping costs, and changes to the exchange rate, all reducing the margins Chinese factories had for obtaining business. Some Chinese factories are said to be experiencing a shortage of manpower, resulting in delivery times becoming longer.

But what about the recession, how has this affected white metal makers? A number have said that they are finding collector enthusiasts turning more to kits to build themselves, firstly to pay less, but also to achieve a unique model. Why else would the 1:76 scale John Day kits frequently seen on eBay be selling so well, when their immediate ready built competitors from Oxford Diecast, Base Toys or Classix are only £3.00?

On the international scene, we may be seeing something of a renaissance. Both Great American Dream Machines and Motor City USA have recently been bought by new and enthusiastic owners, keen to not only maintain but improve the already high quality of these ranges.

New makers such as Simon Elford and Frank Jones have also recently appeared. It now seems very appropriate and constructive to draw this debate, and this book to a close by featuring three white metal makers who, in very different ways, are proving in the UK that the market, and its producers, have adapted successfully.

Simon Elford
Trident Models

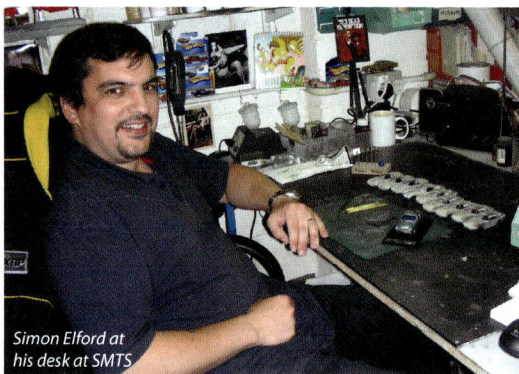

Simon Elford at his desk at SMTS

Whilst the general trend has been one of reducing production runs, some ranges ceasing, and less overall choice, it's very pleasing to find that a new range has been born!

Simon Elford is the brains behind the Selfords range, and his story is a familiar one.

Simon lived in London as a child, but moved to the Hastings and Bexhill area when he was 14. As a teenager in the early 1980s, he recalls building many Tamiya plastic kits, enjoying the precision and detail provided by plastic injection moulding.

His first employment was as a chef in Hastings, which he did for a couple of years until 1992. At the restaurant he met many interesting people, amongst them an Aston Martin Owners Club member who invited him to join him at AMOC club meetings. There he met Keith Williams, of Scale Model Technical Services, who also owns an Aston Martin DB 2/4, which happens to be in pieces in a barn.

Simon had begun collecting basic models from the mass diecast manufacturers, but also continued building plastic kits, and it was this latter skill that interested Keith. He asked Simon if he would be interested in building white metal models for him,

and in 1995, Simon began working full time at the SMTS works.

At SMTS, all the employees had to be able to fettle the castings, spray paint, and assemble, and the amount of work the castings required, together with the quantity of fine pieces to each small 1:43 scale model, presented Simon with quite an initial challenge.

To maximise his income, Simon also worked in a local model shop, Model Supplies, on Sunday mornings. This shop specialised in radio control and wooden assembly kits, but over time, Simon developed the plastic kits and diecast ranges to spread the customer interest. However, after 3 years of working at SMTS, the owner of the model shop wished to sell up, and in 1998 when his buyer dropped out, Simon stepped in and bought it. He had reduced his hours at SMTS in order to learn the shop business thoroughly, but then had to leave SMTS, keeping in touch with Keith, and selling some of the SMTS ranges.

Regrettably, the market for radio control models became heavily influenced by eBay, with traders encouraging younger people to buy complete models, but these traders were less able to repair them when they went wrong. The shop found itself reduced to repairs only, with sales plummeting,

Brass pattern for Trident Models Maserati

and eventually Simon had to close the shop and commence bankruptcy proceedings.

Through his links with Keith, he was able to return to work for SMTS full time, and found a changed workforce, reduced due to the overall decline in the market. However, whilst the team had diminished, the quality of the work done had risen significantly. This was partly in response to customer demand, higher competition from Chinese quality diecasts, and improvements to staff experience, materials and overall precision.

By 2002 Simon was back on his feet, and met Colin Fraser of Formula Models, based with John Simons of Marsh Models. To supplement his income, Simon rented space with Colin, and finally became self employed. This enabled him to undertake building and finishing work for a number of people, including continuing with SMTS, but also taking on work from Formula Models, Illustra, Marsh Models, and Model Assemblies.

This wider world opened his eyes to the great diversity of cars being modelled, but some that had never been made to modern quality standards, such as a Maserati Mistrale. The answer was obvious, he should launch his own range!

Christian Sargant was doing pattern work for John Simons, Keith Williams and Pat Land, so was an obvious choice for a pattern maker, and Keith at SMTS, equally for the castings. After scouring his books, for both pictures and technical data, he

Trident Maserati - the finished model

selected the Mistrale coupe as his first model, followed by a Mistrale Spyder, and then the De Tomaso Mangusta. So far his production has been approximately 50 of each, and he is testing the likely interest with both owners clubs and the international market. A Lister Jaguar XJS Le Mans is the next planned model.

Encouragement has come from many quarters, including Grand Prix Models, which has enabled coverage in the Octane and Classic & Sports Car magazines.

Simon feels optimistic about the future, and is currently working 6-7 days per week as a builder, and now range creator, with both his own range and continuing work for Illustra and SMTS. He recognises that the market has shrunk, and that as a result, the need for pattern makers, casters and builders to 'cross pollenate' their time and activities is essential. Simon is married to Tanya, and has 2 daughters aged 19 and 15, who share his interest in cars.

Frank Jones
British Heritage Models

Frank Jones, of British Heritage Models, hoping to fill the gap caused by the loss of Somerville, Milestone and Western Models, announced his plan to launch three new ranges in late 2010. Frank was born and brought up in Liverpool, a quarter of a mile from the Meccano Dinky Toy factory, and these toys played a big part in his childhood. He began collecting white metal models around 2000, but due to redundancy, his collection had to be sold.

In 2010, Frank returned to white metal as a dealer and it was in March 2010 that he came up with the idea of British Heritage Models, specialising in just British model cars. He hopes at some point to bring out his own range but for the moment will concentrate on the Somerville Collection and The Sovereign Range, both

BHM Triumph Stag

Frank Jones

of which have been very well received.

The Somerville Collection began with re-casting the Vauxhall Velox L-type, whilst his Sovereign range uses the K&R Replicas Triumph Stag, fully built for him by Scale Model Technical Services, as its flagship.

Maroon H Type Vauxhall, re-issue of Somerville Series

Blue Vauxhall Velox, re-issue of Somerville Series

Frank plans on low production runs, together with having some good contacts in the white metal industry, enabling him to gauge demand, and extend the ranges.

Trevor Wright
TW Models

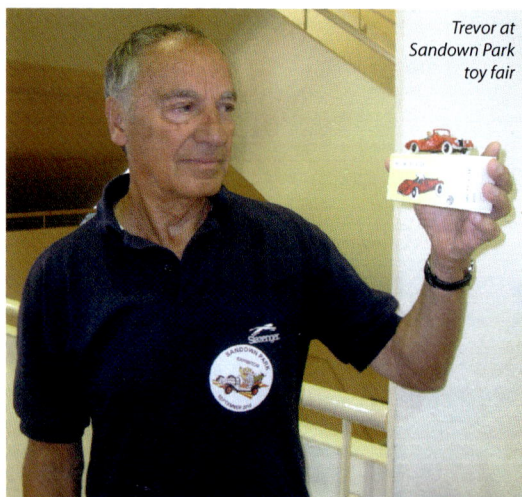

Trevor at Sandown Park toy fair

Responding to the needs of amateur builders, Trevor Wright's TW range has contributed to the revival of the craft side of the industry, whereby he has developed simple artisan examples produced in his own home. Wasn't that where the early pioneers came in?

Trevor's childhood recollections are not so much of Dinky Toys to start with, but of military figures. He recalls that soon after the Second World War, his parents took him to the renowned Hamleys toy shop in Regents Street, and he fell in love with the Skybirds range of soldiers. They were all made to 1:72 scale; a six foot man then becomes 1". Skybirds had originally started manufacture in the 1930s.

In due course, Trevor's most treasured possessions became his Dinky Toys, but as he approached entry into National Service, his toys were all packed away, and largely forgotten about. However, he does recall a visit to Ireland with Royal Air Force colleagues, and spotting a Dinky Toys military Quad field gun set, and with heavy encouragement from his friends, he bought it for 12/6d.

On returning to 'civvy street' Trevor took his experience in Air Traffic Control from Germany to Gatwick, and finally switched to the commercial operator, British United Airways, followed by British Caledonian Airways.

Come 1969, Trevor had begun selling military Dinky Toys, and he recalls being contacted by the Army who were seeking a wider range of military recognition models. In the training room at the Royal Military Academy Sandhurst, tables were laid out with sand, and he recognised dozens of Denzil Skinner's tanks of all nations. Trevor agreed to supply the army with chipped Dinky military vehicles, which they then sprayed all over with desert sand paint.

In due course, he found that he had amassed a considerable collection. He had discovered the model car press, replied to 3 advertisements, and realised that there was money to be made from prudent purchasing.

Dellow

Healey Westland Kit

He borrowed £200 from his father, and with this backing, in six months had built up a 5 page list, and repaid the loan. His trading included regular advertisements in Modellers' World magazine, and the swapping of 45 RPM records with a French dealer in French Dinky Toys.

Trevor soon became friends with dealer Bryan Garfield Jones, and together they would visit the Windsor swapmeet, where he met Mike and Sue Richardson. As Bryan's range of Motorkits took off, Trevor was able to supply him with a few diecast models from European makers to be used as patterns for his white metal ranges. These included the Tekno MGA coupe, Volvo PV544, and others.

During the 1970s Trevor was writing regularly for Modellers' World, and Model Collector, on military vehicles, his first love.

By 1980 he decided that he wanted to make models for his own collection. He then set about teaching himself to cast using rubber moulds, and passed on much of his knowledge to friend Ian Law, founder of PP Copy Models, making replicas of earlier toys. Retirement from his job as an aviation overseas manager arrived in 1986, and Trevor began his creative work with a number of 1:76 scale trucks, including the Canadian pattern Chevrolet, calling them Military Motors. A few years later, he was approached by Chris Fruin, of London Toy Soldiers, asking if he would make a range

Healey Duncan coupe 1947

of soldiers for him. Trevor switched to 1:32 scale, and at his request, focussed on the Royal Medical Corps, creating a number of boxed sets of figures in action, all depicting First World War poses. These included rather large military vehicles, such as tanks, ambulances, etc.

Post retirement business blossomed, and a strong association was built up with London Toy Soldiers. Unfortunately, in 1993, financial difficulties caused Chris Fruin's business to close down, leaving Trevor with many unsold kits.

However, another love for Trevor, came to the rescue. At a Kempton Park toy fair his interest in racing cars, led him to spot that the Dinky 23 series and Crescent ranges omitted some important historic cars, such as the Ferrari Squalo, and Alfa Romeo Bimotore.

Using his innovative approach, he first took moulds from existing castings, and then adapted them, with plasticene, cardboard, paper clips, and matchsticks and in true 'Blue Peter' fashion, any other materials that would create the desired

Nash Healey Le Mans coupe

effect. This provided the masters, from which moulds could then be used to cast new models in white metal. And so a Ferrari Squalo was born, and 5 were sold very quickly!

Through the 1990s, and with the assistance of publicity in journals such as Classic & Sports Car, Trevor realised that 1:43 scale was the universally recognised scale for model cars, and in 2000 talked with Mike and Sue Richardson about their views on him reproducing copies of some of the cars they had modelled in their ranges. Using their original as a pattern, he first made the Squire.

Further exposure in Octane magazine, and Rev Counter, the journal of the Austin Healey club, led Trevor to create new subjects of cars never before modelled, including the range of Healeys made by the Healey Motor Company.

A few famous people have models in their collections made from Trevor's kits, including the late American singer, Frankie Laine, David Coulthard and Sir Stirling Moss.

At the time of writing, models of the little known

Paramount, Warwick and Ogle SX 250 are being developed. Trevor now has many different kits in his ranges, but insists that it continues to be a hobby. The cars produced are those that interest him, and he simply ensures that his costs are covered. He has never advertised his white metal kit ranges, and whilst eBay has increased the demand for them to a world wide market, this has been achieved through the sales of his kits by others.

Reliant Super Sabre

After all our research and interviews with the many innovators in this industry, it is clear that white metal work is a very flexible craft, capable of adapting to new economic circumstances. Indeed, it is now doing just that, with both well established producers and new entrants responding to the changed conditions.

We hope that the histories recalled prove as interesting to readers as they have to us, particularly those of craftsmen and specialists no longer with us. These now form permanent memories for friends, relatives and the wider collecting public.

PATTERN MAKER NETWORK

This table illustrates the wide range of producers for whom many pattern makers work.

PATTERN MAKER	PRODUCER
Dick Armbruster	Durham Classics; Precision Miniatures
Lloyd Asbury	Precision Miniatures
Steve Bates	John Day Models; Mikansue; Little Smashers
Martin Beacom	Pirate Models
Ian Birkinshaw	Modified existing patterns
Reg Bishop	Grand Prix Models
Neil Bollen	Max Kernick/Top Marques
Bill Brown	Durham Classics
Alastair Duncan	Pathfinder Models; A&S Model Makers; American Automobile Miniatures; Crossway Models
Andy Dunn	Scale Model Technical Services; Wargames South
Pat Evans	Bellini; Little Smashers;
Martin Feldwick	Monarch Miniatures; Carthage Miniatures; Omen Miniatures; Phoenix Model Developments; Real Models; Montys Model Railways; SMTS; Fradilro Scandinavian; K&R Replicas; Grand Prix Models; Jameo Kits
Bill Fellowes	World of Miniatures.
Colin Flannery	MiniMarque43; Buccaneer Models
Martin Field	Mikansue; Crossway Models; Minimarque43; Illustra Models
Paul Fisher	Creative Miniature Associates; Legendary Motorcars
Rodney Fox	Piccolino Models; Highlander Models; Four Wheel Models; Pandora Models; Elektra Models.
Lawrence Gibson	Gems & Cobwebs; Crossway Models;

PATTERN MAKER	PRODUCER
Lawrence Gibson (cont.)	Top Marques; J&M Classics
Gerald Gilbert	Top Marques; Milestone Miniatures; GTA Models.
Dave Gilbert	John Day Models; Milikits; Len Buller Models; Pirate Models; DG and DS Models.
John Halcrow	Big River Models
David Hamilton	Grand Prix Models
Chris Happé	Durham Classics
Ian Harrah	Langley Miniature Models
Rodney Henley	Mikansue; John Day Models; Motorkits; C-Scale Models
Bob Hine	Grand Prix Models, Conquest/Madison Models; Formula Models; Historic Replicars; Model Assemblies; SMTS; Wargames South
Robin Housego	Scale Model Technical Services (SMTS); Western Models; Autographic
Mike Karslake	Auto Replicas
Peter Kenna	Kenna Models; Pathfinder Models; N & KC Keyser; SMTS; Conquest/Madison Models; Belgium Trucks/Jupiter Models; Minicar43 Norway; K & R Replicas; Western Models; Promod Models; Brooklin Models; Motor City USA; IMP; Vulcan Models; Jemini Models; Crossway Models; Spa Croft Models: Motor Pro; Somerville Models; Wrightlines; Formula 1 Models;
Brian Lawrence	Pirate Models; Transport Replicas; Western Models; Langley Miniatures; Motorkits; LDM Aeroplane Models. Acorn Models; Helmet Miniature Aircraft.
Barry Lester	Auto Replicas; John Day Models; Acorn Models; Pirate Models; Lowland Models.

PATTERN MAKER	PRODUCER
Don Loos	Motor City USA
Doug McHard	Somerville Models
Andy Martin	Creative Miniature Associates
Mike Murray	Illustra Models
Rod Parker	John Day Models
Ian Pickering	John Day Models; Motorkits; Pathfinder Models; Corgi Toys; Transport Replicas; Durham Classics; Western Models; K&R Replicas; Brooklin Models; Lansdowne Models; Marsh Models; Auto Buff; Great American Dream Machine; Illustra Models; SMTS; Spa Croft Models; Crossway Models; MiniMarque43; Phoenix Miniatures; Legendary Models; Highway Travellers; Illustra Models, J&M Classics; Franklin Mint; Motor City USA; Hawtal Whiting; Castco.
Ian Playfoot	Wills Finecast; South Eastern Finecast.
Greg Roberts	Thameshead Models; Highway Models; Danbury Mint; Brooklin Models; Bellini/RAE Models; Thoroughbred Models.
Doug Roseman	World of Miniatures
Christian Sargant	Marsh Models; SMTS; K&R Replicas; Milestone Miniatures; South Eastern Finecast; David Ferguson; Scale Auto Bodies; MPH Models
Mike Sheppard	Pirate Models
Denzil Skinner	John Day Models
Paddy Stanley	Paddy Stanley
Julian Stewart	Durham Classics; Brooklin Models
Richard Stokes	John Day Models; Mikansue; Grand Prix Models; Scale Racing Cars; Western Models; Danhausen; Abingdon Classics; K&R Replicas; Brooklin Models;

PATTERN MAKER	PRODUCER
Richard Stokes (cont.)	FM Automini; Pat Shrimpton; Ralph Foster; Gems & Cobwebs; The Make-Up Co, Japan; Pathfinder Models; Illustra Models; SMTS; Simon Jones
Adrian Swain	BEC Models; GS Models; John Day Models; Chris Leigh; MOPOK (4mm railway parts); Transport Replicas; Westward Models; Pirate Models; Auto Replicas; Motorkits.
Glenn Thomas	Crossway Models; Alan Smith Automodels; Fire Brigade Models; Traffic Model Cars; Dave Jones; Hart Models; Transport of Delight
Arthur Trendall	Alan Smith Automodels; Fire Brigade Models, Buckingham Pewter; Transport of Delight; Brian Norman's Tractors; A&H; John Winnett; Kingfisher Models; Hart Models; Mayes Models
Dick Ward	K&R Replicas; Brooklin Models; SMTS; Illustra Models; Marsh Models; Aerotech; Motor City USA; Minimarque43; Formula Models; Bellini; Promod Ltd; Scaledown; Develotech; Specialities International Wargames South; Miltra; Great American Dream Machine; Peter Wingfield.
Dave Weaver	SMTS; Lansdowne Models
Ken Wetton	Grand Prix Models
John Wright	SMTS; Brooklin Models; RAE Models; Motor City USA; Western Models; Conquest / Madison Models; Durham Classics.

APPENDIX 2
A WHITE METAL MODEL TIMELINE

1900

1910 • S.R. (Simon et Rivolet) of Paris launched its range of model cars and tanks

1950

1951 • Denzil Skinner set up his company and made small scale war gaming models.

1953 • Frank Vescoe opened his shop BEC Models

1955 • Bill and Ted Friend of Graphic Designers Ltd, launched their Replicars range.

1958 • Bob Wills made his 1st loco kit of LNER J69

1960

1961 • Bob Wills was encouraged by Ian Smith to model the 1962 Stack Pipe BRM

1963 • Carlo Brianza launched his first large scale brass super-detailed model.

1964 • Wills 1:24 scale model cars announced.

• Marc Europa 1:43 range launched by Brian Jewell, cast by Denzil Skinner.

1965 • Pete Atkinson made w/m replicas of the Skybirds range.

1968 • Gene Parrill formed Marque Products

1969 • AP Stanley Models launched first w/m kit cast by Denzil Skinner

• NC Keyser made Craven A LMS 1/2 cab coach

• Pirate Models made their first spare parts.

• Vic Bailey opened Veteran & Vintage shop in Portslade

1970

1970 • John Day launched his first two models

1971 • First Danhausen catalogue appeared.

• Dave Gilbert launched his white metal kits with Austin Chummy tourer

• Ralph & Kathleen Avis opened St Martin's Accessories.

• Pirate Models announced their first bus kit, patterned by LDM.

1972 • Renown advertised a new range of military vehicles in 1:43,
  made by Phoenix Model Developments

• Barry Lester introduced Auto Replicas with his ERA

• Cotswold Model Engineering advertised new range of bus kits

• Dave Jones offered w/m spare parts for Lesney Matchbox

1973 • Bob Wills launched his first 1:43 kit – the Citroen 2CV

- Jim Varney made his first Transport Replicas – Shillibeers horse drawn bus
- Western Models launched their first model – the Mercedes 540K
- Mikansue's No.1 model – Jowett Jupiter launched in October

1974
- FDS launched new range from Italy, of Fiat, Alfa and Ferrari in April
- Marco Bossi announced Idea 3, a new series, from beginning with
  a 1:43 handbuilt Lancia
- SB kits begin with D-Type Jaguars, direct from Mikansue
- Paulo Rampini's Modelli 'R' range of 100 pieces only starts
- Wessex Models started with spare parts and Dinky 35 and 36 series copies
- Dubray of France launched a range of various Peugeot 402s
- Danhausen 1:43 cars arrived
- Brian Harvey of Grand Prix models began his range of
  Classic Car Kits with Allard J2 in 1:43 scale
- Marque Products launched a w/m range with 2 1949 Porsches
- Milikits 1:60 w/m military kits were launched

1975
- Max Kernick began Abingdon Classics
- Jim Varney began his Transport Replicas range of cars
- Dave Jones was now mailing full car kits – 1st a 1902 Renault 16HP
- Brian Harvey's Grand Prix Models launched Buccaneer range of Dinky replicas.
- Walldorf (Model International of Frankfurt) launched a range of kits with a
  Ford Eifel, including chrome parts and opening bonnet and boot.
- H models started with a Fiat Presidentiale
- AMR launched new range with Martini Porsche Turbo
- American Automobile Miniatures – a new range of 1:43 fully assembled models.
- Bill Barnes and Len Buller formed B&B Models
- GDE of Italy launched range of racing cars.
- K models launched new range from Italy
- Project I launched with a Lotus Elite
- John Gay began trading in model buses
- Car Cast launched with a Lancia
- Motorkits launched their 1:43 car range

1976
- MetalModels launched Morris Commercials range from Norfolk
- Equipe Gallois started a range of copies of French Dinky
- Midget Models began a range of 00 scale w/m kits
- Brooklin Models launched with the Pierce Arrow from Brooklin, Ontario.

- Tron began with a Ferrari.
- Steve Flowers established his spares business.
- Western launched their kit range from South Nutfield
- Hobby Technica began.
- Bryan Garfield Jones launched MotorModels – 1:43 fully finished commercials
- Conti Models launched with a Lancia from Italy.
- Reen Replicas, the 1st range of w/m from Japan.
- Norman Miniatures, 1:32 horse drawn series from Brighton
- Circuit Series racing cars began.

1977
- A Smith Automodels was formed
- VdeC Replicas/LM Replicas began their Equipe range of 2 seater racing cars
- Gene Parrill launched the Precision Miniatures range
- Brown's Models – launched a range of 1:32 tractor kits.
- Veteran & Vintage began their range of fully finished Dinky copies iPortslade.
- Lawrence Design and Models 500th master released – a 1:48 Pitt S2A bi-plane
- Big Six Classic Replicas launched from Goodwin Street, London.
- Calibri launched
- Plumbies launched
- C-Scale kits launched
- Bryan Garfield Jones opened his Autoroute shop in Horsham

1978
- DG models launched range of 28 Series 1st type Dinky van copies.
- Doug McHard started Somerville Models in Liverpool with the Austin FX4 taxi.

1979
- Playtoy Models launched from Belgium with Rover P2 kit
- Julian and Margaret Stewart founded Durham Classics Automotive Miniatures in Oshawa, Ontario.
- Heavy Goods was placed on the map by Geoff Moorhouse
- John Martin opened Cowplain Models

1980

1980
- Len Buller and Bill Barnes launched Military trucks range

1981
- Model Tractor Co. launched by Scaledown Models of Havant.
- John Hodges launched his 'Odgi' Toys of Yesterday – models in Dinky Toys Style.
- Little Smashers launched by Dave and Carrie Wade
- John and Pam Simons formed Marsh Models

1982
- Graham Ward opened his Promod shop
- Model Road & Rail opened Worcester Park shop in April.

1983
- LSR Productions was formed by Howard Statham, Mike Stanton,

and Fred Kaesmann.

- SMTS was formed by Keith Williams, John Allen, and Steve Overy.

- Modellers' World shop opened in Bell Lane, Eton Wick

- Richard Briggs released his first Minimarque43, a Riley RMB

- Sun Motor Co. set up by Rod and Val Ward

1984 • Top Marques began making models.

- Vic Trimble of Henley on Thames launches range of 1:200 Dinky Style

- aircraft with a fully finished Lancaster.

- Maurice Bozward became self employed as White Metal Assemblies

- Mike Coupe began trading as Brock Miniatures

1985 • Milestone Miniatures launched

- John Fisher registered Kingfisher Models

1985 • David Buckle founded Formula One Models & Prints

1986 • MiniMarque43 took over Abingdon Classics range

- Sue and Jeff Sharrock launched Pathfinder Models in Leeds

- Colin Fraser started Formula Models

1987 • Hart Models took over the former Denzil Skinner range

1988 • Peter Stoyle launched Peregrine Models

- Bob Wills retired, and Dave Ellis took over at South Eastern Finecast

1989 • Ian Law launched his PP Copy range

- Brian and Linda Harrison set up B&L Models

- Marshall Buck launched his Creative Miniature Associates model range

1990

1990 • MICA produced their first w/m model – figure of Les Smith

- The first ModeleX show took place on October 13th

- World of Miniatures launched by Adrian Towner

- Penelope Pitlane launched by Steve Ward

- CMA Mouldcast created by Chris Arnott and Dave Buttress.

1991 • Transport of Delight was registered by Brian Salter

- Barry Wright launches BW Models

- Minichamps launched by Paul Günter Lang

1992 • Mach One Models was founded by Ian Jones

1993 • Ted and Joan Webber set up Specialties International

1994 • John Halcrow founded Big River Models with a range of Australian 'utes'

- Frank Vescoe retired and sold BEC models to Brian Robinson

1996 • Gary Oxley founded Classic Jaguar Miniatures

1996	• Colin Massingham died
1997	• Max Kernick moves Top Marques to Honiton.
1998	• Ian Law began producing models for Club Dinky France members
1999	• Mike Rogers began trading as J&M Classics
	• Greg Roberts began trading as Thoroughbred Models

2000

2000	• Hartsmith was founded
	• Trevor Wright began making copies of Mikansue models.
	• Barry Lester sold Auto Replicas to Adrian Swain
2001	• Jean Francois Consille launched Imit'Toys range
	• Max Kernick moved to France
	• Barry Lester moved to France
2002	• Pathfinder range ceased due to ill health of Jeff Sharrock.
	• Simon Elford launched a new range – Selford Models
	• Rae & Ann Dobbins bought MerryMeet Model Cars
	• Richard Briggs, John Haynes, Ernie Knott and Doug McHard died
2004	• David Buckle died
	• Ted Webber died
2005	• Amanda and Carl Merz bought the Crossway business from Roger Tennyson
2006	• Frank Vescoe died in October.
2009	• Jeff Thomas acquired Motor City USA from Alan Novak
	• David Austin died

2010

2010	• Barry Lester died.
	• Frank Jones launched his British Heritage Models.
2011	• Bill Barnes announced his retirement from model making.

We appreciate the support shown for this book by the following specialist manufacturers, pattern maker and retailers, past and present.

(International calls to the UK should be preceded by +44 and delete the 0)

Ralph & Kathleen Avis
St Martin's Accessories Ltd
Tel. 0207 836 9742
mail@stmartinsmodelcars.co.uk
www.stmartinsmodelcars.co.uk

Charles Barnett's Midas Models
67, Coniston Avenue, Queensbury, Bradford
West Yorkshire BD13 2JD
Tel. 01274 816437
charles.barnett@virgin.net

Brooklin Models Ltd
Unit A3, Pines Way, Industrial Estate
Ivo Peters Road
Bath, Avon BA2 3QS
Tel. 01225 332400
brooklin_models@talk21.com
www.brooklinmodels.co.uk

Marshall L. Buck
Creative Miniature Associates
New York, USA
Tel. 631-563-2876
info@cmamodels.com
www.cmamodels.com

CMA Moldform
Unit 17a Spitfire Park
Ashold Farm Road,
Birmingham B24 9PR
Tel. 0121 350 7707
Fax 021 333 6010
info@cmamoldform.co.uk
www.cmamoldform.co.uk

Mike Coupe
Spa Croft Models
98, High Street, Tibshelf
Derbyshire DE55 5NU
Tel. 01773 872780
SpaCroft@aol.com
www.spacroftmodels.co.uk

Andy Dunn, Pattern Maker
1, The Blythe, Stowe-by-Chartley
Stafford ST18 0LT
Tel. 07772 955992

Colin Fraser
Formula Models
Unit 3, Old Stable Studio, Court Lodge Farm,
Wartling, Hailsham BN27 1RY
Tel. 01323 833866
formulamodels@freeserve.co.uk
www.formulamodels.co.uk

John Hodges
'Odgi' Toys of Yesterday

J&M Classics
Tel. 01903 732660
Tel. 01404 815735
www.marqueart.com

JM Toys
32 Aston Road
Waterlooville
Hampshire PO7 7XQ
Tel. 02392 262446
sales@jmtoys.net
www.jmtoys.net

Minichamps GmbH & Co. KG
Postfach 500505 - D-52089 Aachen
Tel. +49-241-9672 300
www.minichamps.de

Pier van Netten
Model Cars of the World
39 Benwerrin Drive
Burwood East, Vic 3151
Australia
Shop hours Thurs. & Fri. 11.00 – 4.00
Tel. 61(03) 9887 9929
Fax 61(03) 9887 8336
eBay Store Australianmodelcars
sales@modelcars.com.au
www.modelcars.com.au

Steve Overy & Mike Murray
Illustra Models
20, Caves Road
St Leonards, East Sussex TN38 0BY
Tel. 01424 722007
mail@illustramodels.com
www.midlanticmodels.com

Promod Ltd
PO Box 366
Stafford ST16 3UR
Tel. 01785 224212
sales@promod-diecast.co.uk
www.promod-diecast.co.uk

Keith Pillinger
Bristol Ambulance E.M.S.
www.bristolambulance.co.uk

Peter Stoyle
Peregrine Model Cars
Peregrine Cottage
Challaborough,
Nr Kingsbridge
Devon TQ7 4HT
Tel. 01548 810844
peter@peregrinemodels.entadsl.com

Scale Model Technical Services
10 Moorhurst Road
Hastings
Sussex TN38 9NA
Tel. 01424 853353
smts.models@btconnect.com
www.smts.models.co.uk

Geoff Sear
Sear Models
sear@telkomsa.net

John & Pam Simons
Marsh Models
Unit 2, Old Stable Studio
Court Lodge Farm
Wartling, Hailsham
East Sussex BN27 1RY
Tel/Fax. 01323 833717
marshmodels@aol.com
www.marshmodels.com

Julian, Margaret & Nicholas Stewart
Durham Classics Automotive Miniatures
27-1300 King St East,
Suite # 239,
L1H 8J4 Canada
Tel. 905-244-5205
info@durhamclassics.ca
www.durhamclassics.ca

Bob Wills
Wills Finecast

INDEX - CHAPTERS & PROFILES

INTRODUCTION

CHAPTER ONE
WHERE DID IT ALL START? 1
Pete Atkinson | Acorn Models | 3
Peter Cox & Guy Harrison | Pirate models | 6
Bill & Ted Friend | Graphic Designers Ltd | 10
Brian Jewell | Marc Europa | 12
Denzil Skinner | | 13
Paddy Stanley | | 14
Frank Vescoe | BEC Models | 14
Bob Wills | Wills Finecast | 19

CHAPTER TWO
MAKING MODELS FROM WHITE METAL 23
John Allen | Scale Model Technical Services | 25
Maurice Bozward | White Metal Assemblies | 25
Dave Buttress & Chris Amott | CMA Moldform | 26

CHAPTER THREE
PATTERN MAKERS – THE HEART OF THE BUSINESS 29
Steve Bates | | 30
Neil Bollen | | 31
Martin Feldwick | | 32
Rodney Fox | Concours Auto Models | 34
Lawrence Gibson | | 36
Gerald Gilbert | | 37
Brian Lawrence | Lawrence Design & Models | 38
Pete Kenna | Kenna Models | 39
Ian Pickering | | 41
Greg Roberts | Thoroughbred Models | 44
Christian Sargant | | 45
Richard Stokes | | 46
Adrian Swain | | 48
Glenn Thomas | | 51
Max Tomlinson | | 52
Arthur Trendall | | 53
Richard 'Dick' Ward | | 54
John Wright & Dave Weaver | John Wright Model Makers | 55

CHAPTER FOUR
THE EARLY PIONEERS 57
Graham Bridges | Milikits | 57
Peter Comben | Enco Models | 58
John Day | John Day Model Cars | 62
Bryan Garfield Jones | Motorkits | 64
Dave Gilbert | DG Models / Autocraft | 66
Brian Harvey | Grand Prix Models | 69

Max Kernick	Top Marques and Autotorque	71
Barry Lester	Auto Replicas	73
Mike & Sue Richardson	Mikansue	75
Mike & Joyce Stephens	Western Models Ltd	79
Jim Varney	Transport Replicas	81
Keith Williams & John Allen	Scale Model Technical Services Ltd	83

1980s and 1990s

David Baulch	Classic Model Motorcycles	86
Richard Briggs	Minimarque43	86
Boston-Nicholls		87
Ian Burkinshaw		87
Alistair Duncan	A & S Modelmakers	88
Keith Edney	RAE Models	88
Dave Ellis	South Eastern Finecast	90
Martin Field	Guild Master Models	91
Brian Gildea	Mascot Models	91
Pat Land	Model Assemblies	92
Mike Michelak	Cheshire Scale Models	93
Steve Overy & Mike Murray	Illustra Models	93
Gary Oxley	Classic Jaguar Miniatures	94
Gerry Pettit	G P Mobilia	95
Graham Price	GTA Models	96
Mike Rogers	J&M Classics	97
John & Pam Simons	Marsh Models	99
John Shinton	Model maker	101
Ted Webber	Specialties International	101
Phil Winslade	Scale Model Technical Services	102

CHAPTER FIVE
THE MODELEX ERA — 104

CHAPTER SIX
INTERNATIONAL CONNECTION — 109

Phil Alderman & Paul J. Burt	The Great American Dream Machine	109
Henk van Asten	Conquest/Madison Models	110
Carlo Brianza	ABC Brianza	111
Marshall Buck	Creative Miniature Associates	112
Jean Francois Consille	Imit'Toys	115
Otto Duve	Walldorf Miniaturen	116
Dave Eames	Automodelli Studio	118
Lee Elmes	American Automobile Miniatures	119
Ged Fitzsimmons	Fimcar, and other white metal model car manufacturers in Australia	120
Sergio Goldvarg	The Goldvarg Collection	124
John Halcrow	Big River Models	125
Bob Hooper	Dominion Models	126
Buz Kirkel	Route 66 Model Car Store	126
Paul Günter Lang	Danhausen and Minichamps	127
BS MacReynolds	Autobuff	129
Mike McNally	Model Auto Emporium	130

Pier van Netten	Model Cars of the World	131
Alan Novak, Gene Parrill & Jeff Thomas	Motor City USA	132
Gene Parrill	Precision Miniatures	134
Arjan de Roos	de Roos Miniaturen	135
André-Marie Ruf	AMR	137
Dave Sinclair	Miniauto	138
Julian, Margaret & Nicholas Stewart	Durham Classics Automotive Miniatures	139
Thomas Wolter	Tin Wizard Model Cars	141
Robert Budig	Modellautos	143

CHAPTER SEVEN
COMMERCIAL BREAK — 144

Bill Barnes	Nene Rubber & Plastics	144
Derek Barratt	MetalModels	146
John Fisher	Kingfisher Models	147
Mike Forbes	Marquis Models	147
Geoff Moorhouse	Heavy Goods	149
Frank Rice-Oxley	Roxley Models	150
Brian Salter	Model Historian	151
Tony Molay & Alan Smith	Hartsmith Models	152
Adrian Towner	World of Miniatures	154
Barry Wright	BW Models	156

CHAPTER EIGHT
ON THE BUSES — 157

Anbrico Model Buses and Railways	157
John Gay	159
Model Bus Federation	161

CHAPTER NINE
TRAINS, PLANES AND BOATS — 163
Trains - 163

K's	163
Cotswold Models	163
Nu-Cast	164
Wills Finecast	164
GEN	165
MTK	166

Planes – 166

John Alcott	Veteran & Vintage	168
Michael Armitage		170
CA (Tommy) Atkins		169
David Austin	The Aerodrome	168
Derek Barratt	MetalModels/ Airpower	170
Martin Beacom	Small World	168
Richard Bizley	Eclipse/Bizleyart	169
Wojtek Benzinski		168
Ron Crawford	HBM	169
Leighton Fletcher	Aerocrafts	168
Paul Howard	Helmet Historical Aircraft	169
Fred Hempsall		169

Melvyn Johnson	Miniature Aircraft Models	169
Brian Keates	Vapour Trail	168
Dennis Knight	Helmet Models	169
Langton Miniatures		169
Ann Lister	Helmet Historical Aircraft	169
Simon de Montfalcon	Aircast	168
Norfolk Group		170
Chris Sayer	Shed Models	170
Boats -		171
Alan Dixon	D & M Casting Company	171

CHAPTER TEN
BREAKING THE RECORDS | | 173 |

Jason Ferns	HB Models	173
Ralph Foster	Pandora Models	174
Ian Jones	Mach One Models	175
Howard Statham	LSR Productions	177
Mike Stanton	Mayes Models/MS Models.	179

CHAPTER ELEVEN
THE CHEQUERED FLAG | | 182 |

Colin Baxter	Scale Racing Cars	182
David Buckle	Formula 1 Models & Prints	183
Colin Fraser	Formula Models	184
John Haynes	Historic Replicars	185
Roger Taylor	Autographic	185
Carrie & Dave Wade	Little Smashers	186
Steve Ward	Penelope Pit Lane	188

CHAPTER TWELVE
THE SHOP FRONT | | 190 |

David Angel	The Angel Collection	190
Ralph & Kathleen Avis	St. Martin's Accessories Ltd	192
Charles Barnett	Midas Models	193
Mike Coupe	Spa Croft Models	194
Rae & Ann Dobbins	MerryMeet Model Cars	196
Les & Peter Duplock	Model Road & Rail	196
Brian Harrison	B & L Models	198
Nigel Judge		199
Tony Mclellan	Langley Miniature Models	200
John Martin	JM Toys Ltd	202
Bob Pitkin	Tober Models	204
Peter Stoyle	Peregrine Model Cars	204
Steve Traffic	BMC Garage	206
Graham Ward	Promod Ltd	207
Rod & Val Ward	Modellauto Ltd, Sun Motor Co.	208

CHAPTER THIRTEEN
THE VOLUME PRODUCERS | | 212 |

Bernie & Graham du Cros	Gems and Cobewbs	212
John & Jenny Hall	Brooklin Models Ltd	213

Nigel Parker & Tim Fulford	Brooklin Models Ltd	213
Doug & Roly McHard	Somerville Models	217
Jeff & Sue Sharrock	Pathfinder Models	219
Roger Tennyson, John Billinger,		
Carl & Amanda Merz	Jemini Models and Crossway Models	221

CHAPTER FOURTEEN
THE PARTS BIN

		226
Steve Flowers	Steve Flowers Model Supplies	226
Martin Jewell		226
Colin Penn	Motorail	227
John and Chris Stockton	Photo Etch Consultants (PEC)	229

CHAPTER FIFTEEN
The ADAPTERS & FLATTERERS

		231
Victor Bailey	Veteran & Vintage	231
Dennis Goodman	Debo Toys	232
John Hodges	'Odgi' Toys of Yesterday	232
Ian law	PP Copy Models	233
Fred Lewis		235
Barry Lloyd	B–Line Models	236
Kevin McGimpsey & Stewart Orr	MICA and Perfect Toys	237
Colin Penn	Copycat Models	240
Keith Pillinger	My Way models	243
John Roberts	Master Model Maker	244

CHAPTER SIXTEEN
THE INFLUENCE OF CHINA &
THE 21st CENTURY SCENE

		247
Frank Jones	British Heritage Models	248
Trevor Wright	TW Models	249
Simon Elford	Trident Models	250